Experimenting with the Consumer

Experimenting with the Consumer

The Mass Testing of Risky Products on the American Public

Marshall S. Shapo

Westport, Connecticut
London

Library of Congress Cataloging-in-Publication Data

Shapo, Marshall S., 1936–
  Experimenting with the consumer : the mass testing of risky products on the American public / Marshall S. Shapo.
    p. cm.
  Includes bibliographical references and index.
  ISBN 978–0–313–36528–7 (alk. paper)
  1. Products liability—United States. 2. Technological innovations—Law and legislation—United States. 3. Human experimentation in medicine—Law and legislation—United States. I. Title.
  KF1296.S428 2009
  346.7303′8—dc22   2008033664

British Library Cataloguing in Publication Data is available.

Library of Congress Catalog Card Number: 2008033664
ISBN 13: 978–0–313–36528–7

First published in 2009

Praeger Publishers, 88 Post Road West, Westport, CT 06881
An imprint of Greenwood Publishing Group, Inc.
www.praeger.com

Printed in the United States of America

The paper used in this book complies with the Permanent Paper Standard issued by the National Information Standards Organization (Z39.48–1984).

10 9 8 7 6 5 4 3 2 1

For Helene
the nonpareil

And for

Nat and Robin   Ben and Jackie

Aaron, Gabrielle, Josh, Noah

Contents

Preface

I owe much to many people for the genesis, and the research, for this book. I can mention only a few, a list that encapsules an important set of personal and professional influences.

Law has diplomatic relations with many areas of intellectual endeavor, among them philosophy, economics, sociology, political science, and anthropology. Today, an especially important area is science. I can trace my family interest in that subject back two generations. In the late 1940s, my father, Mitchell Shapo, told me about a remark made to him by his father, Rabbi Julian Shapo, probably around 1940. It concerned the great vistas and problems that the power locked inside the atom would present for mankind.

During World War II, my father worked as an expediter for a coppersmithing firm. Sometime later, he told me that during the war he had begun to sense that the plans he locked in his safe at night had "something to do with atoms." Security was tight, and vast war projects were highly compartmentalized. But I remember that my father was convinced that his wartime work had something to do with the Manhattan Project.

This surely was one of the earliest seeds of my continuing curiosity today about how science and technology relate to the law. My scholarship has focused in large part on torts, the law that applies to civil actions for injuries, and the more specialized field of products liability. It has also encompassed government regulation of safety, including the many statutes and administrative rules that govern the production and sale of products with proved, and potential, risks. Those interests have grown to embrace questions about how policy makers gauge and weigh the risk of injury from modern products and processes, and how courts and lawyers wrestle with questions of scientific causation in civil cases.

My father's remarks stand in the background of my reading and writing about these issues over the course of my career. Among the many people who have helped enlarge that background are students, librarians, faculty assistants, faculty colleagues, and practicing lawyers.

My student assistants have greatly aided my research. I want to single out, in particular, David Lee, Matthew Burke, and Laura MacDonald.

The librarians at Northwestern University School of Law have helped me enormously. I thank our head librarians, Chris Simoni and now Jim McMasters. The captain of these research efforts on the ground has been Marcia Lehr, unfailingly competent and cheerful. Adding to her consistent and timely work have been Pegeen Bassett, Irene Berkey, and Heidi Kuehl.

Foremost among my faculty assistants in the production of the manuscript for this book has been Derek Gundersen, and I also appreciate the help of Mike Sobczak.

Deans at three law schools have encouraged me in progressive parts of this quest. At Texas, Page Keeton, my first dean and collaborator, instilled in me an interest in the problems of evidence and proof. Monrad Paulsen at Virginia provided research opportunities that laid a foundation for the work I now do in this area. At Northwestern, I am grateful for research time provided by David Ruder, Bob Bennett, and David Van Zandt.

Members of law faculties depend on colleagues for continuing stimulation of ideas. I have been fortunate to have coworkers who continue to enrich my understanding of the law and related areas of knowledge. Many years ago at Texas, I had the good luck to have an office near Leon Green, perhaps the most creative legal mind I have personally known. I cannot link particular ideas in this book to any specific things he said to me, but he surely educated me in an approach to legal problems that endures. At Virginia, I had the valuable colleagueship of Richard Merrill, with whom I conducted a seminar in law and science, and who sympathetically criticized prior work of mine.

At Northwestern, the interchange in 30 years of faculty workshops has rounded my background in diverse areas of inquiry in many ways. I retailed various ideas that have come to fruition in this book in some workshops overseas, particularly with Professor Eiji Maruyama at Kobe University and Norio Higuchi at the University of Tokyo.

I have been able to sharpen my practical understanding of the interaction of law and science in a number of consulting capacities. I benefited in various ways from the decade I spent in a counsel role at Sonnenschein Nath and Rosenthal. Most recently, Ray Mullady of Orrick Herrington and Sutcliffe instructed me in various practicalities of the law when I served as an expert witness in an asbestos litigation, an experience that provided an extra dimension to my thinking about this book.

My family has been a continuing inspiration. My son Ben, a research engineer who was investigating gravitational lenses when he was 17, has clarified basic scientific ideas for me. My son Nat, a lawyer, is a master at weighing complicated problems of law and policy, and making them understandable. Their families are continuing joys to me: Ben's wife Jackie and their children Gabrielle, Aaron, and Joshua; and Nat's wife Robin and their son Noah.

Helene S. Shapo has been my boon companion for 49 years. Time after time, she has exerted her moral authority and exercised her analytical talents in ways that have enhanced my work: generally as a critic, particularly in her hostility to cant and jargon, and most specially in her ability to cut a problem back to the core—an attribute that many years ago my father told me was a signal quality of the lawyer.

Introduction

Consider a forbidding catalog of events in medical and environmental research:

- On July 30, 2007, an FDA advisory committee concluded that the antidiabetic drug Avandia "was associated with a greater risk of myocardial ischemic events"—heart attacks—than placebo or two other antidiabetic drugs.[1] Despite this, the committee decided to allow the drug to stay on the market, although most of its members "call[ed] for strict warning labels."[2] Five months later, a newly published study concluded that users of Avandia over the age of 65 had "significantly elevated risks of heart attack and death."[3]
- The next month, a study in a medical journal counted a doubling in the number of "serious adverse drug events" reported to the FDA between 1998 and 2005.[4]
- In September came a report that the inspector general of the Department of Health and Human Services had concluded that "federal health officials do not know how many clinical trials are being conducted" on drugs, that the government audits "less than 1 percent of the nation's testing sites," and that "on the rare occasions when inspectors do appear," they "generally show up long after the tests are completed."[5]
- That same month, a story appeared on "[a]n apparent breakdown in biosafety at Texas A&M University," a description that covered "three missing vials" of highly contagious *Brucella* bacteria, "a faculty member performing a recombinant DNA experiment without the necessary" approval from the Centers for Disease Control and Prevention, and "three unreported cases of individuals exposed to the bacterium *Coxiella burnetii*, which causes Q fever, a treatable but infectious disease."[6] A month later, an official of the Government Accountability Office reportedly said that there was "[n]o single government agency ... responsible for tracking the rising number of laboratories qualified to handle the most dangerous infectious agents," including anthrax, West Nile virus, Q fever, and avian flu.[7]
- In November, the drug maker Merck announced that it would pay $4.85 billion to settle lawsuits filed by users of its painkiller Vioxx who ascribed heart

attacks and strokes to the drug.[8] One scholar noted that after the risk of "serious cardiovascular events" at a high dosage of Vioxx had been first discovered, "Merck and the FDA debated for quite some time about the need for a change in labeling." She referred to Merck's "demanding test for determining an adequate basis for warning, withdrawing the drug only when a clinical study found risks at the normal dosage level."[9] The amount of the litigation settlement was about nine months of profits for the company.

- The next month, a Congressional committee began pressing Merck and Schering-Plough about their failure to release results of a clinical trial for the cholesterol drug Zetia, a study completed more than a year and a half previously.[10] In March 2008, a news report summarized findings that Vytorin, a combination of Schering-Plough's Zetia and Merck's Zocor, had been found "no better at fighting heart disease than a far-cheaper generic."[11]

- In the fall of 2007, there came to light a "disease cluster"—reportedly "dozens of cases" of the dreaded Lou Gehrig's disease—"centered around a downtown industrial area" in Middleborough, Massachusetts.[12]

- In early 2008, a summary of the "largest workplace health study ever conducted" described the beginnings of the research in "an apparent cluster of brain cancers" at the North Haven, Connecticut, plant of Pratt & Whitney Aircraft. With final results of the study not expected until 2009, a journalist noted that there was "a good chance" that it would "wind up like so many other workplace health investigations: inconclusive."[13]

What ties together all of these items—from the laboratory to the industrial plant to the urban environment? It is the use of human populations, in both large and small groups, for experimental purposes. That phenomenon is not surprising, when you think about it. Indeed, a hallmark of humanity is experimentation. We are always trying out new ways of doing things, even seeking ways to improve our lives. We make a little change here, occasionally a big change there, and we always are on the lookout for some advantage over the way we do things now.

This proclivity for experiment attacks many of the great enemies of humankind—disease, pain, hunger, all kinds of deprivation. It also targets areas of human activity where desperation, having shaded into need, shades further into desire. Almost every television show gives us examples in its lengthy batches of commercials. We move from trying to stay alive in the face of a dread disease to urinating less frequently to having better sexual experiences. Our needs then extend to more responsive automobiles to slimmer cell phones to more fragrant substances to clean the toilet bowl.

That innovation is a modern mantra does not make it a new concept. The person who discovered that putting loads on a cylinder could enable him to transport the loads more easily, the person who first cross-bred plants, the individual who first scratched out symbols for things on a rock—all of these were experimenters.

This very selective catalog only symbolizes the many benefits of innovation, but the experimentation that produces benefits to many sometimes entails risk to some. In some cases, that risk is known, and in others, at least the zone of uncertainty attending it is known. Columbus, mountain climbers of all eras, and skydivers would understand. All chose, or now choose, a dimension of risk and uncertainty for themselves.

However, there are many people who are subjected to risk by others who do not mention the existence of the risk or its nature. Moreover, some of these hazards threaten not just one uninformed person, but rather large groups of people who are continued subjects of experimentation. Women prescribed estrogen for their postmenopausal symptoms may not know of risks already defined by experts, nor may they know that there is controversy among distinguished scientists about risks that are uncertain or at most dimly perceived. Indeed, estrogens provide a striking case in point. In their pharmaceutical heyday, these hormones acquired the reputation of a panacea: a product that prevented hot flashes and decreased the risk of heart disease as well as reducing the ravages of osteoporosis. After many years of marketing success for the drugs, however, a series of research reports indicated that many of the claims made for the products may not have been well founded and that, indeed, estrogens might even be increasing certain kinds of risks they had been asserted to minimize.

For most people, the term human experimentation connotes a well-defined step in the process of developing medical products. The predominant image is of physicians and scientists setting up tests to assess the benefits and risks of those products. A modern version of this process, labeled the "gold standard," involves double-blind studies in which neither doctor nor patient knows whether the patient is receiving an investigational drug or a placebo. Beyond these structured settings, though, a much broader process of market experimentation embraces a wide range of products, including products that we ordinarily would not associate with experimenters in hospital coats. With the expansion of our cornucopia of consumer products, the experimental society that is the United States—and, in fact, all industrialized nations—pushes inexorably onward with not only clinical tryouts but mass testing of products on human beings. This occurs across the spectrum of consumer goods, from prescription drugs and quasi-pharmaceuticals like herbal supplements to all kinds of specialized machines, including motor vehicles and both large and small machines used in industrial settings.

A well-publicized example of the use of consumers as test subjects for workaday products is one in which, literally, the rubber meets the road. This is the case of Bridgestone/Firestone tires used as original equipment on the Ford Explorer sports utility vehicle. As is so with medical products that have become causes célèbres in regulation and tort litigation, the risks of these products became evident only over time. At first, one could discern only a blown out tire here and an overturned Explorer there. But after a time, a familiar pattern emerges. The pins in the map become clusters. Then, the National Highway Traffic Safety Administration becomes involved. Running on their own legal trail, claimants' lawyers begin to see patterns and file claims. In the course of courtroom events comes multidistrict litigation, which involves hundreds of cases brought against the tire maker and against Ford, with the companies lobbing shells at each other on the side.

This episode is emblematic of another facet of modern product making—that of coordinating different components that make up complex products. Market experimentation presents especially difficult problems when there is more than one cook in the experimental kitchen. Products liability law has developed a set of responses to such problems. The working solution is that component makers will not be civilly liable for injuries caused by fully assembled products into which components have been integrated if the components are not in themselves defective. That result holds particularly when the assembler of the completed product was in the best position to control risks or the component maker could not foresee the way the injury occurred.

The consumer in these cases is in an especially disadvantaged position, having even less theoretical chance to avoid risk or to bargain to minimize it than when the maker of a product has fabricated it all on its own. In the case of products used in ordinary consumer life or in the workplace, for which regulatory surveillance often is less stringent than with drugs and medical devices, solutions to the injury problem will likely reside more with the tort system than with regulation.

This book draws lessons from a group of histories that have emerged from mass experimentation on people with a spectrum of needs and desires for new products, and with an equally broad spectrum of knowledge about risk. The principal focus is on health care, broadly defined, an area that presents many issues of mass experimentation at points of high tension. In that area, both needs and desires are often at a peak, and the risks of both illnesses and projected cures can be very serious. The tendency to ignore risk—by sellers, medical providers, and patients alike—is substantial and often understandable. At the same time, newly published information on risk may generate hysteria among consumers, an emotion born of concerns that turn out to be unjustified by the facts. The very mention of "the facts," it should be stressed, leads to the point that in science, "truths" are developed, criticized, revised, and sometimes fall by the wayside.

The histories reviewed here are replete with human stories. They are stories of dedicated scientists at work and of physicians coping not only with the problems of their patients but with a deluge of communications about medical products. They are also stories of consumer-patients who want help. Some patients serve knowingly as subjects of formal experimentation; many others undergo the informal experiments that occur on everyday markets without thinking of themselves as vehicles for tryouts.

There are a lot of actors in this drama who are trying to do their best—for their careers, for their employers, for consumers, even for society. But make no mistake about it, this is partly a book about wars: scientists against scientists, scientists against doctors, product sellers against other sellers, manufacturers against government agencies, sufferers against agencies, consumers against consumers, and lawyers against sellers and other institutions.

An important feature of this book is the interaction of technology, consumerism, and views of risk. We do not perceive many of the effects of technology on the simplest products. A commonplace example lies in the mechanization of the production of bread, which culminated in changing the nature of bread to adapt it to machine production.[14] The "nature" of bread thus changed, evolving into a different biochemical substance to fit the needs of technological methods.[15] Efforts to transform products that are even more "natural" involve the cultural definition of objects. The use of additives to make oranges more orange is an example of technology responding to acculturation in a way that establishes a marketing standard.

Questions about the safety of even some familiar products present thorny issues for government regulators, who provide oversight for the American people as they search for pleasure as well as relief from pain and disease. What regulators often must do is try to divine the willingness of people to accept risk to secure certain benefits, and its counterpart, their aversion to risk. Regulators serve as watchdogs, and sometimes as brokers, for the people at large, who are simultaneously awed by science and distrustful of it because of the conflicting messages they receive from continuing investigations that are conducted on mass markets. Only illustrative of the conflicting nature of those messages is the history of the science and marketing of postmenopausal estrogens, analyzed in Chapters 5 and 6.

Regulators also must provide correctives for gullibility, including gullibility fueled by hope and gullibility attributable to a lack of education or intelligence. They must seek to insure, so far as possible, voluntariness in encounters with risk. And they also serve as arbiters of sacrifice in the case of people who encounter risk, at least in part, out of a desire to serve humanity.

Industry keeps putting new products on the market, and they survive or pass into oblivion on a Darwinian basis. There will be those who criticize the products that survive and those who mourn the products that did not succeed. Those are often judgments of taste, sometimes even of morality. But as modern society works, we are all the subjects of market experimentation, an ongoing process during which sellers constantly try out innovations on us, often with some degree of risk.

Reflecting both tensions between science as a search for truth and science as a handservant to commerce, this book presents a moving picture, filmed through a series of different filters and from different angles, about several aspects of the problem. These include the incentives of experimenters—both entrepreneurial scientists and commercial entrepreneurs; the impact of media, both promotional and reportorial; and the social background that often transforms desires into needs. An important lens through which it surveys this landscape is that of law. A principal question it asks is when law should take a hand in environments of uncertainty in which persons exposed to risk have relatively little information about its severity or the frequency of their exposure to it.

I examine several levels of the problem of mass market experimentation—levels involving science and public understanding, and lack of understanding, about science; the concept of experimentation; the nature of risk and people's attitudes toward risk; and the boundaries of knowledge and uncertainty about the hazards of products and processes. Those at risk include people who directly consume products and people exposed to the byproducts of many kinds of substances and processes in the environment at large or in the more limited environments of workplace and home. Chapter 7, in particular, focuses on the accelerating development of nanotechnology, which may pose both process risks to workers and product risks to consumers.

Attitudes toward risk are crucial. Anthony Giddens has written of a world in which we live "after tradition"—"a world where life is no longer lived as fate."[16] In this world, one lives in a "risk society," one "increasingly preoccupied with the future (and also with safety), which generates the notion of risk."[17] An important characteristic of this society, Giddens says, is the "transition from external to . . . *manufactured risk*," that is, risk "created by the very progression of human development, especially by the progression of science and technology."[18] With the advent of "manufactured risk," "there is a new riskiness to risk. In a social order in which new technologies are chronically affecting our lives, and an almost endless revision of taken-for-granted ways of doing things ensues, the future becomes ever more absorbing, but at the same time opaque."[19] Moreover, "[i]t is characteristic of the new types of risk that it is even disputed whether they exist at all."[20]

I treat issues that affect millions of people directly and have implications that extend to the population as a whole. They range from the effects of prescribed hormones on the bodies of women (Chapter 5) to the effects of drugs intended to produce erections for men (Chapter 4). They include the kind of scientific proof it takes to persuade regulators, or courts, that silicone gel breast implants have caused serious systemic disorders (Chapter 3). Parallels will appear between misconduct that is of particular interest to the scientific community—for example, the faking of research data on products that have not nearly come to market—and various forms of experimentation that bring products and processes to market with insufficient knowledge about their potential risks.

I will discuss at least three ways in which innovators try out their novelties on people. One method is direct experimentation without any indication to the human subject about what role he or she plays, even about the topic of the experiment. That was the case in some episodes that I describe in Chapter 1. A second method, also examined in that chapter, is clinical experimentation in a controlled setting, in which the experimenter provides at least some information on risks and hoped-for benefits to the subjects of the experiment, and typically elicits their consent—a consent that is more or less "informed." A third method is the more masked method of acquiring information by putting a product or process into general circulation and awaiting data about risk and loss, data derived from reporting systems with varied abilities to dig out details and to classify them. This third method is mass market experimentation. Throughout the analysis, awareness of these different kinds of experimentation—these diverse ways to employ human beings as "guinea pigs"—will inform the development of principles applicable to the full spectrum of testing on human beings: the good as well as the bad and ugly.

The questions of whether to regulate and how much to regulate become intertwined with the questions of what persons to trust, and how much to trust them. What stakes do decision makers—scientists, industry personnel, and consumers themselves—have in assuring that the collection of data on risk, and the assessment of risk, are accurate?

I emphasize that most of the experimenting that goes on in this society is not really conceived that way by the people who do it. Their focus is on the innovative part of their behavior, and often they would profess amazement at the idea that they are deliberately using others as "subjects" of their innovations. Yet, there is abundant evidence that, even though innovators may not conceptualize what they do as experimental, they are well aware of that feature of their development and marketing of products. A notable example in the law of products liability was the decision of Ford Motor Company to forego the use of design features in the Pinto automobile, estimated to cost $4 to $8 per car, which allegedly would have prevented gruesome injuries caused by fires occurring when other vehicles collided with the rear end of Pintos.[21] This evidence sufficiently enraged a California jury that it awarded $125 million in punitive damages to a young teenager who was hideously burned in a rear-end collision that sparked a fire in the Pinto in which he was a passenger. Although requiring a reduction of the punitive award to $3.5 million, an appeals court accepted a jury finding of "corporate malice," which the trial court had said could "be inferred from acts and conduct, such as by showing that the defendant's conduct was willful, intentional, and done in conscious disregard of its possible results."[22] The appellate court said there was evidence that the manufacturer had "engag[ed] in a cost-benefit analysis balancing human lives and limbs against corporate profits,"[23] which it found qualified under the verbal formula for punitive damages as "conscious and callous disregard of a substantial likelihood of injury to others."[24]

The California appellate court's opinion in the Pinto case was, to say the least, controversial. In defending the case, Ford had pointed out that the phrase "conscious disregard of its possible results" would allow plaintiffs "to impugn almost every design decision as made in conscious disregard of some perceivable risk because safer alternative designs are almost always a possibility."[25] Without judging the strength of the arguments on both sides in that case, I am only making the point that entrepreneurs often are aware, sometimes almost to the dollar, of the comparative costs of certain choices they make and of the injuries those choices may cause.

The concept of the human guinea pig is an emotively powerful one. And, indeed, we are all guinea pigs, much of the time. A major challenge to policy makers and courts in the new millennium is to fashion reasonable controls against the natural tendency of entrepreneurs to conduct risky broad-scale experiments with people in order to gather useful information, including information about risk. I stress that there is general agreement that experimentation is necessary to the innovation that often improves human welfare. The question is what boundaries the law should set for experiments that take chances with the safety of others.

A first line of defense against unreasonable risk is the market. Common sense, not to mention economic theory, tells us that when people are properly informed about risk and able to make choices about it, the market often provides the best solution. It emphasizes freedom of choice, it is not burdened by the administrative costs of regulation, and it is a self-correcting mechanism. Most of the cases that are the subject of this book, however, arise from situations in which the market cannot bring to bear its well-known advantages—for example, because persons at risk do not have sufficient information to avoid the risk at issue or because they are not in a position realistically to make a choice to avoid or minimize it. Yet, one remarkable saga shows how a relatively small, articulate community of sufferers, persons afflicted with HIV, brought pressure against a federal agency to allow them to accept a set of risks of which they were painfully cognizant. This is the story of Chapter 2.

In all of the cases discussed here, law plays a central role. It seeks to encourage technological development and the benefits it brings society, while taking into account the dangers that development poses to society. Sometimes, it must confront the question of whether a clear advantage of benefit over risk should be dispositive when a product or process will cause severe injury to a relatively few people, often people who lack the ability to protect themselves against that harm. Besides deciding when the many who benefit from innovation may ride on the backs of those injured by innovation, the law must decide when to spread the risk of injury to the beneficiaries. It also must provide a matrix for societal judgment of questions that are basically scientific questions—for example, what are the incremental risks to women who take estrogens over their sisters who do not? And it must provide answers to mixed questions of procedure and substance, like those tied up in the issue of what sort of proof it takes to convince a court that a product has caused a particular disease.

Using a broad range of legal, scientific, and journalistic materials, I focus on a few dramatic episodes of perceived threats of harm to consumers and workers. In the background are other, well-publicized controversies about alleged risks of innovation that provide examples of how we serve as experimental vehicles each day. Analysis of these cases yields an anatomy of the law's response to risk, often in the context of fast-moving events, and suggests some lessons about how to deal with a cluster of uncertainties that involve us all.

CHAPTER 1

Experimentation: A Survey at Trench Level

Few hazards to human health and safety inspire as much fear as radiation. It would seem that people who employ radiation would be exquisitely careful, as a matter of ethics, not to mention public relations, in their deliberate use of it on human beings. It is therefore remarkable that the 1990s brought to public light several episodes concerning the experimental use of radiation on people, going back as far as a half century. These included:

- Studies conducted as early as 1945 at three universities and the Oak Ridge National Laboratory, involving the injection of plutonium into terminally ill persons to investigate its effects in the body.[1]
- The use of partial or whole body radiation on 88 cancer patients, of whom more than 50 were black and many indigent, in experimental treatments at the University of Cincinnati over an 11-year period beginning in 1960, allegedly to determine the effects of battlefield radiation on soldiers.[2]
- The irradiation of the testes of 161 prisoners in Oregon and Washington in the 1960s, with the goal of finding the lowest dose that would produce temporary sterility.[3]
- The feeding of radioactive milk to young boys at a state school in Massachusetts, under the pretext that this was part of joining a "science club."[4]
- The use on terminal brain cancer patients of neutron radiation from a boron compound, employed by a national atomic laboratory and a consortium of universities—a procedure allegedly done after the patients were misled about the possibility of medical benefits to them.[5]

These are some of the more horrifying examples of the use of human beings as experimental animals. I shall discuss others in this book, but I stress that the idea of people as guinea pigs has a much broader connotation with more benign aspects. Seeking a theory of regulation that minimizes the adverse effects on people of scientific and technological progress, the book deals primarily with the relatively masked form of experimentation that takes place on the general market with all sorts of products. However, it is useful to begin with a review of principles that have been developed, often as the products of vigorous argument, to govern the rawer forms of human experimentation. In those situations, modern law requires experimenters to identify themselves in that role to persons who become "subjects" of their experiments. It is true that although people undergoing such tests often make their choices under the pressure of terrible diseases, the experimenter does not create that aspect of the grim wager for them. It is also true, however, that in some instances the experimenter seeks only data and not the cure or alleviation of disease in the particular person.

Antecedents of Informed Consent

In 1914, Judge Benjamin Cardozo articulated the proposition that "[e]very human being of adult years and sound mind has a right to determine what shall be done with his own body."[6] This is the standard quotation on the subject, but Cardozo cited a Minnesota Supreme Court case[7] that quoted eloquent language in an even earlier Illinois opinion. In the Illinois case, the appellate court had declared that:

> [u]nder a free government at least, the citizen's first and greatest right, which underlies all others—the right to the inviolability of his person; in other words, the right to himself—is the subject of universal acquiescence, and this right necessarily forbids a physician or surgeon . . . to violate, without permission, the bodily integrity of his patient by a major or capital operation . . . operating on him without his consent or knowledge.[8]

With the rise of a doctrine of informed consent in American tort law involving medical cases—which took place only beginning in the 1970s[9] —Cardozo's pithy declaration has become a traditional rhetorical device. But it was after World War II, in the wake of the Nuremberg trials for Nazi war crimes, that the idea of informed consent acquired its most powerful articulation.

The Nuremberg Code

The seminal document in the modern history of control of experimentation on human subjects is the Nuremberg Code, which came into being in 1947 as the judgment of the Nuremberg Tribunal in the so-called "medical case."[10] Based on ideas originally articulated by two medical witnesses for the prosecution in the trial of Nazi doctors at Nuremberg,[11] the ten principles of the Code reportedly were fashioned principally by a judge on that tribunal.[12]

The first sentence of the Code declared that "[t]he voluntary consent of the human subject is absolutely essential." The first principle continued by requiring that the subject "have legal capacity to give consent; should be so situated as to exercise free power of choice, without the intervention of any element of force, fraud, deceit, duress, overreaching, or other ulterior form of constraint or coercion." It also said that a subject must "have sufficient knowledge and comprehension of the elements of the subject matter" of the experiment "to enable him to make an understanding and enlightened decision." The elements of that knowledge included "the nature, duration, and purpose of the experiment; the method and means by which it is to be conducted; all inconveniences and hazards reasonably to be expected; and the effects upon his health or person which may possibly come from his participation in the experiment."[13]

Another principle declared that "the experiment should be so designed and based on the results of animal experimentation and a knowledge of the natural history of the disease or other problem under study that the anticipated results will justify the performance of the experiment."[14] The Code also said the subject must "be at liberty" to end the experiment "if he has reached the physical or mental state where continuation of the experiment seems to him to be impossible."[15] Moreover, it required investigators "to be prepared to terminate the experiment at any stage" if they had "probable cause to believe . . . that a continuation of the experiment is likely to result in injury, disability, or death to the . . . subject."[16]

Although there have been several more detailed summaries of principles concerning human experimentation over the last 60 years, the Nuremberg Code has not gone out of style. In the case of the boron neutron experiments mentioned previously, a federal district judge quoted language from the Code[17] in concluding that the defendants could not raise the defense of qualified immunity against claims that they violated the "constitutional right to bodily integrity" of the plaintiffs. He declared that "at the very least, the judgment of the Nuremberg Tribunal regarding fundamental legal principles of human subject experimentation served as an explicit international declaration" that the allegations about the conduct of the defendants in the boron neutron case "'shocked the conscience' within the meaning of Justice Frankfurter's words" in a famous Supreme Court opinion.[18]

The Declarations of Helsinki

Following the Nuremberg Code, over a period of more than 30 years beginning in 1964, came a series of detailed codes on human experimentation, collectively titled Declaration[s] of Helsinki. The first Declaration, adopted by the World Medical Association (WMA) in 1964, distinguished "between clinical research in which the aim is essentially therapeutic for a patient, and clinical research the essential object of which is purely scientific and without therapeutic value to the person subjected to the research."[19] The Declaration did allow that doctors could "combine clinical research" for acquiring "new medical knowledge" with "professional care," but cautioned that this could be done "only to the extent that clinical research is justified by its therapeutic value to the patient."[20] The category of "clinical research" obviously responded to the horrors of Nazi experimentation that employed human beings entirely as experimental animals without their consent. The Declaration established firmly the need for consent, "as a rule . . . in writing," obtained from subjects who were "in such a mental, physical, and legal state as to be able to exercise fully [their] power of choice" after explanations of "[t]he nature, the purpose, and the risk" of the research. One principle in the Declaration stressed that investigators "must respect the right of each individual to safeguard his personal integrity, especially if the subject is in a dependent relationship to the investigator."[21]

A second Declaration (Helsinki II), adopted in Tokyo in 1975, added a requirement for a "specially appointed independent committee" to consider protocols for experimentation involving human subjects. It also stressed the need for "careful assessment of predictable risks in comparison with foreseeable benefits to the subject or to others" and specified the weighing of potential benefits and risks "against the advantages of the best current diagnostic and therapeutic methods." This Declaration amplified the concept of consent, using the language "freely-given informed consent, preferably in writing." Another principle required researchers to "cease any investigation if the hazards are found to outweigh the potential benefits."[22] Helsinki II further specified that subjects for "non-therapeutic research" "should be volunteers—either healthy persons or patients for whom the experimental design is not related to the patient's illness."[23]

After a Helsinki III, which made a change concerning the consent of minors, the Association proceeded to Helsinki IV, adopted in Hong Kong in 1989. An important change in that document recognized the potential conflict of interest posed by the professional incentives of investigators and sponsors of research. Helsinki IV required that committees reviewing research protocols be "independent of the investigator and the sponsor provided that this independent committee is in conformity with the laws and regulations of the country in which the . . . experiment is performed."[24]

Placebo Controls

Controversy erupted over a rather fuzzy provision on the use of placebo controls in Helsinki V, which was adopted in 1996. This "Principle" declared:

> In any medical study, every patient—including those of a control group, if any—should be assured of the best proven diagnostic and therapeutic method. This does not exclude the use of inert placebo in studies where no proven diagnostic or therapeutic method exists.[25]

The placebo question already had been a live one. The authors of a 1994 journal article, for example, condemned as "unethical" research experiments in which, even with informed consent, plaintiffs were "assigned a placebo instead of a therapy effective in treating their condition."[26] The authors noted that Food and Drug Administration (FDA) officials believed that placebo controls were "the 'gold standard.'" So strong was this conviction, they observed, that for lack of a test using placebo, the agency had refused to approve a beta-blocker drug for angina pectoris "even though the application showed that the new drug had an effect similar to that of . . . an already approved drug."[27]

The authors found unpersuasive two ethical justifications for the placebo requirement. One was that to withhold accepted treatments "may not lead to serious harm." This rationale, they declared, "concedes to individual investigators and to institutional review boards the right to determine how much discomfort or temporary disability patients should endure for the purpose of research." They pointed out that "[e]thical codes in medical experimentation have been developed expressly to shield patients from such vulnerability." They also criticized an argument based on informed consent, saying that "investigators should not put patients in a position in which their health and well-being could be compromised, even if the patients agree." Among other concerns, they referred to disparities in information between researchers and patients and the distinct possibility that patients in such circumstances might not be able to make rational decisions.[28]

Thus, even before Helsinki V, the battle lines had been forming on the question of whether researchers must use treatments in active use as comparisons with the treatments that are the subject of their experiments. And a principal touchstone of critics was the welfare of the individual patient in situations in which various incentives existed for researchers to reach for the rationalization that they were serving the overall welfare of sufferers.

The placebo issue generated a spirited exchange that continued through the late 1990s. Benjamin Freedman and two collaborators identified what they viewed as several "myths" about placebo-controlled trials, at least in the case of diseases for which treatments already had been developed and were being used in practice. One of these "myths" was that such trials "provide[] an accurate baseline measure of a treatment's biological effectiveness." The authors noted, for example, that the psychology of patients who hope for improvement might make the "placebo effect of effective drugs . . . greater than the placebo effect associated with placebos"[29]— in other words, that their minds could make them feel even better on the real thing than with a sugar pill. Freedman and his colleagues also challenged the premise that placebo-controlled studies were in fact blinded, finding it "dismaying that relatively few studies attempt[ ] to check whether the blind was maintained."[30] Also classifying as a myth the idea that "[p]lacebo controls are simpler than active controls"—that is, existing, standard treatments—"in testing the effectiveness of new drugs,"[31] they raised the possibility that placebo studies would tend to miss differing effects of drugs on different groups in the population.[32]

Although viewing the then-current Helsinki principles as badly worded, Freedman and his colleagues found substance in what they viewed as a core idea of the principles—that is, that those who enrolled in a clinical trial "should not be agreeing to medical attention that is known to be inferior to current medical practice."[33] They attacked the defense of placebo trials based on patient consent, saying that "a poor risk/benefit ratio cannot be compensated for by consent."[34] They argued that it was justifiable to be skeptical about the ability of patients such as those with psychiatric problems "to make an informed choice," noting that "patients in such circumstances have substantial difficulty distinguishing research from treatment" and that "they find it hard to understand that staff would not act in their best interests in all circumstances."[35] Generally, they criticized the premise that "effectiveness" of new drugs meant "absolute effectiveness— better than nothing," a premise on the basis of which they said the FDA required "placebo controls rather than active controls" instead of employing "a more useful measure, such as clinical effectiveness."[36]

Experimentation on Third World Populations

A particular focus of the debate over placebo controls as it developed was experimentation outside the United States, particularly in Africa, where a combination of drugs was being tested for its ability to minimize the transmission of HIV from afflicted pregnant women to their children. In an essay in the *New England Journal of Medicine*, Peter Lurie and Sidney Wolfe, of Public Citizen's Health Group, criticized the use of placebo in these tests instead of other antiretroviral drugs that already were being used for HIV therapy. A particular object of their ire was pressure from a study section of the National Institutes of Health (NIH), brought to bear on investigators at the Harvard School of Public Health, to use a placebo-controlled trial in a study in Thailand. Lurie and Wolfe argued that use of existing drugs as controls would "provide even more useful results than placebo-controlled trials, without the deaths of hundreds of newborns that are inevitable if placebo groups are used."[37]

Marcia Angell, then executive editor of the *New England Journal of Medicine*, spoke of a "slavish adherence to the tenets of clinical trials" in discussing the "strong temptation" of researchers "to subordinate ... subjects' welfare to the objectives" of their studies. She suggested that "[w]ith the most altruistic of motives, researchers may find themselves slipping across a line that prohibits treating human subjects as a means to an end." One focus of her critique was a Uganda study that compared a placebo-controlled group with prophylaxis treatments aimed at reducing tuberculosis in patients with HIV. Although she acknowledged that it was fair to argue that a placebo-controlled trial was ethically justifiable because it was still "uncertain whether prophylaxis will work," she excoriated the argument that it was ethical to use such a trial "because prophylaxis is the 'local standard of care' in sub-Saharan Africa."[38]

Two other commentators focused their guns on the potential phoniness of "informed consent," saying that "[i]n most settings in Africa, voluntary, informed consent will be problematic and difficult, and it may even preclude ethical research." This, they wrote, was "because, in the absence of health care, virtually any offer of medical assistance (even in the guise of research) will be accepted as 'better than nothing' and research will almost inevitably be confused with treatment, making informed consent difficult."[39]

The unrelenting search for pools of impoverished research subjects has continued. A 2005 essay by Indian authors in the *New England Journal of Medicine* criticized a new government rule that allowed trials of new drugs to be conducted in India "at the same time that trials of the same phase are conducted in other countries." This rule replaced a prior directive that limited Indian trials in earlier phases of drug investigations to times only after later phases were tested in other nations. The authors attributed the new rule to "vociferous demands from multinational drug companies and private organizations that conduct clinical research." They noted the advantages that India presented for such trials, including a "genetically diverse population of more than 1 billion people who have not been exposed to many medications but have myriad diseases," doctors who almost all speak English, and "cheap labor and low infrastructure costs."[40]

These critics capsuled several episodes of "illegal and unethical trials" that had recently taken place in India. Pointing out that "[i]n a population such as India's, a large proportion of the subjects in any trial will inevitably be disadvantaged persons," they said it was "of paramount importance to protect the most vulnerable" by assuring "genuinely informed" consent and voluntariness of choice. They targeted one specific concern, which has been raised before in the United States: the offering of "financial inducements to participants." They noted, for example, that researchers were "paying illiterate blue-collar workers more per month to participate in a trial than they earn at their jobs and . . . providing medication that is worth more than their annual salary." With respect to the latter inducement, they said that "no protocol we have ever seen has promised to continue to supply the studied medication free of charge after completion of the trial, if it is found to be beneficial."[41]

A complicating factor with respect to alternative therapies in clinical tests in underdeveloped countries is the cost of the alternative therapy. Barry Bloom, dean of the Harvard School of Public Health, noted that the cost of the "best proven therapeutic" could range up to $15,000 annually per patient and raised questions about who would absorb that cost.[42] One writer who reviewed the controversy essentially lamented that it is, literally, a poor world. He sorrowfully indicated that it was the "maldistribution of wealth and resources that both mandates these [placebo-controlled] studies and, at the same time, renders them so troubling."[43]

Cost was a consideration in what began as placebo-controlled studies in Thailand on pregnant women with human immunodeficiency virus (HIV). One such study was terminated as an existing drug became available through a Red Cross donation program and funds provided by the country's Ministry of Health. However, other placebo-controlled studies continued, even though one Thai commentator said that the cost of the existing drug "would constitute only a small fraction of the . . . budget" for one of those studies.[44] In reply, letters from investigators in one of the Thai studies stressed that the existing HIV drug AZT, (zidovudine), was not available for distribution to provincial hospitals when their study began. They argued that "[s]ince zinovudine is not the standard of care in the region, its availability solely through the research study would represent an unethical coercive enticement or inducement to participate."[45]

As these arguments continued, there came an announcement that a Thailand study of the relatively short-term administration of zidovudine—which cost approximately $50 per person for the pregnant women on whom it was being tested—had shown that that drug worked "almost as well" as a much more expensive, longer term treatment. That study had involved placebo controls, but after its results became clear, officials of the Centers for Disease Control and Prevention (CDC), NIH, and the UN AIDS program said they would recommend stopping several other placebo studies that were going on across the world on mother-to-child transmission of HIV.[46]

Harold Varmus of the NIH and David Satcher of the CDC joined the debate with an emphasis that a placebo-controlled study "provides definitive answers to questions about the safety and value of an intervention in the setting in which the study is performed," asserting that "these answers are the point of the research." Vigorously answering critics, they said such studies were "not a case of treating research subjects as a means to an end, nor does it reflect a callous disregard of their welfare." Rather, they declared, "a placebo-controlled study may be the only way to obtain an answer that is ultimately useful to people in similar circumstances." They capped their argument by saying that to "enroll subjects in a study that exposes them to unknown risks and is designed in a way that is unlikely to provide results that are useful to the subjects or others in the population," would be to "fail[] the test of beneficence."[47]

The term "beneficence" in this context is freighted with academic meaning. John Harris, an English professor of bioethics, has written of "a powerful obligation to pursue support, and participate in scientific research." He refers, in this connection, to the "duty of beneficence, our basic moral obligation to help other people in need."[48] He asserts that "[w]e all benefit from living in a society and, indeed, in a world in which serious scientific research is carried out and which utilises the benefits of past research." Working from this premise, he contends that "there is a clear moral obligation to participate in medical research in certain specific circumstances," although stressing that he is making an ethical argument and not "advocating mandatory participation."[49] Arguing against "a narrow interpretation of the requirement that research be of benefit to the subject of the research,"[50] Harris asserts that "we are justified in assuming that a person would want to discharge his or her moral obligations in cases where we have no knowledge about their actual preferences." He even pushes the argument to the point of saying that "[t]o do otherwise would be to impute moral turpitude as a default."[51]

Advancing a somewhat different line of argument, Robert Levine found it "necessary to acknowledge with regret that there are great imbalances in the distribution of wealth among the nations of the world." This led him to contend that "[d]eveloping countries that cannot afford all the goods and services" available in industrialized nations "must be allowed to develop treatments and preventive interventions that they can afford."[52]

Levine was a disputant in a controversy that cropped up in 1999 when a study group set to work drafting a revision of the Declaration of Helsinki. A medical school professor who was chair of the Human Investigations Committee at Yale, he headed the group. Its draft declared that a patient who was a research subject should have "the best proven diagnostic, prophylactic, or therapeutic methods that would otherwise be available to him or her." However, according to one account, critics complained that this language "legitimized a two-tier standard of care and the exploitation of poor societies"; Peter Lurie characterized the draft as "an attempt to water down the declaration to introduce economic relativism." The debate culminated in Levine's "ouster from the revision process."[53] Subsequently, in 2000, the WMA adopted a revised Declaration that said that "the benefits, risks, burdens and effectiveness of a new method should be tested against those of the best current prophylactic, diagnostic, and therapeutic methods." A qualification was that this did "not exclude the use of placebo, or no treatment, in studies where no proven prophylactic, diagnostic or therapeutic method exists."[54] The new version added the phrase "no treatment" to the latter clause as it was worded in Helsinki V in 1996.

That hardly ended the argument. Levine, for example, said that to have forbidden placebo trials in the past would have been to sacrifice the development of drugs for high blood pressure and stomach ulcers, because there were existing treatments that research eventually showed were less effective than the new drugs. Robert Temple, director of medical policy at the FDA's Center for Drug Evaluation and Research (CDER), called the revision absolutist and asserted that it would keep researchers from using placebo testing on new drugs for hay fever and migraine.[55]

Apparently with these arguments in mind, in 2001 the WMA appended a "note of clarification" to the 2000 revision. This note "reaffirm[ed]" the WMA's "position that extreme care must be taken in making use of a placebo-controlled trial and that in general this methodology should only be used in the absence of existing proven therapy." However, the note said that such a trial "may be ethically acceptable, even if proven therapy is available," when there were "compelling and scientifically sound methodological reasons" that made "its use . . . necessary to determine the efficacy or safety of a prophylactic, diagnostic or therapeutic method" or where such a method was "being investigated for a minor condition and the patients who receive placebo will not be subject to any additional risk of serious or irreversible harm."[56] Another clarifying note, added in 2004, was appended to a principle that required that subjects of a study "should be assured of the best proven prophylactic, diagnostic and therapeutic methods identified by the study."[57] The clarifying note stressed the necessity "during the study planning process to identify post-trial access by study participants" to procedures "identified as beneficial in the study or access to other appropriate care."[58]

This episode, drawn from classic, controlled experimentation, gives us several lessons for the broader topic of this book, which focuses on much larger scale, uncontrolled experimentation on the general public. One lesson is the controversial nature of some established scientific methodologies, even if they are "gold standards." Another lesson concerns the problem that ordinary people face in making up their minds about choices in consumer goods. Despite the premise of consumer sovereignty that infuses much economic theorizing, lay persons are quite dependent on experts' views of risks and benefits—and are likely to be frustrated when the experts disagree, as is often the case. This state of affairs casts a shadow over the idea of "informed consent," whether it is employed in a controlled setting or stretched to cover broad-scale experiments on mass markets. These observations spotlight not only the need for information but the frequent existence of uncertainty in the choices we make in our daily lives. The best available information may turn out to be only information about the range of uncertainty, and this is a difficult point to put across to people who are not experts.

The issue of placebo trials in underdeveloped countries adds another set of dimensions to the problem—those of scarcity and affordability. It is a commonplace among economists that requiring only the best will be costly to poor people who would be willing—if they were properly informed—to use a product or service that is of relatively low quality but is better than no product at all. However, one must also keep in mind the slipperiness of the slope that descends from the argument that for the poor, something is better than nothing. At the bottom of that slope, disadvantaged and ignorant people can become no more than experimental animals.

Some Recent Case Histories

As successive revisions of the Helsinki principles were published, from time to time tragic stories surfaced about experiments allegedly gone wrong. These cases did not have the horrific overlay of the radiation cases that introduced this chapter, from which there emanates the odor of governmental officials imposing on extremely vulnerable people like prisoners and persons in poverty. Rather, they arose from seemingly conventional clinical experimentation. However, taking the allegations at face, these episodes were at the least troubling.

The Hepatitis Drug Cases

One group of cases, which came to light in 1994, involved the deaths of five patients who had taken a drug designed for treatment of hepatitis B. In the background were failures to "connect the dots" on the deaths of four patients who took the drug earlier. Those events had not been reported to the FDA because investigators believed that the deaths had been "associated with . . . underlying illnesses" rather than the toxicity of the drug. The principal scientist at the NIH for the later experiment reportedly said that he thought that the symptoms of some of the people who died in those tests were linked to underlying disease "until the deaths [in his experiment] began to occur."

Controversy arose in the wake of this incident because of the FDA's proposal of new rules for drug investigations, which included a presumption that adverse reactions were caused by a drug being tested unless there was proof to the contrary. The proposed rules also mandated use of "safety monitor[s]" approved by the agency, and they required more frequent detailed safety reports on drugs. However, scientists who had reviewed the deaths from the hepatitis drug said they wished that the agency had postponed its proposal until an investigation of the deaths that was in progress was completed. That inquiry, conducted by the Institute of Medicine (IOM), was the third one that had been held on the cases, the first two having been mounted by the FDA and the NIH.[59] The fact that three important bodies had investigated this small group of deaths and that two scientists involved in the NIH inquiry had called for patience underlined the scientific complexity of such matters. Sotto voce, there also was a suggestion of politics about turf.

After a series of amendments, the FDA's rules for reports on investigational drugs now require reporting of "serious and unexpected" "adverse drug experience[s]" in connection with new drug investigations.[60] The rules define "serious adverse drug experiences" as "[d]eath, a life-threatening adverse drug experience, inpatient hospitalization, or prolongation of existing hospitalization, a persistent or significant disability/incapacity, or a congenital anomaly/birth defect."[61] The definition of "unexpected" gives a description of events where the "specificity or severity" of an "adverse drug experience" was "not consistent with the current investigator brochure," or if there were no such brochure, where "the specificity or severity" of the event was "not consistent with the risk information described in the general investigational plan or elsewhere in the current application, as amended."[62] The amended regulations require reports to the agency of "serious and unexpected" adverse drug experiences that occur after the marketing of a drug, "as soon as possible, but no later than 15 calendar days" after the sponsor receives the information.[63] Their definition of "serious" is identical to that for investigational new drug reports. The definition of "unexpected" simply includes "[a]ny adverse drug experience that is not listed in the current labeling for the drug product."[64]

Jesse Gelsinger

A much-publicized case involving the death of a human subject was that of Jesse Gelsinger. He died at 18 years of age after a gene therapy experiment fashioned in the Institute of Human Gene Therapy at the University of Pennsylvania. Gelsinger suffered from ornithine transcarbamylase (OTC) deficiency, which leads to high levels of ammonia in the blood, but he was able to keep this metabolic disease under control with a low-protein diet and 32 pills a day.[65] Allegedly, he entered the experiment knowing that it was not designed to benefit him directly but to test the safety of a therapy for babies who had a fatal form of OTC deficiency, although there apparently was some indication of hope for alleviation of his disease in the future.[66] His father, Paul Gelsinger, told Stone Phillips of NBC that his son had believed "he was going to help others. Like he said, 'Help the babies.'"[67]

The experiment involved the infusion into Gelsinger of genes via a "vector," a weakened form of the cold virus adenovirus. The lead scientist was James Wilson, who the director of the NIH later said was at the time "at the top of the world," "one of the touted stars of biomedical research."[68] The dose given to Gelsinger had been tested in various animals and then in one woman, who was said to have "done 'quite well,'" although three monkeys reportedly had died from an administration of the vector that was "20 times the highest dose planned for the study."[69]

At the time Gelsinger received the infusion, September 1999, there had been biting criticism by some scientists of what they viewed as the unmerited trumpeting of the potential of gene therapy. Dr. Harold Varmus, the formidable director of the NIH, had said researchers were creating "the mistaken and widespread perception of success." Ruth Macklin, a member of the Recombinant DNA Advisory Committee (RAC), which has oversight of research on gene therapy, said that "Gene therapy is not yet therapy."[70] And one scientist who had reviewed the Penn experiment for the RAC was said to be "troubled" by reports on the three monkeys who had died. Moreover, the investigators injected the vector used in Gelsinger directly into his bloodstream, which had never been done before. Two reviewers had opposed the test, at least for volunteers who did not have active symptoms.[71]

Within four days after he received the infusion, Jesse Gelsinger died. He went into a coma the day after the infusion, overwhelmed by a blood clotting disorder—a problem that had been observed in the monkeys who had died—and then suffered multiple organ failures.[72]

One RAC member, Louise Markert of Duke University, said the death "really came as quite a surprise." She said she did not "think that anyone could barely conceive that this would happen and it's just a tragedy."[73]

Gelsinger's father Paul, a handyman, who had been "enthusiastic" about the experiment,[74] now spoke of a lack of advance information about prior animal data and about risks. He said, as one report summarized it, that "[n]either he nor his son knew that despite 300 clinical trials, gene therapy had never cured anyone." He also claimed that one of the principal investigators said that "the treatment was already working in some patients" and that his son's particular illness would make it possible to "'show exactly how well this works.'"[75]

Problems that wove in and out of the Gelsinger episode involved independence of opinion, defined both in terms of professional and financial incentives, and informed consent. With respect to the need for information or opinions independent of investigators, Paul Gelsinger said he "would have liked to have had somebody there who was not affiliated with Penn that could have assisted in describing the whole process of gene therapy." And Ruth Macklin of the RAC pointed out that one factor that distinguished the area of gene therapy from "general run-of-the-mill research" was that "large numbers" of gene therapy researchers "themselves have a financial stake." As to informed consent, one piece of the Gelsinger episode was that the Gelsingers' informed consent form did not contain information about the monkeys who had died from a stronger dose. Paul Gelsinger also said that he had not known about the existence of the RAC until after his son died, let alone about the opinions of some members that the experiment should not be done.[76]

Agonizing over his son's death, Paul Gelsinger had a "heart-to-heart talk" with Wilson on a "late night hike...through the Arizona desert." During that conversation, Gelsinger later told a reporter, Wilson "express[ed] his concern with losing his institute...250 people depended upon his institute remaining open." Gelsinger said that at this point during the walk, "I put my hand on his shoulder, and I looked him in the eye, and I said, 'You know Jim, it could be a whole lot worse.' I said, 'You could lose one of your kids.' And that stopped him cold. And he stopped and nodded his head and said, 'Yeah, you're right.'"[77]

With all this, though, Paul Gelsinger revealed an inner torment about what should be done. He reportedly said that he wanted gene therapy work to go forward and expressed concern that other researchers were "backing away" from Wilson: "They'll sacrifice Penn, they'll sacrifice Jim Wilson," he said. "These guys screwed up, yes. But they should not be put out of business....I want them to make this thing work, and do it right."[78] In the jargon of biomedical ethics, this seemed a hymn to "beneficence."

The Penn Institute for Human Gene Therapy, in a response to some "Inspectional Observations" by the FDA, insisted that "each and every patient who participated in the [OTC deficiency] trial gave informed consent to participate" and that the Institute had "contemporaneously documented each patient's eligibility to participate." It noted that three primates in a prior animal study had "received a dosage approximately 17 times higher than the highest dose in the OTCD trial."[79]

Despite Penn's defense and Paul Gelsinger's initial plea on behalf of Wilson, however, some planks undergirding the Penn experiment began to fall—and then the roof caved in. It collapsed with Paul Gelsinger testifying to a Senate committee, independent lawsuits by Gelsinger and the federal government, and the administration of some severe sanctions.

In January 2000, the FDA—which had suspended the trial in which Gelsinger participated after he died—stopped all of Penn's other human trials of gene therapy. The agency later acknowledged that its own monitoring "was sometimes 'less than adequate,'" in part because sponsors of research did not have to disclose potential financial conflicts of interest until after the completion of a drug trial.[80]

In February, Paul Gelsinger testified to the Public Health Subcommittee of the Senate Health, Education, and Labor Committee. Now, his ambivalent support gave way to a detailed indictment. He told the committee that he and his son had been told that "a prior patient, the patient before him, had shown a clinical improvement of 50 percent in her ability to eliminate ammonia from her system following gene therapy," but that he had "discovered that no efficacy was achieved at all in this patient." He declared also that he and Jesse had been "unaware of the severity of liver injury incurred by several of the patients prior to Jesse" and that "Penn . . . removed from the information they gave Jesse and me any reference to deaths of monkeys which had previously appeared in their documents." Moreover, he said, he learned at an "RAC meeting in December . . . that at least one other monkey died in a related study using the same adenoviral[81] vector used on Jesse."[82]

Paul Gelsinger's bill of particulars continued. He also learned, he said, that "Penn neglected to follow its own and FDA protocols when it found that Jesse had ammonia levels about the permissible limits, a clear danger sign, and yet went forward with the procedure anyway." Further, he said, he learned that a drug company that had conducted similar experiments had "obtained adverse results which, if disclosed, would have fully informed Jesse and me of the real risks of this procedure." He also discovered, he said, "that only six percent of nearly 700 adverse events were reported properly to the NIH."[83]

Gelsinger also criticized the "short statement" in the consent form that "The University of Pennsylvania and Dr. James Wilson" had a "financial interest in a successful outcome"; he told a committee that he could not have imagined what that meant.[84] What it meant was that Wilson "had founded a private research company, Genovo, in which he held stock," and which "contribute[d] a healthy portion" of the "overall budget" of the Penn Institute, although it had not funded the study in which Jesse Gelsinger died.[85] (It should be noted that the notoriety of these events did not prevent the Seattle-based firm Targeted Genetics from acquiring Genovo in August 2000 to try to "consolidate its position using adeno-associated vectors in gene therapy.")[86]

In late 2000, the FDA sent Wilson a letter that proposed to disqualify him for clinical investigations—as one account put it, the rough equivalent of disbarring a lawyer. The agency said that the experiment "repeatedly or deliberately violated regulations governing the proper conduct of clinical studies." It declared that people coming into the study "were misled" into thinking that the FDA "was comfortable with the study . . . when the researchers had failed to inform the agency about instances of serious toxicity in previous volunteers that should have resulted in the study being halted." It also noted that the informed consent form did not mention the monkey deaths and further said that the investigators had enrolled Jesse Gelsinger "and another volunteer . . . despite medical tests results that indicated that they were ineligible for the study."[87]

There were simultaneous developments on the litigation front. As Paul Gelsinger's disaffection came to a boil, he brought a civil suit against Penn, the Genovo firm, Wilson, two other scientists, and those scientists' institutions. The defendants settled for an undisclosed amount in November 2000. Gelsinger said that "[d]ealing with the money end of this . . . was probably one of the most difficult aspects . . . because this experiment was all about money, and it was never about money for Jesse." He said he would use part of the settlement money to raise "public awareness of the need to protect human subjects."[88]

Another shoe was to drop in the civil litigation area, but the end of that story was not written until five years later. In 2005, the U.S. Attorney's office in Philadelphia announced it had arrived at civil settlements with Penn, Wilson, two other scientists, and the Children's National Medical Center (CNMC), where one of the other scientists worked. Ending a suit brought by the Government under the federal False Claims Act, this settlement administered more than a spanking. Besides requiring substantial payments of money, it imposed many conditions. Penn and the CNMC agreed to pay more than a half million dollars in fines each, and each committed itself to a variety of activities designed to increase patient safety in human research. Penn, for example, committed itself to "[m]andatory training for all investigators and clinical coordinators" in various aspects of patient protection and to "[i]nitial monitoring and oversight of clinical research through an independent Contract Research Organization," as well as the creation of an "Office of Human Research" under a vice dean.[89]

The terms of the settlement were particularly rigorous for Wilson. Having been shut out of human clinical trials since 2000, he now faced five more years' deprivation of sponsorship of clinical trials regulated by the FDA. He would have to "meet imposed training/educational requirements applicable to human research participant protection and clinical research." Besides that, he would have to have a "Medical Monitor" for three years while conducting "restricted clinical activity" in order "to gain practical experience." And he would have to submit to a "Special Monitor" who would "oversee" even animal research where it "could influence the safety of human research participants." Just to insure that the message was clear, the settlement said Wilson had "agreed to lecture and author an article on the lessons learned from this study" and that he would "advocate for the inclusion of any statements from those affected by the study, e.g., the Gelsinger family," with such statements to be "at the discretion of the Gelsingers."[90] No defendants admitted liability, and CNMC and its researcher denied that "they engaged in any unlawful activity" and indeed said that "their conduct was at all times in good faith, appropriate, and in the best interest of the study participants."[91]

For his part, Wilson commented that the settlement would allow him to "continue to devote myself fully to my laboratory research" on gene transfer vectors.[92] Indeed, as early as 2001 the British journal *Lancet* had reported that Wilson's laboratory had developed "an HIV-based viral vector that carries envelope proteins from the Ebola virus." As the *Lancet* report summarized it, Wilson's group said it hoped that the vector could be useful in fashioning "an effective gene therapy for cystic fibrosis." A Berlin researcher, although saying that the research was "intriguing," reportedly commented that "safety concerns" were "under-represented in the study."[93]

The Gelsinger episode presents, in cameo, several significant elements of the process of human experimentation, both in clinical settings and on the mass market. These include the problem of how technical information about risk can be communicated to lay persons and the necessary element of uncertainty in collection and interpretation of data at the frontier of research. They involve disagreement among experts on matters where the stakes include life and limb for human subjects and innovation for the benefit of society more generally. How does one strike the proper balance between running with the caution light on and fostering medical progress?

The scope and complexity of the enterprise of gene therapy is evident not only in the holes in the regulatory fabric revealed in the Senate hearing at which Paul Gelsinger appeared, but also in assertions by scientists at that hearing about the promise of gene therapy. The magnitude of the research is evident in two colloquies that Senator Frist, himself a physician, had with witnesses at the hearing. One of those witnesses, director of the FDA's Office of Therapeutics Research and Review, said there were 212 Investigational New Drug (IND) projects that were "active"—they were "authorized to proceed"—and that "[m]any or most would be enrolling patients." Another witness, the director of the NIH's Office of Biotechnology Activities, said that her agency had "funded or supported" 160 clinical trials. Frist queried both witnesses on the difference between these numbers: "why do you have 212 and she has 160?" Told that the difference could be ascribed to the fact that an IND application could "encompass a number of trials," he asked the NIH official, "are there gene therapy trials that you see that aren't conducted at those institutions that are not NIH funded that you would not see?" She replied, "You'd have to call on my colleagues at FDA to answer that question," and the FDA witness said, "I don't have awareness of that but [sic] I cannot give a definitive answer." Frist responded to both witnesses, "[a]s we struggle to make sure . . . what you're doing and what you're doing, which are two different things, both of them important, we need to have that information."[94]

Frist also found intriguing, if not encouraging, testimony that only 39 of 691 "adverse events . . . in adenoviral trials" had been the subjects of "timely" reports to the NIH.[95] One hears the edge in his voice in the printed record when he says to the NIH official, "based on your past experience the last several months, they have not been reporting to you, you sent a letter out [on adenovirus alone], 600 report all of a sudden and now we have 75 percent more experiments that you have sent, you've sent a letter out to them as well?" The official's reply was, simply, "Yes."[96]

As one reflects on the massive noncompliance with regulatory requirements these numbers reflect, the picture becomes further complicated by a story of early triumph and sobering second looks. The gene therapy enthusiast Theodore Friedmann, speaking at a meeting of the American Association for the Advancement of Science in 2000, favorably referred to French experiments with small boys who had a form of severe combined immune deficiency (SCID). As he summarized the results of this research, which he said involved "nothing new in method," the children "are now to all appearances immunologically reconstituted entirely." However, clouding this picture of progress was later news that the French scientists halted their trials because three patients out of ten who had done well in the early phases of the research had developed a "leukemia-like disease." One died; the other two, treated with massive chemotherapy, were "doing well, as well as the other seven."[97]

Friedmann, described by one writer as "gene therapy's most ardent advocate," extolled what the writer characterized as "the unprecedented possibilities" in gene transfer—of a world in which medicine could reach "underlying causes" rather than only treat "signs and symptoms." Yet, Friedmann encapsuled the problem of scientific experimentation that is at the base of the regulatory problem: "medicine has always had to work with imperfect knowledge and technology."[98]

The topic remained a live one at the FDA. In late 2006, it issued a "guidance for industry" document that focused on "delayed adverse events" rather than the type of sudden reaction that took Jesse Gelsinger's life. This document, which included a chart with sequential questions to be answered by investigators, included recommendations for risk assessment and "specific advice regarding the duration and design of long-term follow-up observations." Of general relevance was a section labeled "Informed Consent in Trials Involving Retroviral Vectors," which required the provision to "[e]ach subject in an investigation" of "a description of any reasonably foreseeable risks from participating in the investigation." This section provided, as a highly specific example of the kind of language that should be used to inform patients of risks, a description of the French SCID study. The illustration included references both to the children who developed a "leukemia-like malignant disease" and to the fact that most of the children in the experiment had "not been found" to have the disease, although cautioning that "[a]lthough they appear healthy, we still do not know whether they, too, will develop a malignant growth."[99]

A remark of James Wilson epitomizes an important aspect of the broader problem illustrated by gene therapy experiments. A journalist reported a dinner conversation in which Wilson expressed his worry about "the morale of his staff," who was concerned about whether the institute would lose its financial sponsors and whether volunteers would stop coming. One of his most telling expressions of anxiety, though, was, as the reporter put it, "whether he would lose his bravado—the death knell for a scientist on the cutting edge." As the reporter quoted him, "My concern is, I'm going to get timid, that I'll get risk averse."[100]

Ellen Roche

A death in 2001 at another prestigious institution, Johns Hopkins, taught more lessons. These included the lesson that even top-of-the-line research centers could have been much more careful than they had been about human experimentation. The episode also suggested that although independent review of research protocols can be costly, it can save lives.

The person who died—this time a volunteer in an experiment without any projected direct benefit to anyone—was 24-year-old Ellen Roche. She was a laboratory technician at Hopkins, which, incidentally, stoutly denied that employees were "expected to volunteer as part of their work[]."[101] Roche died four weeks after she inhaled hexamethonium bromide, which the FDA had not approved for clinical use. The purpose of the experiment, as a science publication explained it, was "to examine two aspects of normal lung physiology," namely bronchoprotection and bronchodilation.[102] Roche was the third volunteer to inhale the chemical, which was described as "a ganglion blocking drug that affects the nervous system, lowering blood pressure and relaxing the airways,"[103] but the first to inhale it from a "more powerful spray mechanism" than was used on the first two. Her death, on June 2, 2001, must have been agonizing: the chemical irreversibly damaged her lung sacs, causing slow asphyxiation over the period of a month, and ultimately she had multiple organ failure.[104]

The lead investigator on the Hopkins study, Alkis Togias, notified the institutional review board (IRB) at the school on May 9 of "a serious adverse event," and on May 17, a vice dean at Hopkins notified the U.S. Office for Human Research Protections (OHRP). Hopkins made the matter public June 13, announcing, "with deep regret, the recent death of a volunteer research subject."[105] A few days later, a spokesperson in the university's public relations office said it was "proper to characterize this as a mysterious death."[106]

By July, the FDA declared that Togias had not reported "an unanticipated adverse event"—a persistent cough—in another volunteer. The agency also criticized the "failure to follow the approved scientific blueprint in preparing the . . . drug" and "failure to inform participants that the drug . . . was experimental." Later that month, the medical dean at Hopkins, Edward Miller, took "full institutional responsibility" for Roche's death, although saying that "[t]he precise cause is likely to remain uncertain."[107]

After a preliminary internal report, the university suspended Togias from other research. The Hopkins report said that Togias "did not initially ask the FDA for permission to have volunteers inhale drugs that would trigger asthma-like reactions in their lungs" and had changed the method of administration without notifying anyone. It also noted that Roche's consent form did not identify the dangers of the chemical. Hopkins officials did say that Togias and the IRB had not thought they had to get FDA approval because hexamethonium was "already being used for basic physiology tests." But although they asserted Togias had "made a good effort," they acknowledged that "the consent form would not have been granted if the dangers of this drug were concealed."[108]

The OHRP, which like the FDA was investigating the case, was not that forgiving. On July 19, it imposed a suspension on all federally supported research at Hopkins that used human subjects. The vastness of Hopkins' involvement in what might properly be called the business of science is evident in the fact that the University's researchers were then conducting 2,800 clinical trials. The OHRP lifted the suspension for most Hopkins studies after three days,[109] although a reinstatement of all studies except Togias' studies took up to six months.[110] By September, the FDA had reached the harsh conclusion that, as David Lepay, a senior adviser to the agency, expressed it, "there was a systemic problem in the whole oversight scheme" that the university used for clinical research.[111]

Hopkins had a tremendous stake in its image: with funds tied to clinical trials amounting to over $300 million, it received the most federal research money in the country.[112] An article by medical dean Miller, in a university publication dated Fall 2001, detailed a number of improvements the institution was making in its systems. Saying that he "was stunned by the magnitude of the action by" OHRP, he announced that Hopkins was creating "additional Institutional Review Boards and enhanced IRB training for faculty." The university also would "require[] investigators who use any non-FDA-approved substance to file an application for an Investigational New Drug (IND)" and to "provide substantial evidence of safety for human use" where the FDA did not require an IND. Dean Miller also mentioned "[a] special committee" that would create "a policy that requires involvement of an investigational drug service in all studies using drugs or substances in human subjects" at the Hopkins hospital and at its Bayview Medical Center, where Roche died. He wrote also of a "team of faculty and staff volunteers that has devoted countless hours, including nights and weekends, to . . . developing our corrective-action plan" and which had been working "with the federal agencies re-reviewing hundreds of protocols."[113]

This broadly gauged response from a vast research institution drew praise from the FDA senior adviser, Lepay, who said that by contrast with the university's early reactions, "we do feel that Hopkins is now taking this very seriously."[114] One question that did present itself, however, was this: Given the large gaps that the agencies found in Hopkins' oversight, and Hopkins' contrite and time-consuming response, why did it take a death to generate large-scale reform? Stuart Finder, who directed Vanderbilt's Center for Clinical and Research Ethics, said it had been the Gelsinger case that "was the wake-up call for many institutions." He added, "[h]ere at Vanderbilt, we said, 'We need to devote more resources to make sure we're doing things the right way.'"[115]

The existence of many pockets of lax oversight—a situation, I would observe, that is not limited to medical research—indicates a need for entities that experiment with human beings to institutionalize Cassandras, either within or without their formal structures. These institutions require people whose job it is to raise alarms before deaths and injuries inflict costs not only on those who serve as experimental subjects, but on the entities themselves. Only one of those costs is that of civil litigation: Roche's parents, who had had to decide to take their daughter off life support, sued Hopkins, which settled.[116]

If Hopkins had begun to reform itself, Alkis Togias remained in a pitiless spotlight. At the end of March 2003, the FDA sent him a "warning letter" saying that he had violated the Food, Drug, and Cosmetic Act and agency regulations "by initiating a clinical investigation . . . without submitting an . . . IND." The agency said Togias had not provided "adequate animal toxicity data," which was "an essential basis for you . . . to have concluded that it was reasonably safe" to use the product in humans. It asserted that he had "not describe[d] adequately the clinical procedures and other measures" to "minimize risk to these subjects." It noted the failure to report a change in the saline solution in which the hexamethonium bromide was suspended. It also pointed out that the investigator had not reported to the IRB that Roche had fatigue or drooping eyelids after two successive administrations of the product.[117]

A fundamental point in the FDA letter with respect to informed consent was that "the consent form failed to disclose that the inhalation of hexamethonium bromide was an experimental use of the drug." The letter also observed that the consent form had said that the drug was "a medication" and did not disclose that it would be "chemical grade, labeled for laboratory use only and not for drug use." The letter added that this catalog of criticisms was "not intended to be an all-inclusive list of deficiencies with your clinical studies of investigational drugs." It ordered Togias to respond on what "specific corrective actions" he had taken or would take and "recommend[ed]" that he sign a "restricted agreement . . . regarding your future use of investigational new drugs." [118]

At this point, Hopkins had made an internal investigation and the OHRP and FDA had conducted inquiries into the case. Hopkins had undertaken a comprehensive reform of its clinical research program. The FDA had sliced and diced Togias' research procedures. Yet, even then, a member of an external committee set up by Hopkins to review its human research reportedly said that it was "still unclear when researchers who aren't developing drugs need FDA clearance for human tests." A news report summarized this person—Alastair Wood, an assistant vice chancellor at Vanderbilt—as saying that "[f]or years . . . many researchers have used substances already present in the human body to trigger reactions such as the raising or lowering of blood pressure without seeking FDA approval." The reporter, noting that "[h]examethonium bromide is not naturally present [in] the body," explained that these studies were "precursors to later, FDA-approved studies in which drugs are tested in people to see if they counter these reactions." She quoted Wood's laconic statement, "I think clarity would be useful."[119]

A Damaging Antibody

Episodes of drug trials gone wrong continue to crop up. A publicized case in 2006, involving frontier biotechnology, arose from "severe inflammatory reaction[s] and multi-organ failure" in six men who were test subjects for a monoclonal antibody, a so-called "superantibody," in a London hospital. The maker of the product, the Wurzburg company TeGenero, had developed it to treat leukemia, rheumatoid arthritis, and multiple sclerosis.[120] As a press report described it, within hours of injection of the drug all six men "were . . . experiencing . . . cytokine storm, where an outpouring of immune molecules attack organs of the body." Several months later, tests indicated that all the men were "suffering from severely damaged immune systems that will probably leave them vulnerable to disease for life."[121]

A preliminary investigation by the U.K. Medicines and Healthcare Products Regulatory Agency "concluded that the root of the problem lay not in contamination or incorrect dosages" but in the effects on the body of the drug itself.

Scientists speculated to a reporter that the product had activated many more T cells than it was supposed to target, unleashing the "cytokine storm." The reporter said that "[s]everal medical experts" had opined that the incident "highlight[ed] the need for caution in designing trials of biotechnology drugs that work through novel mechanisms."[122]

Lawyers will tell you that as activities become more complicated, it becomes difficult in proportion to their complexity to write detailed codes to cover those activities. The episodes described earlier, viewed in progression, suggest that at some point the question becomes one of institutional culture. I have served on IRBs at two excellent medical schools. Most of the members of those boards demonstrated significant sensitivity to the issues of human dignity and effective communication of relevant information that brought IRBs into being. However, I have witnessed discussions of research protocols in which the investigators have shown themselves—to use modern jargon—to be clueless about fundamental principles governing human research. As the Hopkins story and the quotation from Stuart Finder of Vanderbilt indicate, attitudes at specific medical centers require particularized scrutiny.

Alphabet Soups

The twenty-first century brought a new tangle of issues about clinical experimentation, featuring applications ranging from the battlefield to the cancer clinic and bureaucratic warfare over turf fought in a jungle of overlapping jurisdictional interests. In 2001, the National Bioethics Advisory Commission (NBAC) recommended the establishment of a single office to monitor research by private parties as well as governmentally funded investigators. NBAC suggested that this office, which it titled the National Office for Human Research Oversight, should not be subject to the jurisdiction of the OHRP, which is under the Department of Health and Human Services. Although the executive director of NBAC acknowledged that the commission had not found "evidence of widespread problems in either public or private human subjects research," he said that it "felt that the principle of respect for participants in human research is one that extends to all participants, regardless of funding source."[123]

Disagreement came from the president-elect of the Federation of American Society for Experimental Biology (FASEB), Robert Rich, who said that OHRP had "all the tools it needs" and contended that the proposed independent panel "would be subject to greater political pressures." At the same time, a half dozen university and research groups, which included FASEB, announced that they had formed an association to "operate a voluntary national accreditation program to monitor clinical research carried out with either public or private funding." The name of this group was the Association for the Accreditation of Human Research Protection Programs.[124]

This soup of acronyms symbolizes the complicated politics of formal experimentation on human beings. Enriching the soup, not only of institutions but of issues, was a proposal by the Environmental Protection Agency (EPA) for a regulatory standard on human subjects research. Commentators raised concerns about this proposal, in which the EPA took note of the fact that "third-party" data—summarized by critics as being data "from academia, industry, or public interest groups"—was "not legally subject" to what is known as "the Common Rule."[125] In the commentators' summary, that Rule, administered by the Department of Health and Human Services, sets out "accepted ethical standards for the protection of human subjects in research conducted or sponsored by all federal agencies."[126] These critics found "troubling the notion that the ethical standard for a human toxicity test or a clinical trial would be different when conducted by a nonprofit organization or an industry." They faulted a suggestion by the National Research Council to create "an EPA review process and review board for human studies proposed for use in formulating regulations," under which "[p]rivate entities would submit research plans before beginning a study, and again before submitting the study results." Dryly, they commented that "[i]t is unclear how post-study review can contribute to protection of research subjects." They suggested that "EPA require that private entities obtain review under the Common Rule or its foreign equivalent before undertaking a study and provide documentation of this review in order to submit their data for regulatory purposes."[127]

The fall of 2002 brought into the field yet another acronym—SACHRP, the Secretary's Advisory Committee on Human Research Protection. In early 2003, the Bush administration ignited a controversy with its appointments of members to the committee, which had been created to advise the Secretary of Health and Human Services on protection of human subjects. Critics complained that most of the new appointees were "representatives of research institutions with financial stakes in human experiments while none of the 11 members is a professional patient advocate."[128] One of the new appointees, Jonathan Moreno, a University of Virginia bioethicist, said he did not intend to serve. He commented, "[y]ou can say that all heads of research are patient advocates, but institutional roles do mean something, and when it comes time to take a position on research protections, the institution or business that you represent makes a difference." Summarized as saying that he did not think the administration "care[d] much about human subject protections," he suggested the presence of a political agenda: "I think they do care about finding any way they can to advance their platform on the protection of embryos, in general, and on stem cell research, in particular."[129]

Contemporaneously, scientific issues arose within the multitude of disputes associated with the invasion of Iraq. In early 2003, the FDA first applied a rule that allowed approval of "critical drugs and vaccines" based on a showing of effectiveness in animal tests, with only "scaled-back human trials" for safety. A reporter wrote that this "animal rule" would apply "when full-scale clinical testing would expose humans to a life-threatening disease such as the plague or smallpox or when the cost of [a] trial would be impractical." Robert Temple of the FDA explained that "[t]he reason you're doing this is to save someone's life," and Roy Gulick, who directed the FDA's advisory committee on antiviral drugs, acknowledged that "[a]nimals may react differently" to drugs than humans, but said that "animal data is better than no data at all."[130] The reporter summarized the position of FDA officials as being that the rule was not "to be applied broadly."[131] However, early criticism focused on the agency's initial application of the rule—to the drug pyridostigmine bromide (PB), intended for use by troops "facing an imminent threat from the nerve gas soman." One medical professor said that to apply the "animal rule" to PB "might lead to confusions about safety and effectiveness."[132] The executive director of the National Gulf War Resource Center was less gentle: "They might as well have said FDA approves gasoline as a mouthwash."[133]

"Experimental Medicine"

Meanwhile, industry pushed ahead with drug research on human beings. Some companies began employing volunteers—both healthy volunteers and patients—for what was labeled "experimental medicine." This term was applied to very small-scale clinical trials that used precise measuring techniques to determine the effectiveness of new treatments. As a reporter described it, these tests might expose subjects "to more scans, blood tests and biopsies than in a more conventional trial." A biotechnology company executive put it more colorfully, but literally: "You're squeezing the last drop of data out of every patient you treat."[134]

This kind of investigation, which might shuttle "back and forth between human and animal trials," could be extremely expensive—on the order of $100,000 per subject instead of $10,000 to $15,000 in standard trials. The potential payoff, though, lay in the possibility that this kind of research would avoid "late failures"—the discovery in the latter stages of the development of drugs that they should not be marketed.[135] A patient with a gastrointestinal tumor who was undergoing such tests articulated an informal model of informed consent: "There's always a risk, but there's a larger risk when you don't do it." He commented, "I don't feel like you go into these things feeling like a guinea pig."[136] This comment assumed the pejorative connotation of the term "guinea pig" as it has come to be used. However, the patient appeared simply to be expressing a neutral recognition, and acceptance, that he was, literally, an experimental animal. "Guinea pig" terminology, it would seem, reflects attitudes—including attitudes about the ability to make a choice under constrained circumstances and about the incentives of investigators.

Prisoners as Subjects

A particularly challenging issue from the standpoint of humaneness and public policy, one that had been settled for more than a quarter century, reared up again in 2006. This was the question of using prison inmates for testing of investigational drugs. Because of some notorious episodes of prisoners being subjected to potent and highly dangerous products, federal regulations promulgated in 1978 required investigators to insure that experiments on inmates subject them to no more than "minimal" risks. However, a 2006 report by the IOM proposed, as a reporter described it, that experiments with greater risks be allowed "if they had the potential to benefit prisoners."

Responses to this proposal occupied a broad spectrum of opinion. A Nebraska genetics professor who chaired a Health and Human Services committee that requested the IOM study said that the existing regulations were "entirely outdated and restrictive," and that they "arbitrarily" excluded prisoners "from research that can help them." By contrast, a New York dermatologist who had worked at a Pennsylvania prison during an infamous group of experiments said that his "first-hand" experience showed him that "[w]hat started as scientific research became pure business." He concluded that "no amount of regulations can prevent that from happening again." Clearly, economics was a big factor, specifically as it related to the pharmaceutical industry's need for human subjects. Illustrative of the size of this part of the business was an estimate that revenue from the "contract research industry," which "recruit[s] volunteers" for drug trials, grew from $1 billion in 1985 to $7 billion in 2005.[137]

The new proposal was in effect a post-modern thought experiment that brought full circle a story that ran back to the raw experiments of as long as two generations ago, some of which are described at the beginning of this chapter. Repeat ingredients included vulnerable patient groups, ambitious scientists, and potential large savings in research costs. Was the ingredient of potential benefit to inmate subjects enough to save the IOM proposal, or did prison walls make such experiments duress per se? One of the larger questions explored in the next chapters is how much ordinary consumers are prisoners of their own desires and their lack of scientific expertise, and how much they are able to be captains of their own fates.

CHAPTER 2

HIV/AIDS Drugs: Speeding up Science under Political Pressure

Picture yourself with a dread disease for which up to the time it begins to ravage your body there is no known cure. A group of researchers say they have developed a medicine that may give you a shot at a cure, or at least a substantial prolongation of your life. But the government says that the research on the product does not pass its standard tests. This chapter tells a story from one of the multifront wars that are constantly fought in the process of human experimentation: how a small group of desperate sufferers, persons with AIDS, pushed the FDA to bend its rules on "good science" to provide quicker access to drugs. It also shows how the full bench of a federal appellate court established limits to the battles that victims of dread diseases could wage against the agency, in the process overruling a panel of the same court.

★ ★ ★

The system that the U.S. Government uses to screen new drugs is one of the most complex filters for product innovation that exists. In the early stages of new drug development, companies employ computer models and animal tests to investigate the effects of the drug. Once a manufacturer has developed a drug to a point that the firm wants to start the product on its way to market, it encounters the application process for Investigational New Drugs (IND). A drug maker—the "sponsor" of the drug—must submit an IND to be able to ship the product across state lines and must wait 30 days after submission to start clinical trials.[1]

The principal type of IND—the classic model of the process—is an "investigator IND," under which the sponsor must jump three staged hurdles that involve tests on human beings. The first of these hurdles, Phase 1 in the jargon, typically employs fewer than 100 healthy volunteers. They serve as biochemical black boxes—true guinea pigs—"to determine the metabolic pharmacological actions of the drug in humans, the side effects associated with increasing doses, and, if possible, to gain early evidence on effectiveness."[2] Even at this stage, though, the sponsor must tell the FDA whether it believes that either the chemistry of the drug or the way it is manufactured "presents any signals of potential human risk" and must describe "the steps proposed to monitor for such risk(s)."[3]

Effectiveness moves to center stage in Phase 2, in which tests, typically carried out on several hundred people, seek "preliminary data" on the ability of a drug to treat particular illnesses or conditions. Phase 2 tests also investigate "common short-term side effects and risks" of a drug.[4]

Phase 3 studies, which involve "several hundred to several thousand" subjects, probe further into effectiveness and safety in order to establish the comparative risks and benefits of a drug. The FDA's description of Phase 3 studies says that they "provide an adequate basis for extrapolating the results to the general population and transmitting that information in . . . physician labeling."[5] Yet this is, in a sense, more of an intermediate hope than an established fact—a state of affairs that weaves through this book. The relatively small size of the sample and the relatively short time during which investigators perform Phase 3 studies limit the ability of scientists to project their results to the general population. It may be only after hundreds of thousands or millions of people use a drug, over a period of years, that unwelcome side effects become apparent in statistically significant ways. This is part of the reason that some drugs find their way into harsh media spotlights after hopeful beginnings.

Compassionate INDs

There is a special set of IND categories that project a sense of drama and embody feelings of compassion; indeed, these categories are known are "compassionate INDs." A special statutory basis for this legal treatment is the so-called "Orphan Drug Amendments," which tell the FDA to

> encourage . . . sponsor[s] . . . to design protocols for clinical investigations . . . to permit the addition to the investigations of persons with the disease or condition who need the drug to treat the disease or condition and who cannot be satisfactorily treated by available alternative drugs.[6]

One kind of compassionate IND responds to scattered individual cases in emergency situations that do not permit the kind of long-term, carefully staged experimentation typical of investigator INDs.[7] It may also be used in cases where, as the FDA has summarized it, patients do "not meet the criteria of an existing study protocol, or if an approved study protocol does not exist."[8]

Emergency INDs are drama on a small scale. The other type of compassionate IND—the "treatment IND"—has provided drama on a larger stage. The development of this regulatory category is, in fact, one of the most interesting stories of our time concerning human beings as subjects of experimentation.

Before we plunge into that story, however, we must sketch the step after INDs in the process of bringing drugs to market: the New Drug Application (NDA). After the maker of a drug has completed clinical trials, it will submit an NDA to the

FDA's Center for Drug Evaluation and Research (CDER). By this time, as CDER officials point out, data on the drug may mount into "the hundreds of thousands of pages and are delivered to the agency in tractor-trailers."[9] The advent of online submissions may make the process less paper-heavy, but it is still weighty with data. Platoons of specialists—doctors, pharmacologists, chemists, and statisticians—then review these mountains of information to decide if a drug shows substantial evidence of effectiveness and is safe enough to send onto the general market.[10]

The Emergence of AIDS

It was AIDS that came barreling into the carefully built world of controlled clinical investigations followed by rigorous review by the FDA. A relatively small community of sufferers proved to be an engine for change in that structure, bringing products to market in an environment in which afflicted people were willing to take more risks than the law then allowed.

The earliest chapter was written in March 1987, with the agency's approval of zidovudine, which has the acronym AZT, for a specified group of persons with AIDS and advanced AIDS-related complex (ARC). These were people shown by laboratory tests to have "severely depressed immunity" or a history of the pneumonia often associated with AIDS, pneumocystis carinii pneumonia (PCP).[11]

Robert Windom, Assistant Secretary for Health, pointed out that the FDA's review and approval of AZT, under a priority review process, occurred in fewer than four months. Dr. Windom called the approval of the drug "an important demonstration of FDA's ability to move swiftly, with impressive scientific precision, to review and approve promising treatments for AIDS, when such action is justified by sound and convincing clinical evidence."[12] But that event was just the beginning of a movement, spurred by persons with disease, to expedite the bringing to market of drugs that under traditional tests would be viewed as experimental.

Two months later, the agency put the finishing touches on a set of regulations that provided principles for the approval of treatment INDs for drugs like AZT. The agency was operating in the shadow of at least two major Supreme Court decisions concerning the approval of new drugs. In one of those cases, the 1973 decision in *Hynson v. Westcott & Dunning, Inc.*,[13] the Court dealt with the withdrawal of an NDA for a drug whose maker recommended it for use in premature labor. In the background of that case was a massive evaluation by panels of the National Academy of Sciences/National Research Council of 16,500 claims made for 4,000 drugs that had NDAs in effect. Remarkably—as the Court summarized the data—"[s]eventy percent of these claims were found not to be supported by substantial evidence of effectiveness, and only 434 drugs were found effective for all their claimed uses."[14] The Court concluded that the manufacturer could not escape the requirements of the "new drug" provisions of the statute, given what it summarized as the manufacturer's attempt "to rely solely on the testimony of physicians and the extant literature, evidence that has been characterized as 'anecdotal.'"[15] This conclusion fit into the Court's declaration that "anecdotal evidence indicating that doctors 'believe' in the efficacy of a drug" did not measure up to the "strict and demanding standards" of the governing statute. That legislation requires that a drug maker show "substantial evidence" of effectiveness, derived from "adequate and well-controlled clinical investigations." Those standards, the Court said, were "amply justified by the legislative history."[16]

The other case, *United States v. Rutherford*,[17] decided in 1979, dealt with efforts by terminally ill cancer patients to obtain Laetrile, a substance made from apricot pits that had not been recognized as "safe and effective." In his opinion for the Court, upholding a ban on the interstate distribution of Laetrile, Justice Marshall declared that "[t]o accept the proposition that the safety and efficacy standards of the [Food, Drug, and Cosmetic] Act have no relevance for terminal patients is to deny the Commissioner's authority over all drugs, however toxic or ineffectual, for such individuals." Summarizing the history of quack remedies like turpentine, mustard, and peat moss as cures for cancer, he said that history suggested "why Congress could reasonably have determined to protect the terminally ill, no less than other patients, from the vast range of self-styled panaceas that inventive minds can devise."[18]

The Treatment IND

These two decisions provided by interpretation a rigorous framework of Congressional intent concerning the approval of new drugs under the IND/NDA process. Mindful of that, the agency tried to situate its 1987 regulations governing the treatment IND category in the overall framework of the IND process, justifying the departure of those regulations from the usual requirements of that process. Thus, it spoke in terms of appropriateness of the use of the drug for "patients not in . . . clinical trials, in accordance with a . . . treatment IND."[19] The standard for fitting in that category was "a serious or immediately life-threatening disease condition in patients for whom no comparable or satisfactory alternative drug or other therapy is available."[20]

The agency announced as its purpose the facilitation of "the availability of promising new drugs to desperately ill patients as early in the drug development process as possible, before general marketing begins, and to obtain additional data of the drug's safety and effectiveness."[21] This rationale clearly made patients taking drugs under treatment INDs into a special class of experimental subjects for the development of information. Moreover, it was implicit that if a treatment turned out not to be effective, or tolerably safe, it would never reach the general market. Thus, these patients were very much volunteers, trading hopes for amelioration of their disease against the risk of unwanted side effects. Part of that trade was the agency's requirement that there be no "comparable or satisfactory alternative"; thus, the patient would know that the only other branch for decision was to let nature take its course.

The Standards and Their Inherent Tensions

The standards the 1987 regulation set for the FDA Commissioner's decision on whether to allow a treatment IND were heavy with discretion, featuring the language of "may" and, repetitively, variations on "reasonable." The Commissioner could deny a request involving "immediately life-threatening disease if"

the available scientific evidence, taken as a whole, fails to provide a reasonable basis for concluding that the drug:

(A) May be effective for its intended use in its intended patient population; or

(B) Would not expose the patients to whom the drug is to be administered to an unreasonable and significant additional risk of illness or injury.[22]

Presumably, the principal standard for reasonableness would be an objective one within the confines of the general drug regulation scheme, including the IND process. But, given the political pressures that produced this set of regulations, the standard of reason appears to tilt toward the reasoning process of patients whose treatment options are running out. Thus, the treatment IND seems to move in the direction of the consumerist society even for a set of products whose marketing has been tightly cabined.

Illustrative of the tensions reflected in the regulations were explanations by the agency that emphasized both the need for "good science" in deciding on treatment INDs and discretion in making those decisions. On the one hand, an FDA document featuring "highlights" of its rule insisted that the rule "provide[d] for a standard of medical and scientific rationality—a requirement for sufficient scientific evidence on the basis of which experts could reasonably conclude that the drug may be effective in the intended patient population."[23] And the agency stressed that it "continue[d] to believe that the absence of alternative therapy should be prerequisite to granting a treatment IND because one of the major principles underlying the treatment IND policy is that these drugs would be necessary to fill an existing gap" in available therapies. On the other hand, the agency "agree[d] that there should be flexibility in applying this concept so as best to serve desperately ill patients," saying that "the mere fact that the disease in question has existing approved therapy does not mean that the approved treatments are satisfactory for all patients."[24] Thus, consumerism becomes ever more individualized.

Informed Consent

As more of the decision swings toward the consumer, the concept of informed consent moves more into the policy spotlight. The FDA made clear that informed consent was "a crucially important safeguard" in treatment INDs, defining the term as requiring the provision by doctors of "information in lay language that truthfully explains the possible benefits and potential risks" of an investigational drug.[25]

It is interesting, in this regard, to refer to a critical article on the ethics of clinical research that was published just after the FDA released its final rules on treatment INDs. In this article, Benjamin Freedman described two concepts of "equipoise" in clinical research. "Theoretical equipoise," an "overwhelmingly fragile" concept, exists "when, overall, the evidence on behalf of two alternative treatment regimens is exactly balanced."[26] This kind of equipoise would be "disturbed" when a clinician has what "'even might be labeled a bias or a hunch,' a preference of a 'merely intuitive nature.'"[27] By contrast with this concept, one that "is most appropriate to one-dimensional hypotheses and causes us to think in those terms,"[28] Freedman presents the "robust" idea of "clinical equipoise," which "places the emphasis in informing the patient on the honest disagreement between expert clinicians." Thus, if the investigator has a decided "treatment preference," "based on something more than a hunch," she could disclose it; in fact, it might be "ethically mandatory" to do so while "emphasiz[ing] that this preference is not shared by others," because "[i]t is likely to be a matter of chance" that the patient is being treated by a clinician with one preference or the other.[29]

In this framework, the self-conscious provision of information by investigators themselves about their preferences enhances—perhaps even defines—informed consent. The consent procedure underlines the individualized choice involved. And even if the investigator's preference is pinned to a fairly specific reading of the data at hand—that is, "more than a hunch," it would seem that the patient's consent will depend significantly on his or her hunch about the investigator's competence and canniness, given that the patient is not a scientist.

The FDA's Response to Criticism: Some Bending, Some Holding Firm

The 1987 rule did not stem complaints from people—particularly AIDS sufferers—who thought the FDA was not acting swiftly enough. One landmark incident occurred in October 1988, when more than a thousand protesters trapped FDA staff in their own headquarters.[30] Sensitized to such protests, in the same month the agency issued a new "interim rule" on treatment INDs.[31] In terms that built on its 1987 rule, the agency said its purpose was to "expedite the development, evaluation, and marketing of new therapies intended to treat persons with life-threatening and severely debilitating illnesses, especially where no satisfactory alternative therapy exists."[32]

Explicitly recognizing the "urgency associated with life-threatening illnesses," the agency said it would "begin implementation of these procedures immediately,"[33] although it did invite public comment. Despite acknowledging the urgency in such cases, though, the FDA stood its ground on the requirement of placebo testing in situations "where no therapy has been shown to be effective." It contrasted the situation in which there was "known to be an effective therapy"—where it said that it was not appropriate to require placebo controls.[34] The rationale was that, in the long run, "controlled clinical trials" would provide better results. In this connection, the agency quoted a report by the Institute of Medicine (IOM) that said that "[p]oorly designed trials, or administering drugs without controls and 'observing' the course of the disease" would "risk being inconclusive or drawing incorrect conclusions."[35]

An insistent theme of the new rule was that safety is a relative concept, requiring regulators to take into account "the severity of the disease and the absence of satisfactory alternative therapy."[36] As the agency explained, this was "particularly true in the case of drugs to treat life-threatening diseases, where drugs that are quite toxic may nevertheless be considered safe under the circumstances."[37]

The rule permitted submission of treatment protocols if "preliminary" results of phase 2 testing—testing for effectiveness in a few hundred people—"appear[ed] promising." These protocols would "normally remain in effect while the complete data necessary for a marketing application are being assembled by the sponsor and reviewed by FDA."[38] Evidently prepared to skip the larger scale clinical testing on Phase 3 studies, the agency said that "[t]he treatment IND, as appropriate, would continue to serve as a bridge between phase 2 trials and the point of marketing approval."[39] Within a month after the issuance of these regulations, Congress passed the AIDS Amendments of 1988, which encouraged the sponsors of AIDS drugs to submit IND applications for them and authorized the Secretary of Health and Human Services to "provide technical assistance" in the submission of such applications.[40]

A Cluster of Markets

This interim rule pushed further along the path to the ideal of the market overt—a literally open market. In a consumer bazaar at its fullest, it would be possible for ailing consumers to buy anything they desire, so long as adequate information about risks and benefits is provided to them—by government, by doctors, and by product makers.

In fact, as this new rule was being printed, desperate people seeking drugs were creating their own markets outside the process. An advocacy group for AIDS sufferers, Project Inform, was distributing a pamphlet with the title "Federally Unapproved Medications for Treatment of AIDS (How to Get Them; How to Bring Them Home; How to Use Them)."[41] The same group even began to run its own "clandestine" tests on Compound Q, a substance "reputed to have an amazing ability to kill cells infected with AIDS in a test tube," which the group had smuggled into the country.[42] A remarkable indicator of the effects of these activities and the political pressures associated with them was an FDA directive in July 1988 that allowed people suffering from any illness "to import a three-month supply of FDA-unapproved drugs into the United States for personal use while under the care of a doctor."[43]

A Political Struggle Intensifies: Sufferers and Scientists

These events were the subject of much discussion, reflecting the passion of many contentious groups—persons with AIDS, different kinds of scientists, manufacturers with direct commercial stakes in drug development and sales, the NIH, and the FDA. The arguments on the speeding up of IND investigations in the AIDS area made it clear that what might be at stake was the entire process of clearing new drugs for the market. One person who raised this concern was Michael Peskoe, a lawyer for a drug manufacturer, who expressed concern that "all of the FDA's official publications appear to group AIDS with other life-threatening conditions."[44] He said that AIDS was "clearly creating far more interest in changing the underlying rules of the system than" other serious illnesses.[45] In this environment, Peskoe said, "the treatment IND and related provisions seem . . . to be a part of the mainstream of the approval process of AIDS drugs." This might "get[ ] to the end result faster," he said, but it would also "accept[ ] more risk for patients as part of the process."[46] Peskoe set these developments in the framework of a concern about the "fragile" nature of the system under which new drugs are approved, which he said "does poorly in the spotlight where it can be easily and unfairly attacked."[47]

Intensifying the spotlight were pressures generated by "AIDS activists," including desperate sufferers and people living with the continuing horror of seeing their friends die awful deaths. Commentary by one such person, James Eigo, captured the concentrated impatience of the AIDS community. He noted that about 400 members of an AIDS coalition in New York City, ACT UP, met weekly. Members of such groups were making themselves expert on both regulation and pharmacology. Forty members of a "Treatment and Data Committee" of ACT UP were "track[ing] the progress of investigational AIDS drugs" through the FDA's processes. In 1989, Eigo said, the organization "played a large part in the institution of a federal registry of AIDS-related clinical trials, . . . securing final approval for the drug ganciclovir . . . as well as the pre-approval availability of a potential anti-AIDS Drug . . . (DDI) for sick people without treatment alternatives."[48]

Accentuating the pressures on the FDA was an early version of the 24-hour news cycle. As drug company official David Barry put it, it was "not unusual for a patient to have heard information on the morning news, to have gone to the doctor requesting that drug, and the doctor not to have known anything of the information." A further problem, he explained, was instant analysis by media savants.[49] A related source of pressure, as a Washington food and drug lawyer explained, was that "in the world of AIDS drug development, things change virtually every day."[50]

The effects of the politics of AIDS were evident in a narrative by A. Bruce Montgomery, a scientist who had spearheaded the early development of an aerosolized version of pentamidine, a drug that had been used for 50 years against parasites, which Montgomery and his team began trying to use against PCP. Their first studies indicated that the aerosolized drug was "strongly positive in curing acute cases of pneumonia." There was, however, a contemporaneous irony of progress: the success of AZT, which was approved in 1987, lengthened the average life of AIDS patients by more than a year—and this led to more cases of recurrent PCP. Now, a coalition of "AIDS patients, activists, and some practicing physicians" began to "advocate[e] aerosolized pentamidine as the standard of care to prevent PCP in spite of a lack of long term data on its safety and efficacy." And, with intense demand, a "gray market" developed. Prescription pentamidine was "commercial[ly] available" for intravenous use. The solution, literally, was for people who wanted an aerosol to dissolve the drug in water and put it in a nebulizer.[51]

Montgomery and his associates put together "the first successful community based treatment trial," which used 400 patients and yielded diverse assessments depending on one's status in the struggle against AIDS: "The patients were happy, but some wanted to change dosage based on the first adverse event." "The FDA remained neutral," not commenting "on the study's probability of success" and saying, in effect, "'prove efficacy to us.'" Moreover, the NIH "rejected a grant that would fund the trial because the trial design was not scientific enough." Meanwhile, the media "began to hound the clinical investigators for results that would take up to eighteen months to obtain." But after a while, "[t]he AIDS activists had gotten their message through and the NIH was reacting." Even though it had refused to give the Montgomery team the grant it sought, it "wanted to modify many of [its] studies by adding aerosolized pentamidine."[52] Then, after "countless meetings," the FDA agreed that the team's "data had proven efficacy by showing a dose response," and finally, in June 1989, the agency gave full approval. This, Montgomery asserted, would "delay death in up to 20,000 people and . . . save over $500 million in hospital costs" in one year.[53]

Freedom of Choice and Scientific Rigor

If the message had gotten through, though, some concerned citizens in the scientific community raised questions about the balance of costs and benefits from the speedups. True, in some respects, the system was becoming "something approaching patient freedom of choice."[54] But "the issue of freedom of choice" was "confounding the science of drug approval."[55]

A major issue in such situations is how free a choice can be about scientific matters when the evidence has not been developed according to the standard tenets of science. A complicating factor was the process by which information about drugs gets communicated to patients. As a lawyer noted, "[p]racticing physicians are often unaccustomed to presenting a detailed explanation of risks and benefits to patients—at least to the extent risks and benefits are ordinarily explained in research settings."[56]

Beyond that, there arises the question of how to define good science in the vortex of politics. A fascinating set of undercurrents on the question of what good science is flows from rivalry between scientists who do basic research and those who apply drugs in clinical settings. Montgomery has pointed out that "bench scientists . . . view clinical researchers with some apprehension and make academic tenure difficult, if not impossible, to obtain." Moreover, he says, "clinical researchers are often excluded from the most prestigious scientific organizations and committees that review most . . . NIH . . . grants."[57]

Ellen Cooper, director of the FDA's Division of Antiviral Drug Products, captured the tension at one point of application, concerning the conflicts often inherent between basic science and aggressive patients. On one hand, she said, "few would argue against the ethical principle of individual autonomy." On the other hand, though, there exist competing "ethical principles," including "social benefIcence requiring the systematic collection of data that are critical for determining the safety and efficacy of new drugs."[58] "Freedom of choice" might involve no freedom and no meaningful choice when speedups in availability of drugs in the early investigational stage "create[ ] the potential for false hope among physicians and patients," possibly "persuad[ing] them not to use effective therapies."[59] As one commentator warned, "[i]nappropriate early expanded access could create a disaster in the HIV-infected patient population."[60] The "social beneficence" of traditional methods of drug investigation might, on balance, yield individual beneficence for patients who could otherwise be led astray by premature optimism.

Dr. Cooper identified some other problem areas that are primarily peculiar to new drug investigations, but which in their broad outlines relate to the price of products in a society that has a lengthy continuum of income levels. A salient question is who pays the price of product development. Should the money for drugs used in treatment INDs come from the public treasury or from drug companies? Dr. Cooper pointed out that "[m]any . . . smaller companies do not have the resources." Or should it come from patients, many of whom themselves may not be able to afford the drugs? Another problem with "parallel track" investigations— where treatment INDs exist side by side with "carefully monitored" controlled trials—is the collection of data for the treatment INDs.[61]

Who Gets the Experimental Drugs

Still another issue concerns the possible tendency of "parallel track" trials to render participation in controlled investigations an inferior alternative in the eyes of potential subjects. The problem here is simply that the patient in a randomized controlled trial has an even chance of getting standard therapy and not the experimental drug.[62] James Eigo, the AIDS activist, provided at least a partial answer to this concern, noting that there were "waiting lists around the country to get into trials" for the drug called DDI (didanosine), "because of the interest in parallel track, not despite it."[63]

Especially symbolic of the rending nature of these problems was the selection process for those eligible for treatment INDs. The standard approach, Dr. Cooper noted, was to give those products only to patients who could not use standard therapies. She acknowledged that the process of making that distinction was not "easy, scientifically or emotionally." Yet, she observed, "if patients and their physicians refuse to accept the protocol definitions of eligible patient populations," it might "jeopardize[ ]" "the whole concept of early expanded access."[64]

This chapter focuses on the complex political and scientific background of the effort to expand early access to investigational new drugs. In the landscape of consumer products, new drugs are undoubtedly a special case. There is no governmental investigational process for new models of automobiles, or farm tractors, or punch presses. However, although prescription drugs get special treatment, many of the elements of the problem are common to the ongoing process of nonclinical experimentation that wins the benefits of innovation for consumers of many kinds of products as well as subjecting consumers to the risks of newness. These factors include the technical nature of information about the innards of many products, the relative inability of consumers to acquire that information—or to understand it—and the strong desire of consumers to acquire products whose risks they may comprehend only dimly, if at all.

Speedups Codified

A new subchapter unfolded in the early 1990s, when the "parallel track" program became concretized in government agencies. In May 1990, the Public Health Service (PHS) published a proposed policy statement, "Expanded Availability of Investigational New Drugs through a Parallel Track Mechanism for People with AIDS and HIV-Related Disease." The agency designed this "parallel track" scheme to make "more widely available" "promising investigational agents" to patients who had "no therapeutic alternatives" and "who cannot participate in . . . controlled clinical trials."[65]

In April 1992, the FDA and the PHS simultaneously published documents on the subject. The FDA proposed a rule that said it would consider accelerated approval "in two situations."[66] One involved a showing of the effects of a drug on a "surrogate endpoint" or "marker"—that is, "a laboratory measurement or physical sign that is used in therapeutic trials as a substitute for a clinically meaningful endpoint of how a patient feels, functions, or survives and that is expected to predict the effect of the therapy."[67] The effect on a surrogate endpoint had to "reasonably suggest[] clinical benefit" or there had to be "evidence of the drug's effect on a clinical endpoint other than survival or irreversible morbidity, pending completion of any necessary studies to establish and define the degree of clinical benefits to patients."[68]

The FDA's explanation implied the tentative nature of such decisions against the background of political pressures to move drugs onto the market more quickly. It said it was "proposing to approve new drugs for serious or life-threatening illnesses at the earliest possible point at which safety and efficacy can reasonably be established under existing law,"[69] stressing that the program "should only apply to drugs that provide meaningful therapeutic benefit over existing treatment for patients with serious or life-threatening diseases."[70] The other element of the FDA's regulation involved situations where the agency decided "that a drug, effective for the treatment of a disease, can be used safely only if distribution or use is modified or restricted."[71] It gave as illustrations the restriction of "distribution to certain facilities or to physicians with special training or experience," or the "[c]onditioning [of] distribution on the performance of specified medical procedures," for example, blood tests to monitor toxicity.[72]

On the same day, the PHS issued a "final policy statement," following up on its proposed statement of 1990,[73] with the purpose of expanding the availability of "promising investigational drugs for AIDS and other HIV-related diseases . . . under 'parallel track' protocols while . . . controlled clinical trials essential to establish the safety and effectiveness of new drugs are carried out."[74] Among other criteria for this parallel track use were "[e]vidence that the investigational drug is reasonably safe, taking into consideration the intended use of the drug and the patient population for which this drug is intended" and "[e]vidence of a lack of satisfactory alternative therapy for defined patient populations," as well as "[a]n assessment of the impact that the parallel track study may have on patient enrollment for the controlled clinical trials." Factors to be considered in determining eligibility of patients included patients' inability "to participate in . . . controlled clinical trials"—for example, because they were "too ill to participate," or clinical trials were "fully enrolled," or the patient "cannot take standard treatment because it is contraindicated, cannot be tolerated, or is no longer effective."[75] The PHS said that it might approve protocols under this policy "when the evidence for effectiveness is less than that generally required for a Treatment IND."[76]

As with the FDA's proposed rule, the pragmatic solution of the PHS policy effectively permitted different levels of safety for different types of patients. The PHS policy reflected the great tension between an emphasis on individualization, with much more pressure for personal choice, and the desire of scientists to preserve the standard guideposts for scientific inquiry.

The FDA issued its final rule—one covering new drugs, antibiotics, and biologicals for "serious or life-threatening illnesses," where the PHS rule focused on HIV/AIDS drugs—in December 1992. The FDA rule set in concrete requirements of a showing of effects on surrogate endpoints[77] and restrictions necessary to ensure safe use.[78] Responding to comments on its initially proposed rule, the agency rejected concerns that "reliance on surrogate endpoints will become routine," making that "the 'normal' way drugs are brought to the market." Calling this fear "groundless," the agency pointed out that "[t]he vast majority of drugs are directed at symptomatic or short-term conditions . . . whose response to drugs, if it occurs, is readily measured and where there is no need to consider or accept surrogate endpoints." By contrast, the agency said, "[s]urrogates . . . are of interest" when "the clinical benefit, if there is one, is likely to be well in the future," and when "the implications of the effect on the surrogate are great because the disease has no treatment at all or the drug seems to treat people with no alternative"—for example, "because they cannot tolerate the usual effective treatment."[79]

This document, too, revealed the ongoing struggle about the definition of safety in particular circumstances. The agency noted a comment that the approval of the use of "unvalidated surrogate endpoints" seemed "to represent a significant departure from traditional agency interpretations of 'substantial evidence'" under the Food Drug and Cosmetic Act "because it allows belief rather than evidence to serve as the basis for a conclusion about the effectiveness of a new drug." To this concern, the agency responded that "[t]he evidence available at the time of approval . . . will meet the statutory standard," because there would have to be "evidence from adequate and well-controlled studies showing that the drug will have the effect it is represented to have in its labeling." That, the agency explained, would "be an effect on a surrogate endpoint that is reasonably likely to predict a clinical benefit," and it pointed out that "labeling will refer to the effect on the surrogate, not to effect on clinical outcome."[80] The agency insisted that the rule was "not intended to place into the market drugs with little evidence of usefulness." It said that "[a]lthough there is no statutory requirement for significance testing of any particular value, there are well-established conventions for assessing statistical significance to support" the statutory requirement "that the well-controlled studies have demonstrated that a drug will have the effect it is represented to have."[81]

The profile of the FDA rules by 1992 reflected the battering on the agency's walls by patients who were willing to make high-stakes wagers on experimental products. The agency was attempting to adhere to the letter of Congressional intent, recognizing that it now operated in a vortex of political pressures previously unknown. Ironically, the major prior landmarks in drug regulation—in 1906, 1938, and 1962—had been constructed because people wanted more oversight by the government. Now the agency's lens revealed a preference for more room for individuals to experiment. In the developing societal mix were activist organizations who did their own monitoring, the instantaneous effects of media, and the rise of underground markets. All these factors created a new experimental philosophy for product distribution. A restricted market was loosening up.

Congressional Confirmation

In 1997, Congress essentially confirmed this new universe in the FDA Modernization Act.[82] It set in a legislative foundation the emergency IND and the treatment IND, and it established a "fast track" for new drugs.

The statute provides a striking historical illustration of agency experimentation, deemed successful by Congress, that finds its way into legislation. Allowing the Secretary of Health and Human Services to authorize the shipment of investigational drugs and devices for "emergency situations,"[83] the Act permitted "individual patient access" to such products in certain cases. These are cases where a doctor "determines that the person has no comparable or satisfactory alternative therapy . . . and that the probable risk" of an investigational drug or device "is not greater than the probable risk from the disease or condition" of the patient[84] and the Secretary decides that the provision of the drug or device "will not interfere with . . . clinical investigations."[85]

The treatment IND provisions of the statute required a finding "of a serious or immediately life-threatening disease or condition"; a showing that "there is no comparable or satisfactory alternative therapy"; the existence of a "controlled clinical trial" or a showing that "all clinical trials necessary for approval" of the product had "been completed"; and, in the case of drugs or devices in controlled trials, that the treatment IND would "not interfere with the enrollment of patients" in clinical trials.[86] For uses of such products for "serious diseases," Congress required "sufficient evidence of safety and effectiveness to support" the proposed uses. It said that for "immediately life-threatening diseases," the "available scientific evidence, taken as a whole," must "provide[ ] a reasonable basis to conclude" that the product "may be effective for its intended use and would not expose patients to an unreasonable and significant risk of illness or injury."[87]

The "fast track" section of the statute defined the drugs eligible for that process as products "intended for the treatment of a serious or life-threatening condition" that "demonstrate[ ] the potential to address unmet medical needs for such a condition."[88] Congress authorized the Secretary to require that sponsors of fast-track products "conduct appropriate post-approval studies to validate the surrogate endpoint or otherwise confirm the effect on the clinical endpoint."[89] This provision, enacted in 1997, is particularly interesting in light of the emphasis during the intervening decade by legislators and commentators on the need for postmarketing surveillance of medical products.

The statute made clear Congress' commitment to public information about experimental drugs, ordering the Secretary to "operate a data bank of information on clinical trials for drugs for serious or life-threatening diseases and conditions." Moreover, the Secretary was to "disseminate such information through information systems, which shall include toll-free telephone communications, available to individuals with serious or life-threatening diseases and conditions, to other members of the public, to health care providers, and to researchers."[90]

Consumerism: Benefits and Cautions

The FDA Modernization Act's refinement of the agency's lengthy development of procedures for accelerated testing of new drugs, and Congress' emphasis on public information, thrust in a consumerist direction. However, the legislation raises the question of how much information consumers are capable of absorbing and understanding. It is interesting, in this regard, to contemplate a hypothetical patient who is thinking about joining a clinical trial and who goes online to find out about such trials. The NIH put a document titled "An Introduction to Clinical Trials" on the Internet.[91] This document was a dozen pages long. Its bullet point list of questions that people might want to ask included 13 separate points. It had a five-page glossary of terms.[92] One might ask how well the average patient would fare on a written examination on this document, which happens to be written in reasonably plain English for a document that deals in science and medicine. One potential good outcome is that an interplay of patients and their families with primary physicians and investigators might produce at least some enhancement of personal choice. When patients become organized in communities centered on particular diseases—the classic example is HIV/AIDS—there is more of a chance for enhancement. Generally, though, there is the undesirable possibility of premature enthusiasm for treatments that prove relatively unsafe or ineffective (and thus sometimes unsafe because of that). In the scientific community, the more basic the scientist, the more uneasy he or she is likely to be about processes as they move away from the classic model of research.

Expanding Expanded Access

A decade after Congress passed the FDA Modernization Act, the war over access to experimental drugs heated up, and the front moved. In late 2006, the FDA proposed a rule it summarized as designed to enhance "expanded access to investigational drugs for treatment use."[93] The proposed rule sought to even out the availability of experimental drugs to the broad class of sufferers from serious diseases. But it also evidenced a desire to hold the line for "good science," even though some of its language reflected sensitivity to a history that included underground drug markets.

The agency defined the "fundamental problem" the rule was designed to solve as "one of incomplete information." It referred to "a lack of clearly defined eligibility criteria and submission requirements" that "results in disparate access to treatment use for different types of patients and diseases." One particular concern the agency addressed was that "cancer and AIDS patients have had better access to investigational drugs than patients with other serious diseases or conditions" and that patients with doctors in "academic medical centers" had similar advantages over those whose doctors "practice outside such centers." With more of an economic focus, the agency said that the lack of precise criteria "has created inefficiencies that limit patient access to potentially beneficial investigational drugs," noting that this state of affairs had "led some physicians and drug sponsors to devote more resources than necessary to the preparation of expanded access submissions."[94]

The rule defined three categories of sufferers from serious diseases: "individual patients, including emergency procedures; intermediate-size patient populations (smaller than those typical of a treatment IND or treatment protocol)"; and "larger populations under a treatment protocol or [a] treatment . . . IND." The agency noted that existing programs for expanded access had already made drugs available for large numbers of people, using as an example a population of 10,000 patients who had gotten access "to the first cardioselective beta-blockers and the first calcium channel blockers for vasospastic angina."[95]

The agency made clear that it hoped to generate more business for the expanded access program, saying that "[i]ncreased knowledge and awareness about expanded access options should make investigational drugs more widely available in appropriate situations."[96] It suggested specifically that reclassification of open-label protocols as treatment INDs or "treatment protocols" might "increase publicity for, and awareness of, the access program."[97] It noted that "[t]he primary purpose of the treatment IND or treatment protocol" was to provide seriously ill patients with investigational drugs when there was "a reasonable evidentiary basis to support the use in a substantial population, but the evidence needed for marketing approval either has not been entirely collected or has been collected but not yet analyzed and reviewed by the agency."[98]

The agency set out three criteria to govern all the categories of expanded access uses, echoing and elaborating the language of the FDA Modernization Act:

(1) there must be a "serious or immediately life-threatening disease or condition" for which there was "no comparable or satisfactory alternative therapy"[99];

(2) "potential patient benefit" must justify "the potential risks of the treatment use," and those risks could not be "unreasonable in the context of the disease or condition"[100]; and

(3) the expanded access use must not "interfere with the initiation, conduct, or completion of clinical investigations that could support marketing approval of the expanded access use or otherwise compromise the potential development of the expanded access use."[101]

To these general criteria, the agency added specific standards for treatment INDs and treatment protocols. These included a requirement that either the drug be "being investigated in a controlled clinical trial under an IND designed to support a marketing application for the expanded access use" or that "all clinical trials of the drug have been completed." Another requirement was that there "be sufficient clinical evidence of safety and effectiveness to support the expanded access use." A special subcategory applied to the case of an "immediately life-threatening disease or condition": that "the available scientific evidence, taken as a whole, provides a reasonable basis to conclude that the investigational drug may be effective for the expanded access use and would not expose patients to an unreasonable and significant risk of illness or injury." In that circumstance, the proposed rule said, the evidence "would ordinarily consist of clinical data from phase 3 or phase 2 trials, but could be based on more preliminary clinical evidence."[102]

As was the case throughout the history of expanded access, the agency reflected the political and scientific struggles over the proper balance of regulation of human experimentation, including experimentation in which the chief movers are people who want products that scientists do not think are ready for marketing. The agency itself described the rule as "attempt[ing] to reconcile individual patients' desires to make their own decisions about their health care with society's need for drugs to be developed for marketing." Noting this was not always easy to do, it specified the danger that allowing "relatively unfettered access to an investigational drug at a preliminary stage of its development" might expose patients to "significant and unacceptable risks." It referred to the concern that to allow such access might drive enough patients away from controlled trials that they could not meaningfully be conducted. In trying to strike an "appropriate balance," the agency said, it had to assure that "its rules should not compromise the integrity of the drug development process."[103]

With the agency expressing concern that "allowing expanded access to investigational drugs before they are fully evaluated for safety" might "have adverse consequences for the seriously ill patients who receive them,"[104] the proposed rule catalogued a list of "safeguards" for all expanded access uses. The proposal designated doctors who administered drugs while having submitted INDs for expanded access as "sponsor-investigator[s]," with the responsibilities attached to both roles. Investigators' responsibilities included reports to sponsors of "adverse drug experiences," the insuring of compliance with informed consent requirements, and the provision to doctors of "information needed to minimize the risk and maximize the potential benefits" of drugs.[105]

As the FDA was completing its proposal on expanded access, a dramatic confrontation was shaping up in the United States Court of Appeals for the District of Columbia. The first clash of arms occurred in May 2006, and the stakes were high for parties arguing over the correct legal dividing line between untrammeled individual decision making and governmental controls on the ability to purchase experimental drugs. The case was *Abigail Alliance for Better Access to Developmental Drugs v. Eschenbach*.[106] The patient whose plight provided a basis for the suit was Abigail Burroughs, who at age 21 had "exhausted conventional . . . treatments" for head and neck cancer. She tried to get the experimental drug Erbitux, but her frail condition made her ineligible for research trials that were going on and she died three months after her conventional treatments ended. As a commentator summarized it, her father started the Abigail Alliance as an advocacy group "to ensure that cancer patients, no matter how sick and weak," could "have their insurance companies buy any experimental drug that has passed safety testing."[107] The Alliance's suit sought to prevent the FDA from enforcing a policy that kept patients from getting experimental drugs after those products had cleared Phase 1 trials. This meant, as a majority of a three-judge panel for the Court of Appeals for the District of Columbia Circuit put it, that the agency had decided that the drugs were "sufficiently safe for expanded human testing."[108]

In the background, among other precedents, was the Supreme Court's 1979 decision in the Laetrile case, which had kept cancer patients from getting the apricot-pit remedy in interstate shipment. However, remarkably, the panel majority issued a ruling that, although technically limited, favored the plaintiffs.

Writing for the majority, Judge Judith Rogers viewed the question as one of whether the FDA's policy violated a "fundamental right." Drawing on Supreme Court precedents, she discerned two "distinct approach[es]" to the subject. One relied on the "concepts of individual rights to autonomy and self-determination," which led to judicial "unwillingness to countenance state intrusion into certain protected domains such as the bedroom, the clinic, and the womb."[109] Judge Rogers found part of the answer to the problem in history. She observed that until the passage of the original Food and Drug Act in 1906, "a person could obtain access to any new drug without any governmental interference whatsoever." She further noted that "[e]ven after the enactment of the [Food Drug and Cosmetic

Act] in 1938, Congress imposed no limitation on the commercial marketing of new drugs based upon the drugs' effectiveness." And she pointed out that "even today, a patient may use a drug for unapproved purposes even where the drug may be unsafe or ineffective for the off-label purpose." Judge Rogers reasoned from this that "[d]espite the FDA's claims to the contrary, . . . it cannot be said that government control of access to potentially life-saving medication 'is now firmly ingrained in our understanding of the appropriate role of government' . . . so as to overturn the long-standing tradition of the right of self-preservation."[110]

The other "approach" to the subject that the majority identified focused on rights "implicit in the concept of ordered liberty," a phrase used by Justice Cardozo in a 1937 opinion.[111] Even under this "more restrictive" approach,[112] the majority found support for the Abigail Alliance in a Supreme Court "right to die" case, decided in 1990, which it characterized as holding that "an individual has a due process right to make an informed decision to engage in conduct, by withdrawing treatment, that will cause one's death."[113] It found it a "logical corollary" "that an individual must also be free to decide for herself whether to assume any known or unknown risks of taking a medication that might prolong her life."[114]

The majority's constitutional analysis led to the conclusion that "where there are no alternative government-approved treatment options, a terminally ill, mentally competent adult patient's informed access to potentially life-saving investigational new drugs determined by the FDA after Phase I trials to be sufficiently safe for expanded human trials warrants protection under the Due Process Clause." The procedural outcome hinged on the fact that the trial court had not "reached the question of whether the challenged FDA policy violates" the "liberty interest" protected by the due process clause, and the court of appeals remanded to the district court to decide whether the FDA's policy was "narrowly tailored to serve a compelling governmental interest."[115]

Judge Griffith's dissent provided several answers to the majority. One of these had to do with the distinction between safety and effectiveness. He read the majority to imply "that the FDA is primarily concerned with effectiveness after Phase I and that the right argued for by the Alliance would only override FDA regulation for effectiveness." By contrast, he said, "all phases of the FDA's testing process for new drugs involve testing for safety."[116]

With respect to the standard of meaningful consumer choice, Judge Griffith referred to a statement by the FDA that after Phase 1 testing, "'with so little data available, it is hard to understand how a patient could be truly informed about the risks—or potential benefits—associated with the drug.'"[117] Indeed, referring critically to "[t]he majority's vague allusion to potentially life-saving drugs," he spoke of the "difficulty in explaining what drugs [the majority's] constitutional right protects." He said "[t]hat the difficulty arises because at issue here is a novel and unfamiliar area of science," declaring that the "concept of ordered liberty" "does not contemplate that judges should resolve the scientific uncertainties presented by experimental drugs."[118]

Judge Griffith also took issue with the majority's reference to the lack of federal regulation of access to drugs before 1906. Calling this an "unremarkable proposition," he countered with history reaching back to guild regulation of drugs in England in the seventeenth century and to American state statutes, dating to 1736, which had regulated various aspects of drug marketing. Pointing out that this history did "not evidence a tradition of protecting a right of access to drugs," he said that, rather, "it evidences government responding to new risks as they are presented."[119]

Digging to a foundational level of politics, Judge Griffith relied on the power Congress had given the FDA to regulate new drugs, and the processes the agency had developed. He referred to the "judgment of the scientific and medical communities, expressed through Congress and the Executive Branch, that science does not warrant allowing the early access to experimental drugs the Alliance demands."[120] Framing that judgment were the "carefully constructed programs" of legislation and regulation that had been "refined over the years by experience."[121]

The panel majority denied a rehearing in November 2006. As a bad example of the effects of the FDA's policy, it instanced a patient with multiple myeloma who had been "denied access to a medication that had saved others' lives." Although this patient eventually was able to join a clinical trial, the court said, "years of delay had severely diminished [his] chances of responding to the medication" he sought.[122] Indicative of the importance of the question was that on the same day, the full court of appeals said it would review the panel's decision.[123]

Ezekiel Emanuel, a breast oncologist and bioethicist, provided several lessons in a critique of the panel decision in *Abigail Alliance*. One lesson was the story of the use of bone marrow transplants for metastatic breast cancer. "It took years," Emanuel wrote, to enroll 1,000 women to complete "[l]arge, government-funded, randomized clinical studies" of the effectiveness of the transplants. However, with many states responding to political pressure with laws that "mandat[ed] insurance companies [to] pay for transplants," more than "20,000 women got transplants outside the trials." The process of transplantation was "grueling," and entailed serious risks, even including death. Ultimately, the clinical research showed that transplantation "was not effective compared with regular chemotherapy." This wasted "[p]recious time" because of "delayed enrollment" in the trials, and "unnecessarily subjected" thousands of women to transplants, with "hundreds [dying] in the process, often in isolation rooms separated from their families." The dollar costs were "[m]illions, if not billions" for what turned out to be a "substandard treatment."[124]

Emanuel also presented an individual poster person, a contrast to the myeloma patient mentioned in the appellate court panel's denial of rehearing. This was a teacher, a mother of four with metastatic breast cancer, for whom two experimental drugs had proved unavailing. Although Emanuel explained to her that her physical condition excluded her from candidacy for another trial, she "still wanted access to experimental drugs." After conversations in which Emanuel conveyed the inevitability of death in the near term, she became "more accepting" and somewhat resigned herself to her fate.[125]

Emanuel noted that "[a]s every oncologist knows, maintaining a dying patient's hope is essential to their quality of life." However, echoing supporters of placebo controls for experiments with AIDS drugs described in the last chapter, he declared that "maintaining hope should never be confused with delaying the research studies that could give hope to future patients or administering ever-more ineffective and unproven treatments."[126]

Emanuel reserved his most focused scorn for the panel decision, which he saw as returning "to the snake-oil days[ ]." The result, he said, would be "access to unproven experimental agents for a few patients at the expense of more, faster research and access to proven treatments for every patient." This, he said, was "the height of irrationality born of desperation" and indeed was "the major reason why many, if not most, cancer advocacy groups oppose the Abigail Alliance's effort." Moreover, he said that if insurance companies paid for such treatments, "[c]osts would skyrocket as we pay billions through our insurance premiums and Medicare taxes for worthless drugs."[127]

Essentially ratifying Dr. Emanuel's argument as well as confirming Judge Griffith's dissent to the panel decision, eight of the ten judges of the full court then turned around the panel decision, holding for the FDA. Judge Griffith himself wrote for the 8–2 majority of the en banc court. He rehearsed his recounting in his prior dissent of the history of safety regulation for drugs, extending even to colonial times.[128] After summarizing the modern history of food and drug regulation,[129] he instanced the Supreme Court's rejection of the claims of cancer patients that the FDA's ban on Laetrile violated their rights.[130]

Judge Rogers, joined by Judge Douglas Ginsburg—who with her had made the majority on the panel—dissented from the en banc decision. The main argument was over Judge Rogers' reiteration of the idea that the right asserted by the Alliance was a "fundamental" right. Invoking established constitutional principles, she said that this right was one that required "strict scrutiny" of any governmental action that would deny it and thus mandated a showing on the part of the agency of a "compelling governmental interest."[131] She found the right to rest on "core" ideas of "personal autonomy, self-determination, and self-defense,"[132] tying the "self-defense right" to the "'doctrine of necessity.'"[133] She also invoked the historic tort-based "right of protection against interference with rescue"—that is, "rescues that are reasonably necessary"—and commented acidly that "[n]o doubt the deceased members of the Alliance who were denied access to experimental drugs that were subsequently approved by the FDA would have been surprised to learn that these drugs, under the [majority's] analysis, were unnecessary to the preservation of their lives."[134] Twisting in a conservative's knife, she employed an argument based on the Supreme Court's abortion decisions, saying that the majority was "forced to conclude that when a patient's life is on the line, medical procedures like abortion are to be analyzed differently than medical treatments consisting of prescription medications."[135]

Judge Griffith, for the majority, rejected all of these analogies. As to the argument from "necessity," he pointed out that the drugs at issue were "experimental and have not been shown to be safe, let alone effective at (or 'necessary' for) prolonging life."[136] He found unpersuasive the analogy based on the abortion cases because the Alliance's claim was "not about using reasonable force to defend oneself (as in most cases involving self-defense)," and was not "about access to life-saving medical treatment." His characterization of the "access" point drew the line on the asphalt. The question, he said, was "whether there is a constitutional right to assume" what the Alliance conceded were "enormous risks" "in pursuit of *potentially* life-saving drugs." He distinguished abortion decisions involving the "life of the mother" from cases where drugs had not been shown to have a "proven therapeutic effect."[137]

Rejecting the "rescue" metaphor, Judge Griffith said it was "difficult to see how a tort addressing interference with providing 'necessary' aid would guarantee a constitutional right to override the collective judgment of the scientific and medical communities expressed through the FDA's clinical testing process."[138] It was that process that provided the "rational basis" for the impingement of the Alliance's claim of "right," the "fundamental" character of which he denied.[139] He summarized his view as that "the FDA's policy of limiting access to investigational drugs" was "rationally related to the legitimate state interest of protecting patients, including the terminally ill, from potentially unsafe drugs with unknown therapeutic effects."[140]

One particularly interesting exchange of volleys between the en banc opinion writers featured, on one hand, the trench-level decision making of doctors and patients, and on the other, a reference to the essentially political character of the dispute. Judge Rogers drew on the fact that many doctors prescribe "off label," that is, they give patients drugs for purposes "other than that for which the FDA has approved the use of the drug." Noting that "[e]ven today, a patient may use a drug for unapproved purposes where the drug may be unsafe or ineffective for the off-label purpose," she declared that "encumbrances on the treatment decisions of a patient and her physician lack the historical pedigree of the right that the Alliance seeks to vindicate."[141]

Perhaps the last word, though, came from Judge Griffith for the majority. He pointed out that the FDA's process was not set in stone, for the issue could be taken to Congress. He noted that "[t]he Alliance's arguments about morality, quality of life, and acceptable levels of medical risk are certainly ones that can be aired in the democratic branches, without injecting the courts into unknown questions of science and medicine." He concluded that the majority's holding "ensures that this debate among the Alliance, the FDA, the scientific and medical communities, and the public may continue through the democratic process."[142]

However politics might play out on the issue, the Supreme Court refused to get involved. Without issuing an opinion, it denied a petition to review the D.C. Circuit's decision.[143]

Interwoven with the question of how fully the law should take into account prevailing concepts of good science are the questions of how much lay persons are able to understand about science, and, ultimately, the question of what is effective "consumer protection." One object lesson, favoring more traditional scientific methods, involves what appeared to be a promising drug that foundered on experimental data. This was the case of Remune, an AIDS drug originally conceived by the polio vaccine pioneer Jonas Salk and tested on more than 2,500 volunteers beginning around 1996. The lead investigators, university scientists, stopped the study in 1999 because, as one of them explained, "preliminary data showed that the drug was ineffective."[144] This led to a series of bitter battles over the scientific facts about the drug and their dissemination—or withholding. The sponsor of the drug, which reportedly did not provide the investigators with data on the final check-ups of the participants, refused to consent to publication by the investigators of their data.

However, the investigators proceeded to publish an article in the *Journal of the American Medical Association*, concluding that the data to which they had access failed to show that the addition of the drug to existing antiretroviral therapy (ART) "conferred any effect on progression-free survival relative to that achieved by ART alone."[145] Susan Haack reports in her summary of this history that in the wake of the article, and various responses, "[p]articipants in the study, who now learned for the first time why it had been halted in 1999, expressed concern that they had not been informed earlier of the unfavorable results."[146]

The FDA's proposed new rule in 2006 and the opposed opinions of the panel and the full court's majority in *Abigail Alliance* were thus markers in a war within a war. The larger war was the fight against disease. On one side were the strictures, and the needs, of science. On the other were the fierce desires of patients to try out the newest experimental vehicles. The history detailed in this chapter indicates that over time, politics and science sometimes find ways to live together. It also suggests, however, that they will not always be loving couples.

CHAPTER 3

Breast Implants: A Parable of Law's Response to Improvements on Nature

Many women desire devices that will replace breasts lost to surgery or that will make their breasts more attractive. One center of controversy has been the silicone gel-filled breast implant. It has been estimated that between 1 and 2 million women received those implants between 1963, when the devices were introduced, and 1992,[1] when the FDA severely limited access to the implants.

An alternative product is the saline-filled silicone inflatable breast prosthesis, defined by the FDA as "a silicone rubber shell made of" specified materials "that is inflated to the desired size with sterile isotonic saline before or after implantation," which is "intended . . . to augment or reconstruct the female breast."[2] Despite the regulatory action taken by the FDA against silicone gel implants in 1992, saline-filled implants remained on the market after that year, with the numbers of women having "breast augmentation" increasing from 32,607 in 1992 to 132,378 in 1998. Although 60 percent of women who had implants in 1998 were between the ages of 18 and 34 years, one-third of the total number were between 35 and 50 years of age.[3]

During the 1990s and into the new century, many studies on the effects of breast implants appeared. They ranged from particularized investigations of specific effects to broad summaries of the literature. One very large summary was the product of a judicial inquiry, a multidistrict litigation involving hundreds of thousands of plaintiffs. Although that study—and others—basically exonerated implants from an association with connective tissue disease (CTD), a principal maker of the implants eventually reached a multibillion dollar settlement with claimants.

This chapter analyzes the multifaceted drama—human, scientific, and legal—of this long episode of mass market experimentation. It involves a welter of information that would confront a consumer who wanted to know, at any point in time, about the risks of the products involved. As we present that history, it is well to keep in mind this hypothetical consumer and the uncertainties, even the anxieties, that this data would generate.

A Rigorous Early Classification

The legal basis for regulation of breast implants appears in the Medical Device Amendments of 1976, which establish three classes of "devices" for human use. Classes II and III are relevant to this story. Class II devices are products for which the general legal controls of the statute are "by themselves insufficient to provide reasonable assurance of . . . safety and effectiveness," but "for which there is sufficient information to establish special controls," including performance standards, "to provide such assurance."[4] Class III devices are devices that cannot be classified in class II "because insufficient information exists to determine that . . . special controls . . . would provide reasonable assurance of . . . safety and effectiveness," or where a device "presents a potential unreasonable risk of illness or injury." Such devices must obtain "premarket approval to provide reasonable assurance of . . . safety and effectiveness."[5]

An FDA document published in 1982 reflected the potential for scientific disagreement on both silicone gel-filled prostheses and the inflatable products. An FDA panel recommended that silicone gel-filled prostheses be classified in class II, saying it believed that "this device has demonstrated a reasonably satisfactory level of performance over a long period of time." The panel concluded that a performance standard "would provide reasonable assurance of the safety and effectiveness of the device and that there is sufficient information to establish a standard."[6]

However, the FDA disagreed with its panel and proposed class III classification for silicone gel-filled prostheses. It declared that premarket approval should be required because of a "potential unreasonable risk of injury" from three potential hazards:

> (1) possible migration of silicone gel from the interior of the prosthesis to adjacent tissue (with or without rupture of the silicone rubber shell) (2) contracting of the fibrous tissue capsule which forms around the implanted prostheses and which can also lead to marked asymmetry in breast contour, hardness, and pain [designated fibrous capsular contracture],[7] and (3) possible long-term toxic effects of the silicone polymers from which the prostheses are fabricated.[8]

The agency said that "some of the medical literature indicates that a significant portion of patients experience complications directly associated with implantation of these devices."[9] It noted that studies on the "toxicology of liquid silicone" were "limited in scope and require further experimental confirmation," and it more generally referred to "ongoing scientific debates on the safety of breast prostheses."[10]

The same document also featured a parallel set of developments on inflatable breast prostheses. As with the silicone gel-filled products, an FDA panel proposed to classify inflatable prostheses as class II devices because it "believe[d] that the device has an established history of safe and effective use." The panel based its recommendation on its "members' personal knowledge of, and clinical experience with" the products. In particular, it referred to the opinion of one physician, who presented studies to support his belief that "inflatable breast prostheses are superior to gel-filled prostheses" because of studies showing leakage of silicone gel and "the possibility of unknown hazards from ... leaking gel such as foreign body reaction and long-term toxic effects."[11]

Again, the FDA disagreed with its panel and proposed class III classification for inflatable breast prostheses. The FDA took note of the conclusion of its panel that "the valves have been improved to the point where the incidence of complications is remarkably low," specifically noting that "there was substantial reduction in the incidence of valve leakage during ... 1969 to 1974." Yet, it noted "cautions" raised by "early evaluators" and "in recent clinical literature." In that context, in language that partially echoed its proposal on silicone gel implants, the agency said that it thought premarket approval was necessary. It opined that these products "present[ ] a potential unreasonable risk of injury," citing "the primary health hazard associated specifically with this type of breast prosthesis" as "leakage of the contents of the silicone shell and subsequent collapse or deformity of the breast."[12] One lesson of this slice of history, it should be noted, is the way it reflects a course of market experimentation during the early years of the selling of this product. That process evidently improved the safety of the product, but it did so with the active use of consumers as vehicles for safety testing.

Clearly, the developing concerns about the products penetrated the corporate offices of Dow Corning, a principal maker of the implants, resulting in a substantial increase in risk information. By 1985, the company's cumulative package inserts ran to at least seventeen paragraphs on "[p]ossible adverse reactions and complications," ranging from capsular contracture and "reports of suspected immunological sensitization or hyperimmune system response" to rupture of implants and "gel bleed," although the 1995 insert stressed that there was "no evidence of metabolic products of this silicone bleed." The insert stressed in capital letters that it was "THE RESPONSIBILITY OF THE SURGEON TO PROVIDE THE PATIENT WITH THE APPROPRIATE INFORMATION PRIOR TO SURGERY."[13]

Stepped-Up Requirements

In 1988, the agency issued a final rule that classified the silicone gel implants in class III.[14] Then, with the arrival of the 1990s, the FDA began in earnest to build a wall against the marketing of silicone gel implants. In May 1990, it proposed a rule to require premarketing approval or the completion of a "product development protocol" for silicone gel implants.[15] It catalogued in nine paragraphs a list of "significant risks associated with the use" of those implants—risks that ranged from currently identified injuries to "potential risk[s]" to "unknown" ones. It focused initially on the problems of fibrous capsular contracture and the migration and leakage of silicone gel. The agency also referred to "several reports" that the silicone gel implants "may interfere with" tumor detection by "standard mammography procedures" and to knowledge that polyurethane material used on foam-covered silicone gel implants could produce a "potential breakdown product" that caused cancer in animals. Acknowledging that "relatively purer medical grade silicone" was being used in the implants, the agency also said that "the potential for developing cancer as a long-term complication related to silicone migration remains a potential risk." A risk it specifically labeled "unknown" was the risk that silicone could cause birth defects in the children of women who had the implants.[16]

Even as to the risks it put front and center, the agency indicated how experimental the mass marketing of the implants was. It said it was "seeking further information" on "safety and effectiveness" with respect to a number of questions that included "[t]he incidence of fibrous capsular contracture" and leakage and migration of silicone gel. It also mentioned the need for information on "[t]he potential long-term adverse effects" of the implants, including "cancer, autoimmune disease," and causation of birth defects.[17]

The next year, 1991, the FDA issued a final rule that required filing of a PMA application for the silicone gel implants.[18] The agency summarized and responded to comments on the rule as it had proposed it. It acknowledged improvements in technology as they might bear on the problems of contracture, rupture, and leakage. However, it expressed its belief that "neither the literature nor other data currently available . . . describe differences in the incidence of problems attributable to device design and/or variations in surgical procedures." Rather, it said, there was "[s]ufficient information" that identified "contracture, rupture, and leakage as risks to health associated with" the silicone gel products.[19] Marching through its accumulating list of risks proven or potential, it said that leakage and migration "represent[ ] a risk associated with the use of this device," that the implants "may interfere with . . . standard mammography procedures" and that the risk of birth defects "remains a potential risk." On a topic that increasingly became controversial, it declared that "[i]mmunological sensitization may be a serious risk associated with" the silicone gel implants, noting that "[q]uestions have been raised about the relationship between silicone and various connective tissue disorders, including scleroderma."[20]

As the agency developed these rules over the period of a decade, the arguments about the quality of risk information and the interpretation of data became a drama of consumer life in a technologically advanced society. Regulatory actions in the fall of 1991 and early 1992 provided a bridge into a new decade of even more intense theater.

In September 1991, the agency directed one salient of attack into the realm of consumer information. Declaring that it had identified "significant deficiencies" in premarket approval applications for silicone gel implants in particular, it effectively required the disclosure of "written information to patients on the risks associated with" breast prostheses, including also the saline-filled implants.[21] The FDA was plain about its policy premises on personal choice, saying that "[b]ecause breast prostheses are implanted at the patient's own choosing . . . , it is of particular concern . . . that patients receive all of the information pertinent to their decision." Moreover, the agency specified the kinds of information that must be provided to avoid the fate of products being declared "misbranded"—in effect a death sentence for marketing. In terms that might have provoked cries of "governmental nanny" from the manufacturers, the agency said it was providing manufacturers "patient risk information sheets" that the firms could print and send to doctors "so that they can provide them to patients." The document summarized the catalog of risks the agency had been building up, including capsular contracture, ruptures, and "[i]nterference with mammography." One item simply said that "[q]uestions have been raised about whether . . . escaped gel might cause autoimmune diseases . . . or whether it might increase the risk of cancer."[22] The agency's declaration that these sheets were "provided for guidance only" did not disguise the mailed fist of the misbranding remedy.

Early the next year, regulation moved to a new level of intensity on the silicone gel implants. In January, the FDA called for a voluntary moratorium on use of those implants pending review of "new information on their safety." That data included what FDA Commissioner David Kessler called "additional evidence that implants could possibly cause autoimmune or connective tissue disorders."[23]

Then, in April, the agency said it would only allow those implants to be available "under controlled clinical studies," stressing that it would assure access to those trials for women who needed the products for "reconstruction after cancer surgery or traumatic injury or for certain congenital disorders." Although Commissioner Kessler said the policy was "meant to be compassionate toward these patients," he stressed that it was not "'business as usual.'" The severity of the agency's approach was evident in his insistence that all women covered by "open availability protocols" for such purposes as "the correction of severe deformities" would have to have certifications from their doctors "that saline implants are not a satisfactory alternative and that in clinical studies they would be "carefully monitored and followed for years to come."[24] In May of that year, the agency announced that makers of implants—both silicone gel-filled and inflatable—must track them on the market.[25]

Kessler then editorialized in favor of the policy in the *New England Journal of Medicine*. He emphasized the length of "the list of unanswered questions" and the differences in sets of data that had been offered. He noted, for example, that "[a]lthough manufacturers' reports suggest a frequency of asymptomatic rupture" for silicone implants "between 0.2 and 1.1 percent," preliminary data presented to an advisory panel "suggested that 4 to 6 percent of asymptomatic women" had suffered ruptures of the devices. At the same time, he sought to respond to the argument that the implants should not be used at all, based on the theory "that no one should be exposed to a risk that he or she cannot assess." Although he acknowledged that "women who receive implants under the new protocols will be taking a risk of unknown magnitude," he pointed that the provision of information that "implants are not risk-free" was "a decided improvement over the previous state of 'informed consent.'"[26] Trying to shore up his other "flank" against arguments based on personal choice, he stressed the force of the public policy decision embodied in the legislation that created the FDA. He said that to allow people "to make their own decisions about the entire range of products for which the FDA has responsibility" would destroy "the whole rationale for the agency," returning those products to the realm of "caveat emptor."[27]

Kessler concluded on a note that stressed the special limits the law placed on mass market experimentation with products regulated by his agency. He said that if the agency had not taken the action it did, "the uncontrolled and widespread availability of breast implants would probably have continued for another 30 years—without producing any meaningful clinical data about their safety and effectiveness."[28]

The FDA tightened the screws still further on the silicone gel implants. Illustrative is an agency notice in October 1992 that partially denied approval of a premarket approval (PMA) application for a silicone gel implant for use in "augmentation of the healthy female breast," saying that "the device [has] not [been] shown to be safe and effective" for that use. The agency did say that the device could be made available "under strict controls" for conditions with serious health consequences, such as reconstruction surgery after mastectomy, burns, or "surgery to correct serious congenital deformities."[29]

A Catalog of Risks

In early 1993, the agency followed up this and other similar actions[30] with a proposed rule that would require filing of PMAs or product development protocols (PDPs) for the inflatable prostheses, that is, silicone shells inflated with saline. It set out a list of "significant risks associated with" those products, including fibrous capsular contracture, deflation of the devices, and interference with early tumor detection. It also referred to possible cancer risks, saying that "[c]ases of several types of cancer in humans have been reported in association with various forms of implanted silicone," and said that "[p]rolonged contact with the silicone membrane and its components might present a potential risk" of birth defects.[31]

Paralleling and following these regulatory developments were a series of scientific tennis matches between critics and defenders of the devices—contests that a conscientious patient would have found especially difficult to follow because sometimes the players seemed to be serving and returning on adjoining courts. These matches played out against the background of litigation that had been filed as far back as the 1970s on behalf of women who claimed injury and illness from implants. Perhaps the first lawsuit in what became a wave of litigation was brought by a woman suing for a ruptured implant. It yielded a $170,000 jury verdict, which was affirmed on appeal in 1978.[32] A mid-1980s case led to a substantial jury award, and later a settlement, in favor of a woman who claimed that silicone implants caused autoimmune disease. Her attorney employed documents found in Dow Corning archives to support the claim.[33]

The Multidistrict Litigation

By the 1990s, in the midst of an outpouring of scientific studies on the topic, nationwide litigation on breast implants developed and ground along. After 16,000 women had brought suits following the FDA's clampdown on sales of implants, the litigation was consolidated in the federal district court in the Northern District of Alabama,[34] where Judge Sam Pointer sought to implement a class action settlement for all the claims. For a tantalizing period in 1994, it appeared that the parties—women suing for implant-caused injuries and manufacturers—had arrived at a settlement based on a fund of $4.25 billion. However, the pressure of numbers—claimants and the amount of money they sought—forced the settlement to collapse. About 440,000 women made claims against the fund, seeking even more money than the massive amount set aside in the fund, and 7,000 others brought individual suits. Dow Corning went into bankruptcy in 1995, and three other manufacturers started negotiating for a new settlement.[35]

A fascinating development that occurred parallel to this litigation was the involvement of various interest groups in public discussion—an analogue of the political involvement of HIV/AIDS groups in the arguments about IND speedups. An example of this type of activity was a statement published by the National Multiple Sclerosis Society in 1993 that declared that there were "no valid scientific data indicating that silicone implants are related to the onset of typical multiple sclerosis." After referring specifically to the proposed court settlement of the implant claims, the group said that since it was "clear that there are many hundreds of thousands of people with" various immune disorders "who have never had silicone breast implants, silicone cannot be a sole, or even primary, cause of such conditions." What would be helpful with respect to questions of causation of multiple sclerosis, the statement said, would be completion of a study that was underway on "the association of silicone breast implants with immunological disorders."[36]

An Early Warning

A contrast, illustrative of preliminary warning signs that filtered through generally benign results, appeared in a study published in 1993 on patients with complaints about rheumatic disease who happened to have had silicone implants. Alan J. Bridges and colleagues noted that "most women with silicone breast implants and symptoms of rheumatic disease have normal results of common immunological tests." However, they identified a small subset of women with "findings that were unusual even for patients referred to rheumatologists." One of these findings was a "distinctly unusual autoantibody response characteristically found only in patients with connective tissue disease." Referring to the result of other research, although emphasizing that that data was not from "controlled epidemiological studies," the Bridges investigators found support for "a hypothesis that silicone may . . . be a 'trigger' for a scleroderma-like illness in small numbers of patients." They were careful to say that because each of the patients in their study "was referred with existing symptoms of rheumatic disease," they could not ascertain "the degree of risk for development of rheumatic disease" from breast implants. They advocated testing of their hypotheses "in large, population-based studies."[37]

This report was in line with many studies coming out over a period of several years: no concrete findings of risk, some disturbing hypotheses, and calls for data from larger numbers of people. A particularly interesting feature of the report by Bridges and his coauthors, however, was the way it spotlighted a profile of disease that might be related to a product but that affects a relatively few number of people who cannot be identified in advance. Whether one calls the development of such a disease a result of hypersensitivity or something else, it poses a problem both for regulators and judges. How should policy makers, and courts, react to the case of a product or activity that benefits many but severely harms a few?

The scientific battle heated up. The end of 1993 brought a debate in the *Journal of the American Medical Association* between the Council on Scientific Affairs of the American Medical Association (AMA) and Commissioner Kessler. The AMA Council acknowledged that there was "considerable public anxiety concerning the safety of breast implants," but stressed its view that "[t]his anxiety is not warranted based on current scientific evidence." It specifically criticized "a number of journalists and media organizations," which it said had "not presented a balanced and informed view on the safety of breast implants during the past year." The Council recommended that "the AMA support the position that women have the right to choose silicone-gel filled or saline-filled breast implants for both augmentation and reconstruction after being fully informed about the risks and benefits."[38] Kessler's response, joined by two colleagues, was tart and unusually condemnatory of doctors. He said that then-current statistics indicated that 75,000 women "with implants would be at risk for potentially serious adverse health effects." This, he said, was "not a safety standard that the FDA can accept." He declared that "[f]or 30 years, physicians implanted silicone gel implants in women without having adequate information on what risks they might pose to their patients and without insisting on that information. Such practice represents an abrogation of responsibility on the part of physicians."[39]

Studies Showing No Risk

Appearing to confirm the AMA Council's position was a stream of reports that showed no elevated risk. One such report was a study on CTD by a Mayo Clinic group led by Dr. Sherine Gabriel, published in 1994, that compared two sets of women in one Minnesota county who had had mastectomies for breast cancer.

The women in one group had received breast implants. A second group of control subjects included pairings of two women who had had mastectomies but no implants for each woman who had an implant. The study was retrospective, with the authors noting the expense and time it would take to do a prospective study. Their basic conclusion was that there was no "statistically significant elevation in the relative risk of any" of several "specified connective-tissue diseases or disorders"— a dozen, all told—"among the women with breast implants as compared with the control subjects."[40]

A summary of another study, tying it together with prior research, said there had been no showing of a "statistical association" between silicone gel implants "and the development of connective tissue diseases." An editorial by the leader of the study, Dr. Marc Hochberg, cautioned that "[a]ll studies ... lack adequate statistical power to definitely exclude a small excess risk, and may not have adequate follow-up to account for a long latency period between implantation and the development of disease." He concluded that "the issue of causation remains unresolved" and observed that "there are no uniform guidelines for the management of patients with rheumatic symptoms and/or connective tissue diseases with silicone gel-filled breast implants."[41] Dr. Hochberg told a reporter that "women with breast implants should be somewhat reassured by these data." However, he also pointed out that his investigation did not seek to find out whether "there was any relation between the implants and other disorders, or between ruptured implants and connective-tissue diseases."[42]

More support for the view that there was no link to CTD appeared in a 1995 study that employed the Nurses' Health Study cohort, using questionnaires sent to all female, married nurses between 30 and 55 years of age in several populous states. Sifting a total of more than 87,000 women who responded to questionnaires, these investigators analyzed 516 women who had confirmed connective tissue disease of some kind and 1,183 women who had had "some type of breast implant." They also did a "validation study" that compared self-reports by members of the cohort with reviews by physicians of the medical records of a small sample of women. They found no "increased risk of any connective-tissue disease or of 41 signs or symptoms of connective-tissue disease among women with any breast implant or with specific types of breast implants," although they referred to certain limitations of the study that kept it from being "considered definitely negative."[43]

The appearance of this study cast a spotlight on the intersection of science and the legal system, specifically with reference to the enormous class action in progress on the implants. At the time the study was published, approximately 400,000 women had registered to participate in what looked like a settlement, whereas more than 11,000 others had sued individually. A lawyer who had worked on insurance coverage issues on implants predicted that the new study would make more women "inclined to join the global settlement" because of "'the mounting evidence of lack of connection'" between the implants and connective tissue illnesses.[44]

The close interaction between law and science was evident in mid-May 1995 when Dow Corning, the maker of the silicone gel implants, filed for bankruptcy protection. The owners of Dow Corning were Dow Chemical and Corning, Inc., and a news report said that most of those firms' stock in Dow Corning would go into paying implant claimants. Dow Corning had originally pledged $2 billion for the settlement pool—which it said was all it could do over a 30-year period, given the individual suits also pending against it—and other implant manufacturers had pledged a little over $2 billion more. Judge Sam Pointer in the federal court in Alabama had said that the money pledged to the pool would not cover the claims before him and "sent the parties back to renegotiate." Dow Chemical announced that it would "write off its entire $374 million investment in Dow Corning," and its shares promptly rose 62.5 cents on the New York Stock Exchange.[45]

Scientists Collide with the Legal System

Meanwhile, various members of the medical community expressed anger and trepidation about the burdens imposed on researchers by implant litigation. Dr. Shaun Ruddy, the president of the American College of Rheumatology, said "he knew of academic doctors who starting filling out forms for lawyers 'at 1,000 bucks a pop.'" Dr. Gabriel of the Mayo Clinic said that the demands of plaintiffs' lawyers for documents had "taken a huge amount of time and it has been extremely stressful." She said the lawyers were demanding "over 800 manuscripts . . . , they want hundreds of data bases, dozens of file cabinets and the entire medical records" of all women in the county where the study was done, "whether or not they were in the study." She said the process had "severely compromised my ability to do research." Dr. Marcia Angell, the executive editor of the *New England Journal of Medicine*, added that she had been subpoenaed twice, with demands for "a large number of documents that don't even exist." A plaintiff's lawyer responded by asking, "Why doesn't she come clean and show us the documents?" and declared, "I'd like to get her under oath."[46]

Dr. Angell wrote an editorial accompanying the Gabriel study in which she spoke critically of "[m]ultimillion-dollar settlements" "[d]espite the lack of published epidemiological studies" showing causation of connective tissue diseases by the implants. "The effect of breast implants on the human body is not a matter of opinion," she declared. "Like other scientific questions, its resolution must await the marshaling of a sufficient amount of carefully gathered and analyzed data."[47] A committee of the American College of Rheumatology, which labeled claims by trial lawyers against one scientist as "baseless," said in May 1995 that rheumatologists who had "expressed opinions or published work viewed as contrary to the interest of plaintiffs and plaintiffs' attorneys" had been "subjected to various forms of harassment in the work place or even at their homes." A committee document said that the College's board of directors "should not underestimate the vigor with which" the "agenda" evident in criticism of rheumatologists "could be pursued, given the resources at stake."[48]

Studies and commentaries now multiplied that in effect emphasized the positive—that is, by citing and presenting negative data on disease-causing propensities. A 1995 report based on data from a rheumatology practice in Atlanta concluded that there was "no evidence" that women with breast implants are at an "increased risk for having rheumatoid arthritis or other diffuse connective-tissue disease" such as lupus or scleroderma.[49]

A somewhat more nuanced picture concerning the risk of breast cancer, but one that showed no increased risk on balance, appeared in a reanalysis of data on implants done in the Canadian province of Alberta—from a group that totalled more than 10,000 women in a 13-year period in the 1970s and 1980s. A prior study had shown that women with implants had "a significantly lower risk of breast cancer than the general population." The investigators who did the reanalysis concluded that "the apparent risk of breast cancer cannot be said to be either higher or significantly lower than that of the general population."[50]

It is worth dwelling for a moment on the number of women who had had breast implants by the 1980s—both with respect to the undoubtedly broad geographical spread of the devices and to the great uncertainty about just how many women had received the implants. The Alberta numbers alone symbolize the breadth of distribution of the devices. Statistics frequently cited about the total number of implants demonstrate the uncertainty. Another 1995 study, referred to earlier, cited sources for the proposition that "[s]ince 1982, approximately 1 million to 2.2 million women in the United States and Canada have received silicone breast implants," either in reconstruction following surgery or "for cosmetic reasons."[51]

The American College of Rheumatology issued another pronouncement later in 1995, expressing its belief that there was "compelling evidence that silicone implants expose patients to no demonstrable additional risk for connective tissue or rheumatic disease." The organization extended this statement with a jump into the political waters, opposing lawsuits brought on behalf of women with implants. It declared that "[c]linicians, scientists, academicians, and editors who have been harassed by plaintiffs' attorneys for their involvement in scientific research efforts related to silicone implants deserve the continued support of their institutions and professional societies." Accompanying this was a sideswipe at "anecdotal reports." The organization acknowledged that such evidence was "of importance to call attention to a potential problem," but declared generally that it "should not be utilized to formulate decisions and regulations." It said specifically that anecdotal evidence "should no longer be used to support" the relationship between implants and rheumatoid arthritis or CTD "in the courts or by the FDA."[52]

Some Risk Data

Although the scientific case in defense of the implants appeared strong by the mid-1990s, some emerging data cast shadows on the products. A retrospective study in the *Journal of the American Medical Association* in 1996 analyzed self-reported data from a large sample of female health professionals, including 10,830 women who had had breast implants and 11,805 who reported CTD over a period of 29 years. It concluded that the data were "compatible with prior reports from other cohort studies that exclude a large hazard," but that the data did "suggest small increased risks of connective tissue diseases among women with breast implants." The researchers, led by Charles Hennekens of the Harvard Medical School, said that the large size of the sample made "chance an unlikely explanation for the results," although a "plausible alternative explanation" was "differential overreporting of connective-tissue diseases or selective participation by affected women with breast implants." They stressed that "[t]he major contribution of this and other observational analytic studies" was "to exclude large risks of connective-tissue disease following breast implants."[53] A slightly different set of nuances appeared in Hennekens' statement to a television reporter that the study "provides reassuring evidence against any large hazard of connective tissue disorders" in women with the implants. He then presented a kind of double qualification that the study "raises the possibility but by no means documents a small hazard of connective tissue disorders."[54]

A much more critical slant came from some journalistic sources, who focused in part on what they viewed as distortions in public relations campaigns on behalf of Dow Corning. One pair of reporters presented what they claimed was an internal document from a public relations firm that suggested that women satisfied with implants be trained to give testimony, which would be written for them, to give to Congressional committees. Another document ascribed to the company suggested the use of "spokespeople drawn from women's cancer support groups . . . to defend implants by writing letters to the editor, participating in media interviews, and communicating positive messages to women's groups in their regions."[55]

One writer identified as "the biggest myth" the "notion that scientific studies had disproved suffering women's claims." She noted that Dow Corning, now functioning in bankruptcy, had taken out "full-page ads in a dozen national papers" which emphasized that studies "showed no link between breast implants and disease." This writer said that some of these studies "were directly funded by Dow Corning" and that others, including the Mayo Clinic study, had been "made possible by grants from a foundation whose chair . . . admitted that it acted as a 'facilitator' delivering" funds from the company. Condemning "junk journalism," the reporter complained that journalists had "become captives of corporate P.R.," "accept[ing] . . . corporate-funded research as the only 'real' science," and "adopt[ing] the implant manufacturers' preferred framing of the story."[56]

Critique of Risk Evidence

A stern response to these arguments came from *New England Journal of Medicine* editor Angell. In a "Special Article," she decried people who "naturally assume that implants are the cause of any illness or symptoms that occur after they were inserted." She declared that "the watchword of some women with implants, 'We are the evidence,' seems reasonable to many people, although it is logically meaningless." Borrowing a favorite metaphor of scientists arguing against false inference of cause and effect, she said, "[i]t is as though the rooster who crowed before dawn took credit for the sunrise, and thought the sequence of events was evidence enough."[57]

Referring in particular to the Hennekens study summarized previously, Angell expressed anxiety about the problem of "reporting bias," which cast doubt on the validity of unverified self-reporting of CTD. She vented a particular concern about "the fact that the questionnaires" for the study "were sent to the women after the publicity surrounding the FDA ban." The problem of reporting bias, she predicted, would "increasingly plague[ ]" research. She opined that "[e]ven attempts to validate self-reports by medical records will be subject to bias, because there are now a number of doctors whose patients are referred to them by plaintiffs' attorneys and who diagnose implant-related illness so often that their records would be highly suspect."[58] Summarizing anxieties already mentioned by researchers, she lamented "the encroachment by tort law on the conduct of research studies," instancing "intimidating" demands by plaintiffs' lawyers who sought "enormous amounts of research data" by subpoena. The "implied message" to "both institutions and researchers" was that "research on breast implants could easily cost them vast amounts of time and energy, as well as large legal fees."[59]

The most troubling thing, Angell said, was the reflection in the "breast-implant story" of "what appears to be a widespread distrust and misunderstanding of science in American society." She noted that "several jurors who participated in implant decisions, as well as the head of a powerful advocacy group, have publicly said that the results of scientific studies did not matter to them." This attitude, she suggested, illustrated an alienation on the part of "many people" "from science and scientific habits of thought." This was occurring, she said, "at a time when we need science more than ever to help us find our way through an increasing number of serious and complicated questions involving risks to health and safety."[60] Some of the later chapters in the story would provide more evidence supporting Dr. Angell's concerns.

The National Science Panel Report

The end of the 1990s brought some major studies and summaries on breast implants, which might be said generally to exonerate the devices from causing increased risk in the general population, but which in proper scientific fashion urged more research. The weightiest document, literally, was a report of a "National Science Panel" to the Alabama federal court in which the multidistrict class action resided. Judge Pointer of that court, who was overseeing the litigation, posed a set of questions to the panel that focused on whether silicone gel implants "cause or exacerbate" CTDs and immune system dysfunctions of various kinds.[61]

One chapter of the report dealt with "animal studies relevant to silicone toxicity." It summarized research indicating that silicone exposure had "a modest and somewhat consistent effect" on the activity of natural killer (NK) cells.[62] However, it found "little evidence from controlled animal studies that suggest silicone causes systemic inflammatory responses."[63] It reported that 17 experiments had "indicate[d] that silicone did not induce or promote the development of autoimmune disease and/or alter diagnostic clinical endpoints," although it said that two other experiments "must be viewed as providing weak but suggestive preliminary evidence of a promotional effect."[64] Although it referred to various limitations on the data, the report concluded that "the preponderance of the evidence from animal studies indicates little probability that silicone exposure induces or exacerbates systemic disease in humans."[65]

A chapter on clinical immunology suggested the need for further data on "potentially susceptible individuals." This, the author indicated, was because the information on what are known as haplotypes—certain versions of genes—lent itself to two different hypotheses. One was that silicone implants "trigger disease in a susceptible population." The other was that they "are unrelated to the development of disease."[66] The chapter also summarized studies indicating that women with implants "do not reproducibly demonstrate an increase in autoantibodies," although it indicated inconsistencies in studies of antinuclear antibodies and various gaps in desirable knowledge.[67] The general conclusion of the immunology chapter was that there were "no consistent data to suggest systemic inflammation or systemic induction of anti-silicone or autoreactive responses."[68]

However, the writer of the clinical immunology chapter acknowledged that "[m]ost studies on the immune system in women with SBI [silicone breast implants] have design flaws such that they do not, in fact, address the existence of SBI-indicated immunologic abnormality." It also said that it "remains possible that we do not yet know how to recognize an affected subset of individuals or that we have not analyzed the relevant parameters of immune activation."[69] Thus, a haunting question resounded about the effects of a particular stimulus on vulnerable segments of a population, most of whose members do not suffer effects from that stimulus. That topic recurs, in one form or another, throughout the law governing product risks.

A separate chapter dealt with epidemiology with respect to CTD. This chapter included "meta-analyses" that surveyed "various sets of studies" from statistical and epidemiological points of view.[70] The authors acknowledged early that most of the individual studies of silicone implants and CTDs had "insufficient numbers of women to provide precise estimates of the possible association between implants and disease."[71] With technical qualifications, however, the chapter concluded that for each of the CTDs analyzed, "the findings are consistent with a lack of association between breast implants and connective tissue diseases." In fact, it noted that for several diseases, the statistics would, "if interpreted literally... imply that breast implants protect against these conditions."[72]

The authors of this chapter found it appropriate to deal textually[73] as well as in an appendix[74] with the Hennekens study, summarized previously.[75] Echoing Dr. Angell's earlier critique, the authors noted features of that study that "could bias the results." They referred to the fact that all the data came from self-reports in answers to questionnaires, during a time when "publicity concerning silicone breast implants and their possible adverse effects, particularly for CTD-like syndromes, was intense in the scientific and public media." They suggested that "[t]his high media visibility could be conducive to reporting bias, i.e., women with implants and perceived illness would be more likely to respond to the questionnaire than would unaffected women." The authors also suggested that the fact that only 24 percent of people to whom the questionnaire was sent responded to it could possibly introduce bias.[76] The intensity of media publicity was clearly a nettle for the authors. Referring specifically to a 1990 television program in which Connie Chung discussed breast implants, they concluded that such publicity was "likely to have sensitized implanted women to their symptoms and resulted in over-reporting of disease relative to nonimplanted women."[77] These concerns simply underlined the difficulty of doing good science—both biological science and social science.

The final chapter of the panel report, written by a kidney rheumatologist, dealt with clinical cases and clinical associations. It was clear enough, the author said, that "a wide variety of connective tissue/autoimmune diseases and symptoms" appear in women with silicone breast implants.[78] The question was whether the implants were causing additional cases of the diseases. Seeking an answer, the author examined data from many studies in detail.[79] Analyzing that data, the author slanted toward a lack of statistical association, but there were some grays, rather than blacks and whites, in his conclusion. With respect to the "Classic/Accepted Diagnosis" of CTDs, there was no "'appreciable' association" shown with silicone implants. The survey included "[p]atients with one or more symptoms and signs" who did "not meet the criteria" for a "classic/accepted" CTD or for an "atypical" syndrome called "Undifferentiated Connective Tissue Disease." For those women, there were "few symptoms and signs for which a single study found an appreciable association, but in all cases, there were other studies of the same symptom or sign that did not confirm this association."[80]

One problem inhered in the fact that "many of the signs and symptoms including the rheumatologic and psychological complaints are so common in the general population and as presenting complaints in physician's offices, that a possible increased frequency of these complaints among those with implants would be difficult to discern."[81] The executive summary of the panel report summarized this point by saying that "[n]o distinctive features relating to silicone breast implants could be identified."[82]

The overall conclusion to the clinical chapter was scientifically careful, and gray: "No substantive data was found that allowed a rigorous assessment of any difference in the clinical course from those with the conditions but without implants; thus no conclusion can be reached due to the uncertainty arising from a lack of research addressing this question."[83]

Remaining Uncertainties

The court in the multidistrict litigation had before it a report it had commissioned totaling hundreds of pages and laden with appendixes. On the whole, that report seemed to indicate that breast implants were not increasing the level of CTD in the general population. However, as scientists properly will do, the panel raised many questions about gaps in existing knowledge—gaps that might be expensive to fill, sometimes requiring research that would take many years. There lurked the specific question of whether significant numbers of women had been affected adversely by the implants, effects perhaps attributable to genetic make-ups on which the implants worked badly, with the bad fit being undiscoverable in the state of present scientific knowledge: undiscoverable before the implants were done and perhaps even after they were done. The case of silicone breast implants, therefore, was another classic case of experimentation on mass populations. These experiments were conducted at the hands of scientists with high technical knowledge and skills, but still yielded some uncertainty for those researchers—and they took place under conditions of significant uncertainty with typically little knowledge available to the mass market subjects.

The U.K. Report

Just before the National Science Panel made its report, the British Independent Review Group [IRG] published a set of conclusions that essentially paralleled those of the Panel. The fact that the group was set up at the request of the Minister of Health indicated the level of concern in the United Kingdom, where breast enlargement was "the most common cosmetic procedure performed on women" in the U.K., with about 8,000 operations a year.[84] Overall, the report found no hard evidence that the implants were causing problems. However, it bowed to evident political pressure by suggesting the need for more research. And, interestingly, it recommended a standardization and increase of the amount of information given to women contemplating implants.

A feature of the Group's report that it shared in common with the work of the National Science Panel was the analysis of "immense amounts of complex evidence."[85] Another—commonplace among those who deal in safety regulation issues—was the relativity of the concept of safety, which requires "[b]alancing risks and benefits." The Group emphasized that the fact that "safety is not an absolute concept" is "particularly so in medical practice, where deliberate invasive procedures carry a risk to health."[86]

A "principal question[ ]" on which the Group focused was whether silicone gel implants "*lead to the development of an autoimmune disorder?*"[87] The Group considered testimony[88] asserting that it does. However, it concluded to the contrary. Specifically referring to material provided by the Tennessee scientist Radford Shanklin, it said it "did not agree with him that any of the changes seen constituted evidence of an immune response."[89] However, again, the possibility of vulnerable subgroups reared its head. This was with particular reference to "inflammatory reactions that indirectly provoke immune responses to the recipient's own tissues[]." The Group said it could not "rule out the possibility that a sub-group of the women who develop an autoimmune response do so as a consequence of their implant rather than due to other factors."[90]

On the whole, though, the Group arrived at a series of conclusions indicating that evidence was lacking for an association between the implants and adverse reactions. It found "no histopathological evidence or conclusive immunological evidence for an abnormal immune response to silicone from breast implants in tissue" and "no epidemiological evidence for any link between silicone gel breast implants and any established connective tissue disease."[91] It found, indeed, that there was a "slightly reduced incidence of breast cancer in women with breast implants."[92] It also concluded that "[g]ood evidence" was "lacking" for "the existence of atypical connective tissue disease or undefined conditions such as 'silicone poisoning,'"[93] and noted that it was "difficult on the available data to identify a specific syndrome associated with silicone gel breast implants when the symptoms are so diverse and could be related to other conditions, occurring in women with an implant but unrelated to it."[94]

The Group did observe, however, that "chronic infection around breast implants has been reported" and that this "could account for the fatigue and musculoskeletal pains noted by some women." It said "further research would be required to determine the presence and frequency of such infection associated with implants and its relationship to the level of symptoms reported."[95] It also "recognised that there were issues such as the precise incidence of rupture where the scientific data were incomplete so that rigorous conclusions could not be drawn."[96]

A very interesting aspect of the Group's recommendations was its emphasis on consumer information. This was interesting not only as applied to breast implants but because of its ramifications for medical care generally. The Group presented a "checklist" in double columns spread over a full page of "issues to be discussed" by surgeons with patients considering implants.[97] Notably, it recommended a "'cooling off' period of several days between the initial consultation with the surgeon and the operation."[98] Moreover, it recommended the development of a "specific consent form" for such operations that would "incorporate[ ], as an integral part, the checklist."[99]

This degree of standardized, specified information is rather unusual from the standpoint of informed consent doctrine generally, even though that doctrine itself requires fairly high levels of specificity about risks and benefits. These particularized recommendations seem to have arisen from the special set of angers that fueled political controversy about breast implants. This intensity of focus is also evident in several elements of another of the Group's recommendations. It suggested setting up a "small steering group . . . to prioritise, plan and monitor" a "programme of research" that would include "research into the true incidence of rupture" and "into the aetiology of symptoms exhibited by a number of women who have had implants, in particular to elucidate the role, if any, of sub-clinical infection."[100]

Fascinating, in view of the fact that the Group had more or less categorically concluded that there was no evidence of an association between the implants and disease, was a recommendation referring to studies that the Group termed "not conclusive and . . . open to legitimate scientific criticisms."[101] One of these studies, which had to do with the use of an assay test for antibodies,[102] provoked some side arguments about financial conflicts of interest on the part of the investigators.[103] Despite its quizzical judgments about those studies, the Group said that "in view of concerns expressed by women's groups, the IRG recommends that there would be scientific merit in determining whether the results of these studies can be reproduced by independent laboratories."[104] It would seem that in this case, politics pushed against establishment science and gained a few yards of ground.

The Institute of Medicine Study

Another major study appeared in 1999, this one from the prestigious Institute of Medicine.[105] Much of what this study did was to go over ground already plowed. However, it was impressive in the amount of literature it surveyed—it cited almost 1,200 references.[106]

As was so with prior estimates, the IOM's range of estimates for the number of implants done was pretty large, although the gap had narrowed to 1.5 to 1.8 million.[107] On the whole, the report underlined the lack of evidence on systemic effects of the devices, marching through a list of illnesses that had been attributed to the implants.[108] However, the report did refer to significant numbers of problems of "local complications" as well as "perioperative" complications—those associated with surgical processes like removal, surgical revision, or replacement of implants.[109]

One theme that comes through the IOM report is that of manufacturers experimenting with consumers across a long period of years: try out, and revise, try out, and revise. In fact, a remarkable factual aspect of the report is its notation that "[t]here is no such thing as a 'standard' breast implant." In fact, there were "more than 240 U.S.-made breast implants and expanders," with implants coming "in a great range of sizes," ranging "generally from 80 to 800 cubic centimeters . . . in volume." Although many of the different features of this variety of implants were inconsequential, "at least some of them have, or are reported to have, important influences on the biologic responses to, and complications of, implantation."[110]

The report was fulsome in its description of the "thoughtful and detailed comments provided by women with implants, not only for the sake of their own health but also out of concern for other women who are considering breast implants." Although the IOM committee noted that its "mandate focuse[d] primarily on peer-reviewed scientific evidence," it said that these women "provided an extremely valuable context for its deliberations."[111] The sum of the committee's view, however, was that although it was "moved" by these witnesses' suffering,[112] it was not persuaded by the hypothesis of systemic effects. Yet, it did observe that "[l]ocal complications and reoperations have significant implications for the safety of silicone breast implants, because they may involve risks themselves and may lead to medical and surgical interventions that have risks."[113]

An illustration of this kind of effect was a study of women who received implants at the Mayo Clinic: more than 23 percent "had clinical indications requiring reoperation"—"amount[ing] to 18.8 percent of the 1,454 breasts implanted" with "multiple complications" in 61 percent of those cases.[114] The report described "the odds of a woman needing more than one implant per breast over time" as "high," with at least one woman having had 16 implants. In three small groups of women surveyed, the numbers of implants were, respectively, 3.19, 2.78, and 3.45.[115] The commission's data indicated that "women, historically, could expect early (postoperative) complications, up to 30%–40% after reconstruction with implants."[116]

There was an astonishing range of statistics on ruptures of gel implants—from less than 1 percent to 77 percent.[117] That problem typically manifested itself only over time: 96 percent of ruptures of gel implants occurred "at or beyond 10 years."[118]

One event sometimes associated with breast implants is capsular contracture—the formation of a lining around the implant that makes the breast feel hard and distorts its appearance. The rate of serious contractures reportedly improved over time, presenting a cameo of positive results of experimentation. The IOM committee found in the scientific history "a continuing willingness of surgeons (and women) to experiment with a series of technologies that have progressively improved contracture rates."[119] One question in the background, though, was how well informed were the patients—putting aside the surgeons—and how willing they were to "experiment."

Rates of infection for implant surgery "range[d] around 1–4% after augmentation and significantly higher after reconstruction." In at least two studies the infection rate accompanying reconstruction was as high as 13 percent.[120]

A general chapter on immunology pointed out that studies on the activation of T cells in women with gel implants were "limited" and that "the technical problems associated with available studies are substantial."[121] On the whole, however, the committee found "no convincing evidence to support clinically significant immunologic effects of silicone or silicone breast implants."[122]

Risk Hypotheses Unproved

Several chapters included attacks on allegations about dangers said to be associated with the silicone implants. The IOM authors judged "insufficient or flawed" proffered proofs for an association between silicone implants and antinuclear antibodies.[123] The same language appeared in its conclusion on "atypical" CTD[124] in a chapter that generally found no showing of association between the silicone implants and CTD.[125] Adding a statistical dimension to the critique of the Hennekens study in the report to the court handling the multidistrict litigation, the IOM committee pointed out that the proportion of women with breast implants who responded to the Hennekens questionnaire "was more than twice the estimated national frequency of these implants," a figure that it said "suggest[ed] selection bias."[126]

The committee reserved a special level of criticism for the hypothesis of a "new syndrome associated with" the silicone implants. Some authors had "noted that there are few objective signs" for such an illness and that "the majority of these signs and symptoms are common in the general population or frequently seen in other defined diseases."[127] The committee found "no rigorous, convincing scientific support for atypical connective tissue or any new disease" associated with the implants.[128]

There also was "no convincing evidence" for a cancer risk; in fact, "epidemiological studies of breast cancer and silicone breast implants are strikingly consistent in showing no association."[129] The evidence for a connection with "a general neurologic disease or syndrome" was "insufficient or flawed."[130] So was the evidence for an association with "children's health effects."[131]

To be sure, the lay instinct that implants would "interfere with screening mammography" was correct.[132] Even with a technique designed to correct for implants, "the amount of breast tissue visualized will be limited by the implant."[133] With "[d]ata on whether cancer detection is impaired by implants" not allowing "definite conclusions," the committee thought that "[s]pecial attention to detection is required in women with silicone breast implants."[134]

Although the bill of health for systemic effects was pretty clean, the committee concluded that "reoperations and local and perioperative complications are frequent enough to be a cause for concern"; in fact, they were "the primary safety issue with silicone breast implants."[135]

More Research Recommended

Against this background of light and shade, the committee set out some "recommendations for research." One was the development of "[r]eliable techniques for the measuring of silicone concentrations in body fluids and tissues" for the purposes of comparing those concentrations in people who did or did not have silicone implants.[136]

Another recommendation, reflecting continuing pressure from patients, advocated "[o]ngoing surveillance of recipients of silicone breast implants...for representative groups of women, including long-term outcomes and local complications." Among other things, the committee recommended attention to the "physical and chemical characteristics" of implants and the tracking of "identified individual implants." Beyond that—perhaps a token of the fact that good science could be better—it specified the use of "appropriate, standardized, and validated technologies for detecting and defining outcomes" and the "ensuring" of "representative samples, appropriate controls and randomization in any specific studies, as required by good experimental design."[137] How much of this was simply a rehearsal of what had gone before and how much an exhortation to do better was not clear.

The final recommendation reflected the importance of consumer information in a model under which the consumer was viewed as capable of being queen. Aligning itself with the U.K. Group, the IOM committee advocated "development of a national model of informed consent for women undergoing breast implantation" and the "monitor[ing]" of "the continuing effectiveness of such a model."[138] The era of comprehensive assessment of massive collections of data had apparently closed. The warfare continued.

Rule on Saline Implants

Despite the force of studies that negated many of the risks ascribed to the silicone gel implants, the FDA still walked gingerly as it turned its attention to saline implants. With the IOM study quite fresh in the background, coming hard on the heels of the National Science Panel report and the U.K. Group's study, the FDA issued its final rule on the "silicone inflatable breast prosthesis"—that is, the saline implants.[139] Observing that the gel implants and the saline-filled implants had in common "a silicone elastomer shell," the agency noted the distinction that the IOM study had made between systemic illnesses and "local complications." It concluded that "local complications" should "be addressed" by a premarketing approval application or a product development protocol (PDP) submission, saying that those submissions should cover "the risks to health identified in" its proposed 1993 rule.[140]

The uncertainty about data that still existed was evident in the FDA's repetition of a 1995 request for "time-course data on the rate and frequency of fibrous capsular contracture."[141] Moreover, the agency expressed its belief that "the potential carcinogenicity for this device remains unknown," and said it "continues to believe that carcinogenicity is a potential risk that must be assessed in PMA or PDP."[142] Acknowledging that "no definitive causal relationship has been established" between saline implants and "immunological effects and/or connective tissue disorders," it even said that it "continue[d] to believe that adverse immunological effects and/or connective tissue disorders remain potential risks that must be assessed in a PMA or PDP." It added, however, that it did not "believe that 10 years of prospective data collection on a specific product will be necessary to do so."[143]

Crossfire: Consumer in the Middle

At about this time, a women's group that was becoming heavily involved in the topic began to explore the limitations of the IOM study. Its Web site displayed a "fact sheet" that noted that "several" of the studies surveyed by the IOM "evaluate[d] only a few hundred women" and that "even the larger studies do not include enough implant patients to study rare diseases like scleroderma." The release from this group, the National Center for Policy Research (CPR) for Women & Families, declared that "[m]astectomy patients who have breast implants have many more problems than cosmetic patients." The release noted that the implant maker McGhan had reported that "more than 20% of ... mastectomy implant patients have an implant removed after two years, as do 30% after four years" and said that "[m]ultiple surgeries are even more common." The release also referred to "new research" that included an "FDA study of 150 women" suggesting "that women developed the kinds of antibodies in response to silicone breast implants that are typically associated with autoimmune diseases."[144]

The crossfire continued as the new millennium arrived, with the publication in 2000 of a new set of "meta-analyses"—studies of studies on autoimmune and connective tissue disease—in the *New England Journal of Medicine*.[145] This report included a survey of several studies that had not been included in prior meta-analyses. The authors' conclusion, "[f]rom a public health perspective," was that "breast implants appear to have a minimal effect on the number of women in whom connective-tissue diseases develop," and that "elimination of implants would be unlikely to reduce the incidence of connective-tissue diseases."[146] This report, like others before it, found the Hennekens study wanting. It referred to "various methodologic problems" in that study, "including the lack of validation of disease diagnosis by review of the medical records." It criticized "[s]elf-reports of connective-tissue disease" as "inaccurate." And again, it found a potential for bad science in the context of adverse publicity about implants. This, the authors said, was "likely to have made women with implants more aware of their symptoms and to have resulted in overreporting of diseases among women with implants as compared with women without implants." The biases thus introduced, they said, "probably" made the relative risks in data "that included the study by Hennekens" and his colleagues "overestimates."[147]

These conclusions threw a spotlight on the problem of the lay consumer, presumably the sovereign in a free market. At this point, the weight of scientific opinion fell heavily against an association of breast implants with immune system and connective tissue diseases. And it is a fact of our media-soaked lives that scare stories will sometimes keep people from doing what, on balance, is good for them. An angry report under the imprint of the American Council of Science and Health, also published in 2000, premised that "much media coverage of implants continues to be irresponsible."[148] The writers of this report instanced Connie Chung's 1990 broadcast, as well as magazine articles with titles like "Toxic Breasts" and "Time Bombs in the Breasts."[149] Noting studies that indicated increased levels of "well-being" and "a new sense of physical integrity or wholeness" in women who had implants,[150] the writers also referred unfavorably to "vocal and influential feminists" for whom "a preference for big breasts represents female oppression."[151] Journalism that attempted to heal mistaken public impressions of the effects of implants came "too late," said the authors: "The damage had been done."[152]

The cannonading went on with a reply volley from the CPR aimed at the meta-analyses in the *New England Journal of Medicine*. This report found "a number of flaws" in the *Journal* article, including the fact that 5 of 20 studies analyzed "were not published in peer-reviewed journals" and that many of the studies did "not evaluate.... 'atypical' connective-tissue disease symptoms or fibromyalgia-type symptoms that many patients report." (Fibromyalgia has been described as "a syndrome characterized by widespread pain, fatigue, and sleep disturbance.") The CPR writers also faulted the fact that most of the studies analyzed "relied on medical records, which might omit vague symptoms that would be reported in the early stages of disease," and declared that "[i]n order to conduct an accurate study of implant patients' health, patients should undergo a comprehensive medical exam."[153]

This critique highlighted some important areas of controversy: the argument about whether "atypical" symptoms were real diseases, or perhaps the products of the minds of patients overconditioned to worry about implants; the always-present tension between individual complainants and medical statistics; the expense of digging deeply into individual medical profiles.

The FDA sought to summarize the state of the science in a relatively nontechnical "Information Update" in 2000.[154] In this document, it stressed the IOM's conclusions that "'reoperations and local and perioperative ... complications are frequent enough to be a cause of concern and to justify the conclusion that they are the primary safety issue with silicone breast implants.'"[155] Following up on this point, the "Update" pointed out that "[b]reast implants **are not lifetime devices** and cannot be expected to last forever"[156] and told women contemplating implants, "[y]ou should understand that there is a high chance that you will need to have additional surgery at some point to replace or remove your implant(s)" because of "problems such as deflation, capsular contracture, infection, shifting, and calcium deposits."[157] This advice appeared within a list of 15 "Breast Implant Risks,"[158] also including "pain," "dissatisfaction with cosmetic results," and "changes in nipple and breast sensation." A condensed version of that list appeared on the Internet.[159] The "Update" also included a discussion of "other illnesses," consuming several pages, although the agency said that "most studies of these illnesses have failed to show an association with breast implants."[160]

The "Update" presented a cautious rehearsal of the prevailing opinion on connective tissue and autoimmune diseases, saying that taken together, the studies on the topic "indicate that the risk of developing a typical or defined CTD or related disorder due to having a breast implant is low."[161] However, the agency also said that the existing studies could not "completely resolve" the question about the "risk of CTDs and related disorders" and "do not resolve the question of whether the variety of signs and symptoms some women report might be related to their implants."[162]

Thus, science and politics moved in uneasy harness. On balance, there was little positive proof about the most targeted concerns of immune system diseases. However, the Hennekens study always lurked in the background. Moreover, there was always room for more studies on established disease; scientists usually will agree that you can always go deeper. And there was some consensus about the risks of surgery and local complications, with lingering questions about "atypical" disease that were charged with individual anger and political controversy.

What was occurring was a cross-country conversation about the meaning of risk, in which participants seemed to be arguing as much about the definition of terms and the reality represented by the data as about the data itself.

A Cluster of Risks beyond Connective Tissue Disease

A diverse set of statistics appeared in a study emanating from the FDA itself, published in 2001. This study focused on the health effects of ruptured silicone gel implants. The authors concluded that "breast implant rupture alone was not associated with self-reported physician diagnosed FM [fibromyalgia] or other CTD." However, a "statistically significant" association existed between those illnesses and extracapsular silicone.[163] The agency scientists who wrote the report said that if the association persisted "in other studies," women with silicone gel implants "should be informed of the potential risk of developing fibromyalgia if their breast implants rupture and the silicone gel escapes the fibrous scar capsule."[164]

The next year, FDA analysts with the same lead author lamented the gaps in research on fibromyalgia, saying that "additional observational studies of women from nonreferral populations are necessary to validate an association."[165] They repeated that if their findings were confirmed, "women considering silicone-gel breast implants should be informed of the risk" of fibromyalgia "before implantation," and they delivered a policy message: "This information should be considered by the FDA when they adjudicate on the safety and effectiveness of silicone gel breast implants."[166] It should be noted that fibromyalgia is not a crisply defined illness. The authors employed a standard general definition of fibromyalgia as "a disorder characterized by pain, tenderness, and stiffness of muscles surrounding joints," noting that the American College of Rheumatology's "criteria for the classification of fibromyalgia" included "a history of widespread pain and pain at 11 of 18 specific tender points."[167]

At the same time, an interesting exercise in spin and counterspin developed around studies of health effects and mortality in more than 13,000 women with cosmetic implants—research of particular interest because its subjects had been followed for an average of 13 years after they had implants. As a 2001 release from the National Cancer Institute (NCI) summarized one of these studies, conducted by a group led by Louise Brinton, cancer rates "for nearly every cancer . . . were not increased among implant patients." The only rates that were higher for implant recipients were "respiratory and brain cancers . . . and only the rate of respiratory cancers reached statistical significance."[168] Another article that year, also by a group of researchers led by Brinton, presented a complex set of results: "[B]reast implant patients had an increased risk of death compared with other patients undergoing plastic surgery," but "both groups of patients actually had a lower mortality than the general population." What mostly created a "slight excess risk of death among implant patients" was their "higher risks for malignancies (primarily respiratory tract cancers) and all external causes, particularly suicide."[169]

Commenting on the first of these studies, the NCI said that "[t]he increased risk of respiratory cancers," which was "mainly due to the large number of lung cancer[] cases," was "difficult to interpret." It also noted findings that "implant patients were two to three times more likely to develop stomach cancer, leukemia, and cancers of the cervix, vulva and brain." It said, however, that it was "possible that the increased risk of these cancers was related to factors common to women undergoing plastic surgery"—for example, "socioeconomic status, sexual and reproductive behavior, and cigarette smoking"—"rather than to the effects of silicone exposure."[170]

Writing for the women's group CPR, Diane Zuckerman and Rachael Flynn presented the same data in a different perspective. They characterized one of the studies as finding "a 21% overall increased risk of cancer for women with implants, compared to women of the same age in the general population." Because these were the first studies of women who had all "had implants for at least eight years," the authors said, their data "indicate a potentially serious risk for the health of women with breast implants." The authors also commented that increases in suicide levels "seem[ ] to contradict the manufacturers' assertion that implants improve a woman's feeling of self-worth." They offered a dark interpretation of "why so many previous studies focused on just a few, rare diseases, rather than a more comprehensive evaluation of" patients' health. This was that "plastic surgeons and the implant manufacturers helped design and fund much of the previous research on implants."[171]

A Maker's Catalog of Risks

While the arguments progressed about the silicone gel implants, the FDA approved PMA applications from at least two makers of saline-filled implants—McGhan Medical Corporation and Mentor Corporation.[172] It is interesting to examine a booklet on breast implants that Mentor designed for patients.[173] One interesting aspect of the booklet is its fairly detailed rehearsal of the "complications" that the FDA detailed on its own patient "Update."[174] Early in the booklet, the company emphasized that women should "be aware that breast implantation may not be a one time surgery" and that "[b]reast implants are not considered lifetime devices."[175] One especially interesting statement in the booklet is its suggestion of a cooling-off period, as the British Independent Review Group had recommended. The booklet advises patients "to wait a week after reviewing and considering the information in this brochure before deciding whether to have augmentation surgery."[176]

Another interesting aspect of the Mentor booklet is its effort to share risk with physicians, in the form of an "ask your doctor" catalog. The company lists ten questions to ask surgeons about breast augmentation and 19 questions about breast reconstruction.[177]

Perhaps the most interesting things about the Mentor booklet, though, are features that can be sensed only by an overall examination of it. Notably, these are its length and its complexity. An early printout I have, probably from about the year 2001, is 22 pages long. The 2004 version, under the logo of the FDA, prints out to 33 pages from the Internet.[178] Moreover, although the writers of the earlier version evidently strived for readability by patients who are not in the health care profession, it included a significant amount of statistical detail. Graphs on types of treatments and complications occupy more than four pages in the company's original version.[179] In addition to graphic drawings of implants, the booklet also lists no fewer than 11 different styles of implants and gives simple diagrams of three types.[180]

This is a good example of a problem that faces manufacturers of many different kinds of medical products and indeed many other kinds of technically complex products. There is often tension between the legal requirement that information be full and fair and the relative lack of ability, and inclination, of nontechnical consumers to absorb and understand information that is put before them. It is not just a matter of more or less information, but one of greater or lesser levels of detail. And—as our summary of just a few of the many studies on the subject indicates—sometimes the devil, as well as the angel, is in the details.

A Divisive Topic

Experts involved in the area of breast implants noted that the issue had a remarkable tendency to divide people. A medical professor, who was on an FDA advisory panel considering whether to reauthorize broad marketing of silicone gel implants, said after a meeting on the subject, "I sat there wondering, why, why, why is this such a polarizing topic?" He answered his own question; the matter went "far beyond medical considerations. . . . It involves society and womanhood." One speaker at the meeting, the president of an organization called Dads and Daughters, spoke of "the pervasive cultural messages that devalue girls and women" and declared that "[w]e are hammering our children with the notion that how they look is more important than who they are and what they can do. . . . And that is just wrong."[181]

This quizzicality, and querulousness, were in the background in early 2004 when the FDA announced that it was deferring a decision on whether to approve sale of the silicone gel implants again. An agency official, Dr. David Feigal, acknowledged that "a lot of information has been developed" to demonstrate safety since 1992, when the FDA first called for a voluntary moratorium, and then tightly limited access to the silicone gel implants. However, he said that "there is additional information that we think is necessary for this product to pass the threshold of what we would consider necessary." Gina Kolata of *The New York Times*, who has long reported on medical news, noted that the decision was against the agency's usual practice because it opposed a 9 to 6 vote by the agency's advisory committee to let the products come to market. She described the issues as "particular[ly] fractious." Feigal observed that "[t]his was a very visible product, and we had input from almost everybody and anybody." One notable feature of this train of events was that after the advisory panel had voted, Dr. Thomas V. Whalen, its chairman, had written the agency to ask that it not approve the implants because, as Kolata summarized his views, "they had not been shown to be safe." Cynthia Pearson, executive director of the National Women's Health Network, thought the decision was "as good as it gets," declaring that "we want implants but we want safe and effective implants."[182]

Thus, the active struggle over the safety of silicone gel breast implants began moving toward the 25-year mark. The FDA had first proposed a rule on the subject in 1982. Paralleling the story of speedups of IND applications, the moratorium that followed and the long debate that ensued reflected the political content of the idea of "safety." Here, a significant wedge of the scientific establishment had concluded pretty firmly that the silicone gel implants did not have a set of frightening effects that had been ascribed to them. Marcia Angell's concerns about public devaluation of science, forcefully expressed in 1996,[183] may have seemed poignantly confirmed.

However, there was a certain irony in the developing history, for it is scientists who insist on the continual formulation and testing of hypotheses. The relative certainty, if not certitude, of those who argued against the existence of extra risk encountered a strong demand for more information. In the grandstand were consumers, most of them nonspecialists, including both those who desired the products at even moderate levels of risk and those who believed that the products had harmed them. For women arrayed along that spectrum and their families, the government's decisions about both marketing and the quantity and quality of information would be significant.

Drama at a Hearing

A mini-drama on the silicone gel implants played out on the public stage in April 2005. The actors included manufacturers, women testifying on their travails with implants, practicing physicians, and members of an FDA advisory panel.

A prologue occurred on April 6, with publication on the FDA's Web site of statistics indicating that "74 percent of a cross-section of women would suffer implant failures in 10 years"—a figure that increased to 93 percent "[f]or women undergoing reconstructive surgery, mostly breast cancer survivors."[184] These numbers became prominent in the background of a theatrical event that was a prologue to the advisory panel's projected decision a week later on whether to recommend reapproval of the implants.[185]

A feature of the event was a series of confrontations between advocates and opponents of the devices. One 74-year-old woman told the panel that after her implants ruptured, "strings of silicone started coming out of her eyes and ears." Some women exhibited "poster-sized photos of deformed breasts as wrenching as the photos of aborted fetuses" used by anti-abortion groups. By contrast, a

35-year-old woman told the panel that her implants "helped her 'to feel whole,'" and criticized opponents of the products for "making a moral judgment, not a medical one." The debate at the panel hearing spilled into the hallway, where some young women opposing implants sported T-shirts with the words "100% all natural," and were confronted by a woman with saline implants who said she was "offended that you're saying I'm not natural." Her statement that "[w]omen need choices" was met by the remark of the president of the National Organization of Women, "Choice? The choice is to be sick."[186]

Divided Advisory Panels

The uncertainty about data that plagued the broad controversy came to the fore on April 13, when a 5 to 4 majority of the FDA advisory panel voted against approval of silicone implants made by Imamed Corporation, on the ground that the firm had not provided enough data on ruptures. The state of the statistics, as a reporter put it, was that the FDA "was forced to make assumptions about whether implants were more likely to rupture as they aged." Under the company's assumptions, analogizing stereo equipment that was "no more likely to break in [its] 10th year of use than in [its] first," "14 percent of implants would have ruptured after 10 years." The FDA's assumptions, which yielded a figure of up to 95 percent ruptures in ten years for silicone implants used in reconstructive surgery, posited that "implants might be like cars or tires, which wear out with age." The degree of frustration among even experts was apparent in a remark of Dr. Pablo Bonangelino of the FDA that "[i]n fact, we really don't know." In this zone of uncertainty, a panel member who was a plastic surgeon made the case for consumer choice. Michael J. Miller of the University of Texas said that there were "women who would benefit from these devices who don't have access to them. . . . If there's any motivation to resolve this, it's because of the women I'm going to see."[187]

The very next day, in a development that the chair of the panel termed unexpected, the members voted 7 to 2 to approve silicone implants made by Mentor Corporation for cosmetic surgery. The panel majority appeared to be impressed by data offered by Mentor that the company said indicated a rupture rate of 9 to 15 percent after 12 years. In an interesting manifestation of a perceived need for public belief in the rationality of scientific decision making, Dr. Stephen Li, a panel member, thought out loud: "I want to explain to myself and everyone else why I could vote yes on one application and no on another." His explanation for a yes vote was that the Mentor implants "had an extremely low rupture rate."[188] Even so, one FDA official said that even if Mentor's numbers were correct, 22,500 women would have ruptures every year. Panel member Barbara R. Manno, a psychiatry professor at Louisiana State University, presented some astringent philosophy as she ruminated on the panel's apparent rationale, summarized by a reporter as being "to give women a choice of implants." She said, "it isn't to have a choice. It is to make a choice. And tough luck if it doesn't work out."[189]

Lifting of the Ban

A year later, the FDA reversed its 1992 ban on silicone implants for most uses. In November 2006, it approved products made by Mentor and Allergan for breast augmentation as well as reconstruction, although not for cosmetic use for women under 22 years of age.[190] This decision contained many of the elements of the larger problem this book analyzes: arguments about what good science is, with disagreements about the quality of data; questions about the glories, and the limitations, of consumer choice; the responses of regulators who must make what are at least partly political decisions in conditions of scientific uncertainty; and the never-failing insistence that more data are necessary even when products are cleared for the market.

The president-elect of the American Society of Plastic Surgeons, Dr. Richard D'Amico, called the decision a "triumph of science." Dr. Sidney Wolfe of the Public Citizen's Health Research Group, responded that "[t]he approval makes a mockery of the legal standard that requires 'reasonable assurance of safety.'" An FDA official, Dr. Daniel Schultz of the agency's Center for Devices and Radiological Health, insisted, as a reporter characterized it, that the decision was "in the best interest of American women." Yet he cautioned about the statistics on rupture—one of several studies had put that number at 69 percent. He repeated what now had become a mantra: that "[w]omen should know that breast implants are not lifetime devices."[191]

One of the most remarkable features of the FDA decision was an aspect of it that confirmed a basic theme of this book, which is that we often accept that the entire nation is an experimental laboratory for products and processes. Accenting the experimental aspect of the marketing of breast implants was the way in which, like waves breaking on a beach, new billows of risk entered the catalog of concerns. For many years, the focus of research was on immune system and connective tissue diseases. But building up during that time were statistics on ruptures and the need for reoperations. The striking experimental aspect of the FDA's decision lay in the agency's requirement that the manufacturers must monitor 40,000 women who received implants for the safety of the devices. As a reporter summarized it, Dr. Schultz said that this would involve collection of data on "rates of rupture, cancer and autoimmune diseases and effects of the implants on reproduction."[192] A lay consumer familiar with the history recorded in this chapter might well comment, in current street jargon, that she thought we had "been there and done that." However, these new studies would be quintessentially science at work—in consumer markets.

Civil Actions

The principal focus of this book is on regulation by public agencies of hazardous products and processes. There are, however, other legal instruments that are part of the way that our society responds to injuries. One powerful, and controversial, tool is civil litigation: in tort actions, judges may order makers and sellers of dangerous things to pay people who are harmed. It is therefore useful to compare the branch of tort law called products liability with the regulatory history on which we have been focusing.

We have noted that an important legal process that paralleled the regulatory process for breast implants was the vast multidistrict action in an Alabama federal court. Eventually, the multibillion dollar settlement proposed for that litigation, of which an important scientific paper was a byproduct, collapsed. However, a number of cases have proceeded to appellate decisions on injuries attributed to breast implants, and they have some interesting lessons to teach.[193]

The plaintiff in one important case, Charlotte Mahlum, alleged that Dow Chemical was responsible for a painful set of injuries from two implants, made by Dow Corning, which were done after a double mastectomy. Five years after the implants, her "health began to deteriorate." Three years after that, one implant ruptured.[194] Suffering from "muscle tremors, skin rashes and bouts of incontinence,"[195] she had to have both devices removed. However, the surgeon could not remove all the silicone gel from her body, leaving about "ten percent of the silicone materials embedded in muscle, tissue, and blood vessels under her arms and ribs." Her health "continued to deteriorate after the explantation surgery,"[196] and she said that "small slivers of the substance" continued to "push through the skin on her arms, chest, and face."[197]

Dow Chemical had what the Nevada Supreme Court called a "parent/subsidiary relationship with Dow Corning, including some control over Dow Corning's products and significant control of testing and protocol." Dow Chemical possessed "fifty per cent control of Dow Corning's shares," and had "the control inferred from . . . various agreements with Dow Corning."[198] Charlotte Mahlum and her husband sued Dow Chemical after Dow Corning went bankrupt.[199]

A trial yielded a substantial verdict for the Mahlums, totalling a little over $4,000,000 in compensatory damages and $10,000,000 in punitive damages.[200] The state supreme court ultimately affirmed the plaintiffs' judgment on compensatory damages. How it got there provides some interesting insights about the law as it relates to complex corporate structures as well as science.

The trial court had accepted a theory that Dow Chemical had a "'tacit understanding'" with Dow Corning to "misrepresent the safety of the silicone used in breast implants, withholding information regarding the adverse consequences of such silicone from physicians and patients." The Nevada Supreme Court, however, found that the plaintiffs had not proved "the existence of an agreement" of this sort, "tacit or otherwise." It said that "Dow Chemical's few public statements about the potential safety of silicone" could not "support an inference that Dow Chemical and Dow Corning had an agreement to misrepresent the safety of silicone breast implants."[201] This finding contributed to the supreme court's decision to vacate the award of punitive damages.[202]

There was another theory of liability in the Mahlums' quiver, however. This was negligence on the part of Dow Chemical with respect to the tests it had conducted on the silicones used by Dow Corning. Here, the supreme court opined that once Dow Chemical had undertaken "to test the safety" of those silicones, it had "to fully complete [the] testing until a reliable safety determination was made." Part of the court's determination of negligence rested on its judgment that it was foreseeable that continued marketing of the implants without warnings about "the potential dangers of silicone fluids would result in women electing to receive the implants without a full appreciation of the risks involved." In a notable statement on the duty of one who undertakes to do something for someone else that will affect the safety of third persons, the court said that given Dow Chemical's knowledge of silicones and its corporate relationship with Dow Corning, Dow Chemical "should have used its influence to halt the marketing of Dow Corning's silicone breast implants until the long-term effect of silicone breast implants on humans was understood and these products were determined to be safe."[203]

A finding of substandard conduct, however, is not enough to carry the day in a negligence case. Plaintiffs must also prove that there is a probability that the defendant's negligence caused the harm at issue. The Mahlums also jumped that hurdle, with the aid of testimony from an immunologist that "liquid silicone impairs the body's immune system," triggering a process in which the body "turn[s] on itself." The court also referred to the testimony of a rheumatologist who had treated more than 100 women with silicone gel implants. He said that the plaintiff shared many symptoms of "atypical autoimmune disease" with other recipients of implants.[204]

The Nevada court acknowledged that causation was a "scientifically controversial" aspect of litigation on breast implants, but declared that plaintiffs "did not need to wait until the scientific community developed a consensus that breast implants caused [Charlotte Mahlum's] diseases." The court said that the plaintiffs' case "was not tried in the court of scientific opinion, but before a jury of [Ms. Mahlum's] peers who considered the evidence" and decided there was causation. "Science," the court said, "may properly require a higher standard of proof before declaring the truth." But, the court explained, "that standard did not guide the jury," and it said that it did not "use that standard to evaluate the judgment on appeal."[205]

This opinion highlights a difference between court decisions and science. Where science can wait indefinitely to accumulate data considered reliable, courts have to decide the case before them. Indeed, there are constraints on how long plaintiffs can wait to sue; the *Mahlum* court specifically referred to statutes of limitations and repose, for example.[206]

One also finds a significant temporal difference between the judicial process in civil litigation and the regulatory process. This chapter has summarized a history of a quarter century during which the FDA approved silicone implants, sharply restricted their use, and then substantially opened up the field for marketing them. Again by contrast, courts must give decisions that irrevocably resolve individual cases that press on them. There also exists a parallel between the systems, however. It lies in the uncertainty that has dogged regulators—and does to this day in the case of breast implants—as well as afflicting courts.

Expert Testimony in Tort Suits

Another area in which there are significant differences between tort law and regulation, but also some overlaps, involves the role of experts. A group of other decisions illustrates how plaintiffs can succeed in tort suits with plausible expert testimony, with juries being permitted to choose among conflicting opinions.

The Massachusetts Supreme Judicial Court found sufficient evidence in a silicone implant case in which the plaintiff offered a variety of experts. One was a professor of materials science and engineering who testified that animal studies "demonstrated migration of silicone to various organs both from ruptured gel implants and after intramuscular injection" of a particular type of liquid silicone. The plaintiffs also offered the chief of a medical school division of rheumatology, immunology, and allergy who had done research and treated more than 700 women with silicone gel implants. He said there was a "unique constellation of symptoms" in about 5 percent of women with those implants and that those symptoms in combination presented "an atypical autoimmune disease." Another witness, a rheumatologist, opined that the plaintiff suffered from "atypical autoimmune disease." The court favorably cited the qualifications of each witness, ranging from a variety of researches and publication in "peer reviewed journals on silicone related topics" to clinical treatment of women with implants.[207]

Federal appeals courts have made similar references to the research and clinical work of experts for plaintiffs in implant litigation. In one such case, regarded as a principal trigger for breast implant litigation, the plaintiff was Mariann Hopkins. She won a jury verdict of $840,000 in compensatory damages and $6.5 million in punitive damages. Affirming the judgment for Hopkins, the Ninth Circuit said that even without a "solid body of epidemiological evidence to review," it would allow testimony by a "recognized expert on the immunological effects of silicone on the human body." This was a witness who based his testimony on "his experience as a toxicologist, his review of medical records," studies by the defendant, and "his general scientific knowledge of silicone's ability to cause immune disorders as established by animal studies and biophysical data." The court also allowed testimony by an expert that was "based on scientific studies he authored, his participation in a preliminary epidemiological study involving over 200 women, and his examination of [the plaintiff] during which he discovered evidence of silicone in her tissue and detected symptoms consistent with exposure to silicone."[208] Another federal appellate court found admissible the testimony of witnesses who "had conducted research, published in peer-reviewed journals and treated hundreds of women with silicone gel implants."[209]

Some expert testimony falls short. A Maryland federal decision refers to a group of deficiencies in testimony offered by a chemist in an implant case, having to do with both his qualifications and his methods. As to the witness's qualifications, the court noted that he was "not a medical doctor," a pathologist, or a toxicologist, although he was proposing to opine that an implant was "defective because it presents medical and toxicological risks." As to methods and substance, the court noted that he had "not done general testing to confirm or refute the presence of many alleged harmful chemicals" he claimed were present in the implant, had "not done specific testing on the implant," and had not provided evidence that "the alleged harmful chemicals were found" in the body of the plaintiff's mother, who had died by the time of the litigation.[210]

Sometimes a witness may be qualified but his methodology and his evidence do not convince the judge. In a D.C. Circuit case, it was the "heavy reliance on case reports" by experts for the plaintiff, who claimed that implants caused her scleroderma, that proved "her undoing."[211] The court noted that one witness who had written on scleroderma and on "silicone-related disorders" had "acknowledged that there is no proof that silicone breast implants cause scleroderma." It said that the witness's reliance on "'differential analysis' to eliminate alternative causes" was "misplaced," noting that his methodology assumed that "whatever factors remain after other alternative causes have been eliminated is at least capable of causing the disease in question." It concluded that the witness's "reliance on case reports, temporal methodology," and the plaintiff's "atypical symptoms" were not "sufficient to show that silicone breast implants are capable of causing scleroderma."[212] For good measure, the court noted that another of the plaintiff's witnesses had "acknowledged that ongoing research investigating the cause of scleroderma" had "merely given rise to ideas about an association between certain environmental factors and scleroderma" and had "not yet shown a causal relationship."[213]

Yet, experience can tell, even when an expert has not secured peer review for his opinions, when there is a certain degree of precision in his testimony. Illustrative are opinions of the Oregon appellate court and the Oregon Supreme Court in a case in which the appellate court acknowledged that the witness's ascription of neurological injuries to exposure to silicone "appear[ed] to be novel." Despite that, the court found the testimony admissible, noting that the witness's hypothesis was "based on his own experiences and observations as well as on scientific methodology." It observed that he had tested his hypothesis on "50 patients who exhibited unique symptoms and conditions similar to [the] plaintiff's and who all had been exposed to silicone from breast implants," and that he "conducted those evaluations by using neurological examination techniques generally accepted by the medical field . . . with an error rate of five to seven percent." The court was not persuaded by the defendant's argument that the testimony should not be admitted because it had not been peer reviewed or even by the witness's admissions that he did "not understand the mechanism" that he thought caused neurological harm. The court said that "[t]he proper focus" was whether the witness "had a basis for his hypotheses that depends on relevant, empirical data derived from scientific methodology." It emphasized that Oregon's rules on scientific evidence did "not preclude the admission of novel scientific evidence."[214]

The Oregon Supreme Court used much of the same language in affirming its appellate court. Also pointing out that "neither peer review nor publication is a *sine qua non* for the admissibility of scientific evidence," the supreme court said that the witness's testing methods and the clinical history of his patients were subject to checking by "[a]ny scientist." Moreover, it noted that his results could be tested, as by a neurologist who could examine "women with silicone breast implants to see if they had the same neurological conditions" the witness had identified. In an interesting differentiation of the scientific and legal issues, the court said that "[a] conclusion about causation ultimately is a qualitative decision." It quoted a reference on epidemiology on the proposition that "[w]hile the drawing of causal inferences is informed by scientific expertise, it is not a determination that is made by using scientific methodology."[215]

Criticism of the results that could flow from judicial hospitality to such testimony, even when there was vigorous argument in favor of its validity, focused on a cluster of costs, both corporate and social. During the period in which the cases discussed earlier went to appeal, a report in *Scientific American* referred to the "steep" expenses to which manufacturers were subjected by litigation. The result, the reporter said, was that "[s]ome businesses have stopped making silicone and other materials used in medical implant devices, ranging from pacemakers to hormone-releasing implants for post-menopausal women." Illustratively, Dow Corning—which at that point had filed for bankruptcy protection—had "stopped supplying implant companies" with silicone.[216]

It took more than nine years for Dow Corning to emerge from the tunnel of bankruptcy it entered in 1995. In June 2004, the company announced that it had completed negotiations on a settlement that provided $2.35 billion for claimants[217]; incidentally, company chair Gary Anderson said the firm would "continue to explore high-potential applications for silicone materials and services in a wide variety of industries."[218] A 74-page "Claimant Information Guide," initially published in late 2002, appears on the Web. It describes a group of settlement options: (1) An "Explant Payment" of $5,000 for women who have had an implant removed, (2) a $25,000 "Rupture Payment" for women who show that their "Dow Corning silicone gel breast implant was removed and was ruptured," (3) a "$2,000 Expedited Release Payment," available on proof that a woman had been "implanted with a Dow Corning breast implant," and (4) a "Disease Payment."[219] Disease payments ranged from $13,000 to $300,000, with the highest awards reserved for "Systemic Sclerosis or Lupus Severity A."[220] The Information Guide listed no fewer than eight documents in a "Claims Package."[221] The Settlement Facility-Dow Corning Trusts, which had prepared the Guide, had obviously tried to make it user-friendly. Ironically, though, its complexity seemed to rival that of the scientific data that had been amassed over a generation.

Desire and Uncertainty

The events on the civil litigation side added to the burdens of regulatory constraints on implant makers. The question of whether tort law provided an oversupply of ammunition in the battle against injuries caused by mass market experimentation presented a continuing policy issue. The problem involved not only the continuing desire of companies to try out potentially risky products on mass publics, but the desire of consumers to use those products. The woman who wanted to take a chance on silicone gel breast implants was cousin to the person with AIDS who wanted to try the latest antiretroviral drug, without waiting for double-blind testing. Yet, she was also cousin to the woman who told an FDA panel that strings of silicone were leaking from her eyes and ears.

In the background was the expense of research that could tend to confirm or reject causal linkages between consumer products and illnesses, and the complex judgments that go into the allocation of research resources. An observer of this medical and regulatory history will be struck by the amount of scientific firepower that was concentrated on the hypotheses that implants cause immune system dysfunction and connective tissue diseases—this at the same time that thousands of implants were rupturing and many other problems, like capsular contracture, were occurring.

It has never been suggested that once the FDA clears a product for the market, manufacturers should be required to have consumers sign formal informed consent forms, as surgeons have patients do for operations. That would be extravagantly impractical. Yet it was clear, after a generation of market tryouts of breast implants, that an ideal statistical profile about those products would require still more data. And it was equally clear that the only way to acquire that data was through mass experiments beyond the reach of clinical research committees.

CHAPTER 4

Treating Thyself with Drugs—For Men Only: The Saga of Viagra

Does the product name sildenafil citrate mean anything to the average guy? Probably no more than the chemical name of that product, which is 1-[3-(6, 7-dihydro-1-methyl-7-oxo-3-propyl-1H-pyrazolo[4,3-d]pyrimidin-5-yl)-4-ethoxyphenyl]sulfonyl]-4-methylpiperazine citrate.[1]

That formula, however, is just the technical description for a trade name that every American with access to a television set knows: Viagra, a drug designed to overcome the cluster of problems that result in erectile dysfunction (ED). The complex chemical name is symbolic of the fact that the average person has no idea of what is in the pills he is pumping into his body. This is not sodium chloride. Even the average health care professional may not have a very crisp idea of the pharmacological pathways that such products take into the body.

The story of Viagra weaves together threads of science, regulation, marketing, and consumer perceptions. Flitting across the foreground are images of the famous—a former Senate majority leader and a baseball player with potent statistics—as well as cuddling actors playing ordinary people in prime-time advertisements. At this writing, the story appears to be one of much-desired benefits and risks that are quite tolerable overall. In the background, though, are effects of the sort that crop up over time when drugs reach mass markets. Complicating the story is scientific uncertainty about the causes that produce those effects. All of this poses continuing puzzles for regulators and at least a little grist for the mills of litigation.

The Market

Product innovators respond to existing markets and they develop new ones. The case of Viagra is illustrative. For a variety of reasons, physical and psychological, many men who desire sexual pleasure cannot develop or sustain erections. The category shades over into a class of men who, in today's dating environment, have become anxious about their ability to "perform" and wish to be sure that they literally will be able to pump themselves up when the occasion arises.

A newspaper feature describes the second category graphically—"an increasing number of sexually healthy men, many in their 20's, 30's and 40's, who doctors and sex therapists say are using impotence drugs . . . as psychological palliatives against the mighty expectations of modern romance." A poster child in this feature is a lawyer, 41, named and pictured embracing at least three women, who described an encounter with a female lawyer who was "very wired" and told him that she could not "judge a man without having first had sex with him." He described his first sexual encounter with her—for which he primed himself with Viagra—as feeling like "this test—like passing the bar." As he recounted it, "I'm thinking to myself, I haven't had this sort of performance anxiety since I was 17."[2] What goes for straights goes for gays as well. The same feature quotes a "54-year-old Manhattan gay professional who uses Viagra regularly": "A lot of it's about the sexual adventure—you want to have sex for four or five hours. It relieves any concern about performance."[3]

Early Medical and Regulatory History

An Accidental Discovery

The discovery of Viagra was accidental—a not uncommon story with useful drugs. Around 1985, Pfizer researchers in Sandwich, England, had been searching for a treatment for angina. It was only in Phase 1 trials of the drug in 1991 and 1992 that they noted "the unique 'adverse event' of causing penile erection." This, a summary of the history of the drug laconically reports, "led to a change in the focus of the clinical research program." It was in 1993 that the company recruited men for the first study of sildenafil to treat ED.[4] During clinical trials on 3,000 to 4,500 men, eight or nine died, although Pfizer said that the pill had not caused these deaths.[5] The FDA approved the drug in March 1998.[6]

A Burst of Promotion, with Some Cautions

The product burst on the mass marketing scene, so to speak, that spring. It appeared to a marketing accompaniment of trumpets and drums and, almost immediately, to reports of a few deaths among men who took the first batches of the pill.

The strongest caution in Pfizer's package insert for the drug was a contraindication for the use of "organic nitrates in any form"—which included nitroglycerin, often prescribed for heart patients. The insert referred, generically, to "a degree of cardiac risk associated with sexual activity," and therefore suggested that "physicians may wish to consider the cardiovascular status of their patients prior to initiating any treatment for erectile dysfunction." It then set out a catalog of reported "adverse events" in which the percentages for Viagra were significantly greater than those for patients with placebo, a list led by headache (16 percent), flushing (10 percent), and dyspepsia (7 percent). A textual reference and daggered footnote both referred to "abnormal vision" as one effect, listed at 11 percent, and said to be "more common at 100 mg than at lower doses"; the recommended dose for "most patients" was 50 milligrams (mg). Changes in vision were described as "[m]ild and transient, predominantly color tinge to vision." The document also mentioned "increased sensitivity to light or blurred vision," but noted that in clinical studies, "only one patient discontinued due to abnormal vision." The insert set out a fairly long list of events for which "a causal relationship to VIAGRA" was "uncertain" but which were said to have "a plausible relation to drug use."[7]

An FDA "talk paper," announcing the agency's approval of the drug, tracked the most common side effects mentioned in the labeling. It enjoined patients contemplating the use of Viagra to "[h]ave a thorough medical history and physical examination to diagnose impotence, determine underlying causes and identify appropriate treatment," as well as to "discuss the cardiac risk associated with sexual activity prior to initiating any treatment for impotence."[8]

Within two months of marketing, sales rocketed upwards: 900,000 prescriptions by late May and 1.7 million by early June.[9] It was the sliced bread of pharmaceuticals. During this period, the *New England Journal of Medicine* published an article, based on studies supported by grants from Pfizer, that concluded, overall, that Viagra was "an effective, well-tolerated treatment for men with erectile dysfunction." The main side effects the article reported were those identified in the manufacturer's package insert. The statistics on effectiveness seemed impressive, ranging from 56 percent "improved erections" at the low dose of 25 mg to 84 percent for men who took 100 mg.[10] There is something almost hilarious about the precision with which the investigators asked their questions, which included "the hardness of erections" and "a global efficacy question," namely, "Did the treatment improve your erections?"[11] Indeed, the standards and standard setters to which the researchers referred are symbolic of the fact that erections are good business. Not only is there a panel of the American Urological Association on the Treatment of Organic Erectile Dysfunction, but there is an International Index of Erectile Dysfunction.[12] The author may be forgiven for recalling a morning on his junior high school playground where one of the coaches at a summer program displayed to fascinated pubescents his "peter meter."

A "Dear Doctor" on Nitrates

Simultaneously with the publication of the *New England Journal of Medicine* article, the medical director for the "Sexual Health Team" of the U.S. Pharmaceuticals Division of Pfizer, Richard Siegel, sent a "Dear Doctor" letter to emergency physicians. Noting that this group of doctors might not ordinarily be privy to warnings about Viagra, he advised them about the serious side effects that could accompany the combination of nitrates with Viagra, which could well require treatment in ambulances or emergency rooms. He cautioned about the routine administration of nitrates by emergency room doctors or ambulance personnel to patients with chest pain without questioning if the patient had used Viagra. One interesting sidelight was the letter's reference to Pfizer's belief—though not its knowledge, as the letter emphasized—that "nitrates that are inhaled for recreational use ... will have the same effect when combined with Viagra." Dr. Siegel also noted the company's awareness that "women have started taking" Viagra, "either on their own or via an off-label prescription from a physician," and that this entailed the same kinds of risks for women that use of Viagra with nitrates could pose for men.[13]

Early Deaths

During the spring of 1998, an increase in deaths among Viagra users accompanied the surge in prescriptions. Despite press reports that focused on a total of 16 deaths since the introduction of the drug, however, the evidence weighed against a linkage to the drug of the deaths, most of them in men over the age of 60 with histories of cardiovascular problems. An FDA spokeswoman said that the deaths were not "related directly to use of the drug."[14] A doctor described as "an adviser on impotence to the American Urological Association" commented that he "had a lot of patients say, 'If I have to go, that's the way I want to go out.'"[15] As is so with other products we have analyzed in this book, it is often difficult and sometimes impossible to ascribe causation of a particular illness to a product used on a population in which there is an established statistical probability of deaths without use of the product. A Pfizer spokesman, commenting on the 16 deaths, pointed out that the expected monthly number of deaths nationally from cardiovascular disease, in men over 45, was 185 to 275 per million.[16]

More deaths, and more concerns, carried through the summer and into the fall, as the universe of information about Viagra expanded. By July of 1998, the British medical journal *Lancet* referred to "media reports that the FDA has received about 30 reports of deaths among men who have taken the drug."[17] The journal also referenced to "doubts" having "been cast on the objectivity of" the *New England Journal of Medicine* study, mentioned earlier, that judged Viagra effective.[18]

Over the next few months, it became apparent that the FDA was stepping up the pressure on Pfizer to provide more cautionary information about the drug. By August 1998, the company had made available a patient package insert for Viagra.[19]

Heightened Warnings

The end of November saw a small watershed in the story, reflecting the pressure from the agency. An FDA "talk paper" said that "FDA and Pfizer Inc. are advising doctors about new warnings and information in the product labeling for Viagra ... in response to postmarketing reports of serious adverse events." The release effectively noted the status of consumers of new drugs as subjects of nationwide experiments, saying that "[a]s with all approved drugs, there have been postmarketing reports of important side effects with Viagra." Noting that "a causal relationship cannot be established from these reports," it stressed that the reports "involving Viagra constitute only a small fraction of the more than six million prescriptions written for this drug."[20]

The cool language of the November revision of the package insert for doctors became more focused on conversations with patients. Including as the first paragraph in the **WARNINGS** section a reference to "a potential for cardiac risk of sexual activity in patients with preexisting cardiovascular disease," the document advised doctors to "discuss with patients the potential cardiac risk of sexual activity with preexisting cardiovascular risk factors." It specifically noted that there was "no controlled clinical data on the safety or efficacy" of the drug in groups including patients who had "suffered a myocardial infarction, stroke, or life-threatening arrhythmia within the last six months" and those who had low or high blood pressure, and said that prescriptions for these groups should be written "with caution." The insert also introduced a warning on a subject that became a target of dark comic commentary: erections that lasted more than four hours after taking Viagra. It said that men experiencing that effect "should seek immediate medical assistance."[21] A brief communication on the Internet to "healthcare professionals," with a black box around the heading "Important Prescribing Information," highlighted these warnings in the professional insert.[22]

Research Flourishes

Research studies continued—some of them financed by the manufacturer—with results that seemed, in the main, reassuring. However, a few new areas of suspicion developed as flurries of information about the drug continued to appear.

A study of "long-term safety and efficacy" over two years, funded by Pfizer, concluded that the drug "continues to be effective and well-tolerated," with 95 percent of a total of 365 patients who completed the study being "satisfied."[23]

A crossover of medical problems became evident in a June 1999 update from MedWatch, the FDA's reporting program for medical products. This was the addition of a warning to Viagra labeling that to take Viagra with the drug ritonavir would "substantially increase[ ]" concentrations of Viagra in blood serum—an "11-fold increase in AUC [a technical concept meaning the area under a statistical curve]."[24] Ritonavir is a protease inhibitor, for which a primary use is reducing the amount of HIV infection. The added warning said "caution should be used" in concurrent administration of the two drugs, specifically recommending a decrease in dosages of Viagra.[25] A new precaution on use of Viagra with other protease inhibitors was added to a prior precaution on interactions with the antibiotic erythromycin.[26]

The appearance of Viagra on the market provided a stimulus for medical research analogous to the physiological effects of the drug on the men who took it. The authors of a 1999 article in the journal *Circulation* based on 1998 data described "an expert consensus," derived from a review by ten anonymous exter-nal referees as well as opportunities for comment by both Pfizer and the FDA.[27] This report laid special emphasis on the prohibition of the use of Viagra with long-acting nitrates—which was "absolutely contraindicated"—and stressed that patients taking a combination of medications to lower blood pressure "should be cautioned about the possibility" that Viagra would induce low blood pressure.[28] It solemnly set out guidelines for doctors and patients about the "risk of car-diac ischemia"—basically cardiac blockage—during intercourse for "patients with overt and covert coronary artery disease." Delving into the most intimate details of relationships, it provided quantitative guidelines involving metabolic spikes for "woman-on-top" and "man-on-top" intercourse. If a patient could achieve these metabolic levels "without demonstrating ischemia" while having intercourse "with a familiar partner, in familiar settings, without the added stress of a heavy meal or alcohol ingestion," then his risk of ischemia was "probably low."[29]

Unresolved Issues

The authors of the *Circulation* article identified several areas in which data were limited or there were otherwise "unresolved issues." The areas in which data were limited included patients with heart failure or who had heart attacks or strokes within six months or uncontrolled high blood pressure. The unresolved issues included "interaction with nonaspirin antiplatelet agents," effects on the central nervous system, and the occurrence of low blood pressure in patients with severe heart failure, as well as "[m]usculoskeletal effects," namely, "myalgias with chest pain that could be confused with angina."[30] In scientific argument that followed, one commentator termed this study "the most authoritative and unbi-ased assessment of the cardiac risk" of Viagra, saying it was surprising that a letter from Pfizer representatives did not cite the study.[31]

The Question of Consumer Information

It is an empirical question as to how much of this information appeared on the active mental screens of users of Viagra. The solemn advice from the authors of the *Circulation* article might generate some satiric merriment as they detailed metabolic effects in given sexual positions, but it might not influence lovers' choices at romantic moments. This is a constant problem in market experimen-tation; ordinary people—and perhaps many nonspecialized physicians—may not be up-to-the-minute on information about drug hazards. And certainly, the ability of lay persons to translate the most responsible medical advice into daily activities is limited.

Conventional analysis of product risks focuses on comparative risks and ben-efits. Drugs are sold on the basis of their benefits. Some users, because of their medical histories and general sophistication, may learn as much about risk as any user needs to know. We have seen in Chapter 2 that many HIV patients have become expert about the risks of various drugs. Because of the relatively intense interests of HIV patients in their drug regimens, it may be that they became aware of the warnings and precautions about ritonavir interactions relatively early. However, one may wonder how much information like data on risks associated with the combined use of erythromycin and Viagra ran below the radar, including the radar of busy doctors. It seems probable that information on such interactions is not in the mental stores of many Viagra users.

We may compare the risk profile faced by users of folk remedies in preregulatory times. Your great-grandmother may have prepared a brew from the leaves of shrubs for your mother, without knowledge that coffee, taken with that brew, might cause a constriction in the throat. No one would have expected more care from your great-grandmother if the unexpected interaction had taken place. Today, the expectations we have of producers as well as regulators are different, including what we expect about how stringently they will patrol for what would have been the unforeseen to less knowledgeable producers and users. A possible intermediate case is the microclimates of present-day folk medicine, in which some users may be conversant with odd synergies—but many may not.

Reports on adverse reactions continued as the vogue for Viagra carried into the new century. A letter to the editor of the *New England Journal of Medicine* in August 1999 reported an acute myocardial infarction in a man who had taken Viagra and nitroglycerin. The letter writers noted that Viagra "produces a transient reduction in blood pressure" and speculated that the use of the drug with nitroglycerin "may have led to a critical lowering of blood pressure that exacerbated" the patient's ischemia "and resulted in acute myocardial infarction." The writers observed that of "128 nonviolent deaths" that had occurred in Viagra users, "34 percent occurred within four or five hours" after use of the drug and that about "70 percent of the men who died had risk factors for cardiovascular or cerebrovascular disease."[32]

The Web Factor

The writers focused on the difficulty of containing interactions in a world in which the drug was "widely available through the Internet without contact with a physician and through unregulated, illicit trade." They suggested—although their observation about the ready availability of the drug seemed to undermine the practicality of the suggestion—that "men should be warned of the risks of taking sildenafil and nitrates concurrently if they have received a prescription for only one or the other."[33] A study published the next year, which the authors characterized as "the first report on the effect of sildenafil citrate on the systemic and coronary circulation," "demonstrate[d] the cardiac-vasodilating effect" of the product "when used in conjunction with nitrates," an effect the authors warned "might produce a fatal cardiac outcome."[34]

The concurrent rise of the Web and of consumers' belief that they could take control of their own pharmaceutical fates had generated a situation in which the line between prescriptions and over-the-counter medications had become much more blurry than in the days when your great-grandmother concocted her brews. Indeed, the line was blurrier than even in the days when Laetrile, a concoction featuring ground-up apricot pits, was the subject of decision of the United States Supreme Court.[35]

A Spectrum of Opinion

More Warnings, and Some Statistical Fog

At the very opening of the new century, the FDA published a revised label for Viagra. It specified a contraindication for the drug for "patients who are using organic nitrates, either regularly or intermittently," noting that "[a]fter patients have taken VIAGRA, it is unknown when nitrates, if necessary, can be safely administered."[36] A separate warning repeated the 1998 language about the "potential for cardiac risk of sexual activity in patients with preexisting cardiovascular disease," and a prior caution that "treatments for erectile dysfunction, including VIAGRA, should not generally be used in men for whom sexual activity is inadvisable because of their underlying cardiovascular status."[37] Under a category titled "Information for Patients," this labeling repeated a 1998 declaration to doctors that they "should discuss with patients the contraindication of VIAGRA with regular and/or intermittent use of organic nitrates" and "the potential cardiac risk of sexual activity in patients with preexisting cardiovascular risk factors." Also rehearsing the 1998 labeling, it enjoined doctors to warn patients to seek medical assistance immediately for erections that lasted longer than four hours.[38]

The new year of 2000 brought some fog in the zone of medical statistics. Dr. Jerry Avorn, of the Brigham and Women's Hospital in Boston, captured both the uncertainty and the need for research: "If you find old guys on Viagra dying from heart attacks, it's hard to know if it's the Viagra or the sexual activity." But, added Avorn, the chief of the Division of Pharmacoepidemiology and Pharmacoeconomics at the hospital, "that doesn't mean we shouldn't try to find out." Avorn summarized a facet of the problem of market experimentation in the lack of incentive for drug makers to look for bad news: "Manufacturers in general are not eager to look for problems if they are not already evident, and the FDA is chronically impotent in conceptualizing and mandating postmarketing surveillance."[39]

Another pharmacological expert focused on a precise set of comparative statistics—a much larger number of deaths among men who took Viagra than those who took local alprostadils. That group of drugs includes the products Caverject, administered by injection in the penis, and Muse, administered with a penile suppository. This doctor, John Urquhart—who held professorial appointments at the University of California-San Francisco and Maastricht University in the Netherlands—reported 49 deaths per million prescriptions for Viagra users as contrasted with between 1 and 5 for the alprostadils.[40]

A poster presentation at a medical meeting in March 2000 reported 1,473 postmarketing "adverse events" from Viagra. The authors, led by Babak Azarbal, described this as "a high number of deaths and serious cardiovascular events associated with Viagra," saying that "[t]he majority of deaths are due to cardio-vascular causes, mostly occurring in patients" under age 65 "without known cardiac risk factors."[41]

Matching Pfizer's medical and public relations headaches over the drug were two other events in 2000, one with a special celebrity twist. On the legal side, the British Patents Court concluded that Pfizer's patent on a key ingredient of Viagra was invalid because information about it "already was in the public domain."[42] On the celebrity-litigation side, Zsa Zsa Gabor and her husband sued the company on the ground that Viagra had made him dependent to a point that he was impotent if he did not take it.[43]

More data on the potential of Viagra to cause cardiovascular problems had appeared in research dealing with the sympathetic nervous system, excitation of which constricts blood vessels. This study indicated that muscle sympathetic nerve activity increased two to eight times as much in Viagra subjects as in those taking placebo.[44] The researchers commented that "[s]ympathetic excitation after sildenafil use may be implicated in any heightened cardiovascular risk in patients with severe cardiovascular disease,"[45] and the lead investigator told a medical press source, with similarly laconic language, that "[f]or people with unstable car-diovascular disease, this could be a problem."[46]

Positive Conclusions, and Challenges

As these critical perspectives appeared, however, a study of 14 patients pub-lished in the *New England Journal of Medicine* reported that Viagra had "no direct adverse cardiovascular effects in men with severe coronary artery disease," given measurements of a number of variables. Specifically, the investigators found that the product did "not adversely affect coronary blood flow, coronary vascular re-sistance, or coronary flow reserve." Grants from Pfizer supported this research.[47]

Similarly encouraging news for Viagra users came from a Southampton-based study published in the *British Medical Journal* in 2001. Its conclusion was that there was "no evidence for a higher incidence of fatal myocardial infarction or ischemic heart disease among men taking sildenafil." These researchers, led by Saad Shakir, cautioned that although their results were "reassuring," they should not be taken as "definitive evidence" for men in England and that further research was needed. They noted as qualifications that they had used a comparison of deaths from ischemic heart disease in their study population with the "general population of England," that the amount of diabetes in their study group was "much higher than that in the general population," and that it was possible that there was "[u]nderreporting of adverse events" as well a "bias caused by non-response among general practitioners."

Various pressures to get data on Viagra and heart attacks were implicit in the Southampton researchers' decision to report on the "first phase" of an ongoing investigation. They were careful to note that although they had received "financial support from Pfizer to attend conferences overseas," companies that supported the work of their research unit had "no statistical or editorial control over analysis or reporting of results."[48]

Dr. Avorn of the Brigham and Women's Hospital expressed caution about possible statistical gaps in the Southampton study, including the comparison of Viagra users with the general population and, according to a news report, "the lack of information about underlying disease and medications." According to the report, "Avorn said he was reassured that men who received sildenafil did not have a higher rate of cardiac events, but that he could not promote the safety of the drug based on Shakir's study."[49] In a later response to another criticism of their use of the general population for comparison, the Shakir group said it thought that population was an "appropriate" comparator "for two reasons"—that "a valid external comparator cohort of sufficient size, comprising similar proportions of diabetic to non-diabetic men and for which cardiovascular mortality was reported, was not available" and that "such comparisons are useful from a public health perspective."[50] The first reason, in particular, seems subject to criticism, for it can be viewed as rationalizing the use of not very good data on scientific matters of great public interest because people are clamoring for conclusions.

In another study published in 2001, a researcher employed a comparison of deaths associated with Viagra and alprostadil, the injectable product used for ED, in stressing that the issue of Viagra and "cardiovascular events and deaths deserves further study." As he summarized his results, "the number of reported deaths is 6.28 times greater" for Viagra than for injectable alprostadil. He carefully noted that one should apply "caution . . . in interpreting the results," in part because the "intense media attention" given to Viagra might be producing more physician reports of adverse effects, and also because there might be differences in the populations who were using the two products. However, he suggested that this cautionary stance should also apply to doctors considering prescription of Viagra.[51]

A fiery skirmish in the Viagra wars took place in the British urology journal *BJU International* in 2000 and 2001. An editor for the journal, referring to "[t]he large number of poorly explained deaths in patients taking Viagra," cited studies "suggesting" that the drug might cause cardiac arrhythmias. He concluded that these things "reinforce the need for vigilance and caution in prescribing Viagra," which he characterized as "this potent cardiovascular drug."[52] Replying, two Pfizer scientists wrote to the journal that a "variety" of human and animal studies showed "no detrimental effect of Viagra on a range of variables of cardiac function."[53] They referenced a prior study as "[s]howing no difference in the incidence of myocardial infarction or all-cause morbidity between Viagra and placebo."[54]

A reply from the *BJU International* editor, Gordon Williams, declared that "[o]bjective, peer-reviewed epidemiological data assessing the safety of Viagra are remarkably scant." Williams said there had been no adequate explanation for the "[m]ore than 500 deaths . . . associated with the use of Viagra in its first 15 months of marketing." He raised a number of questions about the conditions of use of the product by men who had died, including the suddenness of death and whether death occurred before or during intercourse. He urged "caution and vigilance" in prescription of the drug.[55]

An observer of this history will be struck by certain problems surrounding the marketing of heavily advertised new drugs. One is that because of the time and expense of monitoring side effects, collection and interpretation necessarily lag behind the currents of data that emerge from the use of drugs in wide-scale marketing. Dr. Williams, writing in June 2001, was discussing mortality data going back to 1998 and 1999. At that point, he was asking, "How many more Viagra-associated deaths have now occurred?"[56] Also symbolic of the lag was a review essay published in 2001, accepted for publication in November 2000, which reported on adverse events within eight months of the marketing of Viagra.[57] The authors of this essay summarized cautionary guidelines for the prescription of the drug for men with certain cardiovascular problems and also a three-tiered system of risk categories, ranging from low through intermediate to high.[58]

Scientists as Promoters

An overlapping set of phenomena involves marketers seeking to pump up publicity for their products and scientists who troll for headlines—both in the medical press and the wider press. This is evident in the Southampton researchers' apparent need to explain why they were reporting on the "first phase" of continuing research. There are several competitions constantly on foot here—for sales, for grants, and for scientific recognition. In the extreme case, these factors may combine to constitute a kind of scientific magma, with an occasional resulting explosion. A dramatic recent example is the faking of data on stem cell research by a well-regarded South Korean investigator, whose work was accepted and then, embarrassingly, retracted in a leading journal.[59]

★ ★ ★

The literature on Viagra expanded during 2001 to include effects on various parts of the brain and body, including the nervous system, eyes, and nerves around the heart. It also extended to effects on disease states, in particular Parkinson's disease.

One study "clearly showed" effects of the product on the central nervous system, including "an enhanced ability to focus attention on streams of auditory stimuli." At the same time, it found "no effect" of the drug "[a]t the behavioral level," specifically, "no relevant overt effect on attention and memory functions" in a subject group of young males. However, the investigators said, "inspection of . . . event-related brain potential suggests that there might well be some effects of sildenafil on information processing."[60] The sum of this appeared to be that at least young men should not think that Viagra would enhance their SAT scores in addition to their sexual performance.

The Eye: Initial Problems with Vision

The eyes became a target of research published beginning in 2000, with some interesting disagreements on data emerging even at that early time. A letter to the *New England Journal of Medicine* in 2000 built on prior findings of "[m]ild, transient visual changes such as increased sensitivity to light and color-tinge alterations" in 3 percent of Viagra users. These authors, led by William Sponsel, found an increase in "pulsatile ocular blood flow" in users, although none of their subjects "reported any subjective visual symptoms." Interestingly, the researchers found some possible benefit here because "drugs capable of increasing ocular perfusion might be of therapeutic value in various" disorders of the eye.[61]

Another group led by Juan Grunwald published findings with a different focus. It reported that there was "no significant change in mean optic nerve blood flow" in 15 subjects, although it acknowledged, citing some very specific statistical correlations from their data, that it was "possible that changes may occur in some individuals." These researchers described the Sponsel group's technique as "controversial," and noted that the Sponsel study had not used a placebo control group.[62] A later study by the Grunwald group found "no statistically or clinically significant alteration" in intraocular pressure in a group of subjects with glaucoma.[63]

The first Grunwald study was accepted for publication November 28, 2000, and became available online in May 2001. Paralleling these findings, however, were reports indicating that the eye was an area of concern. A press story in early November 2000 indicated that five Viagra users had suffered what were "essentially small strokes in their eyes," which "permanently damaged their optic nerves, causing some vision loss." Although there was no evidence of causation, the report quoted a researcher as saying that in three of the five cases, "this came on after the first or second time they ever took the medication" and that the stroke-like symptoms appeared "within an hour or two of taking the drug."[64]

One ophthalmologist gave a possible explanation targeted to a physiological peculiarity: four of the five men who had the stroke-type occurrences had a "low cup to disk ratio," a tight bundling of blood vessels and nerves in the back of the eye.[65] This type of problem connects with suggestions that we mentioned in the chapter on breast implants that adverse events may be related to unusual physiologies.[66]

Symptomatic of the uncertainties that accompany such early developments in mass marketing was an observation by Dr. Peter Savino, the director of neuro-ophthalmology at a Philadelphia eye hospital. "Is it a real risk?" he asked, and answered his own question: "Nobody knows...No one is really sure if there is a cause-and-effect relationship." A University of Pennsylvania medical professor, however, had a word for it: "It's the sex, not the Viagra," said Dr. Howard Herrmann. This suggestion appeared to apply especially to men who started using Viagra after many years with no sexual activity—which could be likened to strenuous exercise after years as a couch potato.[67]

Some Complex Results

An interesting set of specific results, emblematic of the experimental nature of drug development on the market, combined good news with bad news. One research group administered Viagra to patients with ED who had Parkinson's disease or the cluster of symptoms called multiple system atrophy, a disorder difficult to define with precision but which includes a group of neurological symptoms often misdiagnosed as Parkinson's disease.[68] The beneficial results of Viagra uncovered by this study were that it was effective for treating ED "in patients with parkinsonism"—that is, a group of symptoms resembling Parkinson's disease—who had that disease itself or multiple system atrophy.

However, the researchers had to stop the study in the group with multiple system atrophy because three of the six patients in that group had a "severe fall in blood pressure," so severe that they were "unable to stand for more than a few seconds." Each of those patients "had to wait"—one of them for four hours—"until the drop in blood pressure became tolerable."[69] Incidentally, these results provide a good example of the incompleteness of subcategorization of many medical conditions—specifically multiple system atrophy as a kind of subset of parkinsonism. Pointedly with reference to the difficulties of determining causation of adverse events, they illustrate the biochemical individuality of human beings, exemplified by the fact that three, but not all, of the six subjects had significant drops in blood pressure. This is simply one instance of the lesson that the only way to develop data that will be useful in the treatment of individual persons is by using drugs on people—a challenge for regulation as well as medicine.

A Party Drug

One other very specific area of concern that surfaced by 2001 was that Viagra appeared to be becoming a "party drug" for some gay men. As a Brown University medical professor explained the potential consequences to a journalist in October 2001, "in a bathhouse or other setting where there's an opportunity to have sex with multiple partners, to have a longer-lasting erection can be a prescription for H.I.V. transmission."[70] Another concern—on the cardiovascular side—was the use of Viagra together with "poppers," a nitrate-based "recreational drug" that could have the same effects as the already well-documented effects of the use of Viagra with nitrates.[71]

On the Treadmill

It was plain that, whatever their level of information, a lot of men thought that Viagra was worth whatever risks it entailed. Pfizer proclaimed on its Web site in the summer of 2001 that 9 million men were taking the drug.[72] And there were reports indicating that for many men, Viagra did not aggravate existing risk. A study sponsored by Pfizer indicated that in treadmill tests, Viagra takers with stable angina fared no worse than subjects taking placebo with respect to how long it took for chest pain to develop. The researchers pushed their subjects to levels of exercise characterized as about double that of sexual activity.[73]

Early in the history of Viagra, medical studies had established the effectiveness of the drug for the desired result—simply, generating and maintaining erections. By 2002, the scientific discussion had settled into a pattern of argument on the kinds of safety problems that frequently arise in mass marketing of medications.

A Run of Mostly Positive Thinking

An article published in 2002 concluded that the product was "effective" in patients with a variety of illnesses or conditions, ranging from diabetes, ischemic heart disease, and peripheral vascular disease to high blood pressure and depression.[74] There was evidence of effectiveness, also, in men who had had prostate surgery, although this differed with respect to whether the surgery spared the surrounding nerves or not. The data in this study, funded by Pfizer, indicated that improvements in erections increased if Viagra was first tried 18 months after surgery (60 percent) rather than six months after surgery (26 percent).[75]

Another study found "marked" improvements in black and Hispanic American men—more than double than those who got placebo drugs. Hispanic men scored higher than blacks—who as the investigators noted had a high percentage of hypertension—and a "mostly white" group scored even higher.[76] These investigators, also funded by Pfizer, reported that 18 percent of blacks and 27 percent of Hispanics had "mild to moderate" side effects and that only one Hispanic patient discontinued treatment for that reason.[77]

The buildup of data was now big enough that scientists began to present review articles consolidating research results. Inevitably, there was a lag between the accumulation of data and reporting, and careful scientists qualified their findings. Illustrating this cautious approach was an article published in the *American Journal of Cardiology* in June 2002 by FDA scientists who analyzed statistics on deaths by myocardial infarction for the first few months of the marketing of the drug in 1998. They found a "peak" in deaths in those months after the initial marketing, noting that "a large proportion of the affected persons had coronary risk disease factors associated with erectile dysfunction and were engaged in sexual activity that has been documented to be a 'trigger' for MI [myocardial infarction]."[78]

Then, having stopped examining "individual case reports" in late 1998, they "analyzed reporting trends that include duplicate reports and follow-up reports having identification numbers different from the original report" and found a decrease in reports through the second quarter of 2001. They concluded that there "did not appear to be an increase in deaths due to MI above expected numbers." They cautioned that "[b]ecause adverse events are submitted voluntarily, the magnitude of underreporting is unknown and possibly substantial." However, they tempered this qualification by pointing out that the "considerable publicity" on Viagra and early reports of sudden deaths "favors more complete reporting of serious adverse events than less publicized drugs." And they then requalified the point by saying that "[n]evertheless, some unknown proportion of deaths probably remained unreported" and that "[t]he secular decline in the number of deaths . . . may not be reassuring because it may only reflect a decrease in reporting with time."[79] This brief review, with its many qualifications, is a nice illustration of the tensions inherent in long-term data reporting on product and process hazards, including possible gaps in the process of data collection itself.

An English review of clinical trial reports, confirming the effectiveness of the drug,[80] reported that "[s]erious adverse events were no more frequent with sildenafil than placebo at any dose."[81] It noted that as dosages went to 100 mg and beyond—100 mg being the top of the "licensed range"—the number of "severe" events "occurred more frequently."[82] However, there was no difference in the number of subjects who discontinued the drug because of adverse effects between those who received Viagra and those who took placebo.[83] A Pfizer grant supported this study, but the authors noted that they had "an absolute right . . . to publish the results" and that Pfizer had not seen the manuscript before they submitted it.

A four-year review of Viagra confirmed that side effects increased with the amount of the dose.[84] Noting the "modest ability" of the drug "to lower blood pressure,"[85] the investigators said that the data indicated that the drug was "well tolerated" by men who took medication for high blood pressure[86] and that less than 1 percent of all patients, including those on blood pressure medication, suffered "treatment-related" adverse cardiovascular effects.[87] On the whole, the investigators concluded that heart attacks and deaths from all causes were "similar" between Viagra users and those who took placebo as well as "men in the same age cohort of the general population."[88]

The authors of this review opined that "heightened concern" about the drug had "stemmed primarily from sporadic case reports of adverse events . . . published in the medical literature and sensationalized by the media."[89] They suggested that "[b]etter controlled studies, such as randomized controlled trials, prospective epidemiologic studies, and large case series" should be used "to determine if any causal relation exists" between use of Viagra and adverse cardiovascular events.[90] The study took note that 2 percent of users in "long-term, open-label studies" had reported effects on the eyes, mostly color tinges to vision, and "increased sensitivity to light or blurred vision."[91] Their overall conclusion was that controlled clinical trials of Viagra showed "an excellent overall safety profile"[92] and that "most patients" with ED "can be safely and effectively treated with" Viagra.[93] This report was part of a supplement to the journal *Urology* sponsored by Pfizer, and four of the five authors noted that they were "paid consultants to, and study investigators funded by" Pfizer.[94] Though this disclosure was "up front," this observer would suggest that value judgments such as "excellent" might be better left to the reader.

Another review essay narrowed in on what was known about side effects as a means to avoiding them. Noting that "[t]he incidence of severe cardiovascular events correlates directly with the severity of pre-existing cardiovascular disease and the dose of Viagra prescribed,"[95] this study concluded that Viagra was "safe under proper conditions" when prescribed without contraindications within the dose range of 50 to 100 mg.[96] It noted that the principal adverse effects of the drug, like headaches and facial flushing, which it described as "mainly symptoms of vasodilation," were rarely troublesome in the context of sexual activity, and . . . short lived."[97] Generally, it emphasized the need for "[a]n assessment of individual cardiovascular risk,[98] and it specifically suggested encouragement to patients and doctors "to seek the minimum effective dose."[99]

An uncontrolled study of ED patients in a British general hospital in 2002 opined that, in general, Viagra "appears to be safe in the treatment of erectile dysfunction in the real world."[100] The investigators, who were supported by an educational grant from Pfizer, found it telling that almost 80 percent of men taking Viagra wished to continue it after the study period ended.[101] They did find that "the incidence of headache, flushing, dyspepsia and abnormal vision [was] higher" than in prior studies. However, besides saying that "in the absence of a control group the significance of this is uncertain," they noted that "13% of men who reported side effects at Visit 2 reported complete lack of them at Visit 3." Yet, they did observe that there was "a 2% incidence each of thirst and 'dazed feeling' (reported by patients as a 'muzzy head')."[102]

Another group of studies that focused on specific physiological areas presented mostly benign results; at the extreme, the picture was almost one of a panacea. A vision study of nine men that employed a single dose of the drug found "[n]o clinically relevant changes" manifested in six tests of visual function.[103] The researchers noted "isolated case reports" of problems with optic nerves and suggested "careful monitoring to detect any emerging pattern."[104]

A hint of the panacea idea came on the hypertension front with the publication of an Israeli report that Viagra caused "small but statistically significant reductions" in blood pressure in men with both high and normal blood pressure, both while ambulatory and at rest. The study group included 49 men who took one 100-mg dose of the drug.[105] Paralleling this was another study summarized as finding that there had been no "serious adverse events related to Viagra treatment" in 562 men who were taking two or more drugs for high blood pressure.[106]

Other positive news—or instances of no news—emerged about cardiovascular effects. A Mayo Clinic study of men with "known or probable coronary artery disease" who were using a supine exercise bicycle indicated that Viagra was "well tolerated" and had "no effect" on abnormalities in the heart wall. The lead investigator, Patricia Pellikka, discerned the "overall message" as that Viagra "does not increase oxygen deprivation to the heart."[107]

There were also encouraging animal studies. One, with rabbits, indicated that Viagra might have effects on the heart analogous to "preconditioning" that would minimize damage from heart attacks. The investigator, Rakesh C. Kukreja of Virginia Commonwealth University, posited that Viagra "causes vasodilatation [dilation of blood vessels] and decrease in the blood pressure," although a press story reported that he said that it would take two or three more years of research and clinical trials to pin down the molecular reasons for the phenomenon.[108] Another study indicated that Viagra reduced the effects of induced strokes in rats.

A researcher said that rats treated with Viagra had better neurological outcomes and more agility, and that indeed the drug created "new brain cells."[109]

Viagra investigations roamed through the male body. Another study, funded by Pfizer, found "minimal effect" of Viagra on sperm counts and sperm movement.[110] There were, however, a few warning flags along the way. In September 2002, the FDA cautioned that Viagra doses above 25 mg, taken together with alpha blockers, could lead to symptomatic low blood pressures "in some patients." The agency concluded that "Viagra doses above 25 mg should not be taken within four hours of taking an alpha blocker."[111]

Concerns in the HIV Community

One specific community—men with HIV—was the target of a warning from the director of sexually transmitted disease (STD) control for San Francisco. This official, Dr. Jeffrey Klausner, urged the FDA to require the labeling of Viagra to warn about transmission of gonorrhea as a byproduct of use of the drug. He reportedly said that men who "often use Viagra as a recreational drug" with drugs like ecstasy and methamphetamines tend to slack off on their use of condoms. Noting that a study at the San Francisco STD clinic indicated that "men who have sex with men were more than four times more likely to use Viagra than heterosexual men," he pointed out that gonorrhea was "much more common than other STDs among men who have sex with men and is 'far more infectious' than other diseases." Pfizer demurred, saying that it thought it had done enough with a label that said that the drug "does not protect you or your partner from getting sexually transmitted diseases, including HIV—the virus that causes AIDS." The company also had warned that using Viagra with the drug called "poppers," amyl nitrate, could cause "a dangerous drop in blood pressure." But a spokesman drew the line at a warning specific to gonorrhea, saying that "any product can be abused, and that's beyond our control."[112]

In the shadows of the Viagra research is the fact of manufacturer-sponsored studies. It is a positive development that journals are now requiring that investigators reveal when funding comes from drug companies, as well as their own stock interests in the firms. Added to this form of disclosure is the limitation on bias placed on investigators by the need to maintain their scientific reputations. It seems reasonable to believe that most researchers will not sacrifice reputation for a single grant. Yet, it also seems reasonable to ask whether, having had bread buttered by a pharmaceutical company, investigators may tilt toward a slightly rosy view of a product when the very nature of corporations would suggest that favorable results are likely to affect future bread, and future butter, from the same source.

★ ★ ★

The year 2003 opened with a worldwide chorus trumpeting the benefits of Viagra, muted only slightly with references to adverse effects. As the year drew to a close, competitors began to move into the market.

More Good News, Including Byproduct Results

In the first week of 2003, the trade press noted a new U.K. study that reported that 51 percent of men taking Viagra had results of "successful sexual intercourse within 20 minutes"—with 35 percent of those men having intercourse within 14 minutes. The leader of the study, Dr. Harin Padma Nathan of the University of Southern California School of Medicine, declared that the study showed the drug "well-suited to meet the needs" of the study population. One could aurally picture the sound track of *La Dolce Vita* in the background as the urology group leader of Pfizer declared that "Viagra's unique clinical profile of a rapid onset and duration of at least 4 hours with minimal side effects...clearly meets the needs of real world ED patients."[113]

At the same time, new data appeared on the vision front—mostly but not entirely positive. A California ophthalmology researcher reportedly found, in a small group study, that Viagra produced "very little change in blood vessels or blood flow" in the eye "in nearly all the patients." He did indicate that with high doses of the drug, there might be some indications that, as a press report summarized it, "people with underlying vascular diseases may experience changes in vision." Moreover, his study confirmed difficulties in perceiving "subtle changes in colour" and that users "had problems picking out a number of colours, not just the blue-green shades reported during...clinical trials."[114]

More review articles came forth, summarizing many studies. Reports on side effects continued generally to be good, and indeed there were more suggestions that Viagra was beneficial beyond helping to sustain erections.

A 2003 review article by Italian researchers had something of a panacea tone. Descriptively, it described Viagra as a "blockbuster" drug,[115] and it mixed description and judgment by saying that Viagra had "revolutionised the management of patients with erectile dysfunction."[116] The authors' overall summary on "[s]afety and tolerability" was that both had "been clearly demonstrated in multiple studies," of which they cited several. They said adverse effects were "usually transitory and of minor intensity," and noted that discontinuance of Viagra "due to adverse effects is very low."[117] They noted that "previous published guidelines suggested that sildenafil could be hazardous in patients suffering from active ischaemic heart disease," but asserted that "more recent data does not support this."[118] They did refer to declarations about the need for careful evaluation of "every single patient...in order to verify his capacity" for sexual activity,[119] stressing that for "patients complaining of coronary artery disease," there should be "thorough discussion with the patient about the risks of physical and sexual activity." At the same time, they pointed out that there was "no evidence of direct effect" of Viagra "on the myocardium or conduction system."[120] The authors also cited research indicating relative safety and efficacy of Viagra in diabetes patients[121] and in men with spinal cord injuries[122] as well as multiple sclerosis, which has very destructive effects on sex life.[123]

Positive byproducts of Viagra appeared in the Italian authors' summary of data from several trials indicating that "the drug is efficacious as a first-line treatment in men with untreated minor depression, in men with ED which is refractory to successful . . . treatment of depression" with selective serotonin reuptake inhibitors (SSRIs), and in men "whose depression was successfully treated but who developed ED as a consequence of SSRI treatment."[124] The latter category was illustrative of the kinds of unintended consequences, sometimes beneficial and sometimes harmful, that often attend the marketing of new drugs. The authors also summarized a report that Viagra was associated with "a clear improvement of depressive symptoms" in 75 percent of men with Parkinson's disease, as well as marked improvements in sexual function in particular.[125] For men who had had radical prostate surgery that spared nerves, it appeared that the best treatment combined early use of injections of alprostadil with Viagra.[126]

The Italian authors' lengthy summary of the effects of Viagra on various conditions is symbolically interesting. It captures the dynamism of the progression of research data on products that are in effect being tried out over time on millions of people.

The globalization of Viagra research encompassed Australia. A review from New South Wales spoke of "emerging evidence for a good safety profile for sildenafil in patients with cardiovascular disease." However, the authors added a hedging note: that there was "no significant experience" about the safety of the drug "in patients who have recently had an acute coronary event, arrhythmia or cerebrovascular event or undergone coronary artery revascularisation, or patients with decompensated heart failure or uncontrolled hypertension." They concluded that "[f]urther experience is required in patients at higher risk of cardiovascular disease."[127]

Even people who are used to there being classifications for everything, from on-base percentage in baseball to rating scales of 1 to 10 for female beauty, may be bemused by the IIEF—the International Index of Erectile Function. A Moroccan study echoed the developing research history on efficacy, finding "significant improvements" in all IIEF categories, "including erectile function, orgasmic function, sexual desire, intercourse satisfaction, and overall satisfaction."[128] The authors of this Pfizer-supported study, published in the *International Journal of Impotence Research*, found five adverse events attributable to Viagra in a group of 71 men, with all but one "mild or moderate in severity."[129] Their study escalated doses over a period of eight weeks, from 25 through 50 and then 100 milligrams. They concluded that Viagra "was very well tolerated," referring to prior studies indicating "that only 25% of patients who received sildenafil in open trials withdrew because of adverse events," with "the most common side effects" being "mild-to-moderate headache and flushing."[130]

Positive results also appeared in a British study of men with chronic stable angina who took a new set of treadmill tests. The authors, led by a paid consultant and adviser for Pfizer and including other Pfizer investigators and employees, concluded that Viagra was superior to placebo "for the time to the onset of angina . . . , the time to limiting angina . . . and the total exercise time."[131] Indeed, they found that Viagra "increased total exercise time in heart failure patients."[132]

How Questions Affect Answers

An interesting combination of results and speculations emerged from a Taiwan study. These researchers noted that the way that questions were asked of research subjects influenced the information collected, pointing out in particular that "[s]pecific and directed questions" about adverse effects produced more reports of those effects than "open-ended questions." They noted, at the same time, that this implied that the adverse effects were "mild in nature."[133] The investigators also discerned "a trend" indicating that Viagra evoked a better response in cases where ED was "milder."[134]

An interesting aspect of the Taiwan data was that the refill rate for Viagra was 58.6 percent for all research subjects and 66.2 percent for those who answered yes to the question, "With Viagra treatment, did you have successful sexual intercourse?" The investigators speculated on "[s]everal possible reasons" for these relatively low rates—time and cost of getting refills, "financial stress, patient and partner motivation, getting old, progression of underlying disease or just for curiosity." They remarked that it would "be interesting to conduct a further investigation into this."[135] These observations provide an added dimension to previous data indicating that very few men stop taking Viagra because of adverse effects.

Some studies focused on particularized groups of patients or effects. In 2003, a Mayo Clinic group presented some very tentative hopeful conclusions for a medical problem quite different from ED. The study involved 13 patients with pulmonary arterial hypertension, which the authors described as a "progressive, debilitating disease with a poor prognosis." They concluded that the drug had an "immediate pulmonary vasodilator effect" in the study patients, who already had been treated with vasodilators. This, they said, made Viagra a "potentially attractive option as adjunctive therapy to current treatment strategies if a sufficient level of efficacy were rigorously shown"—which, they indicated, would require a much larger prospective, controlled study.[136] The existing stresses on the patients in this study presumably contributed to adverse effects and a high number of cases of men who did not continue with the drug. Of the 13 in the group, two "could not tolerate" even a 25-mg dose. A follow-up study found six of the group continuing the drug. A second follow-up found four who no longer took it. The researchers reported that two "experienced adverse effects such as nasal congestion, lower extremity edema, and generalized malaise" and that two others "exhibited signs or symptoms consistent with progression of disease that resulted in discontinuation of sildenafil."[137]

The Costs of Research

Another study published in 2003, based on research done in Germany in 2001, implied the expense of doing such targeted investigations. Using six volunteers aged 21 to 32 who were "seated in a comfortable chair in a quiet room with their eyes shut," the authors concluded that Viagra did not cause "significant changes" in blood flow velocity in the right middle cerebral artery, although there was "a decreasing trend of blood flow that did not reach significance." The authors acknowledged the limitations of the study, which they described as a "pilot" study, and said that "larger studies" would be necessary "[t]o avoid a false sense of safety for elderly males, who are more likely to use sildenafil" than the men in the group studied. They suggested as a "next step" measurements "during sexual stimulation" rather than "under resting conditions."[138] Increases in numbers, not to mention tests held under more athletically realistic conditions, presumably would drive up the costs of studies. This problem constantly attends clinical tryouts of drugs that are simultaneously sold on mass markets.

A Lively Market, Expanding Research, and Continuing Criticism

Competitors Come In

In 2003, two competitors arose to challenge Viagra: Bayer/GSK's Levitra (vandenafil HCL), approved by the FDA in August, and Lilly Icos LLC's Cialis (tadalafil), for which approval was expected by the end of the year.[139] All three products shared a basic biochemistry; they were inhibitors of the enzyme phosphodiesterase type 5 (PDE 5), an action that has the effect of increasing blood flow in the penis and facilitating erections. An early summary of research of the three drugs featured the sweeping conclusion that "none of the PDE 5 inhibitors cause serious adverse events" and that all were "highly efficacious and safe."[140] The author of the study, N.N. Kim, noted that safety and tolerability of the three drugs were dependent on "tissue-specific distribution" of various phosphodiesterase enzymes, although all generally had "excellent selectivity for PDE 5."[141] One specific effect that cropped up with Cialis was back pain, which "tend[s] to increase slightly at higher doses."[142]

As interesting as the science at this point, at least from the consumer point of view, was the marketing competition. One trade journal noted that in searching for "unique product claims," the companies would probably seek to emphasize that their drugs "work[ ] faster (Levitra), last[] longer (Cialis) and [had a] proven track record (Viagra)." The stakes were in the billion dollar range—Viagra had $1.7 billion in worldwide sales in 2002.[143]

Marketing strategies emphasized testosterone values, literally and figuratively. Bayer/GSK signed a three-year deal with the National Football League that gave it exclusive marketing rights for Levitra, among a group of men's health care products. A Bayer/GSK official exulted that this contract would "give us access to the NFL's loyal fan base and an opportunity to reach over 120 million football fans a week." Bayer/GSK also carried the fight to Lilly in Indianapolis, Lilly's hometown, signing its first contract with an individual NFL franchise, the Colts. Lilly Icos made arrangements to sponsor the Western Open golf tournament for three years "on behalf of Cialis." In 2002, Viagra had become an official sponsor of Major

League Baseball. Even as marketing competition heated up among the three products, Vivus Inc. had put into a clinical trial another PDE 5 inhibitor, TA-1790, which it claimed could "restor[e] penile function more quickly than Viagra."[144]

It is worth remarking the role of media in making Viagra and its competitors into national phenomena. The ubiquity of publicity interacted with the commercialization of the product—who could have imagined an official connection between professional football, that most testosterone-laden sport, and a drug designed to combat what lay people would tend to think of as a testosterone deficiency?

A Vast Literature

Viagra provides several sets of lenses for viewing the interaction of law and science. A recurrent problem lies in the task of sorting out relevant information from vast collections of data, and determining its persuasiveness. As the natural history of Viagra and then its competitors on the market continued, one had the sense that investigators, clinicians, and patients were sailing in a small boat on a sea for which there were many charts of varying reliability and on which many currents remained uncharted. The expense of the scientific enterprise already devoted to the ED drugs was manifest in a literature review for an update of American Urology Association guidelines for management of ED, conducted over the period from 1996 through 2004, which yielded 7,067 articles. The variability in perceived reliability of research was evident in the reviewing panel's decision to accept only 85 articles to include in its update. It was telling, as a story in *Urology Times* summarized it, that "[a]ll medical treatment articles were randomized, double-blind, placebo-controlled trials."[145]

Late-Coming Data

In this connection, a study by scientists working for and consulting with Pfizer sheds some interesting light on the appearance of data in the information marketplace that one with a sense of consecutive neatness might think would have appeared earlier. This study, published in 2004, offered "a concise review of our preclinical safety evaluation" of Viagra, focusing on 70 pharmacological studies of dogs and rodents, as well as 30 single-dose preclinical pharmokinetic studies in animals and about 30 toxicology testing studies. Six years after Viagra came on the mass market, the company thought it worthwhile to publish this report "[i]n order to assist physicians in their search for data and to avoid unnecessary additional animal experimentation."[146] The authors concluded that "[t]he favourable results" of this "nonclinical safety evaluation . . . in established animal models have been confirmed by many years of clinical experience during the development and marketing" of the drug.[147] We noted earlier that for various reasons, the publication of research does not always keep up with the 24-hour news cycle. Yet it would appear that the publication of this review in 2004 responded to some level of continuing concern about the drug.

A piece of relatively old news, as measured by the time Viagra had been on the market, appeared in the 2004 publication of a study of more than 24,000 responses to questionnaires by English general practitioners for patients who began taking the drug in 1999. The method of study itself presented a sign of the regulatory times in England: it was "prescription-event monitoring" (PEM), described as "a method of postmarketing safety surveillance of newly marketed medicines."[148] The doctors who responded to the study reported a total of 3,951 reasons given for discontinuance of Viagra. The most common reason given—in 2,339 reports—was that the drug was not effective. The most common adverse event that led to discontinuance—in 135 cases—was ischemic heart disease.[149] The researchers followed up on 1,100 "individual events," finding very few that appeared to be "related to" Viagra. Perhaps the most interesting statistic in this group dealt with 32 events of "visual disturbance," of which there were 13 instances of "blurred vision."[150] There was one case of cerebral vascular accident thought to be related to Viagra. However, there was "no evidence" indicating an association of the drug with fatal myocardial infarctions or ischemic heart disease. Although the authors found their results "reassuring," they said that "because of possible under-reporting and the limitations of using an external comparator," results of their analysis of standard mortality ratios "should be viewed with caution."[151]

Sex and Common Sense

Another study, blending urology and psychiatry, found quite hopeful signs concerning the depression often associated with ED, but improvements appeared to be associated with placebo as well as with Viagra. The heart of the findings of this double-blind study was that treatment with either placebo or Viagra was associated with significant changes in mood, "quality of sexual life . . . , family life . . . , and overall life satisfaction."[152] The investigators ventured several possible explanations for "changes in life satisfaction," including "improved partner relationships; positive changes in sexual confidence, self-concept, or mood."[153] This, perhaps, captured no more than the common sense of the ages: if your sex life is going well, it is probable that you will feel better about yourself than if it is not.

More on Vision

As the study of English general practitioners suggested, Viagra might be shadowing the eyes of some men. A German ophthalmologist, who studied 20 male volunteers aged 20 to 40 years, reported some effects of the drug on certain aspects of vision. One specific effect was "a significant increase in sensitivity for detecting a violet flickering light on a steady yellow background."[154] A summation of several effects, in technical language, referred to a "significant prolongation in the implicit times of the a-wave of the maximum response, the oscillatory potential, [and] the cone-response b-wave." These responses, the report said, "clearly demonstrate[ ] altered retinal function."[155] However, there was "no significant change in sensitivity immediately after extinguishing the yellow background." Moreover, there was "no significant effect" between Viagra and placebo subjects with respect to discrimination between red and green and between blue and green.[156] The investigators offered some technical speculations about the biochemical origins of changes that did take place.[157] As is common, the investigators called for "more extensive and carefully controlled studies," especially of side effects revealed by color and electroretinogram studies, in order "to clarify the mode of action of sildenafil and to resolve the discrepancies between . . . human and animal studies."[158]

Not for Women

It was perhaps inevitable that researchers would inquire as to whether what was sauce for the gander also was pleasing to the goose. The answer was no. Canadian investigators found that Viagra did not provide sexual stimulus to the 34 postmenopausal women they surveyed, although according to a summary of their research, they hypothesized that a "subgroup of women with a low vaginal pulse amplitude response . . . may benefit from" Viagra. These investigators found side effects, akin to the flushing and headaches found in men on Viagra, in 59 percent of their subjects using Viagra and 24 percent of those using placebo.[159]

Wine: A No-effect Combination

On the lighter side, an Edinburgh group concluded that, with respect to such circulatory phenomena as blood pressure and heart rate, there was no significant interaction between Viagra and red wine. Although this may have appeared simply to be a welcome but trivial confirmation to seekers of pleasures in combination, a serious social fact stood in the background. As the investigators noted, Viagra use was on the increase, "both in legitimate users with erectile dysfunction but also in recreational drug users, particularly in combination with alcohol."[160]

That phenomenon was salient as the history of Viagra became deeper and richer. That process featured not only the addition of new data—and hypotheses—but also new social phenomena and a new economy for ED drugs: one characterized by competition and by attendant changes in marketing techniques.

Storm Clouds Thicken over Gay Users

A particular concern about the social reverberations of Viagra related to its recreational use by gay and bisexual males (men having sex with men [MSM]). Some striking manifestations of the problem appeared in answers to a detailed questionnaire by 150 men who attended a sex resort in northeast Georgia. The researchers generalized from these responses that "recreational Viagra use was associated with substance abuse (ecstasy and cocaine), rather than age, income, HIV status, or selected sexual risk behaviours."[161] These findings were particularly interesting because they contrasted in some ways with a San Francisco study showing that Viagra use among MSM was associated with "being HIV positive, older age, and having unprotected sex with risky partners," as well as with "illicit drug use."[162] The investigators on the Georgia study speculated on explanations for their results. On the one hand, they said, their "findings suggest that MSM who attend sex resorts may use or not use recreational Viagra regardless of their sexual risk behaviours." On the other hand, the data suggested "that MSM who obtain and use other illicit substances (for example, ecstasy and cocaine) may be especially likely to also obtain and use Viagra on a recreational basis." The operational conclusion was that in efforts aimed at reducing the spread of sexually transmitted diseases, "recreational Viagra use may be a particularly important issue to address for MSM who abuse substances."[163] An interesting sidelight of this study was the finding that 16 percent of the respondents "reported using nonprescription Viagra in the past 3 months."[164] "Nonprescription Viagra" is technically a contradiction in terms, but purchase of the product is as convenient as establishing an Internet connection using those two words.

A summary of research on recreational use of Viagra by MSM presented trench-level images of party environments in which that occurs—specifically, "raves, circuit parties, or nightclubs." A straight-faced description of "raves" is "all-night parties with a prolonged style of dance to fast-paced, repetitive music often accompanied by laser light displays." "Circuit parties are 2- to 3-day weekend events attended primarily by homosexual and bisexual men from across the country," usually involving "a series of social gatherings that culminate with one main dance event."[165]

One study summarized in this review essay, a study involving men in five London gyms, indicated that one in seven men had taken Viagra. Of 720 respondents, only 17 "had been prescribed the drug, while 83 had used it recreationally." Notably, men who were HIV-negative who had taken Viagra in the prior three months "were significantly more likely"—to the 0.01 statistical level—"to report serodiscordant unprotected anal intercourse" while using Viagra than men who were HIV-negative and had never used the drug.[166] Chilling in this context is the meaning of "serodiscordant"—a sexual union in which one partner has tested positive for HIV and the other has not.

Other data indicated that where just one-fifth of a San Francisco survey population was HIV-positive, that fraction was one-third for Viagra users.[167] Moreover, another San Francisco study found that men who used Viagra with other drugs were statistically much more likely to be under age 35, to have gotten the drug from a friend, and to believe that combining Viagra "with other drugs enhanced sexual experiences."[168] The writers of the review essay were careful to point out various limitations of the latter study, including uncertainty as to whether the association of Viagra with sexually transmitted disease "enabled men to have more partners, increased the duration of exposure to infected partners, or was a marker for higher-risk sexual networks."[169]

The review authors found it "[e]specially concerning that 15% of sildenafil users reported ingesting the drug with amyl nitrites ('poppers')"—the concern stemming from the flouting of the strong warnings against using nitrates with Viagra.[170] However, although "information strategies" are standard prescriptions for minimizing risky behavior, an Internet consultant who used Viagra was dubious about real-life effects: "I don't think guys who are doing crystal (crystal methamphetamine) and Viagra pay much attention to warnings about poppers. All they are thinking about is their erection."[171]

The authors also noted that although most of the epidemiologic data focused on "illicit use" of Viagra, the drug was prescribed to HIV patients for ED and that "the incidence of impotence among patients with HIV is as high as 33%." They pointed out that "HIV disease has itself been speculated to directly produce erectile dysfunction."[172]

A byproduct of these investigations involved an important signal for medical management of HIV patients with ED, namely, that taking Viagra together with protease inhibitors—medications commonly used in the treatment of HIV—significantly drives up the concentrations of Viagra in the blood. This led to the suggestion that men taking protease inhibitors should use the minimum starting dose of Viagra.[173]

The disease-spreading impact of Viagra was not limited to MSM. A press report quoted the sardonic humor of a South Bronx woman attributing the spread of AIDS among women in her neighborhood to heterosexual liaisons. Viagra, she said, "came along and woke the dead." Neighborhood men "started having sex with younger women." This led to communication of HIV to wives who had "never been out of the house, never been on the street, never been with anyone except their husband." The newly adventurous men would use saliva tests on "their family members without their knowing." The environment was that of a conspiracy of silence—as a reporter summarized it, "the stigma is still so great that older people will not discuss the disease even when they know someone has it."[174]

Commercial Erection Wars

Parallel with these developments was the burgeoning competition among the makers of Viagra, Levitra, and Cialis. Concerned about the "real potential for conflicts of interest" in the collection and assessment of comparison data on the drugs, a panel of the American Urological Association updated its guidelines on management of ED. A member of the panel, Dr. Gregory Broderick of the Mayo Clinic in Jacksonville, spoke of the need for "rigorous attention to ensure fairness and accuracy" in the collection of data in trials that compared the drugs. *Urology Times* reported that the panel had proposed the continuation of double-blinding in postmarketing studies of the drugs. The panel also said that reporting of adverse events should focus on the number of incidents in relation to the number of administrations of the drug, rather than the occurrence of adverse events on a per-patient basis. The case for "per-administration" reporting, as a reporter summarized it, was that it provided "information about the consistency, severity, and duration of side effects," all of which were relevant to comparison of the impact of the drugs and consumer preferences.[175]

"Erection wars" had now—so to speak—fully penetrated the media. Criticism of television ads for the three products came from sources as diverse as an industry-focused publication and the FDA. As a writer for *Pharmaceutical Executive* described it, the makers of Cialis and Levitra now "each felt compelled to match" Pfizer's spending on Viagra promotion "to get their messages heard above Viagra's noise." His critique focused on the idea that it was a waste to spend money "encouraging patients to argue with their doctors about brands." He pointed out how much money was being used "to get a patient to a doctor to ask about brand 'X' only to have that physician say that the brand is either inappropriate or not the first choice." It was hardly that writer's goal to minimize sales; the question was how best to facilitate them. The solution, he said, was to convey to consumers that "they have a treatable problem" and motivate them "to seek that treatment." Only then, he said, "individual product teams can use professional promotion to battle for brand share of the newly diagnosed patients in the doctor's office."[176]

A Thing Too Wild

A specific scolding, zeroed in on particular advertisements, came from the FDA in November 2004. This scolding came in the form of a letter to Pfizer that condemned two television ads—of 30 and 15 seconds respectively—as having "misbranded" the product under the Food, Drug, and Cosmetic Act. The longer ad featured a video of a man watching his wife examine a high-heeled shoe in a store with the voiceover "Remember that guy who used to be called 'Wild Thing?'" It also included a man gazing at a black brassiere, panties, and a negligee in a store window with the voiceover, "Remember the one who couldn't resist a little mischief?" The voiceover response, accompanied by trumpet blasts and "blue 'horns' sprout[ing] from behind [the] man's head," was, "Yeah, that guy." Immediately following was the voiceover "He's back," with the horns becoming the "V" in Viagra.[177]

The agency's letter solemnly noted that the ads "make clear that Viagra is intended for sex." The legal basis for the misbranding allegation was that the ads "omit the indication for the drug (namely, treatment of erectile dysfunction) and fail to provide information relating to the major side effects and contraindications of the drug." The letter also referred to the implication of the ads that the man pictured in them had returned to his "previous level of sexual desire and activity," a claim for which the agency said there was no "substantial evidence or substantial clinical experience."[178]

At least two matters deserving comment spin out from the use of television ads for prescription drugs. An obvious point is what gets lost in squeezing into as little as a quarter of a minute a promotional message for a product that has been the subject of 7,000 medical articles. Another, more general issue, concerns the use of direct-to-consumer (DTC) advertising for prescription products. A report on an FDA opinion survey catalogued both benefits and disadvantages of that type of advertising. On the one hand, those messages stimulate consumers to seek information and visit their doctors. On the other hand, both patients and doctors thought that the ads overstated the efficacy of drugs and, as a press report summarized it, did "not present a fair balance of benefit and risk information." It was true that the agency survey did not find that the ads generated more visits to doctors, but it did report that almost half of doctors surveyed felt "at least a little pressure" to prescribe advertised medications.[179]

That ED was big business was evident not only from the sales figures for Viagra and the emerging competition presented by Levitra and Cialis, but from the fact that there were now three different measurement tools for responses to ED treatments. We have referred to the most complicated one, the International Index of Erectile Function, which has a scoring range of from 1 to 30 on a group of questions concerning ability to get and maintain erections. The Sexual Encounter Profile, as a report summarized it, has seven diary questions allowing patients "to record sexual events." The least subtle tool is the Global Assessment Question; as its name indicates, this is a single question, without refinement, to which "even minimal responses will be considered as a yes."[180]

By 2005, it was reported that "more than 750,000 physicians have written a prescription for sildenafil."[181] Research reports continued to come in on the drug. The shadows on vision grew a little darker; if events of this kind were infrequent, they now entered the realms of both public regulation and civil litigation.

A positive summary of the history of Viagra in that year summarized literature on the "safety and efficacy" of the drug in men with cardiovascular disease and congestive heart failure, as well as a variety of other conditions, including Parkinson's disease and kidney failure that required dialysis.[182] This article, two of whose coauthors were Pfizer employees, had something of the tone of a puff piece.[183]

Somewhat less effusively, Thai investigators concluded that "the incidence of adverse cardiovascular events in patients taking sildenafil does not differ from that of the general population."[184] This team did refer, however, to "the increasing incidence of sudden cardiac death in ED patients treated with" Viagra and suggested a need for further research on the effect of the drug on the cardiovascular system.[185]

A Decision Matrix

It had now become possible, given the amount of research on the drug, to develop an analytical decision matrix for treatment. A "consensus conference" in 2004 had approved revised guidelines on "sexual dysfunction and cardiac risk," which proposed a "multi-step process for the assessment and management of cardiovascular risk in patients with ED." The first step was "an assessment of sexual function in . . . initial cardiovascular evaluation . . . to determine the level of risk." The next step included the need to stabilize high-risk patients before they resumed sexual activity or started treatment for ED, with further probing of the risk status of men who at that point had "indeterminate or intermediate risk." Cognizant of the fact that various risk factors for atherosclerotic disease often were risk factors for ED, the guidelines then advocated "routine evaluation of cardiovascular risk factors . . . in patients with ED."[186]

Research on Viagra continued on animals as well as people, and the research on people continued to focus on very specific effects, as well as on uses well beyond that of therapy for ED. One group of researchers found from a study on mice that withdrawal of Viagra after four weeks of use resulted in an upsurge of aggressive behavior. Mice who were taken off the drug had a significantly increased tendency to attack cage mates.[187] The researchers observed, however, that the applicability of these findings to people "remains unclear."[188]

Questions on Discontinuance

On the human front, a subject of some interest was why a significant number of men who had success with Viagra did not continue with the drug. German researchers offered various explanations for data that indicated that about 30 percent of a group of 234 men who found the drug effective did not ask for a second prescription. These researchers said that 45 percent of the men who did not keep using the drug cited the reason as "[l]ack of opportunity or desire for sexual intercourse" and that 23 percent "reported that their partners had shown no sexual interest." Nine percent referred to the cost of the drug. However, the researchers also advanced the common sense rationale that many of the men who discontinued the drug may have drawn sufficient comfort from just the fact that it was available.[189]

Cardiovascular Byproducts

Among the parallel uses for the PDE 5 inhibitors, it was discovered that Viagra had positive effects in treating primary pulmonary hypertension, a use for which the FDA approved the drug.[190] A striking application of this knowledge was the discovery that Viagra produced large increases in the distance that children suffering from pulmonary hypertension could walk—an average of 443 meters, up from an average of 278 meters when they were tested before taking the drug.[191] A negative biochemical twist was the recognition, reflected in Pfizer's labeling information, of the hazard of attacks of low blood pressure in PDE 5 inhibitors used with alpha blockers, which are prescribed for high blood pressure and benign prostatic hyperplasia.[192]

One possible benefit of Viagra under study was protection of heart cells against damage from chemotherapy. Others included potential minimization of neurological effects of liver disease. One study, using Viagra in rats, indicated that the drug "might relieve a rare kidney condition." Another investigation was in progress on the possibility of combatting restricted blood flow to the uterus during pregnancy, and one researcher was doing animal tests as he developed a hypothesis that Viagra could strengthen the hearts of babies who needed surgery for congenital heart defects.[193]

A study at Johns Hopkins indicated that Viagra tended to reduce stress on the heart caused by surges in hormones. Subjects in the research got two injections of dobutamine, described as "a synthetic, adrenalin-like chemical that increases heart rate and pumping strength." Perhaps paradoxically to lay intuition, Viagra cut the heartbeat of these patients by half with the result, as described in a trade publication, of "a smaller increase in blood flow and blood pressure generated by the heart in response to chemical stimulation."[194] Thus, it appeared that a drug famous for helping sexual excitement might functionally be a calmative for people roused to hazardous circulatory conditions by stress.

A drug like Viagra is a continuous font of proposals for more studies. In that sense, the positive things such products do, in addition to the medical benefits they confer, include augmentation of research budgets. Illustrative is an article reporting, among other things, that Viagra had "no significant effect" on blood flow in the middle cerebral artery, nor on resistance indexes in the aorta or in the superior mesenteric artery. However, there was increased systolic flow in bilateral internal carotid arteries, which the researchers theorized "may be responsible for headache." Noting animal tests that showed increased blood flow in the aorta but decreases in the right carotid artery and the left segmental renal artery, the investigators pointed out that there had been only "a limited amount of studies about the side effects" of Viagra on "major vascular structures" like those. These researchers, who thanked Pfizer for "drug support," commented that "further investigations may be necessary for demonstration of the long-term effects of sildenafil use on major vascular structures."[195] A lawyer might ask whether this call for more research would be considered a "material" fact by a physician considering prescription of Viagra or a patient exposed to ads for the product.

Vision Effects, in Sharper Focus

Important emerging news in 2005 concerned effects on vision that pushed beyond the impact on color perception noted in prior years to effects that occasionally included blindness. These events, as they began to occur, posed in stark form the question of how regulators, and the courts, should respond to events attributed to a drug that produces large benefits for many but very serious consequences for a few. A focal point was nonarteritic anterior ischemic optic neuropathy (NAION), which involved a loss of vision. An illustration was a single case report of blindness in one eye involving a dose of 200 mg of Viagra—what the authors of the report termed an "overdose." This patient, a 54-year-old man, had been taking 100-mg doses of the drug two or three times a week for a few months. On the occasion when he took the 200 mg, he had "a sudden and pain-less loss of vision in his left eye." The authors, three of four of whom were based in the Chesterfield Royal Hospital in England, interpreted this event as "the result of increased intraocular pressure . . . superimposed on a state of systemic hypoten-sion . . . both of which are well-known side-effects of sildenafil and were present in this patient." "Speculat[ing]" that Viagra "was responsible for the unique clin-ical scenario," they noted that visual symptoms tended to increase as the dose of Viagra went up, and observed that "[t]here is great potential for self-dosing and overdosing."[196]

Although 2005 seems to be the time when general attention became focused on NAION and Viagra, the phenomenon ran back to 1999. A Minnesota report published in 2005 summarized seven cases of NAION that had been reviewed between 1999 and 2003. All seven patients had at least one risk factor for arte-riosclerosis, such as diabetes or high blood pressure. Some had used Viagra for "months or years" before they suffered a loss of vision—six of the events at issue occurring within 24 hours of taking the drug. This, the authors concluded, "sup-ports an association" between Viagra and NAION.[197] The authors also intimated the problem of underreporting of adverse events in their statement that "ophthal-mologists should ask all men with NAION about the use of sildenafil, given that this information may not be volunteered without specific inquiry." In this connec-tion, they suggested that doctors "report cases of ocular ischemia in patients using sildenafil to the National Registry of Drug-Induced Ocular Side Effects" and also opined that "Pfizer consider investigating this association."[198] As will be noted, Pfizer did respond, but its officials were not the only people who were literally "on the case."

A contemporaneous commentary both noted the "unlikely" nature of such events and suggested the significance of the association, instancing a report ty-ing Cialis to a case of NAION. The comment of these authors was a model of two-sided scientific caution: "men who have suffered an event of NAION in one eye should be cautioned about this association as well as the lack of definite proof of causation so they can make their own informed decisions regarding future usage."[199] A Dutch uncle might have told men who had lost the sight of an eye, "Don't use these drugs any more."

Viagra was, among other things, a symbol of globalization. We have noted research reports from Thailand, Taiwan, Israel, Morocco, and Germany. Now, a Turkish report captured confusion about the effects of Viagra on the eye. This study used 30 subjects, 20 taking Viagra and 10 placebo, to investigate "the effects of a single dose of 100 mg sildenafil on ocular blood flow." The results were mixed with respect to different kinds of flow velocities, some of which were statisti-cally significant whereas others were not.[200] The Turkish investigators found that Viagra "increases the systolic, diastolic and mean blood flow of the ophthalmic and short posterior ciliary arteries in patients with erectile dysfunction," although by contrast with other studies, the drug did not change systemic blood pressure and ocular perfusion pressure.[201] The ordinary consumer might be discomfited to read the Turkish researchers' observation that "the results of different studies are confusing." They did find "importan[t]" the fact that Viagra had "not been found to cause any decrease in ocular blood flow." However, they said that Viagra "may have different effects" in several patient groups, including those "in whom retinal autoregulation is impaired due to cardiovascular risk factors such as arterial hypertension and diabetes," or in patients with several different eye diseases. Not surprisingly, they called for further research on the effects of Viagra "on ocular blood flow in different patient groups."[202]

The sober *Medical Letter* was skeptical about Viagra causing adverse effects on the eye. In a June 2005 issue, it noted that "NAION is an uncommon disorder" and that although "[m]ore than 25 million men have taken *Viagra*, ... no increase in the number of cases of NAION has been reported." It noted some "possible mechanisms" of causation, including the fact that PDE 5 inhibitors "increase local concentrations of nitric oxide" and the "modest effect" of Viagra on systemic blood pressure, both of which could theoretically increase risks to the eye. However, it concluded that "there is no proof of cause and effect."[203]

The Tort Angle

It was about this time, though, that litigation and regulatory action began to focus on ocular effects. In early June 2005, a Texas man brought a class action alleging that Viagra had caused blindness.[204] In mid-June, a New Jersey man sued for loss of vision in one eye.[205] At this writing, in 2007, men with even a whiff of side effects they think might be caused by PDE 5 inhibitors have only to get on the Internet to reach a lawyer. One site says, "Suffered harm from Viagra? You may have a lawsuit. Click here, for a top rated law firm to evaluate your legal rights."[206]

Senatorial Concern and FDA Pressure

Concurrently, allegations of suppression of data began to generate responses in Congress. An FDA safety officer told Congressional investigators that she had discerned the blindness problem in early 2004 and told her supervisors that the agency should give warnings about the phenomenon. By the end of June 2005, Senator Charles Grassley was writing the agency saying that he was "troubled" by its failure to take action on updating the label for Viagra. He quoted the safety officer, who was unidentified, as saying that the agency's Office of New Drugs was "under such time pressure to approve new drugs" that "often safety concerns needed to be 'fit in' where they could."[207] Grassley said that internal FDA documents indicated that Pfizer "resisted the FDA's initial request to update the Viagra label to include information about" the risks of NAION.[208]

Pfizer's 2000 labeling had included a revised sentence under the heading "Effects of Viagra on Vision" that said, "An evaluation of visual function at doses up to twice the maximum recommended dose revealed no effects of Viagra on visual acuity, intraocular pressure, or pupillometry."[209] But under mounting outside pressure, Pfizer said in late June 2005 that it would include warnings on sudden loss of vision in its label for Viagra, as Eli Lilly already had done for Cialis.[210] In early July, the FDA approved updated labeling that required NAION warnings for both drugs and Levitra as well.[211] The agency punctuated this action with an "FDA Alert" that referred to the new labeling. It carefully said, "[w]e do not know at this time if Viagra, Cialis, or Levitra causes NAION," which "also happens in men who do not take these medicines." It listed groups of people at relatively high risk for NAION, including smokers and those with heart disease and high blood pressure, and advised men to "[s]top using Viagra, Cialis, or Levitra if you have a loss in your eyesight" and to "[g]et medical help right away."[212]

Within a month, Pfizer counterattacked. It asserted that a review of post-marketing reports showed "no evidence that Viagra causes blindness or any other serious ocular condition." The company's chief medical officer asserted that "[m]en taking Viagra are at no greater risk for blindness—including vision loss from NAION—than men of similar age and health not taking the medicine." He said that "several studies specifically looking into the effect of Viagra in the eye by Pfizer as well as independent ophthalmologic experts found Viagra to have no serious adverse effects on the eye."[213] But these claims—and even the summer change in labeling—did not satisfy the organization Public Citizen. It petitioned the FDA in October to require a "black box" warning about vision loss and the PDE-5 inhibitors. Public Citizen claimed that Viagra was associated with 48 cases of NAION in the FDA's database of adverse events, 19 percent of the total of those occurrences. It noted that two drugs with fewer adverse reports "had prominent warnings" in their labels already.[214]

Criticism continued, from a number of different points of view. A double-barreled critique—of the prescribing practices of doctors—came from H. George Nurnberg, a psychiatrist at the University of New Mexico. Dr. Nurnberg report-edly told a psychiatric symposium that psychiatrists did not prescribe the PDE 5 drugs enough, although primary care doctors prescribed them "like aspirin to virtually any man who asks."[215] Dr. Nurnberg said that psychiatrists should pre-scribe the drugs to men whose sexual problems were a side effect of antidepres-sant medication, so that these patients would keep taking the antidepressants. By contrast, he declared that for general practitioners to view the drugs "as aspirin for erectile dysfunction" was often to miss the occurrence of sexual dysfunction as a "sentinel marker" for other ailments that were developing in patients, for exam-ple, cardiovascular disease. He said, "If you give the drug and [the patients] get better, that is good, but you have no idea what the etiology is. You have to think about the cause."[216]

Targeting Doctors

The entry of Levitra and Cialis in the field sparked intense competition in marketing, and this competition occurred at a time when sales of the ED drugs had begun to decline. Although all the drugs had significant degrees of success in combating ED, there were some differences. One study, for example, indicated that Levitra was effective in some patients whom Viagra did not help. However, a commentator summarizing the study noted that it "was not a head-to-head trial" and that "[t]herefore, the appropriateness of therapy can be highly individual," concluding that "one can not make assumptions about the efficacy of 1 agent as compared to the other."[217] But even advantages in scientific data did not forestall competitive practices at the edge of medical ethics. Illustrative was an offer by the makers of Levitra to pay doctors $100 for each patient enrolled in a postmarketing study of that drug. Dr. Marcia Angell, former editor of the *New England Journal of Medicine* and a commentator on many medical issues, pointed out that on the basis of the few minutes it would take a doctor to sign up six patients for the study, that would effectively amount to a fee of $600 per hour. The fee, she said, "is a kickback."[218]

Targeting Patients

It has been a time-honored practice for makers of prescription drugs to give free samples to doctors. One competitive ploy in the ED market was to give them to consumers: Eli Lilly began to use its Web site to offer vouchers to consumers for three free Cialis tablets. As a follow-up, consumers could then get three more tablets—either of Cialis or a competing product.[219]

Reflecting the degree of competition were the amounts that the ED drug company spent on advertising—in 2004, amounting to 37 percent of the sales of the three companies, as contrasted with 7 percent for the Ford Motor Company.[220] Pfizer, however, "sharply cut back" on its Viagra ads in 2005, especially after scoldings from the FDA.[221] Global sales for the three drugs were about $2.5 billion in 2004.[222] Viagra had a comfortable lead in the three-way race with a 70 percent market share, but its global sales fell 11 percent in 2004.[223] In October 2005, the number of prescriptions written for the three drugs had fallen off by 10 percent compared with the prior year, with Viagra down 20 percent and Cialis being the only one of the three that increased its sales in that period.[224] Truly, the global sales figures were not paltry. But compared with expectations, they were disappointing: some Wall Street projections had seen Viagra achieving $4.5 billion in sales by 2004.[225]

The potential market still seemed big: there were estimates that only 15 percent of men with some signs of ED had tried one of the drugs.[226] And over the period from 1998, when marketing of Viagra began, to 2002, the market multiplied three times among men aged 18 to 45.[227] However, some critics said that the drugs were oversold to young men. A reporter summarized the views of one sexual medicine specialist as that the drugs made "only a marginal difference" for men under 40; his perhaps strained analogy was that "[i]n many ways, if you have a full tank of gas or half a tank of gas, your car runs equally well." A sex therapist added that some young men were disappointed because they confused the desire for desire itself—which the drugs would not stimulate—with the desire for an erection when they were already aroused.[228] Moreover, despite all the emphasis on sexual prowess in many kinds of media, it appeared that many older men were willing to be content with a celibate state. As a reporter summarized it, men might grow "used to sexless relationships," or their spouses might be "physically unable to have sex," or they simply might no longer be "interested in intercourse."[229]

Long Erections, Long Passes

As the advertising battles continued in a relatively flat market, Lilly took a new tack for Cialis, with what one reporter termed "a soft, relaxed focus on couples and romantic settings." Yet, the theme of the Cialis ads created another regulatory side effect—a special problem that might be characterized as too much of a good thing. Taking advantage of the fact that Cialis could work for more than 36 hours, those ads emphasized "spontaneity": the idea that the drug would provide erections "when the time [is] right." True, the power of Cialis occasionally went out of bounds, causing very long-lived erections known as priapism—an effect that had not been noticed in clinical trials. The result was that just before the 2004 Super Bowl, the FDA required Lilly's Cialis commercials to disclose the possibility of priapism in rare cases, along with the more routine list of headaches, backaches, and upset stomachs. Even so—and despite jokes about four-hour erections by late-night comedians—sales of Cialis increased by two and a half times in the two months after the commercials with a priapism reference were aired during the game.[230]

While the overall sales figures ground slowly through the doldrums, criticism continued about direct to consumer advertising. Interestingly, it was an advertising executive who said that Viagra should focus on insuring that "information about the product is available to doctors should they need it." John O'Shea, managing director of Leo Burnett Singapore, emphasized that "Viagra is a prescription medicine for a medical condition." One way he suggested that marketers could orient themselves to that fact was to employ an "interactive element" on the Internet that would allow doctors to ask questions about the drug. This, he noted, would allow physicians to "log on when it suits them, rather than fit in a visit from a drug rep during a busy day." Commenting on attempts to sell Cialis directly to consumers through e-mail, he said "Frankly, Viagra has to take the position of rising above the competition. Work direct with doctors and get the authority and credibility through them."[231]

A Cluster of Different Realities

In the disagreements thus reflected among marketing experts themselves about strategies, there appeared the intersection of many realities—and of issues about what reality is. One factual element of the puzzle was the existence of two levels of consumers—doctors and patients, in a setting where potent desires of lay consumers could be stoked by advertising. Parallel to that were two sharp edges of consumer autonomy. On one edge was the faith of the market that consumers can decide for themselves what is good for them. On the other was the problem that sometimes consumers lack information essential to rational decision making, in an environment highly conditioned by product promotion.

The rise of the Internet vastly expanded the base of communication to consumers. Complicating the problem was the breadth of the spectrum of consumer sophistication. Further potential complications inhered in the possibility that there was a fairly broad range of sophistication among doctors, with the question arising of how much the average general practitioner knew about the details of product risk. These questions existed in a constantly increasing current of data on developing patterns of risk. Introducing further complexity were disagreements about experts, some of whom were financially beholden to the makers of drugs. Beyond that, we have pointed out that scientists have an interest in marketing themselves—both to potential sources of grants and to other professionals for whom their reputations depend on published discoveries.

We also have noted the vastness of the scientific literature that often surrounds well-advertised products which provide benefits much sought after by consumers. Yet, another element of the problem lies in the expense of the studies that an ideal patient—or regulator—might want conducted about all the biological effects of a drug. As medical journal authors constantly tell us, there is always a need for more research. The issues mentioned in this chapter alone cover many different elements of the heart, the circulation of the blood, the eye, and the mind.

Science can supply averages, and by their nature, averages work well for most people. However, it is clear from many studies of ED, not to mention thousands of studies of other drugs, that responses to particular kinds of medication are highly individualized. Any consumer who watches television knows that a certain percentage of people who take prescription drugs will have side effects, but statistical common sense—as well as hope—will tell him that it probably will not happen to him. Surely, the power of media in promoting sales cannot be ignored. One story with a hilarious thread is the stoking of the demand for Cialis by the Super Bowl ads that first publicized the risk of priapism.

The theme of individualization runs through a wide range of human stories that spans the consumer population. Here is the lawyer who feels that sexual encounters with new partners are like bar exams. Here is the man who says that dying during the sex act is as good a way to go out as any. Here is the man for whom intercourse is no longer the goal he may once have frantically sought—but for whom just the availability of the ED drug may be a comfort. Probably most of the members of the potential customer population for these drugs do not know that there is an International Index for Erectile Dysfunction, and many might be amused to find out that there is. In any event, by the very nature of the scientific enterprise, all those who venture to take the drugs have been, wittingly or not, experimental animals.

Finally, there exists an issue that daily presents itself in many aspects of our lives. How do we weigh the risks—sometimes clear and sometimes not so clear—of products or activities that confer substantial benefits? How capable are even the most mathematically minded among us of comparing a 98 percent chance of a pleasing sexual experience against a range of relatively low percentage risks to the heart, the eye, and the erectile organ itself? These questions simply pile on the issues of how well regulation brings out information about risks and how well the market for information works.

CHAPTER 5

Estrogens: A Gathering of Data, a Gathering Storm

Twenty-nine years ago, I concluded a book titled *A Nation of Guinea Pigs* by pointing out that it was then "not yet twenty years since a young woman bought from her neighborhood druggist a vial of the Pill."[1] In the generation since then, the neighborhood drugstore has pretty much faded into oblivion. And, although the twenty-first century began with litigation in the United Kingdom over injuries from oral contraceptives,[2] the rocketing pace of scientific and commercial change has pushed the birth control pill into the background of medication risks that concern American women.

With the expansion of our cornucopia of consumer products, the experimental society that is the United States—and indeed all industrialized nations—pushes inexorably onward with not only clinical tryouts, but mass testing of products on human beings. This occurs across the spectrum of consumer goods. A striking case in point is that of estrogens, prescribed to postmenopausal women over a period of more than 60 years. During that time, scientists suggested that these hormones were a panacea that prevented hot flashes, reduced the ravages of osteoporosis, and even decreased the risk of heart disease. Their manufacturers hawked them for those purposes. In 2002, however, a series of research reports indicated that many of the claims made for these drugs may not have been well founded and that indeed estrogens might even be increasing certain kinds of serious risks.

The story of postmenopausal estrogens is a complicated one, with many players, and featuring many arguments among them. Research scientists contend with each other about biological facts. Regulators fence with manufacturers. Practicing physicians, sometimes quarreling with their own patients, join the argument with researchers. Patients argue with themselves about choices of health and lifestyle. In the background, the mass media serve as questioners and provocateurs.

Early History

The Flower Blooms, Some Clouds Form

The story of the use of estrogens as a palliative for symptoms that afflict women after menopause is a long-running classic of market experimentation. It is an example of how a drug takes on an aura of wonder for one use after initially being developed for quite another. It shows how an increasing flow of scientific information boosts the qualities of a drug in the public mind, at the same time that some data about it arouse fears. The story continues with the rekindling of the vogue for the drug. Then, new storm clouds come up that cast shadows on the product, after expensive major studies delve further into its biological effects. And even more confusingly overlapping these developments, scientists who reanalyze the data find encouraging signs for some patients while warning others to stay clear of the product. This rendering of the story seeks to capture it as it appeared to both prescribers and patients over two full generations.

The birth of estrogen replacement therapy occurred in an odd way. It was part of a search that, in one way or another, has gone on for millennia—and indeed is a sibling of the subject of Chapter 4: the search for male potency. Reportedly, in the 1930s, Dr. Serge Voronoff engaged in that quest by implanting monkey testicles into the scrotums of men.[3]

It was in 1942 that the Canadian company Ayerst introduced the first conjugated estrogen, which it named Premarin. Approved by the FDA that year for the treatment of menopausal symptoms and related conditions,[4] this product is made from the urine of pregnant horses. It is remarkable that this now famous and widely sold product—sales for the Premarin family of products were more than $2 billion in 2001[5]—should be literally a natural product. It was, indeed, so natural that in a 1997 "backgrounder," the FDA explained that the active ingredients of Premarin had "not yet been confidently defined" and for that reason it could not approve a generic synthetic version.[6]

Specialized, simplified histories of estrogen replacement therapy (ERT) reveal relatively little controversy on the subject through the 1940s and 1950s. A publication of the Hormone Foundation, which describes itself as the "public education affiliate of the Endocrine Society," says that in the 1950s, Ayerst instituted a "massive education campaign for physicians that focuses on menopause, menopausal symptoms and the consequences of estrogen loss."[7] A study published in 1953 summarized research indicating that estrogen would inhibit atherogenesis—the formation of plaques in the arteries, at least in young roosters.[8] One landmark event involving a type of estrogen was the FDA's granting of approval to Searle in 1957 to sell the company's Enovid product as therapy for menstrual disorders. In 1960, the FDA approved large-scale testing of Enovid as a contraceptive.[9]

Feminine Forever

An important popular document in the history of estrogen treatments was Dr. Robert Wilson's book, *Feminine Forever*,[10] published in 1966. Wilson postulated that menopause was effectively a form of castration, with pervasive biological effects that "amount[] to a mutilation of the whole body."[11] Invoking his use of conjugated natural estrogens on "thousands of women,"[12] he claimed that estrogenic therapy gave "[e]very woman alive today" the "option of remaining feminine forever."[13] Premising that "[a] woman's body is the key to her fate," in terms of "her ability to attract a suitable male and to hold his interest over many years,"[14] Wilson asserted that "the twentieth century has produced a cultural climate that puts a premium on femininity."[15]

Wilson's claims were far-reaching. At their broadest, they asserted that estrogen treatment could prevent menopause.[16] Flatly declaring that "[m]enopause is curable,"[17] Wilson wrote that "[i]n the vast majority of cases, the distressing bodily changes following menopause are reversible through estrogen treatment"[18] and that it was "now possible to restore full femininity even to women long past menopause."[19]

As he invited "all women to share" the "great adventure of preserving or regaining your full femininity,"[20] Wilson was at pains to assure his readers that estrogens did not "predispose" women "toward cancer," insisting that "[t]he truth is exactly the opposite." He posited as the "most likely explanation" for this effect that "estrogen therapy, by restoring menstruation in post-menopausal women maintains one of the most important features of internal hygiene," in effect "wash[ing] away" "[c]ongested tissues," which he called "a possible starting point for cancer."[21] He even went so far as to declare that "[t]he myth that estrogen is a causative factor in cancer has been proven to be entirely false."[22] Such was Wilson's certitude about propositions later cast in doubt that he associated himself with Galileo as a persecuted heretic.[23] And such was the cultural climate he described that the fad for estrogen gained strength for a generation.

A Best-Seller

During the 1960s, the use of ERT for postmenopausal symptoms increased to what reportedly was 12 percent of all postmenopausal women. Indeed, by 1966, Premarin became the "#1 dispensed drug in America."[24] The use for post-menopausal symptoms of hormone replacement therapy (HRT), which combines progestin with estrogen, began during that decade.

Science Identifies an Initial Set of Risks

The Cancer Question, Softly

Yet, under all of this marketing success, there was concern about the hypothesis that estrogens caused cancer in women, an effect that had been observed in laboratory animals[25] and which had generated "quite pronounced" fears in the 1930s.[26] A more soothing message, although one qualified by a reference to the limitations of data, came in 1971 from a Vanderbilt University group that focused on breast cancer. These researchers, who surveyed 511 women who had taken estrogens after hysterectomies, concluded that there was "no evidence to support a stand that estrogens contribute to incidence of mortality from mammary cancer."[27] The investigators, who credited a grant from Ayerst for aiding their research, noted that the cases of breast cancer that did occur in their study group tended to develop "10 years later than the cancers in an unselected population group."[28]

Another Vanderbilt study, published in 1973 and aided by a grant from Ayerst, analyzed 713 women who had "been maintained on long-term Premarin therapy" after having hysterectomies. A dozen of these women developed breast cancer while on Premarin—a number that the authors suggested was low. Overall, "[t]here was no increase in mammary cancer" and "[a]ctually there seems to be a delay of some 5 years in onset." The authors thought there could "be little doubt that this group of women had a markedly lower incidence of all cancers and enjoys a much lower mortality rate than one would be led to expect from the available population data." Though carefully couched in its scientific assessments, the article closed with something that sounded like a commercial. Indicating that they were continuing to study this group of women, the authors said that "for the immediate future we must accept the fact that these women are remaining young both physically and emotionally which is reflected in their outlook."[29]

A contemporaneous set of studies that focused on oral contraceptives, summarized by Johns Hopkins University researchers, showed "no evidence that administration of female hormones is associated with the development of breast cancer."[30] That report implicitly referred to the expense involved in meaningful clinical trials: the authors noted that those studies involved 283 cases of breast cancer and 583 control subjects—and that each of these studies numbered "about one twentieth the size required to secure an answer to the question with the indicated degree of accuracy."[31]

Other research reports and analyses in the early 1970s foreshadowed what was to become a war over the endocrine systems of middle-aged women. For the moment, though, there were just hints of battles to come.

Cancer, Some Worries

The encouraging reports did not go unchallenged. Illustrative was a comment in a discussion session on the Vanderbilt paper at the 1972 annual meeting of the Southern Surgical Association. The commentator was George B. Sanders, a Louisville physician who referred to treating three women with inflammatory breast cancer in the past year, all of whom had been taking estrogen. He raised a number of methodological questions about the study, including questions about the treatments of study subjects relative to the type of cancer they had and the question of whether estrogens were continued in patients diagnosed with noninvasive cancer. This physician declared that "the picture described in this paper is at variance with what we know about the clinical occurrence and behavior of mammary cancer in women and especially" in a particular mouse that had been "considered a valid model of the disease in humans." He opined that "it may not be proper to correlate the incidence of mammary cancer in a closed, controlled, small patient population of 700 women with the observed incidence of mammary cancer in the general population at large." He stressed that he did not think that "any of us feel that estrogen *causes* mammary cancer" but hypothesized that "under favorable circumstances," estrogen was one of "several factors" that probably provided "impetus" for the disease to become "clinically active and invasive."[32]

A particular portent in this discussion was a remark by another Louisville doctor, Laman A. Gray. Taking note of the potential significance of only 12 cases of breast cancer in the Vanderbilt study's data, Dr. Gray related that three years previously, he had "presented 21 cases of cancer of the breast in 1200 women who had been receiving estrogen for an average period of 8 years." He noted that more than two years before the time of this discussion, "Dr. Brian MacMahon [sic], the Professor of Epidemiology at Harvard School of Public Health," had "brought in patients repeatedly for me to reexamine" as part of a study whose subjects now numbered 2,040. Dr. Gray said that the McMahon group told him "that in 3 months they will punch the button and tell me whether this is statistically accurate or not."[33]

Other studies in the same year, 1972, yielded a spectrum of opinions. An article reviewing the literature, in which one author reviewed the incidence of breast cancer in 4,900 of his private patients, declared that there had been no "reported increase in the incidence of breast cancer" since the advent of estrogens for menopausal therapy. The authors concluded that "[t]he evidence at hand does not suggest that the administration of estrogens, in the presently accepted preparations and usage, plays a role in the etiology of human breast cancer."[34] The author of a contemporary study, reviewing pathology files of 240 patients with breast cancer, concluded that he could "identify no specific microscopic changes" revealing an association of "exogenous estrogens" and breast cancer.[35] This analyst, Robert Fechner, also said that "controlled studies have shown no convincingly distinctive appearance in the breast tissue of women taking oral contraceptives, including women with breast cancer."[36] He noted that such "distinctive patterns" had, by contrast, been found in the endometrium and endocervix of "women treated with progestin-estrogen mixtures as found in oral contraceptives."[37] He acknowledged that his findings, and the literature, did not "preclude an effect of exogenous estrogens on the breast" but said that any such effect would "have to be determined by other than morphological methods."[38]

A somewhat contrasting conclusion appeared in another morphology study published in the same year, which began with a technical analysis of just three women with breast cancer who had taken oral contraceptives, finding "several features in common" among these women. Although the authors did not draw causal conclusions from this, they did cite other studies for the proposition that "estrogens and progestins are in some instances capable of stimulating metastases of carcinomas of the breast" and indicated that this "conceivably" could lead to a determination that those hormones "may play a similar role regarding the corresponding primary lesion."[39]

A Complex Puzzle

At the same time, an argument occurred in the *British Medical Journal* about a phenomenon involving breast cancer and estrogens that would seem odd, at least to a layperson. This was that estrogen, which sometimes reportedly stimulated the progression of breast cancer, would cause breast cancers to regress in other patients. Thus, estrogen was sometimes used therapeutically in efforts to defeat the disease. The biological mechanisms appear to be complex. Illustratively, Dr. Basil Stoll, a London radiotherapist, referred to data indicating that *"the level of oestrogen dosage at which tumour stimulation is replaced by inhibition tends to decrease with increasing age of the patient."*[40] Just one piece of the puzzle lay in the stimulation by high doses of estrogen of the release of prolactin, the hormone secreted by the pituitary gland that itself stimulates milk production, in postmenopausal women. Stoll noted that "the effect of such therapy is often to inhibit the growth of breast cancer."[41] The paradoxical conclusion was that

> [o]n the assumption that both prolactin and oestrogen are required for maintaining the growth of hormone-sensitive breast cancer there are two ways by which the same tumour can be made to regress—one by depriving it of both prolactin and oestrogen so far as possible by endocrine ablation, and the other by increasing the level of the two hormones at the target as a result of high-dosage oestrogen therapy.[42]

Two commentators, P. Garcia-Webb and M. H. Briggs, raised several opposing points. Among these was that the stimulation of prolactin production by estrogen was "based on an experiment in rats and unpublished findings in man." Another was that "[t]he statement that a tumour might be inhibited by both an absence and a gross excess of oestrogen" was "difficult to understand." Even if this were true, these writers said, "it would again be evidence in favor of at least two clones" in a patient, "one sensitive to oestrogen lack and the other sensitive to oestrogen excess."[43] Their suggestion was that "the theory of different clones within one tumour or its metastases adequately explains variable responses to endocrine manipulation."[44]

With respect to the difficulties facing regulators, perhaps the most meaningful comment of Garcia-Webb and Briggs was an understated, and obvious, one: "we agree that breast cancer response to hormones is a most complex subject."[45] If commentators with such a degree of technical command were puzzling about causation, what was a regulator to do—and how were practicing physicians and their patients to make decisions? One answer, as is the case for many profiles of drug experimentation on a large scale, was to wait a while—perhaps a generation—for more data to accumulate.

As we move to an analysis of the FDA's approval of estrogens for menopausal women, it is worth noting an observation made by Robert Fechner, a physician quoted earlier, who could find no evidence of an association of breast cancer with estrogens. This observation emerged from the need to get information from a group of patients about their use of estrogens. Dr. Fechner noted that "women taking either oral contraceptives or estrogens often do not view these medications as drugs" and therefore "may give a negative response when asked the nonspecific question: 'Are you taking any medications?'"[46] In our analysis of the regulatory response to these hormones, it seems remarkable that people who are ingesting products that alter their endocrine systems do not recognize them as medications.

An FDA Approval

It was in July of 1972 that the FDA gave its blessing to the use of estrogens for "menopausal syndrome." The agency's notice in the Federal Register classified "short-acting estrogens," including Ayerst's Premarin, as "indicated for replacement therapy of estrogen deficiency associated with" several ailments or syndromes, including "[m]enopausal syndrome."[47] The agency also rated "long-acting estrogens," including Ayerst's Estradurin, as indicated for that syndrome.[48] The only explicit "warning[]" for either preparation was in the statement that "the use of estrogen in pregnancy is not recommended."[49]

Parallel Development with the Pill

The case of oral contraceptives was running on a parallel track. The association of the Pill with blood-clotting diseases—at least with the estrogen content the Pill had in the 1960s—had first been documented in 1968 by the British investigators W. H. Inman and Martin Vessey. They wrote that "[o]n balance, it seems reasonable to conclude that the risk of death from pulmonary embolism, during one year's treatment with oral contraceptives is of the same order as the comparable risk of bearing one child."[50] In 1970, after some spirited skirmishes on the issue of blood clots, the FDA decided to require a 150-word package insert directed at patients that referred to "abnormal blood clotting which can be fatal" as the "most serious known side effect" of the Pill. The agency also noted that patients could get from their doctors an 800-word consumer pamphlet about the product.[51]

By 1975, a study led by Inman and Dr. J. I. Mann found an increase in heart attack deaths in Pill users, statistics they characterized as "helpful" in providing a "crude estimate of risk of death."[52] There was at least tentative agreement on the proposition that it was unwise for women who smoked or had other risk factors, like high blood pressure, to use the Pill. A Boston University researcher found risk statistics "reassuring" from a "public-health perspective" for women aged 30 to 39 and said it was "a matter of opinion" whether it was an acceptable risk for women over 40 to use the Pill. But he found troubling the data on the synergy of the Pill with other risk factors and concluded that there was "convincing evidence" that "oral contraceptives cause thrombosis through the vascular tree."[53]

The data on the association of the Pill with clotting diseases and with heart attacks—especially with other risk factors—lay in the background when a pair of reports, published in 1975, focused on an association between endometrial cancer and the use of estrogens during and after menopause. One research team found a "completely unadjusted relative risk of 4.5" for such cancers for women who had estrogen therapy contrasted with those who did not. After adjustment for year and age of diagnosis, that risk factor was 7.5. The researchers noted that the risk was highest for women who had no "'classic' predisposing signs" for cancer. Although saying there were some variables that needed testing, this group found a "credible argument for a causative role of exogenous estrogen in the development of endometrial cancer."[54]

Another study, by Harry K. Ziel and William R. Finkle, reported a risk factor of 7.6 for endometrial cancer in users of estrogen.[55] An editorial commentator suggested that there was much research to be done on many aspects of the question and noted that more than 99 percent of women taking estrogens postmenopausally did not have endometrial cancer. However, he said there was "no question" that menopausal and postmenopausal users who had their uteruses should be checked "quite closely" for the disease.[56] Another commentator soberly added that estrogens had come into "a category of pharmacologic agents that must be used with extreme care," when one considered the "putative" risk of endometrial cancer along with the hazards of clotting diseases, stroke, and heart disease associated with that class of hormones.[57]

A Recommended Warning

By the end of 1975, the hazards of menopausal estrogens had moved into the public spotlight. The FDA's Advisory Committee on Obstetrics and Gynecology recommended that the agency require "strong warnings" to physicians and package inserts for patients on the risk of endometrial cancer. The committee said that the drugs should be approved "only for conditions for which effectiveness has been proven," a category that reportedly included "hot flashes." The committee report also urged lower dosages of the hormones because of data on increased risks of endometrial cancer as dosages increased. It also said that the drugs should be given on "a stop-and-start basis, and discontinued occasionally to detect the need for their continued use, if any, or to consider decreasing the dose."[58] An editorial in the British journal *Lancet* said that until there was more definitive evidence on long-term use of hormones for estrogen replacement, "the only possible recommendation" for candidates for such medication was that they "should have a hysterectomy." Accompanying this emphatic, even startling, recommendation was the terse comment that this was "not a very attractive prospect if the eventual aim is treatment of entire populations."[59]

In early 1976, Ziel and Finkle added a new report of their research, pointing out that of 94 patients they surveyed with endometrial cancer, the disease "appeared five years earlier on the average in postmenopausal women who received estrogen" than in those who did not. Among their other findings on postmenopausal women in their group, "70 per cent of the patients with endometrial cancer had received estrogen," a "sharp contrast" with "23 per cent of . . . control subjects." They also noted that 63 percent "of the postmenopausal patients had received conjugated estrogens."[60] This article ended in a kind of lecture unusual in research journals, aimed at "[t]he endocrinologist who gives estrogen as treatment for the menopause." The authors asserted that "[h]is patient is readily deluded by her wish to preserve her figure and by her physician's implication that estrogen promises eternal youth" (*Feminine Forever* had been published a decade before). Reverting to more dispassionate terminology, the lecture continued with a standard notation that "[i]n a rational approach to therapy, risk is weighed against benefit," pointing out that "[i]n long-term estrogen replacement therapy, particularly where estrone is used, risk may outweigh benefit." It concluded that the authors' data "strongly suggest an association" of endometrial cancer with the administration of estrogens.[61]

The Law Steps In

Public Controversy on Endometrial Cancer

The FDA Commissioner, Alexander Schmidt, told a joint hearing of two Senate committees in January 1976 that a description of Premarin by its maker Ayerst was "misleading and irresponsible." He cited an Ayerst letter's omission of findings about the risks of endometrial cancer in a document that he described as simply "inform[ing] physicians that a controversy has arisen regarding the findings of recent studies."[62]

By this time, the Department of Drugs of the AMA had begun to worry not only about patients but about the potential liability of doctors. In early March 1976, the *American Medical News* reported that "numerous calls" had come into the department from "anxious physicians." An AMA attorney gave the kind of answer that infuriates nonlawyers who want to know about the law, just as it vexes nonphysicians who want definitive answers about their medical situation. Speaking on the assumption that the FDA would be strengthening warnings for the products, she said, "we can't answer [doctors] if they will be held liable for the occurrence of cancer in patients who take the drug after the label change is made." However, she noted, "[p]hysicians can be held liable for not keeping abreast of literature on the dangerous effects of drugs and not fully informing patients of the dangers."[63] Just a couple of weeks later, without waiting for the publication of formal regulations, the FDA issued a warning to doctors about the risk of endometrial cancer. This document repeated the charge that the maker was "irresponsible."[64]

Another issue concerning estrogens and cancer—one that would carry forward for three decades—came into focus in an article concerning breast cancer published in August 1976. Its authors described findings that "clearly indicate that menopausal estrogen use does not protect against breast cancer"[65] and raised questions about the possibility that the hormones caused the disease. These researchers did not identify a causal connection. However, they did note a group of statistics that might "be cause for concern." It was clear enough that women who had confirmed benign breast disease were at higher risk for breast cancer than women without such disease—"about twice that of the general population."[66] Beyond that, "[t]he risk among women with disease diagnosed after they started taking estrogen is seven times greater than that of the general population." One hypothesis was that "benign disease and breast cancer are part of one response to an estrogenic stimulus—at least among some women."[67]

Warnings, More Pointed

The accumulation of evidence on endometrial cancer drove the FDA to issue new regulations in September 1976 on the labeling for estrogens. Leading the labeling directed to doctors was a boxed warning with the heading, *"Estrogens Have Been Reported to Increase the Risk of Endometrial Cancer."*[68]

The agency also proposed patient package labeling for the drugs. Under a subhead in this labeling, titled "THE DANGERS OF ESTROGENS," was a reference to the "increased risk of *endometrial cancer*" when estrogens were "used in the postmenopausal period for more than a year." Giving statistics on the incidence of endometrial cancer with and without the product, the proposed labeling italicized the conclusions that *"it is important to take estrogens only when you really need them"* and that *"it is important to take the lowest dose of estrogen that will control symptoms and to take it only as long as it is needed."*[69] In a release sent out at the same time, Commissioner Schmidt sounded a consumer-choice note. He said that the agency's purpose was "to keep these drugs on the market but to reduce overuse and misuse." He added that the agency "believes it essential that women be informed and that they decide for themselves if the risks are worth the benefits."[70]

Within the month, Ayerst began to comply. An advertisement in the *American Medical News* mentioned the risks of Premarin in the specific context of women who had had their ovaries removed—although it cloaked those risks with a positive mantle. The ad started with the headline, "Surgical Menopause," with the added phrase "The sign . . ." accompanied by a picture of a surgical scar. The next page had a color picture of a fairly young looking woman with a child clinging to her neck, accompanied by the words "without the symptoms." The Warnings section included brief statistical summaries of the risks of endometrial cancer as revealed in three studies.[71]

The Doctors Reply

The American College of Obstetricians and Gynecologists (ACOG) weighed in with a counter-cautionary message. The *American Medical News* reported that ACOG had "warned against 'hasty and ill-conceived termination' of estrogen replacement therapy for symptomatic postmenopausal women." The report quoted ACOG as saying that "no firm conclusions are warranted regarding the carcinogenicity of estrogens," although the organization also said doctors should use caution in evaluating patients' needs for the product and their health status.[72]

Cancer Risks, Identified and Potential

In the summer of 1977, the FDA settled the issue, issuing a final rule on patient labeling. It specified, as the first listed risk, "[e]ndometrial carcinoma," saying that "[t]he importance of minimizing dose and duration of use is to be stressed, as is the importance of using estrogens only when necessary." The rule also referred to risks of "[o]ther possible cancer," mentioning specifically that women with breast nodules or "a family history of breast cancer" should be given "[s]pecial attention."[73] The Commissioner said, in explaining the rule, that he believed that it was "ultimately the patient's decision whether she wishes to take estrogens."[74] He said that risks, including endometrial cancer and birth defects, "must not only be carefully considered by physicians . . . but also by patients."[75]

The same set of FDA documents introduced an attack on another prescription front, the use of estrogens to reduce breast engorgement in mothers who had recently given birth. At this point, the agency was tentative on the issue, saying that patient labeling should include the information that "[t]he dose of estrogen needed to prevent pain and swelling of the breasts is much larger than the dose needed to treat symptoms of the menopause" and that this could increase the risk of blood clots.[76]

Early in 1978, a report of the FDA's Obstetrics and Gynecology Advisory Committee turned the agency to a harsher stance, puncturing what had become a doctors' myth. The agency referred to a report concluding that the evidence did not justify "the feeling" that had been "perpetuated" among doctors that estrogens were effective for breast engorgement, saying that there were "no data . . . available that demonstrate a substantial lasting effect of estrogens when used for this purpose." As the agency summarized it, its committee "concluded that the available evidence does not support the safety and effectiveness of estrogens for the treatment of postpartum breast engorgement." Emphasizing the risk of blood clots, the agency thus proposed "to withdraw approval of new drug applications for estrogen-containing drug products that are labeled for use in postpartum breast engorgement."[77]

Consumer Choice Spotlighted

In 1979, a "consensus report" of a conference on menopausal estrogens organized by the National Institutes of Health stressed that the decision was a personal one for patients, advised by their physicians. The report said that what was "critical" was "the value that each individual patient applies to balancing out her symptoms, expectations for optimizing health and well-being, and her willingness to sustain varied risks in the process." The chairman of the conference, Dr. Kenneth Ryan of the Boston Hospital for Women, introduced a particular note for realism about the nature of consumer choice. A press report summarized him as saying that "women these days tend to choose doctors who support their own views" on whether or not to take the hormones.[78] An FDA report that year had suggested that overall, women were becoming more risk averse about the products, estimating a decline of more than 25 percent in the use of estrogens for menopausal and postmenopausal symptoms from 1975—the year research reports began to cluster on the risk of endometrial cancer—through 1977.[79]

Benefits Discerned

An interesting pairing of risks and benefits—specifically, the risk of breast cancer and the benefit of bone protection–appeared in 1980. This was a study of retirement communities totaling more than 30,000 residents, focusing on 131 breast cancer patients and twice that number of women who did not have that disease. Among women with intact ovaries who took the equivalent of 1.25 mg of conjugated estrogens for three years, the researchers found an "excess risk of breast cancer" of two and one half times, with "some decrease in risk" in women who had had their ovaries removed. The researchers suggested that the risk-benefit tradeoff became more favorable at dosages of half 0.625 mg or less.[80]

On the benefits side of the ledger was a study indicating that women who used estrogen for five years or more had a risk of fracture of hips or forearms that was "only about 40 to 50 percent of that of a nonuser"—findings that were solid in age groups from 50 to 74 years and identical for those who took the 1.25-mg pills and those who took half that dosage.[81] These reductions in fracture risk, the authors noted, were "quantitatively smaller than the added incidence ... of endometrial cancer" in women with intact uteruses. However, there were no data available on the possible benefits in reduction of vertebral fractures. Until data could be collected on that and other possible health benefits, the authors concluded, "the decision to use these drugs on a long-term basis will remain an uncertain one for many women."[82] Thus, as in many walks of life, uncertainty meets, and confuses, consumerism.

Estrogens Go to Court

In the time of Andrew Jackson, Tocqueville observed that most political questions in America tend to become judicial issues.[83] In 1980, that is what happened with the question of menopausal estrogens. That year, the Pharmaceutical Manufacturers Association and a flock of physicians' associations sued the FDA, claiming it had gone beyond its legal power in requiring patient labeling for estrogens. The courts were not sympathetic. Federal District Judge Walter Stapleton of Delaware saw patients as the principal patrons of information about drug risks. He characterized the medical plaintiffs as "urg[ing] recognition" not of doctors' rights "to exercise judgment in prescribing treatment," but "rather of a right to control patient access to information." Reviewing case law on physicians' rights to practice medicine, cited by the plaintiffs to support their case, he declared that the rights recognized in those decisions "were only those necessary to facilitate the exercise of a right which patients were found to possess." Doctors' rights discussed in those cases, he stressed, were "thus derivative of patient rights and do not exist independent of those rights."[84]

Judge Stapleton cited the FDA Commissioner's rejection of the argument that patient labeling "would cause unnecessary anxiety to some." The Commissioner had referred to patient labeling for oral contraceptives as suggesting "that patient experience with drug therapy, rather than written information, primarily determines discontinuance of drug therapy" and noted that patients were "consistently referred to their physician so that decision can be made in the context of appropriate medical advice."[85] Judge Stapleton concluded that the Commissioner's "explication of [his] reasoning" was persuasive that the regulation of patient labeling was "the product of a rational process."[86]

The judge further nailed down his conclusion with the statement that "the Commissioner was entitled to make a forecast" about "possible patient reaction to the labeling information" "without supporting clinical data or expert opinion." The issue, he said, was one about which the Commissioner could make a "rational judgment" on the basis of his "specific knowledge of the information to be conveyed and his general knowledge of human nature."[87] The Third Circuit affirmed in a brief opinion that focused in part on the FDA's statutory authority to ban the "misleading" advertising of prescription drugs.[88] Citing the 1975 studies on endometrial cancer—which the district court had done[89]—the appellate court noted that the FDA had "found that, without the patient package insert, the estrogen labeling was 'misleading' because it failed to reveal facts" about the consequences of taking the drug under normal use.[90]

Lessons of an Early Lawsuit

A fairly accurate harbinger of developing risks concerning a product category appears when trial lawyers show interest in the product. One indicator of lawyers' interest in menopausal estrogens was an item in a regular feature of the *Personal*

Injury Newsletter titled "Lawyers' Medical Report." That article simply summarized medical literature on the risks and benefits of estrogens.[91]

One of the first cases brought on behalf of an estrogen user foundered on a combination of the plaintiff's own conduct and the statute of limitations. This plaintiff took Premarin for six years by refilling a prescription that the original prescribing doctor said "should have required renewal every six months." She saw that physician for the last time a year and three months after she began taking the drug, and on that occasion he did not renew her prescription, but she kept filling it. After six years of taking the hormone, she was advised to discontinue it when she was hospitalized for another purpose. Finding the plaintiff's claim barred by the statute of limitations, the court rejected her argument that she fell under the exception to the statute for "continuous treatment." The court said that exception had "no application to a situation in which the patient undertakes self treatment by continuing use of a drug prescribed many years before, long after she has discontinued treatment by the prescribing doctor."[92] The case does not focus on the merits of the drug, but it is interesting because it reveals the spectrum of knowledge and judgment of the mass of drug consumers—and the inclination of many to treat themselves.

As usually is the case when the calculus of drug hazards and benefits becomes a focus of public as well as scientific interest, research continued to flow out of laboratories. And as is often the case, research results confirmed the complexity of the interaction between many systems in the human body and the complicated molecules introduced into the body by drugs. Estrogens—as they had been for decades and would be for decades to come—were a vehicle of continued human experimentation.

Research on a Spectrum of Risks and Benefits

Combining Progestogens

An evolving set of clinical experiments involved the use of the hormones called progestogens in the same pill as estrogens, to "oppose" some of the dangerous effects of estrogens. The biochemical puzzle was a complicated one indeed, as is evident in two studies published in the *New England Journal of Medicine* in 1981. In March of that year, one trio of researchers focused on the effects of progestogens on high-density lipoprotein (HDL) cholesterol. Increases in that so-called "good" cholesterol, which are fostered by estrogen replacement therapy, are "negatively correlated with coronary heart disease." That, by itself, is clearly beneficial, but—as had been demonstrated already—estrogens by themselves "markedly increase[] the risk" of endometrial cancer. The combination of progestogens with estrogens appeared to "offset this risk."[93] But, as is apparent throughout this book, such benefits often do not come costlessly.

In this case, the difficulty lay in the fact that "progestogens may increase the risk of coronary heart disease and other arteriosclerotic complications"—which happens with the "prolonged use of oral contraceptives" that now combine the two kinds of hormones. What the investigators set out to do was test three different kinds of progestogens (progestins are the synthetic product) in hormone therapy. They found that adding two kinds of progestins—that is, norethindrone acetate and norgestrel—had the undesirable effect of decreasing the HDL levels boosted by estrogen. But one—medroxyprogesterone acetate—at least did not cause a "significant drop" in HDL cholesterol levels, even though it kept those levels from going up, as they would have if women took estrogen alone.[94] This was a particularized example of the deep well of complexity that powerful drug treatments present with respect to both the body of the human animal herself and her choices among families of drugs.

What Can a Layperson Know?

As we describe these mass-market experiments, the reader must consider how a layperson would react to their results; the question insistently poses itself how a layperson can choose among alternatives when the data are so technical. Accentuating this point with respect to consumer choice on risk-benefit tradeoffs was an article published in the *New England Journal* in late 1981 by London researchers who focused on norethindrone and norgestrel. These investigators found that those hormones reduced the adverse biochemical effects of estrogen on the endometrium—which they determined by taking endometrial tissue from research subjects. Their study used Premarin as the estrogen, in both 1.25 mg and 0.625 doses. The researchers acknowledged that a reduction of the dosage to 0.3 mg might reduce the amount of stimulation estrogens gave to the endometrium. However, they pointed out that this would lose the effects of suppressing hot flashes and conserving bone mass—principal reasons for women to take estrogens. They recommended, therefore, the addition of progestins to the treatment of women taking estrogens. They concluded by noting that "[o]ther progestins," like medroxyprogesterone—the hormone used in the study previously described that did not significantly reduce HDL cholesterol levels—might "have beneficial effects on the endometrium without causing adverse changes in lipid concentrations."[95]

But a woman who was privy to the most modern currents of clinical experimentation, and sensitive to the many complications that tend to arise from the introduction of hormones into the body, might ask, "Is there anything more I need to know?" And the answer was yes. An editorial in the very same issue of the *New England Journal of Medicine*, commenting on the study by the London team, offered "a word of caution." This was that although "progestin may reduce the risk of endometrial carcinoma, the addition of progestin may be tantamount to the addition of oral contraceptives to the treatment of postmenopausal women," which required one to think about "a more serious risk than the relatively low risk of endometrial carcinoma." This was, indeed, a group of risks—blood clots, heart attacks, and stroke. And if the "possibility" of those effects were increased, then "the risk to life will be greater than it will be if cancer of the uterus is diagnosed early."[96]

This suggestion itself provides a striking example of the breadth of market experimentation with drugs—the continuing employment of clinical trials while products are on the general market. In a world in which the FDA had extolled the principle of consumer sovereignty, one could pose two questions. In this complicated biomedical landscape, where the experts themselves were trying out ideas, how was the presumably sovereign patient to choose? And what was a regulator to do?

Caution: Do the Minimum

As research on estrogens progressed, the AMA House of Delegates essentially codified what the FDA had already done. In December 1981, the House of Delegates issued recommendations that said, as a press report summarized it, that "[e]strogens should be used only for responsive indications, in the smallest effective dose, and for the shortest period that satisfies therapeutic need." Specific recommendations included yearly monitoring of patients not exhibiting symptoms, monitoring that might "include histologic and cytologic sampling of the endometrium."[97] This philosophy trickled down from specialist level to family practice. In June 1982, the *American Family Physician* published an article by a staff physician who was research coordinator in the Department of Family Practice in the Naval Regional Medical Center in Charleston, South Carolina. He stressed that "[e]strogen replacement therapy should be reserved for women with symptoms severe enough to interfere with normal daily activities."[98]

The Question of Heart Disease Arises

The roller coaster of controversy about menopausal estrogens slowed down somewhat in the 1980s. However, a controversy about effects on the heart lurked. The issue was raised at least as early as 1976, when the Columbia University researcher Gerald Phillips first published data indicating that men with heart disease had "abnormally high concentrations of estrogen in their blood," a finding that he extrapolated over the next two years into the hypothesis that "high concentrations of blood estrogens are a risk factor for heart disease."[99] By the early 1980s, the issue had surfaced enough that the Naval physician in the 1982 article quoted previously had noted that "current literature" showed that "this subject is more controversial and less clearly defined than was previously thought." He referred to a "consensus" that "a personal history of cardiovascular disease, such as stroke, myocardial infarction" or blood clots was "an absolute contraindication to estrogen replacement therapy."[100]

In 1983, two new studies confirmed the hypothesis Phillips had developed in 1976. Most interesting was research that investigators for the famous Framingham Heart Study, a project that had gone on for many years, carried on with Phillips and federal investigators. A report of this research said that "the one thing that distinguishes Framingham men who have heart disease from those who do not is that the men with heart disease have higher levels of the estrogen derivative estradiol in their blood."[101] How firm was the hypothesis regarding men? Researchers at Framingham were starting a study that would follow men without symptoms of heart disease to see whether those who eventually had heart attacks had high estrogen levels. That study, it was reported, would "take 5 to 10 years."[102]

Did these conclusions apply to women? The Georgetown researcher Estelle Ramey was "dubious." A news summary said that she pointed out that estrogen protected against heart attacks in rats and that "[p]ostmenopausal women who take estrogens have fewer heart attacks than those who do not."[103] Research findings published the same year in the *Journal of the American Medical Association* gave good news for estrogen users in a broader sense—they had "lower mortality rates than nonusers." The researchers for this study, after adjusting for such factors as age, smoking, and blood pressure, found that "estrogen use remained inversely and significantly related to total mortality."[104] The investigators noted that estrogen raised HDL cholesterol, but said that this "accounted for some but not all of the lower risk of death in estrogen users."[105] Although the researchers speculated that one "alternative explanation" might be that "estrogen users have health-oriented behaviors that are different from ... nonusers and that may favorably influence mortality," they said their data did not address that question.[106] Whatever the changing calculus of risks and benefits, it appeared that reported risk factors were affecting consumer choice. A reporter who summarized the *Journal of the American Medical Association* study noted that "one estimate" indicated that "only 13 percent of post-menopausal women take estrogens."[107]

Hopeful News on Breast Cancer

Provisional good news appeared in 1984 in a study that found "strong evidence" suggesting that "the use conjugated estrogens and of other noncontraceptive estrogens does not increase the risk of breast cancer," even with conjugated estrogens taken for "many years, even at high dosages, or in the distant past."[108] An editorial commentator noted that "[j]ournals are loath to publish negative results" and that "the public press has little enthusiasm for negative studies"—an important corrective to the tendency of media to emphasize the scariest results of medical research. The editorialist, Barbara Hulka, wrote that doctors and patients would be "vitally interested in negative results" for a drug often prescribed, particularly when the findings related to "the most common cancer among women."[109] A press report said that Hulka indicated that this study and other large studies contravened "[e]arlier, small scale studies" that suggested a link between estrogens and breast cancer. Hulka wrote that it "strains credibility to presume that an important biological effect exists" that could not be detected by the larger studies.[110]

Recommendation on Osteoporosis

The principal problem in osteoporosis, which had become a principal target of estrogen researchers, is a "loss of bone mineral density" that "increases the risk of fracture."[111] This condition is "directly linked to the decreased production of estrogen that coincides with menopause,"[112] typically manifesting itself "within 10 to 15 years after menopause." An important benchmark was a 1984 recommendation by an NIH panel that presented a difficult choice for women: "[w]omen over 50 should consider estrogen therapy to prevent osteoporosis." As a reporter summarized it, the panel's recommendation was "carefully worded": it said that low-dose estrogens "should be considered" by postmenopausal women "if they understand the risks and agree to regular medical evaluations." Research on the subject had been building for a while. The panel referred to studies that showed a "60 percent reduction in hip and wrist fractures in women whose estrogen replacement was begun within a few years of menopause" and also a decrease in spinal fractures that often cause "dowager's hump." One member of the panel, R. Don Gambrell, Jr. of the Medical College of Georgia, issued the qualifier that the panel was "still not ready to issue a blanket recommendation." In words heavy with a principal message of this book, he said this was because "we do not know all the effects of long-term estrogen therapy."[113] Just afterwards, an FDA advisory committee recommended estrogens for the prevention and treatment of osteoporosis in postmenopausal women. Although saying that the boxed warning for estrogens should include the risk of endometrial cancer and "the advice that the lowest effective dose should be used," the committee averred that there was "a lack of evidence" linking estrogens and breast cancer.[114]

The FDA gave the point a regulatory imprimatur in a notice published in 1986, in which it announced that the director of the Bureau of Drugs had concluded that "short-acting orally administered estrogens are effective for the treatment of postmenopausal osteoporosis." The document included language for the patient package insert that concisely explained osteoporosis and said that "[t]aking estrogens after menopause seems to slow down . . . bone loss but there is not enough evidence to show that it prevents the bone from breaking."[115]

The next year, the agency proposed a regulation that would "transform" the regulation on patient inserts "from a listing of specific items to be included" in the inserts to "an enumeration of general categories of information to be included." It also announced "the availability of a revised . . . guideline" for patient inserts.[116] In 1990, the agency made final its proposed rule that made the requirement for patient inserts more flexible.[117]

By 1993, the *Back Letter,* a publication devoted to back problems, reported that the consensus of "four international conferences on osteoporosis" was that "estrogen replacement is the most important mode of primary prevention of hip fracture."[118] A journal article summarized a study indicating that estrogen therapy begun at menopause could "decrease the incidence of osteoporosis-related fractures by approximately 50%."[119] The author of that article, which appeared in the *Journal of the American Dietetic Association,* declared forthrightly that "[a]t the onset of menopause, women who desire to follow ERT should begin to do so," with the qualification that "[w]omen who are hesitant to begin therapy should be screened to determine their risk of fracture based on family history, lifestyle," and bone density.[120]

A Patch of Benefits, Including Cholesterol Effects

Some studies in the early 1990s accentuated the positive: estrogen was good for the bones, good for the heart, good for the blood, and, for good measure, good for teeth. One group studied estrogens, exercise, and calcium supplements, singly and in combination. The results varied with the combinations, with the specific bones being studied, and with the density of the bones of the research subjects. As the researchers summarized their results, bone loss in women with low bone density could "be slowed or prevented by exercise plus calcium supplementation" or by hormone replacement with an estrogen-progesterone combination. They concluded, in part, that an "exercise-estrogen regime was more effective than exercise and calcium supplementation in increasing bone mass."[121] Overhanging the study, as always, were the adverse effects of estrogens. Because of those effects, the researchers concluded that "[i]t may be appropriate to advise women with intermediate bone-density values to adopt the exercise and calcium regime and to reserve estrogen for women with low bone density." They identified as an alternative a treatment for all women that would rely on calcium supplements and exercise.[122]

As to the blood, another research group went deeply into cholesterol levels, even into three different types of HDL (the "good" cholesterol) as well as two types of low-density lipoprotein (LDL, the "bad" cholesterol). They concluded that generally, midlevel (0.625 daily) doses of estrogen decreased LDL cholesterol—which was good—in 94 percent of their subjects and increased HDL levels—which was also good—in 90 percent.[123] These effects, they suggested, "may, if sustained over many years, protect against the development of cardiovascular disease" but they also said that it would require a clinical trial to show that "conclusively."[124]

Almost simultaneously, a vast database of more than 48,000 postmenopausal women in the ongoing Nurses' Health Study appeared to confirm this hypothesis. Estrogen users, compared with women who had never used the hormones, "had about half the risk of major coronary disease or fatal cardiovascular disease and no increase in the risk of stroke."[125] The authors commented that "[t]he consistency of the epidemiologic data, the apparent absence" of statistical bias, and "biologic plausibility" "all suggest a causal association between estrogen use and a reduced risk of coronary disease." They further suggested that, "overall," these benefits outweighed the risks of such therapy. Again, however, they chanted the familiar mantra that the decision must rest with individuals and their doctors after a weighing of "all the relevant benefits and risks."[126] A later study projected estrogen benefits to the teeth. An author of that report said that if a woman had taken estrogen for 15 years, her risk of losing all her teeth was "only about 50 percent" of that of a woman who had never taken the medication.[127]

Breast Cancer, Downplayed

The question of breast cancer prowled in the background. A review essay in 1992, dissecting 24 studies since 1980, concluded that "the answer appears uncertain." The author summarized an important proposition, apparently well accepted, as a foundational point. This was that "endocrine factors, specifically endogenous estrogens [estrogen produced in the body], play a critical role" in the development of breast cancer. However, the role of "exogenous estrogens" was "less certain."[128]

The author of the review essay, Janet Henrich, concluded that with respect to applications for clinical practice, there was "no compelling evidence that, overall, women who have overused postmenopausal estrogens are at increased risk of breast cancer." Indeed, even for women with family histories of breast cancer or long periods of use, reports of increased risk were "inconclusive and not consistent across studies."[129]

As scientists confronted with topics of such tight biological weaves must do, Dr. Henrich proposed more studies, on such topics as lifetime history of estrogen use for both contraceptive and noncontraceptive purposes and progestin combinations, and noted that as "[b]iological and genetic markers of breast cancer" became available, they should be incorporated into research. Finally, she declared that "only a randomized clinical trial can address a causal relationship." And, portentously, she referred to the Women's Health Initiative (WHI) of the NIH—a study "designed to assess the overlapping effects of hormone replacement therapy, low dietary fat, and calcium/vitamin D supplements on cardiovascular disease, osteoporosis, and cancer in postmenopausal women." That study, she said, presented "a unique opportunity to resolve the estrogen/breast cancer controversy in a prospective clinical trial."[130] The answer—or at least an answer—would take a decade.

Benefits for the Heart

The idea that estrogens had a beneficial effect in reducing the risk of coronary artery disease had gained credence by the early 1990s. An article published in May 1993 summarized literature including research that indicated that deaths from heart disease of women taking estrogens were one-third of those for nonusers.[131] Another article published in the same month referred to a reduction in the cardiovascular death rate by 30 to 50 percent.[132] The question of effects on stroke, said the authors of yet another article appearing that month, was "more controversial." But these authors, analyzing Swedish data, concluded that "[h]ormone replacement therapy with potent estrogens alone or cyclically combined with progestins can, particularly when started shortly after menopause, reduce the risk of stroke."[133]

Issues on Combination Products

An illustration of the experimental nature of the multifront inquiry on estrogens, and its necessarily measured pace, was the fact that much of the data accumulated on HRT involved only the use of estrogen without progestin. The point appeared in a summary of a contribution to a symposium on osteoporosis, the author of which observed that "[a]lmost all" of the studies reviewed on the subject had investigated women taking only estrogen. She noted that "[e]ven in the very large nurses' study, it was not possible to study estrogen plus progestin, because only 2.7% were taking" the combination.[134] At that point, she could say only that if one accepted the hypothesis of the "protective effect of unopposed oral estrogen," it would be necessary to do studies on whether the combination "can provide the same apparent cardiovascular benefit without other untoward effects."[135] She noted, moreover, that one study had shown that "a North American woman with no increased risk of heart disease or osteoporosis" could expect to live to age 83 "without estrogen and would not add an additional full year of life by the addition of estrogen."[136]

That researcher, Elizabeth Barrett-Connor, participated in another study on bone density that exhibited the complexities introduced by multiple medications. The problem arose from the fact that women who took thyroid hormone, "one of the most commonly prescribed medications in the United States,"[137] had lower bone density levels than those who did not take that drug.[138] This meant that "postmenopausal women taking higher doses of thyroid hormone are at risk for accelerated osteoporosis."[139] Add estrogen to the thyroid regimen, though, and patients had "significantly denser bones."[140] This pointed, logically enough, to the conclusion that women taking thyroid hormone "appear to be excellent candidates for estrogen replacement therapy" with the usual qualification, "if they have no contraindications to its use."[141]

Estrogens in the Media

Public Information: Positives, Negatives, Confusion

Discussion and debate about HRT in media directed at the general public lagged the research, but it seemed to be a significant factor in women's choices. In fact, various writers stressed the now-familiar idea that it was the patient who must decide, always in consultation with a doctor. A group of articles in late 1993 and 1994 give a flavor of the discussion.

A reporter for *U.S. News and World Report* talked about tradeoffs: that estrogens "might prevent heart disease and osteoporosis—but raise the risk of breast or uterine cancer." And, she noted, "[t]radeoffs don't end there," pointing to less-discussed data on possible "stav[ing] off [of] Alzheimer's disease" and "a slightly increased risk of gallstones." She found "questionable" an analogy that one specialist drew between lifelong HRT for postmenopausal women and insulin for diabetics: "[w]ithout insulin, an insulin-dependent diabetic would surely die," but the average increase in life span for women who took estrogen would be only six to 12 months. Moreover, referring to data indicating the cardiovascular benefits of estrogen, she commented, "[j]ust how much is debatable." She pointed out that one way to acquire the necessary data would be to experiment with groups of women, some using HRT and the others taking placebo, but noted that there could be ethical problems with such a test.[142]

A chatty piece in *Physician and Sportsmedicine* gave a brief summary of osteoporosis and said that "[r]eplacement with estrogen alone or estrogen with progesterone is the single most important thing you can do to prevent osteoporosis." It added, in language that is boilerplate in television commercials today, "[a]sk your physician if such therapy is appropriate for you."[143]

A summary of a consumer survey by the drug manufacturer Upjohn included both data and a little bit of hype. This brief article reported that 77 percent of more than 500 women contacted by telephone said that they had "more concern about osteoporosis than they did about any other health issues that might face them at menopause." It quoted a physician in the Columbia University Department of Medicine who said, without embroidery, that HRT plus calcium could "prevent the loss of additional bone mass and significantly reduce the risk of fractures." One item in the survey reflected what appeared as a parallel to the resignation to growing older evident in the reactions of some men to Viagra therapy, although it related to the aging benchmark and not to medication. Eighty six percent of these women "said they would accept menopause as a natural change in their life" and just 8 percent "viewed it as a serious medical condition."[144]

A feature in the magazine *Health* identified positives, negatives, medical denial—and confusion. It summarized data on reduction of the risk of heart disease and reversal of bone loss. It noted that increases in the risk of breast cancer seemed relatively small for long-term users and that there appeared to be no increase for those who used the drug for less than five years. Yet, the article described one cancer expert as being "rile[d]" by doctors who disregarded fears about breast cancer of women in certain categories—such as women who had no children or had them late. This physician, Robert Hoover, chief of environmental epidemiology at the National Cancer Institute, commented tartly that it was "not a startling observation" that "[w]hen you get women coming into menopause and instead of letting them have a cessation of cyclical ovarian activity, you continue it," they would "have a higher risk of breast cancer."[145]

Perhaps most vexing, however, was the fact that "a slew of best-selling books" had presented views on HRT that were "so wildly divergent" that they "leave readers more confused than enlightened." The ferocity of the controversy was evident in the *Health* reporter's summary of a conversation with Hoover about a study in Uppsala, Sweden. Hoover said, the reporter wrote, that one thing he learned from the study was "that people want to hear good news." He referred to a finding of "an excess risk of breast cancer in long-term use" for 7,000 women on a combination of estrogen and progestin. As the reporter observed it, "Hoover stops, looking sheepish. This is the touchy part, the statistic that brings the wrath of hormone therapy advocates down on his head. 'Uh—the number happened to be fourfold.'"[146] Science and felt needs, or desires, had produced public warfare.

A Popularized Critique

The general public does not read articles in medical journals. It does devour books about medicine with shock value. A benchmark in popular books on estrogen therapy—a sharp contrast to *Feminine Forever*—was the publication in 1996 of Dr. John Lee's book *What Your Doctor May Not Tell You About Menopause*.[147] In a retrospective interview about the genesis of his thinking, Lee reflected on a talk he had heard in the 1970s about "natural progesterone," something he said he had "never [been] taught in medical school."[148] Lee developed his views into a thesis that attacked the use of estrogens, including estrogens in combination with synthetic progestins, and advocated the use of creams based on "natural progesterone." Lee obviously was passionately committed to this thesis, but the idea also had profitable consequences. Not only did the book sell hundreds of thousands of copies, but at this writing, many forms of "natural hormone creams," including "natural progesterone" creams, are available on the Internet.[149]

Ammunition for estrogen advocates, as well as stress on uncertainties, appeared in two settings involving continuing education for pharmacists. In late 1993, the text of one lesson for which pharmacists could receive credit summarized risks and benefits, but the tone of its conclusions seemed to emphasize the benefits. The author referred to "[n]egative beliefs about menopause and its treatment, by both patients and physicians" that might "produce poor patient compliance on HRT." To counteract that problem, he said, it was "desirable to emphasize the positive aspects," "because epidemiological evidence indicates that the benefits of hormone replacement therapy, with or without progestins, strongly outweigh the risks."[150]

Continued concerns about various uncertainties appeared in a report of a discussion at a continuing education program at the annual meeting of the American Pharmaceutical Association. Two pharmacy professors reviewed data on both benefits and risks of HRT, with one pointing out that certain risks, like that of endometrial cancer, could be minimized by adding progestin to therapy. Both stressed that women should discuss relative risks and benefits with their doctors. One, Jean Nappi of the University of South Carolina, focused in part on the lack of hard evidence on various issues. Nappi reportedly "urged that the risks and benefits of HRT be adequately assessed" and said she hoped that the Women's Health Initiative would answer some of the questions at issue.[151]

Against this background, manufacturers still sought product differentiation through innovation. Bristol-Myers Squibb, emphasizing the devastating consequences of hip fracture in "very elderly women," promoted a low-dose (0.5 mg) ERT tablet called Estrace. A release written by a New York University medical professor, reporting that the medication "helped prevent osteoporosis in postmenopausal women," said that "women may want to discuss low-dose estrogen replacement therapy with their doctors—to prevent osteoporosis and to begin their golden years on strong footing."[152]

A Transition Period with Mixed Results

The late 1990s now appear as a transition period, one of mixed results. That period featured some apparent confirmation of the benefits of estrogen, and some research-generated harbingers of darker events, paralleled by the first publication of a popular book attacking estrogen therapy. This period also included a somewhat startling illustration of gaps in basic scientific knowledge, as well as an example of how research proceeds in fits and starts, over long periods of time. The year 1995 opened with an article in the *Journal of the American Medical Association* that concluded that "[e]strogen alone or in combination with a progestin improves lipoproteins"—that is, blood cholesterol levels—and lowers the level of fibrinogen, a protein that is a biochemical basis for blood clots and is associated with coronary heart disease and stroke. These researchers, who conducted a multicenter double-blind, placebo-controlled trial over a three-year period, said that estrogen by itself "is the optimal regimen" for increasing HDL cholesterol, the good cholesterol, but noted that the hormone was unacceptable for women who had their uterus because of its linkage to endometrial disease.[153]

Over the next two years, data from the ongoing Nurses' Health Study provided more reason for good feelings about estrogen. One article reported a "marked decrease[]" in "the risk of major coronary disease . . . among current users of estrogen and progestin, as well as among current users of estrogen alone."[154] This study involved up to "16 years of follow-up" on a population of more than 59,000 women. A second report on the Nurses' Study found a "lower mortality rate" among women taking postmenopausal hormones compared with "women who had never used hormones"—a finding particularly applicable to death from coronary heart disease.[155]

The news on breast cancer presented a contrasting picture. A 1995 article by researchers from the same laboratory that had produced the two studies just mentioned, surveying nurses over a 14-year period, reported a "significant elevation in the risk of breast cancer among women using conjugated estrogens alone . . . , estrogen plus progestin . . . , and progestins alone." This group reported that the "relative risk of breast cancer was highest among the oldest women" in the study.[156] These results motivated the writers of the study that had found a drop in overall mortality to remark on the need for a careful individualized consideration of the risks of hormone therapy. Those researchers observed that "we know many ways to lower the risk of coronary disease, but few to lower the risk of breast cancer."[157]

A Science of Puzzles

The FDA and the Unknowns of Premarin

One way or another, the arguments about ERT were partly about money. A symbolic event was the FDA's refusal in 1997 to approve a synthetic generic version of Premarin—with a notation that after almost a half century, there were some fairly basic things about that product that were not understood. Clearly, the approval of such a product would open up a tremendous market, one that as the FDA itself observed, "would result in significant cost savings for American women."[158]

However, the agency explained in a lengthy document that it would not approve an Abbreviated New Drug Application for such a product. The director of the agency's Center for Drug Evaluation and Research, Dr. Janet Woodcock, summarized the center's conclusion as that "because ... Premarin is not adequately characterized at this time, the active ingredients of Premarin cannot now be definitely identified."[159] To a layperson, this may have seemed an astonishing conclusion about a product for which the first new drug application had become effective in 1942, on the basis that it was, as Dr. Woodcock's memorandum noted, "safe for its intended use in the treatment of menopausal symptoms and related conditions."[160]

As the memorandum encapsuled the history, in 1989, the FDA's Fertility and Maternal Health Drugs Advisory Committee "considered the question of the active ingredients in Premarin." Although it concluded that two chemicals in the product—sodium estrone sulfate and sodium equilin sulfate—were "active ingredients," the committee "could not reach a consensus on whether or not other estrogens in Premarin were active ingredients." The next year, an ad hoc subcommittee reached the same partly conclusive and partly inconclusive result. By 1995, uncertainty about the composition of Premarin replicated itself in the Fertility and Maternal Health Drugs committee, now meeting with representation from two other committees. The committee now concluded, unanimously, that

> insufficient data were presented to determine **whether or not** any individual component of Premarin or any combination of components in Premarin other than estrone sulfate and equilin sulfate must be present in order for Premarin to achieve its established levels of efficacy and safety.[161]

There followed a technical analysis on "Characterization of Premarin" that consumed more than 15 single-spaced pages. A layperson who could follow even the generalizations might have been astonished at the lack of basic knowledge the document reflected, not to mention the biochemical complexity, of this widely marketed product. The memorandum noted that "[u]ntil recently, the scientific belief had been that all estrogens were similar in their pharmacologic actions on the body, i.e., 'an estrogen is an estrogen.'"[162] For that reason, Premarin had "historically been defined in terms of total estrogenic potency rather than the sum of the potencies of various components"[163]—of which "[a]t least ten estrogenic compounds have been identified and quantified."[164]

A striking, broad conclusion was that "[t]he actual magnitude of the contribution of each derivative of any component to the overall estrogenicity"—the estrogenic power—"of Premarin is not well understood."[165] More specifically elaborating the gaps in knowledge, the memorandum specified that "without a head-to-head comparison of the dose-related effects of Premarin, estrone sulfate, and equilin sulfate in the treatment of menopausal symptoms, the extent of contribution of the two components to the overall estrogenic potency of Premarin cannot be determined," even though it was "clear that both contribute."[166]

Dr. Woodcock uninflectedly took note of the "safety concerns about all estrogen preparations currently approved for long-term administration for the prevention of osteoporosis." Re-sounding a prior theme, she then pointed out that there were "[n]o head-to-head studies" that "compared the long-term safety of various estrogen preparations when used chronically for the prevention of osteoporosis" and that there were "no comparative safety trials of Premarin components available."[167]

The memorandum compressed the problem into one laconic sentence in its conclusion: "The reference listed drug Premarin is not adequately characterized at this time."[168] A question-and-answer document prepared by the agency responded to the inquiry of why the announcement had "taken so long[]." Noting that "[m]ore than 8 million American women take Premarin each year for estrogen replacement," the document referred to the "profound medical and regulatory implications" of a decision on the proposal to approve a generic version.[169] Dr. Woodcock commented in a press release that findings so far on components of Premarin "underscore[] the lack of precise knowledge of the makeup of Premarin and the relative importance of its components, and therefore the lack of a standard on which to evaluate a generic copy."[170]

Osteoporosis Alternatives

It should be noted that as the demand for osteoporosis treatment continued—an estimate in a 1998 journal essay was that the condition affected "75 million people in Europe, the United States, and Japan"[171]—various alternatives came into the picture. One increasingly prescribed set of drugs was the bisphosphonates, which appeared significantly to minimize fractures and increase bone density in postmenopausal women, with some research indicating that these drugs produced fewer adverse effects than estrogen therapy.[172] A new entry by 1998 was raloxifene, defined as having an "estrogen agonist effect on bone"—in effect, a bone builder—and "an antagonist effect on both the breast and the uterus." A 1998 report in *The Medical Letter* on one two-year study said that this research indicated that raloxifene "might be effective for prevention of postmenopausal bone loss without increasing the risk of breast or uterine cancer." However, it also noted that "[t]he long-term safety and effectiveness of the drug have not been established, and direct comparisons with other drugs are lacking."[173] By the new century, the entry for raloxifene on Medline Plus, a Web service of the National Library of Medicine and the NIH, was straightforwardly describing the drug as "used to prevent and treat osteoporosis," although listing a number of side effects, including sudden chest pain, coughing up blood, and sudden changes in vision.[174]

The march of accumulation of scientific evidence is apparent in the clinical history of parathyroid hormone (PTH) as a treatment for osteoporosis. The 1998 journal article mentioned earlier summarized a range of effects of this hormone on bone, from increased bone density in the spine to no effect on bone density in the femoral neck and including "an increase in biochemical markers of bone formation and resorption." It noted that at that point, the effects of the product "on the fracture rate are not yet known."[175] By 2002, though, the FDA had approved teriparatide, a "portion" of PTH, "for the treatment of osteoporosis in postmenopausal women who are at high risk for having a fracture" and also "to increase bone mass in men with primary or hypogonadal osteoporosis who are at high risk for fracture."[176]

The HERS Study: Equivocal Evidence

As medicine—and large-scale experimentation—moved toward the turn of the century, research findings became more subtle. They also became more equivocal from the standpoint of estrogen advocacy. Symptomatic was a 1998 report by a group led by Stephen Hulley on a randomized trial labeled the Heart and Estrogen/Progestin Replacement Study (HERS). The Hulley group found that there was no reduction in the "overall risk of nonfatal" heart attacks or deaths from coronary heart disease or "of other cardiovascular outcomes" in women under age 80 "with established coronary disease" who took estrogen plus progestin.[177] They also noted that women who took that combination had more episodes of blood clots and more gallbladder disease.[178] The authors ventured several possible explanations—ratifying some suggestions in earlier commentary—for the divergence of their findings from those of observational studies. Those studies, they said, could "be misleading," in part "because women who take postmenopausal hormones tend to have a better . . . risk profile" for coronary heart disease and get "more preventive care than nonusers." They also noted that "[m]ost of the observational studies" had focused on "postmenopausal women who were relatively young and healthy and who took unopposed estrogen." By contrast, the women in this study "were older," had established coronary disease when the research began, and took a combination.[179] Carefully identifying populations they had not studied—for example, women with no established disease—the Hulley group declared that they did "not recommend starting this treatment for the purpose of secondary prevention" of coronary heart disease. At the same time, they said that "given the favorable pattern of" coronary heart disease "events" "after several years of therapy," it "could be appropriate for women already receiving hormone treatment to continue."[180]

Puzzling out Heart Effects

Biochemistry, of course, does not follow the human calendar. But people have always been fascinated by the turn of centuries. And the Hulley study in 1998 represented a bridge into the twenty-first century. The first paragraph of an article published in 2000 by David Herrington and colleagues described the Hulley results as a "surprise" and then went on to add a new dimension. The Hulley study had employed a combination of estrogen and progestin and found that that regimen did not have a beneficial overall effect on women with established heart disease. The Herrington group essentially duplicated that finding, but it also found the same result in a study that used only estrogen.[181] How could these results be squared with "the established effects of estrogen" on blood lipids, on the inner surface of blood vessels, and on "other factors involved" in the development of atherosclerosis? The Herrington group, whose study was known as the Estrogen Replacement and Atherosclerosis (ERA) trial, searched for explanations. "One possibility" was that "estrogen has proinflammatory effects that offset its beneficial effects."[182] Another hypothesis, linked to the fact that the study used only women with established heart disease, was that "estrogen is more effective in preventing the development of atherosclerosis than in slowing the progression of the disease once it is established."[183] An editorial pointed out that there was other research that suggested that women who wanted to reduce the risk of heart disease should concern themselves with lifestyle. The editorialist, Dr. Elizabeth Nabel, referred to data on more than 84,000 women in the Nurses' Health Study, which indicated that the factors that most influenced the risk of disease were "smoking, overweight, lack of exercise, and poor diet."[184] As had now become almost ritual, Dr. Nabel said that the WHI would "definitively evaluate the efficacy of current hormone-replacement therapy for the primary prevention of" coronary heart disease.[185]

Still, the proposition that estrogen provided health benefits to women commanded assent, with qualifications about such factors as whether women were thin or not. Dr. Carmen Rodriguez and colleagues "corroborate[d] many other studies in finding lower death rates (particularly from coronary heart disease) for women who use estrogen than for those who do not."[186] Dr. Rodriguez, stressing that her study of 290,000 women "looked at the hormone's effect on women with no pre-existing heart disease," commented that her findings did not conflict with the results of studies on women with established heart disease.[187]

Breast Cancer Data and Queries

Data on breast cancer also continued to roll in, with results that might be confusing to nonstatistician women who principally read headlines. A study published by William Dupont of Vanderbilt in the journal *Cancer* in March 1999 concluded that estrogen therapy did "not significantly elevate the risk of invasive breast carcinoma in women" with previously defined benign breast disease.[188] A year later, a group of NCI researchers led by Catherine Schairer reported that "the combined estrogen-progestin regimen is associated with greater increases in breast cancer risk beyond that associated with estrogen alone."[189] An editorial commentary by Walter Willett and others stressed that "the increased risk is largely limited to current or recent users and is directly related to duration of use." They pointed out that this had "major implications for risk benefit considerations because the risks of hip fracture and coronary heart disease" did "not become large until a decade or more after menopause." Acknowledging the "important benefits" of HRT, they said that the Schairer study "highlights the potential hazards and uncertainties that accompany such use." They said it was time to "reassess [the] emphasis" on hormones to the "neglect of diet and lifestyle."[190] Willett was quoted elsewhere as saying that "the potential beneficial effect of hormones of heart disease [has] been 'overpromoted.'"[191]

Still a year later, in January of 2001, a review article on estrogen and breast cancer summarized the medical literature as supporting "the hypothesis that higher serum estrogen concentrations are associated with a higher risk of breast cancer in postmenopausal women."[192] The authors' survey of 102 research sources "support[ed] the hypothesis that estrogen and its metabolites are related to both the initiation and the promotion of breast cancer," although they noted that "these associations are complex."[193] The authors noted that "[g]enetic and environmental factors influence estrogen homeostasis and tissue-specific exposure to estrogen and its metabolites"[194] but in the background was the premise that "[e]strogen-replacement therapy has been implicated as a risk factor for breast cancer in postmenopausal women."[195] One background statistic complicated matters a little more: the survival rate for women who developed breast cancer on estrogen therapy was higher than for those who had breast cancer but "had not taken estrogen."[196]

Alzheimer's: Data Back and Forth

An issue that gained currency concerned the effects of estrogen therapy on the mind, with a particularized issue that touched many families being the question of whether estrogen would prevent or slow the ravages of Alzheimer's disease. One basic finding in a 1993 article, not focused on Alzheimer's, was that researchers found no support for the claim that ERT affected "memory loss in old age."[197] But as early as 1994, investigators reported that "[t]he risk of Alzheimer's disease and related dementia was less in estrogen users relative to nonusers" and that "[t]he risk decreased significantly" as the dose and duration of use increased.[198] Encouraging news on this issue appeared in an announcement by the NIH in 1997 that a study led by Claudia Kawas of Johns Hopkins University had found that postmenopausal estrogens were "associated with a reduction, by over 50 percent, in the risk of developing Alzheimer's disease."[199] Dr. Kawas cautiously commented that her findings gave "additional evidence that estrogen may play a role in warding off the onset of this devastating disease." Some later evidence, however, put a brake on optimism. A group led by Ruth Mulnard concluded in 2000 that ERT did "not improve cognitive or functional outcomes" for women with mild to moderate Alzheimer's who had had their uteruses removed.[200] An official of the National Institute on Aging, calling the study "critically important," said that it "turns our attention to how estrogens may help protect women who, at the start of therapy, are cognitively healthy." He also commented that it was not then clear "whether estrogen therapy may be effective in women" with Alzheimer's who had intact uteruses.[201]

The Clouds Build up, a Single Thunderbolt

A disturbing research finding in 2001, drawn from a prospective study of more than 211,000 postmenopausal women, supported "the hypothesis that ERT increases the risk of fatal ovarian cancer." The investigators, led by Dr. Carmen Rodriguez, found that risk to be "approximately doubled in women who had used estrogens for 10 or more years" in the 15-year period before they enrolled in the study.[202] Yet, noting that the lifetime risk of ovarian cancer was 1.7 percent, they said that "any increase in risk" of death from that disease "must be considered in the context of the overall balance of potential risks and benefits." They also noted that the risk of ovarian cancer from the combination of progesterone with estrogen was "unknown"—and therefore a subject for further research. More generally, they observed that "[t]he mechanisms underlying an association between postmenopausal estrogens and ovarian cancer have not been established."[203]

Hold-the-Line Advice

At the beginning of the new century, with the medical community still awaiting the long heralded results of the WHI study, there were negative rumblings in media directed at nonphysicians. In an article published in *USA Today* in June 2001, Rita Rubin summarized research that suggested that hormone therapy was not as effective for as many uses as touted and presented data on the risks of the products. A problem, she suggested, was a lag in the rate at which negative information reached doctors and their patients. She quoted Rose Marie Robertson of Vanderbilt University, president of the American Heart Association, as saying that "the results, even of a big trial like HERS, take a long time to wend their way out" to doctors and the public. Rubin also noted that many physicians tended to be resistant to negative data. Illustratively, she quoted Jacques Rossouw, acting director of the WHI, as saying that in "trying to lay out the pros and cons" of hormone therapy to gynecologists, he often received "quite a hostile reception for being skeptical." She also quoted Isaac Schiff, head of obstetrics and gynecology at Massachusetts General Hospital, as saying that there were "still . . . a lot of people who lecture on the subject who continue to say estrogens protect against heart disease."[204] And she noted an editorial by Robertson that said that during the period when evidence emerged that HRT did not provide protection against heart disease, the percentage of women who believed that it did had increased.[205]

One important event in the history of hormone therapy, occurring in 2001, was not a research result; rather it was a response to research results. This was the approval by the American Heart Association of a "Scientific Statement" that opposed the use of HRT for "secondary prevention" of cardiovascular disease. The statement also said that the decision of whether to continue or stop the therapy in women who had cardiovascular disease "should be based on established noncoronary benefits and patient preference." As to primary prevention, the statement was severely neutral: "Firm clinical recommendations for primary prevention await the results of ongoing randomized clinical trials," and there were then "insufficient data to suggest that HRT should be initiated for the sole purpose of primary prevention" of cardiovascular disease.[206]

Among other things, the authors of the "Scientific Statement" referred to the findings of the HERS study about "the overall null effect of HRT" on heart disease. They also noted that the data "suggest no overall cardiovascular benefit and a possible early increased risk of CVD [cardiovascular disease] events when HRT is initiated in women with documented atherosclerosis."[207] And the Statement referred to a meta-analysis that summarized "a nonsignificant 39% increase in cardiovascular events" in "predominantly healthy postmenopausal women," for whom there was "no overall cardioprotective effect."[208] The lead author, Dr. Lori Mosca, described the document as representing "a shift in our thinking." She said, "We're not saying, 'Don't start . . . [hormone treatment] for other reasons.' We're saying, 'Don't start it with the expectation that you will have a cardiovascular benefit, because we don't have the data to support that right now.'" JoAnn E. Manson, head of preventive medicine at the Harvard Brigham and Women's Hospital, added a declaration that "[p]revention of heart disease should be removed from the benefit-risk equation."[209]

Meanwhile, a statement from Rossouw, acting director of the WHI, signaled that incoming data revealed more risks of the therapy. He commented, "[b]ecause the overall balance between benefits and risks remains uncertain . . . we need to continue" the WHI trial.[210] The stage was set for the WHI report.

CHAPTER 6

Estrogens—The Storm Breaks: A Struggle of Medicine, Law, and Politics

As 2002 began, the maker of Premarin was upbeat. It had a new corporate name, Premarin was for the moment safe from generic competition, and the company was heralding variations on that product as well as new products. Wyeth's annual report for 2001 announced that "[o]n March 11, 2002, American Home Products became Wyeth."[1] The report exulted that the "continuing popularity of *Premarin*" was "particularly remarkable for a brand that will celebrate 60 years on the market," from its origination with Wyeth-Ayerst, of which American Home Products became the parent company. It noted that "the *Premarin* family of products"—which included the estrogen-progestin products Prempro and Premphase—had increased sales by 11 percent in 2001 and that "*Premarin* became the first Wyeth brand to surpass $2 billion in annual sales." The report specified "relief of menopausal symptoms" and "osteoporosis prevention" as the indications for the "*Premarin* family."[2]

The company also reported that it had filed submissions for lower-dose formulations of Premarin and Premarin-MPA, another combination product. It announced that it would be filing a new drug application for "an HRT product that combines *Premarin* with trimegestone, a novel progestin."[3] And it pointed out that the FDA had not "approved any generic equivalent to *Premarin*," although it observed that the product would still face competition from other products and could "be subject to generic competition from either synthetic or natural conjugated estrogens products in the future."[4]

Bad News, Terminated Research

The good cheer that dominated the Wyeth report on its hormone products was about to be dispelled, by both an international study and the long-awaited report from the Women's Health Initiative. In April 2002 came a report that said hormone therapy was best for menopause symptoms but not necessarily for a variety of postmenopausal problems, including heart disease and fractures associated with osteoporosis. This document, the International Position Paper on Women's Health and Menopause, was prepared by 28 experts from the United States, Italy, Sweden, Switzerland, and Australia, and financed by the NIH and a private Italian foundation.[5]

Dr. Vivian Pinn, an NIH official, commented that longer term and "better defined" studies had indicated that "all these things we've thought about the wonders of hormone replacement may not be holding up under scrutiny." Emory cardiologist Dr. Nanette K. Wenger, chair of the international panel, said that the "stringent scientific evidence" produced by the new studies had produced "enormous surprises" in "many areas." One set of those findings, not spotlighted as much as some of the others, was that HRT did not seem to aid older women with urinary incontinence, and Dr. Wenger suggested that there might even be "a worsening." Dr. Deborah Grady of the University of California at San Francisco (UCSF), who had been the lead author of a set of 1992 hormone replacement guidelines for the American College of Physicians, noted that at that time she had believed that HRT "should probably be prescribed to most postmenopausal women, except those at high risk for breast cancer." She had changed her mind. She said that now she prescribed it for menopausal symptoms but that otherwise she was spending "a lot of my life . . . trying to figure out how to help women taper off estrogen."[6]

At the same time, though, new evidence continued to come in on the beneficial effects on bone mass of HRT—both estrogens and combination drugs. A report published in late May 2002 documented gains in both bone mineral density in the spine and hips and bone mineral content in the whole body—effects achieved with doses below 0.625 mg a day.[7]

HERS, Extended

But in early July, the thunderheads evident in the International Position Paper broke in a full cloudburst. First came an extension of the HERS study led by Deborah Grady, which focused on postmenopausal women with a history of serious heart disease.[8] In the background were data from the original HERS trial that showed a "lower rate of CHD [coronary heart disease] events in the hormone group," and which held the hope that "clear cardiovascular benefit would emerge with additional years of treatment."[9] But Grady and her colleagues said that they found "no cardiovascular benefit of randomized treatment with hormone therapy" and firmly declared that this aligned with recommendations that HRT "should not be used for the purpose of reducing risk for CHD events in women with CHD."[10] Another study published the same day, led by Stephen Hulley and including Grady and Elizabeth Barrett-Connor, said that the combination therapy "increased the rates of" blood clots in the veins and also of surgery on the biliary tract, which includes the gallbladder.[11] A press story quoted Grady: "For women with heart disease, there were harms, and zero benefit."[12]

The WHI Report

Then, on July 9, the WHI issued its long-awaited report on postmenopausal estrogens.[13] The most stunning news of this paper was that the investigators had stopped the part of the study that employed an estrogen-progestin combination because "health risks exceeded health benefits over an average follow-up of 5.2 years."[14] It is worth reviewing the WHI findings in detail.

The study reviewed a combination product that included 0.625 mg daily of conjugated equine estrogens and 2.5 mg a day of medroxyprogesterone acetate— that is, Wyeth's Prempro. It was, the authors noted, "the first randomized trial to directly address whether estrogen plus progestin has a favorable or unfavorable effect" on the incidence of coronary heart disease "and on overall risks and benefits in predominantly healthy women" with intact uteruses. The study did not investigate effects of hormones used for menopausal symptoms.[15]

One Study Ended

The initial plan for the WHI trial was to continue the study until 2005, which would have given the researchers 8.5 years of follow-up, but it was evident that the clouds had been gathering as early as 1999. At that point, interim analyses had shown "consistent early adverse effects" concerning cardiovascular disease and with respect to overall risks. Although these results had not crossed the "disease-specific boundaries" that would set off full-scale alarms, the investigators told participants in the trial in both 2000 and 2001 about increases in several kinds of cardiovascular disease and that "the trial continued because the balance of risks and benefits remained uncertain." It was at the end of May 2002 that the investigators decided that the data on breast cancer had crossed the bridge to unacceptability. They thought that evidence, "along with evidence for some increase" in coronary heart disease, stroke, and pulmonary embolism, "outweighed the evidence of benefit for fractures and possible benefit for colon cancer." They thus recommended termination of the study on the combination product, although they recommended that the study continue on estrogens alone because the "balance of risks and benefits" "remain[ed] uncertain" on that question.[16]

The data on cardiovascular disease—for which the overall rates were labeled "low," included a 29 percent increase in coronary heart disease (CHD) events, most of them nonfatal heart attacks.[17] The writers commented that even though the breast cancer statistics were the reason to stop the study, there were enough CHD events that if the study had gone on, it would have been "unlikely to yield a favorable result for the primary outcome of CHD."[18] The authors noted that the discontinued trial "could not distinguish the effects of estrogen from those of progestin" but said that an ongoing trial was testing whether estrogen could prevent CHD.[19]

The WHI study also found a 41 percent increase in the rate of stroke, which "appeared during the second year and persisted through the fifth year," data "more extreme" than those in two prior studies including the HERS study. The writers concluded that it appeared that the combination "increases the risk of strokes in apparently healthy women." There were twice as many cases of blood clots in the veins, which was consistent with prior studies.[20]

Breast Cancer Increase

There was a 26 percent increase in the rate of invasive breast cancer, a risk that emerged over time, and "[a]fter an average follow-up of about 5 years," this statistic "crossed the monitoring boundary." The authors noted that this was "the first randomized controlled trial to confirm" that the combination "does increase the risk of incident breast cancer and to quantify the degree of risk."[21]

On the other side of the scale was a 37 percent reduction in colorectal cancer, which was consistent with prior observational studies. There were also statistically significant reductions in total fractures, with a hip fracture rate of 10 per 10,000 person-years for those on the therapy contrasted with 15 per 10,000 person-years for those who were not. The authors commented that this was "the first trial with definitive data supporting the ability of postmenopausal hormones to prevent fractures" at various sites.[22]

The "Global Index"

The researchers had developed what they called a "global index" including seven specific diseases to which they gave extra weight, as a tool for measuring overall risks and benefits. This showed a "nominally significant 15% increase" in fractures in the women taking the hormones.[23] To be sure, in absolute numbers, the "excess risk" was "low." Thus, a group of 10,000 women who took the drugs over a year might have seven more "CHD events," eight more strokes, and eight more invasive breast cancers, but six fewer colorectal cancers and five fewer hip fractures. However, the authors pointed out that these absolute numbers "would increase proportionately" over the longer term—"more typical of the duration of treatment . . . needed to prevent chronic disease." If one projected these numbers, the risks and benefits of the drugs "could account for tens of thousands of conditions caused, or prevented, by hormone use."[24] The authors acknowledged that if the study continued, it might show "more pronounced benefit for fractures" and "might have yielded a more precise test of the hypothesis that treatment reduces colorectal cancer." Overall, though, they declared that the "risk-benefit profile" for the combination products was "not consistent with the requirements for a viable intervention for the primary prevention of chronic diseases."[25]

Constituencies in Conflict: Patients, Doctors, and Scientists

Public Reaction

The WHI results reverberated through the scientific and popular press and the communities they served, and rocked the pharmaceutical industry, particularly the world of Wyeth. *The New York Times'* initial report quoted Dr. Wulf Utian, the executive director of The North American Menopause Society, as calling the study "the biggest bombshell that ever hit in my 30-something years in the menopause area." Nanette Wenger, the Emory cardiologist, said that she had "done nothing all day but answer the telephone." Reaction from a professional who was a consumer came from a Colorado pediatrician, Deborah Bublitz, who said, "I may have taken my last pill this morning."[26] However, Norman Ginsberg, a Chicago obstetrician/gynecologist, pointed out that "[t]here are lots of conflicting data in this study" and emphasized that the findings "represent a small incremental risk."[27] Capturing the downside of termination of the therapy, Dr. Linda Hughey Holt of Northwestern University described the misery of some patients who previously had been told by doctors to stop taking the hormones: "They're miserable. Their quality of life isn't as good."[28]

Dr. Marcia Stefanick of Stanford University, the leader of the WHI study, provided historical perspective on the reversal that it represented. She recalled that in prior years, medical groups were saying that doctors should encourage women at age 50 to take the hormones: "They linked up a very beneficial product for treating menopausal symptoms to the answer for treating all of a woman's aging problems." More perspective came from Deborah Grady of UCSF. She said she had "six inches of papers suggesting that [hormones] improve[] coronary vasodilation, that it prevents atherosclerosis." Referring to some of the prior data, she said, "[i]f you look at this evidence—and it's part of the mind-boggling aspect of this whole story—boy, the evidence for estrogen looked really strong." Now, she declared that this was "such compelling evidence that women and their physicians ought to be finding a way to get off estrogen"—although a reporter said she was not sure that would happen.[29] A *New York Times* editorial took Wyeth to task for its advertising. Referring to a statement of Lauren Hutton, a model featured in Wyeth ads that estrogen was "good for your moods, it's good for your skin," the editorial said scornfully that this made the product "sound like a beauty treatment and anti-aging elixir."[30]

The *Times* editorialist commended the NIH and the researchers for terminating the study of the combination and commented, "[i]f only the business world could be so forthcoming."[31] For its part, Wyeth reacted with surface calm. Its chief executive, Robert Essner, said that the study was "somewhat disappointing," but a reporter characterized him as "advis[ing] against a rush to judgment." Essner said, "Let's see how physicians and patients react to it once they understand what the data really say." Although Essner said that Wyeth remained committed to HRT, he noted that the effect on the firm's financial health would be somewhat limited. While "the hormone-replacement franchise" had been "the cornerstone of the company" for many years, he said, Premarin was then bringing in just 14 percent of Wyeth sales and Prempro another 6 percent.[32]

Meanwhile, it appeared that the business world was quick to be forthcoming, if not entirely in the sense that the *Times* editorialist used the term. Less than two months after publication of the WHI study, the veteran science and medicine journalist Gina Kolata reported that doctors had been "deluged" by promotions for "anything and everything that could substitute for Prempro," sales for which had dropped more than 25 percent. The proposed substitutes, she wrote, ran a "gamut": prescription products with "slightly different hormone formulations, nutritional supplements made of herbs and vitamins, soy products said to be natural sources of estrogen," and even "menopause accessories," like towelettes to wipe off sweat from hot flashes. A great concern of doctors, Kolata noted, was that the substitutes might present problems of their own. The American College of Obstetricians and Gynecologists (ACOG) warned that the safety of other prescription hormones "should not be assumed in the absence of conclusive data."[33] Stefanick, the leader of the WHI study, had said that "[w]e can't generalize our finding to other estrogens and other progestins, or other ways of taking hormones like pills or patches." She cautioned that "if pharmaceutical companies or anyone else starts to claim that these other kinds are safer, they really need to prove that."[34] ACOG also warned against alternatives like botanical therapies, saying that "'natural' does not mean safe or effective" and that "potentially dangerous or lethal drug-herb interactions can occur."[35]

Britain Begs to Differ

Within the month of publication of the WHI study, a transatlantic shouting match took place between the United States and Britain, reflecting different approaches to experimentation on general populations. In England, it was reported, an independent panel for the Women's International Study of Long Duration Oestrogen after Menopause (WISDOM) had "unanimously concluded that WHI's evidence that hormone replacement therapy raises the risk of heart disease [was] not convincing." The steering committee for the trial thus determined to continue the British study. Oxford epidemiologist Rory Collins declared that the WHI study had "not determined the size of the risks reliably." A Wake Forest University epidemiologist, Curt Furberg, shot back that the continuation of the WISDOM project "may be good for science" but that "patients will pay the price." Jacques Rossouw, the WHI director, was strident, calling the British criticisms "bogus" and saying that the British researchers were seeking "an excuse to dismiss the [WHI] results," because they had "their own trial to protect." Janet Wittes, an American statistician, ventured a cooler interpretation, saying that "the Brits are much more comfortable proceeding with a trial in order to get statistically significant results."[36]

More Skepticism on Utility

Even if WISDOM was wisdom for British scientists, a U.S. critique of HRT came from the careful *Medical Letter*, for many years a publisher of a four-page assessment of drugs that comes out every other week. It concluded that the results of the WHI study were "clear" "that "[no] cardiovascular benefits were demonstrated" for healthy postmenopausal women, and that "serious adverse effects occurred." The publication added that "[t]he long-term safety of taking these drugs for shorter periods of time to treat postmenopausal symptoms remains to be established."[37]

Yet, another view that the risks of HRT exceeded their benefit came in October 2002 from the U.S. Preventive Services Task Force. This 14-member panel recommended "against the routine use of estrogen and progestin for the prevention of chronic conditions in postmenopausal women." A summary of the panel's findings said that it "advised women concerned about bone loss to consult their doctors about nonhormonal ways to prevent it." The panel's recommendations were significant because, as a reporter noted, "its recommendations are generally adopted by Medicare, health plans and insurers."[38]

The ethics of continuing hormone studies continued in the spotlight. Reporter Kolata described some researchers as saying that the results of the WHI study had made them "think carefully about when, if ever, to subject healthy women to estrogen therapy in scientific studies." One study already had been terminated on hormones and the disease lupus, although it was "nearly completed." An official at the National Institute of Arthritis and Musculoskeletal and Skin Diseases, Dr. Joan McGowan, said that safety concerns about HRT had stopped the study.[39]

By October of 2002, a reporter described an "emerging" "consensus" among scientists, although with some dissenters, that there was "essentially no use for the drugs in the prevention of chronic ailments that come with age." The reporter distilled this conclusion from a two-day conference at NIH. Two Yale University physicians represented conflict on the issue. Florence Comite, founder of the women's clinic at Yale, spoke of a "clear message": "If you're using hormones, try to limit it to short-term treatment for symptoms. It's not a prescription for life." That, she said, was "a big, big change." Frederick Naftalin, an obstetrician-gynecologist affiliated with Yale disagreed: "Is there a role for hormone therapy in prevention? Absolutely." He named the benefits of "[p]reventing bone loss" and "preserving skin," and suggested possible benefits for patients with dementia. He even said he was "still not convinced there is no role in [preventing] cardiovascular disease." But Stefanick, the leader of the WHI study, said there was danger in "trying to find exceptions to the main findings." She declared that "[t]o say that the risks don't exceed the benefits—unless you are focusing on menopausal symptoms—is simply wrong."[40]

Experts continued to reflect on the seismic nature of the change. Dr. Barbara J. Turner at the University of Pennsylvania, whose research was described as dealing with the pace of innovation, reportedly described the change as "an almost unheard of transformation of the medical landscape." She said that doctors had "turned on a dime." Dr. Isaac Schiff, of Massachusetts General Hospital, noted that gynecologists were unhappy because the WHI findings seemed to contradict their own clinical experience. A California gynecologist, Dr. Jan Herr of Kaiser Permanente in San Rafael, viewed the news in terms of the need for women to adjust to aging: "They have to be satisfied with feeling better, not perfect," she said. "They had always said, 'Why should I feel like I'm 55? I want to feel like I'm 30.'" A reporter characterized Dr. Herr as saying that "women have to get used to feeling as if they are 55."[41]

Measured and Meditative Responses

The FDA's response to the flood of information in the WHI study and surrounding its study was measured. The agency had first issued a "draft guidance for industry" on estrogens in 1998[42] and revised it in 1999.[43] In February 2003, the agency announced another revised "draft guidance" that "reflect[ed]" its "thinking after considering the results" of the study on the estrogen-progestin combination. This document recommended various additions to labeling for estrogen products, containing "[i]information from the WHI, including a statement that although only a single dose and type of estrogen and progestin were studied in the WHI, risks for serious adverse events should be assumed to be similar for other estrogens and progestins until data show otherwise." Another recommendation was for a statement "that use of estrogens should be at the lowest doses and for the shortest duration in hopes of minimizing risks."[44] A couple of months later, the agency withdrew its prior approval of combination products that mixed androgens—male hormones—with estrogen for menopausal symptoms.[45]

In early 2003, experts became somewhat meditative about HRT, especially about the "only apparent anomaly" in the WHI study and other studies, namely, "divergent data" on coronary heart disease. Here, the WHI data showed an increase in disease, the earlier HERS study had shown rates of "recurrent coronary events" in women who took hormones "similar to those among women given placebo," and "substantial data from observational studies of hormone therapy . . . indicated that it protects against coronary heart disease."[46] Francine Grodstein and colleagues ventured that "the observational studies and the randomized trials may be answering different questions," for example, questions related to the type of hormones used in the research. They suggested various technical explanations for divergences.[47] They found the "clearest message" to be "that we have much to learn about women's health and hormone use." But they said that on the "current evidence," women should not start or continue hormone therapy "for the purpose of preventing cardiovascular disease" and that use for more than five years should not be "recommended for women of any age for the prevention of chronic disease." They reasoned that "[t]he established increases in the risks of breast cancer, venous thromboembolism, and stroke are too high a price to pay."[48] As if in answer, the next month the FDA approved a Prempro formulation with lower doses of estrogens and progestin.[49]

The question of quality of life lingered, even though evidence for the benefits of hormones had some quality of myth. Illustrative was a quotation from Cindy Pearson, the executive director of the National Women's Health Network, who a reporter characterized as saying that "so many women had told her the drug made them feel better that she assumed it was true."[50] Came now another WHI study that said it wasn't true. This study randomized more than 16,000 women, half on the estrogen-progestin combination and half on placebo. The basic finding was that the hormones "did not have a clinically meaningful effect on any aspect of health-related quality of life"—"general health, limitations (either physical or emotional) or usual role-related activities, vitality, social functioning, mental health, depressive symptoms, or sexual satisfaction." The effects of the drugs "did not vary, even among the youngest women closest to menopause or among women who reported hot flashes, night sweats, sleep disturbances, or emotional or mental symptoms at base line."[51] There were "statistically significant effects" for "physical function, bodily pain, and sleep disturbance," but these were "small and appeared to be restricted to the first year of use."[52] Deborah Grady commented that there was "no role for hormone therapy in the treatment of women without menopausal symptoms."[53]

Cauldrons of Controversy

A year after the release of the initial WHI report, more clouds appeared over hormone therapy and more doubts were raised about it, with reactions ranging from cautious acceptance of the new findings to counterarguments that arose from more than one quarter. May 2003 brought a conclusion that the combination therapy "increased the risk for probable dementia in postmenopausal women aged 65 years or older" and "did not prevent mild cognitive impairment in these women."[54] These results came from a randomized controlled trial of the "Initiative Memory Study" of the WHI, led by Sally Shumaker. The same group reported a month later that "[e]strogen therapy alone did not reduce dementia" or the incidence of mild cognitive impairment and "increased the risk for both end points combined."[55]

This provoked vexation from a geriatrician—a familiar example of the skirmishes that often break out between clinicians and researchers on such matters. This doctor found it "alarming that recent studies about estrogen replacement are scaring women yet again, when several past studies demonstrated the positive effects of estrogen on the brain." Noting that the Shumaker research had used "only women 65 or older and for only four years," she said that "[a] true proof" of the effects of a drug on dementia "would require that the drug be taken for considerably longer than four years for the effects to become obvious on a simple mental status test." She asked whether it would not be "more likely that the 'true' effects of estrogen will become known only if this group of women is monitored over many years?"[56]

Piling on the dementia data came bad news in the realm of breast cancer: not only did the combination drug increase the risk of the disease, but those cancers were "diagnosed at a more advanced stage compared with placebo use." There was also a substantial increase in "the percentage of women with abnormal mammograms."[57] One hypothesis advanced for this group of results was, as a reporter summarized it, that "tissue changes caused by the hormones made . . . mammograms harder to read and hid . . . tumors until they grew large." Another was that "the hormones made tumors grow faster."[58] Rowan T. Chlebowski, the lead author of the study, said this would "give women something to think about"—for example, did they want to take the combination drug to "reduce hot flashes 90 percent, probably, at the cost of having a 1 in 25 chance of . . . this abnormal mammogram, which might be more significant?" He ventured that a "lot of women with modest symptoms will now say, 'Wait a minute.'"[59]

A WHI team led by JoAnn E. Manson, publishing the "final results" on the combination therapy and coronary heart disease, concluded that the drugs together did "not confer cardiac protection and may slightly increase the risk of coronary events" in "predominantly healthy postmenopausal women 50 to 79."[60] At the same time, another team led by Howard Hodis concluded that neither estrogen nor the combination product had a "significant effect on the progression of atherosclerosis."[61]

David Herrington, who had been involved in the HERS study, commented that the WHI group had "clearly demonstrated" these conclusions. He and Timothy Howard suggested that this was just a beginning point, that there existed "a tremendous opportunity" to learn more about hormone therapy. They noted, for example, that "an association between a factor and the risk of a disease does not guarantee that drug-induced changes in that factor will produce a corresponding change in the risk." They gave as an example the need to understand why "a drug that lowers the LDL cholesterol level, increases the HDL cholesterol level, and improves several other risk factors . . . nevertheless fails to produce a cardiovascular benefit and even may increase the cardiovascular risk." They said that if researchers could figure this out, they would know "something fundamentally important about the pathogenesis of coronary disease that currently remains beyond our grasp." This, they said, made it "mandatory" to keep studying the question.[62]

In a commentary, John Bailar of the University of Chicago noted that neither the Manson or Hodis groups had "conclusively demonstrated a cardiovascular effect in either direction." He did agree with the decision to stop the trial on the combination. He said that although it was "faintly possible" that more research "would dilute the evidence of net risk," the chance that more study "would reverse the findings to demonstrate a net benefit is virtually zero." Bailar then went on to frame the question in broad scientific perspective. Writing that he had a large sign in his office that said, "We never know as much as we think we do," he said that although he thought "the current results are likely to hold up, . . . it will be interesting to see what we think we know in another 18 years."[63] This captured a basic idea in the background of all the research that had produced the arguments on the topic: that when science appears to move forward, its progress must always be described as tentative. This leads in turn to the point that regulators must respond to news about risk, but must always act with the knowledge that the news may change.

Bones, Benefits and Burdens

A remarkable conclusion on net benefits accompanied an unremarkable finding on the bone-strengthening effects of hormones—a conclusion sure to infuriate those who wanted to focus on specific benefits. The key to the conclusion was the "global index" of the WHI study. The focused finding was that the combination "showed consistent positive effects" on bone mass density. This surely was significant because the study was "the first randomized clinical trial" that showed that the combination product "reduces the risk of fractures at the hip, vertebrae, and wrist." But for these authors, led by Jane Cauley of the University of Pittsburgh, the question was overall effect, as measured by the WHI global model. Using that criterion, they concluded that "[e]ven among women who were considered at high risk of fracture, the HR [hazard ratio] for the global index did not indicate net benefit." The authors said that their results "imply that the benefit of fracture reduction does not outweigh the risks of cardiovascular disease and breast cancer, even in women at high risk of fracture."[64]

Appeals for Calm

By the end of 2003, though, estrogen support troops were bivouacking for counterattacks, and the main players in the WHI studies were issuing statements indicating the elasticity of the clinical implications of their findings. As one press article summarized it, "an increasingly vocal group of researchers and physicians" thought that "the WHI study itself was limited, and its results may have caused an overreaction." Wulf Utian of The North American Menopause Society said that although the WHI project was "an important study," it had "huge deficiencies." He asserted, for example, that it was "difficult to extrapolate it to younger women who are going through menopause." A nonprofit organization, the Kronos Longevity Research Institute, announced that it would start a new study on HRT and cardiovascular disease. Institute director S. Mitchell Harman expressed hopes that this research, on women aged 45 to 54, would be "the definitive study."[65]

Marcia Stefanick of the WHI was dubious, telling reporters that she thought the WHI Study "'had enough women in their 50's to say' that the hypothesis that hormone therapy may help cardiovascular health in young women 'is unlikely to pan out.'"[66] At about the same time, though, Stefanick was saying that "[n]othing about this study should preclude women who need the hormones to take the hormones unless you're at very high risk." She added, "Whatever was said 15 months ago, that's when it was a shock for everybody. We've had a year to calm down and get back to the fact that there still is a place for hormones for treating women." And JoAnn Manson, lead author on the WHI heart study, said that there might "be an element of going overboard" and that it was "going too far for the study to be interpreted as saying hormone therapy has absolutely no role in clinical practice any longer." Noting that women in their 50s, just after menopause, had a relatively low risk of heart attacks, Manson suggested that the increase in risk caused by the hormones was slight enough that it might "be a price worth paying" to relieve symptoms of menopause. At the same time, she stressed, as a news story summarized it, that the "main point" of her report was that even if there was still controversy about increased cardiovascular risk, the hormones did not protect the heart. She said, moreover, that the claim that the WHI data were not statistically significant was "splitting hairs," and that "[v]irtually no one can look at these results and say there isn't a suggestion of increased risk."[67]

Regulation and Litigation

The developing research, with the WHI study at its center, obviously required some response from the FDA. Following the 2003 version of its "draft guidance"[68] came a fourth draft in 2004 that included references to the WHI study on dementia.[69] The agency's general circulation publication, *FDA Consumer*, ran a brief article in late 2003 that announced a "collaborative" "menopausal hormone therapy campaign." This campaign was "aimed at raising awareness about recent findings on the risks and benefits" of HRT and "making sure that women have the latest information about the safe use of FDA-approved drugs to relieve menopausal symptoms."[70] An FDA official declared that the "main message" of the campaign was that "[i]f you choose to use hormones for treating symptoms of menopause, use them at the lowest dose that helps for the shortest time needed"[71]—language quite similar to that in the 2003 guidance document.

The Lawsuits Begin

Not surprisingly, the WHI study stirred up interest among personal injury lawyers, who are both praised as public servants and criticized as overzealous destroyers of free enterprise for their swift responses to new patterns of risk and injury. Within a week after release of the WHI study, an article in the *Wall Street Journal* pictured plaintiffs' lawyers as "tripping over each over to sue Wyeth" on alleged adverse effects of Prempro, instancing the filing of mass tort suits in Philadelphia and Chicago.[72]

A good index to the appearance of a product or activity in the spotlight of tort litigation is *Trial* magazine, the well-edited publication of the Association of Trial Lawyers of America, now the American Association for Justice. *Trial*'s article, "The Rise and Fall of Hormone Therapy," published in August 2003, described class actions in five states and individual cases in others on theories of negligent design of the drugs, inadequate testing, and failure to warn.[73] It noted that a petition to consolidate the federal actions had been granted in an Arkansas federal court.[74]

The natural history of drugs that allegedly cause serious side effects includes the establishment of Web sites by plaintiffs' lawyers, and the case of hormone therapy was no exception. One site includes the underlined words, "Suffered harm from Prempro? You may have a lawsuit. Click here, for a top rated law firm to evaluate your legal rights."[75] The headline on another Web site says, "While Prempro may cure your hot flashes it may also debilitate or kill you." Listing various "Prempro side effects," it tells readers who have had them, "You may have a Prempro case and could be included in the nationwide Prempro class action lawsuit."[76] Still another Web page says, in bold type, that "**If you or someone you love have taken hormone replacement, estrogen replacement, or menopausal hormone therapy treatments such as prempro, premarin, or premphase, and have been injured as a result of side effects you need to know your legal rights.**" It urges readers to "[c]all our HRT lawyers for a free legal consultation."[77]

Exit the Estrogen-Alone Study

The second shoe dropped from the NIH study in March 2004. The NIH announced then that it had told women with hysterectomies who participated in the estrogen-only study, the one that had continued, that they should "stop taking their study pills." In what was now a familiar pattern in the populations of scientists, doctors, and women, there had been controversy even inside the community studying the issue. The news appeared in a statement by Dr. Barbara Alving, the director of the WHI who was also serving as acting director of the National Heart, Lung, and Blood Institute, a statement which was the body of an NIH press release. Dr. Alving's statement noted that in the prior November and December, there had been a review of the accumulated data from the estrogen-only study by an independent advisory committee, the WHI Data and Safety Monitoring Board. As she described it, there had been disagreement among the members of that committee about "whether the pills should be continued, provided that a letter would be sent to the participants clearly informing them of" various risks identified in the study, including the risk of stroke.[78]

A summary of the study by the investigators said that estrogen alone "increases the risk of stroke." It also indicated that estrogen alone did not "affect" the incidence of coronary heart disease and that it "decrease[d] the risk of hip fracture," and the researchers said that "[a] possible reduction in breast cancer risk requires further investigation."[79] Even so, Dr. Alving's statement in the NIH's release said that NIH had concluded that "an increased risk of stroke is not acceptable in healthy women in a research study." The statement said that NIH had "determined that the results would not likely change" if the estrogen-only trial went on to its planned end the next year and that researchers had mined "enough data . . . to assess the overall risks and benefits of the use of estrogen in this trial."[80]

The Institutes' advice to women taking the drug on prescription was "to continue to follow the FDA guidance regarding hormone therapy." Specifically, the statement said that postmenopausal women who were thinking about hormone therapy with either estrogen or a combination with progestin should "discuss the benefits and risks with their physicians." It added that even though hormone therapy was "effective for the prevention of postmenopausal osteoporosis," it "should only be considered for women at significant risk" for that condition who "cannot take non-estrogen medications."[81] There were shades of meaning in this for women who had been prescribed the medication. Dr. Alving herself said that "[w]omen should not feel that this is some grand emergency for them." Dr. James Simon, president of The North American Menopause Society, termed the findings "quite reassuring" because "the major issue which women fear, breast cancer, was not increased on estrogen alone."[82]

Alternative Possibilities

Relief from menopause was big business, and although the WHI findings were bad news for some businesses, they harbored good news for others. Wyeth's sales of Prempro had dived from $60.7 million in July 2002, when the WHI study was released, to $20.4 million at the end of 2003. And even while the estrogen-only study continued, Premarin—which was only estrogen—had gone down from $116.2 million to $82.1 million in the same period. However, *Wall Street Journal* reporters noted that there were "an increasing number of treatment options for menopausal women." These included patches, the lower-dose pills already approved, and vaginal rings, the estrogen from which was not processed through the liver. They also included estradiol, a synthetic estrogen described as "more closely resembl[ing] the estrogen that a woman's body naturally makes." The *Journal* reporters saw an evolving "landscape" that was "turning hormone therapy from an easy off-the-rack prescription into more of a couture therapy, customized by each doctor to minimize side effects and maximize benefit for an individual patient."[83] But while all this was going on, the FDA and the Federal Trade Commission were warning sellers of unapproved "alternative hormone therapies" that their products had not been found safe and effective for their advertised uses.[84]

The Politics of Science and Medicine

As the story continued, an interesting aspect of some comments from scientists associated with the WHI was their apparent bow to the politics of hormone therapy. They seemed to be saying that they were giving "just the facts," but at the same time they were stressing that the facts were open to interpretation—and that for some women, it would be rational to interpret those facts in favor of taking hormones. It was evident that—as is particularly apparent in our prior chapter on HIV medications—a good part of the story about pharmaceutical regulation is a story of politics, which includes scientists being politic.

JoAnn Manson of the WHI group noted that "[h]ormone therapy has lost its luster for the prevention of chronic diseases," but said it "will still be used for the treatment of hot flashes and other symptoms" and predicted that "short-term use will become nearly as frequent as before." Adding that she did not think that "the pendulum will swing back entirely," she yet opined that hormones would "be used more often than [they] had been after the first trial"—the study of the combinations that was suspended in 2002. A cautionary emphasis came from Amy Allina, an official of the National Women's Health Network. Acknowledging that the WHI study did not "answer every last question we have about hormone therapy," she expressed concern that "the medical community is resistant to accepting the implications of this research" and worries "that some women may be getting false reassurance."[85]

Dr. Susan Love, a medical professor who had set up her own foundation for breast cancer research, acerbically recalled that in medical school she had been taught "that at menopause the ovaries stop functioning, shrivel and dry up." She noted that a lot remained to be discovered about hormones and breast cancer, pointing out that, remarkably, "[h]igh doses of estrogen and progestin have been used to treat metastatic breast cancer with success." However, she wrote that "[t]he one thing we know for sure is that it's time to get the elephant out of the middle of the room"—that "[u]ntil these recent studies overturned the theory, we have blamed all the diseases of aging . . . on 'estrogen deficiency.'"[86]

As one views these events from the standpoint of recent history—medical history, social history, and political history, it appears that a great synthesis was taking place, but slowly and painfully. That is what some researchers thought that the WHI studies would achieve. And those studies did dig out a very important collection of data. But, as is so with science generally, the great synthesis was literally a work in progress.

The 2005 "Guidance"

One milestone, which embodied that point, was the FDA's fourth revision of its "draft guidance" on hormone therapy, of which the first appeared in 1998. This 2005 revision, which said it was "for comment purposes only," contained "Recommended Prescribing Information for Health Care Providers and Patient Labeling."[87] Like its predecessors, this revision said only that "when finalized," it would represent the agency's "current thinking on this topic" and that it did not "create or confer any rights for or on any person" and did "not operate to bind FDA or the public."

Basically, the 2005 "draft" provided regulatory advice based on the research that had accumulated to that time. It included two principal sections, one directed at information for "health care providers" and the other at information directly given to patients. The section for providers began with a lengthy boxed warning that briefly summarized risks reported in WHI studies and concluded with the mantra on "lowest effective doses and . . . shortest duration consistent with treatment goals and risks" for individual patients.[88] A three and one-half page Warnings section detailed the principal diseases that research had associated with hormones. The ailments in that catalog on which this chapter has focused were coronary heart disease, stroke, clotting diseases, endometrial and breast cancer, dementia, and gallbladder disease. The Warnings section also mentioned hypercalcemia—very high levels of blood calcium—associated with breast cancer and bone metastases. And it included various diseases of the eye, some of which could cause sudden loss of vision.[89]

The recommended text for the Patient Information Leaflet—which doctors were "advised to discuss . . . with patients"[90]—began with a boxed warning of several lines. Highlighted in the box were statements about increased risk of several diseases,[91] which were repeated with some additions on a boldface bullet-pointed list of eight in the text.[92] The boxed warning also contained declarations that patients should not use the products "to prevent heart disease, heart attacks, or strokes" or "to prevent dementia"—a remarkable emphasis on what not to use a drug for.[93]

Focus on Age and the Trials of Aging

An Experiment Continues

Over the years 2005 and 2006, there was some consolidation of research on a number of issues, with an emergence of data indicating that the time of hormone therapy (HT) can make a difference with respect to various kinds of risk. There were crosscurrents of opinion and skirmishes on those issues, and some research summaries reflected a scrambling for meaning, but there was definite concern about the perils of estrogens when women began to take them at ages a decade or more beyond menopause. One risk that remained in the foreground from the early days of the birth control pill was blood clots. There also was fairly broad agreement that estrogen use should be restricted as much as possible. And epitomizing a thread that ran through all of the literature was a statement in a physician's editorial, capturing the scientist's perspective on human research as well as the status of patients as experimental vehicles: "Piecing together what we have learned from observational studies and randomized trials, we can slowly find the many truths behind HT in postmenopausal women."[94]

Nuance by Age

An article by Hong Kong authors noted that the HERS and WHI studies had "raise[d] a lot of controversies."[95] These authors cited prior research on the hypothesis that starting hormone therapy "[a]t the time of menopause when coronary atherosclerotic plaque is usually not extensive . . . should mainly produce a decrease in" coronary heart disease. They contrasted the "sharp increase" in heart disease events in the first year of taking estrogen when therapy was started "years after menopause when vulnerable coronary plaque may be extensive," a phenomenon "largely reflecting plaque erosion or rupture." However, they also cited the HERS and WHI studies as indicating that as time went on, there would be fewer such events "because plaque formation will be decreased"—a pattern of "'early harm and late benefit.'" They concluded—a point which itself became quite controversial—that "[w]omen who started hormone therapy at menopause should continue it," whereas "starting hormone therapy late after menopause should be considered on the basis of individual risk-benefit profile."[96]

An editorial by a California physician, referenced earlier, captured the way that big biological science proceeds by fits and starts, with errors in judgment imposed by limitations of data. Dr. Shelley Salpeter set up for attack the "highly publicized" conclusion of the WHI "that HT was dangerous for all postmenopausal women and should not be used, with the exception of short-term use with severe menopausal symptoms."[97] Now, referring to new data on subgroups classified by age, she said it could be "conclude[d] with reasonable certainty that HT reduces cardiac events and total mortality in younger postmenopausal women," a benefit "not seen in older women."[98] She said it might "be important to understand what went wrong with our scientific reasoning about the WHI trials"[99]—an error rooted in the assumption in those trials "that HT would be equally efficacious throughout the postmenopausal age range."[100] The "difference in results found with younger and older women," she said, "could be explained by a primary preventive effect of HT that is seen only when treatment is initiated prior to the development of atherosclerosis."[101]

Shortly thereafter came a reanalysis of data from the WHI, which concluded that "[c]onjugated equine estrogens provided no overall coronary protection in women who had undergone prior a hysterectomy, although there was a suggestion of lower CHD risk" in women aged 50 to 59. The authors noted that their trial might not have been able "to demonstrate a significant difference in the risk of myocardial infarction or coronary death by age group because of the low event rate in young women."[102] They laconically commented that "[t]he views of both the medical and lay communities regarding the role of exogenous estrogen during and after menopause remain in evolution during the current paradigm shift."[103]

In other words, both doctors and patients were riding a whirlwind of data still in the process of being discovered. Commentary in the *Harvard Health Letter* in 2006 said that although evidence from reanalysis of the WHI data and the Nurses' Health Study was "intriguing, it certainly isn't conclusive" for an age effect. The *Harvard Letter* noted the continuation of the national experimental process with "[t]wo clinical trials . . . that may give some answers." A lead investigator in one of these, the Kronos Early Estrogen Prevention Study (KEEPS) was Dr. JoAnn Manson, a member of the WHI group who had had a hand in the reanalysis of both the Nurses' data and the WHI data. The focus of KEEPS was "whether starting hormone therapy within three years of menopause slows atherosclerosis." The other study, funded by the National Institute on Aging, was "comparing the effects of estrogen started within six years of menopause to the effects of starting it 10 or more years after." The *Harvard Letter* characterized Manson as saying that "[c]ardiovascular protection is not a reason to be on hormone therapy." It quoted her as saying that "[t]he pendulum has swung from hormones being good for all women to hormones being bad for everyone." Both, she said, "were oversimplications. The truth lies somewhere in between."[104]

More Unanswered Questions

Another study, led by Pamela Ouyang of Johns Hopkins, cited the balance of biochemical risks and benefits associated with estrogen, including its "potentially beneficial effects" on cholesterol levels and inhibition of atherosclerosis, but also increases in fats in the blood and clotting, as well as increases in C-reactive protein, a marker in the blood for inflammation. This group posed "as-yet-unanswered questions about [HT] and cardiovascular risk."[105] Arising from "conflicting results from animal/observational studies compared with the randomized clinical trials," these questions included "whether some of the discrepancy is related to the age of the women in the studies, the timing of initiation"—that is, in the years just before menopause or after menopause—and "the amount of atherosclerosis at the time of initiation." They also included the "dosage, and the preparation form" (for example, oral, intravenous, or through the skin, and whether the medication included progesterone), "and whether there are genetic aspects to benefit or harm from HT."[106] Just this listing underlined the fact that after two generations on the market, these drugs remained experimental. The "controversy" over hormone therapy, the authors concluded, "has not yet been laid to rest." They acknowledged that "it remains possible that some formulations and doses" of estrogen "may have favorable cardiovascular benefits when initiated earlier in the premenopausal or perimenopausal period in women without pre-existing atherosclerotic disease." However, they insisted that "[c]urrent randomized clinical trial data" supported guidelines that opposed the use of estrogens "for prevention of cardiovascular disease."[107]

At the beginning of 2006, a paper in the *Journal of Women's Health* presented analyses of four more years of "follow-up" on the Nurses' Health Study. The authors were Francine Grodstein, JoAnn Manson, and Meir Stampfer. Their overall findings showed a "30% lower risk of CHD [coronary heart disease] for women using estrogen alone or combined HT compared with postmenopausal women who never used hormones."[108] Specifically, they "found a strong inverse relation between HT and CHD for women who began hormone use near menopause,"[109] although one limitation of their data was that only a "small group" of women surveyed "began hormones long after menopause."[110] Their careful summary was that their findings supported "the possibility that the timing of hormone initiation in relation to menopause onset or age might influence coronary risk," but that their data did not permit "firm conclusions." They also repeated a familiar litany: harmful side effects of hormones "in both randomized trials and observational studies rule out a general indication for their long-term use in chronic disease prevention."[111]

Memory Issues

One matter on which the picture was not distinct was the effects of hormone therapy on the mind. One 2005 article referred to evidence from the Women's

Health Initiative Memory Study (WHIMS), a companion study to the WHI, that "found no support for the use of HT"—either conjugated estrogens alone or combined with a progestin—"to reduce the risk of dementia in postmenopausal women older than 65 years."[112] These researchers flatly declared that conjugated estrogens "should not be prescribed to women over age 65 years to enhance cognition or prevent dementia."[113] An article published in 2006 indicated, contrasting other studies, that hormone therapy "nearly doubl[ed] . . . the risk for all-cause dementia." That article's author also referred to "some evidence that early initiation of hormone therapy might protect against Alzheimer's disease, whereas later use may increase that risk."[114] Noting data on rats that suggested that estrogen could "reverse memory deficits" in younger rodents but not older ones,[115] the author derived from a number of studies the suggestion "that women in the earlier stages of the menopausal transition might gain cognitive benefits from hormone therapy."[116] He also referred to the hoped-for benefits of the KEEPS study, then in progress, saying that "[i]nsights from such studies will be critically important in gaining a better understanding of the impact of hormone therapy on cognitive function."[117]

Weighing in on the memory question, two Canadian researchers found that on most tests of working memory, "[t]here were no group differences" among users of estrogen alone, women who took estrogen plus progesterone and women who did not use the hormones.[118] The only principal difference was that older women who never used HT "made fewer errors" on a letter-number sequencing test than users of the hormones, but this "most likely" was "not clinically significant."[119]

Clots, perennially. Always in the background, whatever the statistical ups and downs and uncertainties about coronary heart disease and cognition, was the tendency of estrogens to cause blood clots. Data from the HERS and WHI studies and a clinical trial on Estrogen Replacement and Atherosclerosis indicated "remarkably consistent findings between" hormone therapy and venous thromboembolism (VTE).[120] The author summarized the literature as indicating that estrogen-progestin combinations were "associated with a twofold to threefold increased risk for VTE," that estrogen-only therapy "seems to be associated with a lower risk," and that hormones administered through the skin "may not be associated with an increased risk."[121] He issued a particular caution for women with thrombophilia, an inherited blood abnormality associated with a heightened risk of clots. For such women, the author said, "the safety of HRT is questioned."[122] There was, moreover, a "markedly increased risk" for women with a blood abnormality known as the factor V Leiden mutation.[123]

An embarrassing byproduct of hormone therapy is urinary incontinence, which comes in two forms. An estrogen-progestin combination increased the odds of "urge incontinence"—that is, unintentional leakage of urine before a woman could get to the bathroom—by 50 percent. And for "stress incontinence"—that is, leakage from such things as coughing, sneezing, lifting, or even laughing—the increase was 70 percent.[124] Researchers commented, simply, that "[w]omen who are using or considering hormone therapy should be informed about this increased risk."[125] On the positive side of the side effects ledger, though, came an indication that both estrogen and combination therapies "are associated with a small reduced risk of cataract."[126]

Just in the span of two years, research results on everything from the veins to the eye to the urinary system presented a complex ongoing tale of mass market research on women. One might take hormones to combat the pain and discomfort of menopause, but there were many different prices that might be paid as well as a number of unbargained for advantages that one might receive.

Consumers, Consumerism, and Uncertainty

Science, Consumption, and Politics

Many shades of motivations and convictions among scientists were evident almost four years after termination of the combination study and two years after the estrogen-only study was discontinued. Jacques Rossouw, the WHI project director, indicated that "he wanted to have the 'maximum effect' on doctors and women to stop the practice of prescribing hormones to protect women's hearts" and that he had never intended "to stop women from using hormones for menopause symptoms." However, Dr. Alving, who had rationalized the discontinuance of the estrogen-only study for the NIH, reportedly said that the investigators "had all the information they needed." A press story quoted her as declaring she had "no second thoughts."[127]

A brief remark by Marcia Stefanick, by then the head of the WHI steering committee, encapsuled the combined problems of science, medicine, media, and the necessarily limited ability of lay persons to understand statistics—and uncertainties. Expressing disappointment over the gaps in communication about both the results and limitations of the WHI studies, she said, "[U]nfortunately, science never works in sound bites."[128]

The history we have summarized is a prism for all the problem areas just mentioned, as well as for the reciprocal relationship between consumerism and science, and the development of myths about medicine. This complex set of circumstances posed a special challenge for regulators, who on this issue moved reactively with the data—but up to the end of 2005 always moved tentatively—as in the still-draft "Guidance." It is interesting that the scientists, at least in the context of the decisions on the WHI studies, were more decisive. An interesting prior parallel was the way that scientists associated with the early development of recombinant DNA technology took the lead in trying to assure themselves, and the public, that the external risks of their experiments were minimal.[129]

Tradeoffs for Bisphosphonates

It should be noted that alongside the multifaceted investigations of the effects of estrogen, the search for alternatives continued. I mentioned earlier that one much-prescribed alternative to hormones for bone loss is the group of chemicals known as bisphosphonates. Some brands, like Fosamax and Actonel, had been shown in pill form to reduce the risk of hip and spine fractures in people with osteoporosis. Other bisphosphonates have been taken intravenously by cancer patients to minimize pain and to preserve bones that were already quite fragile. However, by 2006, there emerged news of a side effect for which "firm data" were "scarce" but about which "worried patients" began to "besiege" doctors. This was osteonecrosis—that is, bone death—in the jaw. Although reports of this effect were quite scattered, perhaps in the low dozens, one estimate held that it might afflict 1 to 10 percent of a population of half a million cancer patients who were taking the drugs. Reportedly, some dentists were refusing treatment to patients who were taking bisphosphonates, and "some doctors and dentists suggested stopping" them "for a few months before and after an invasive dental procedure." The case was a cameo, classic combination of several phenomena in the area. These included tradeoffs—one risk minimized but another generated; uncertainty, following a few initial reports of problems but arising from a lack of hard data; and panicked reaction among patients. An osteoporosis expert at Columbia University, Dr. Ethel Siris, was reported to have said that the sense of alarm among some patients was itself alarming: "[t]he whole thing has spun out of control."[130]

An Estradiol Alternative

On a parallel track, a new candidate for relief of menopausal symptoms with a divinely fanciful name had come along. This was Angeliq, which contained estradiol—a hormone used for estrogen deficiency—and drospirenone, a progestin used in combination oral contraceptives. *The Medical Letter*'s 2007 summary of the literature indicated that this drug was "effective in reducing menopausal symptoms without causing an increase in the incidence of endometrial hyperplasia"—always a concern with drugs in this category—after a year.[131]

★ ★ ★

Reports on estrogen research toward the end of 2006, and continuing into 2007, featured a series of bombshells, punctuated by some sparklers of good news. The factor of age came more sharply into focus. As one might expect in a subject featuring diverse research results and conflicting interpretations in a cultural cauldron, controversy remained the order of the day. As scientific issues verged into political questions, the pressure on regulators was palpable.

Stop Estrogens, Reduce Breast Cancer

The principal bombshells exploded sequentially in late 2006 and the following spring. One early explosion came in a report to a breast cancer conference in December 2006 about a decrease in breast cancer cases between August 2002 and December 2003, which investigators attributed to the fact that millions of women stopped taking hormones after the publication of the WHI study in July 2002.

The medical oncologist Peter Ravdin, a coauthor of the report, acknowledged that "[e]pidemiology can never prove causality," but as a reporter summarized it, he opined that "the hormone hypothesis seemed to perfectly explain the data." The senior investigator on the study, Donald Berry, said that the linkage between the decreases of both hormone use and cancer rates was "astounding."[132] This report followed by less than a month the publication of a California study that reported a decline of 10 percent in breast cancer rates of Kaiser Permanente members between 2001 and 2003, a period when hormone use declined 68 percent for combination hormone therapy and 36 percent for estrogen-only medication.[133] Marcia Stefanick, chair of the WHI steering committee, commented that "[t]he best explanation is hormone therapy." A spokeswoman for Wyeth responded that "breast cancer is a complex disease and the causes are not known," saying that it was "simply inappropriate to make any speculative statements" and that "clearly more studies are warranted."[134]

A Philadelphia cancer specialist, V. Craig Jordan, told *New York Times* reporter Gina Kolata that the heightened number of hormone prescriptions in the 1990s had "increased the rate of breast cancer in the whole country" and underlined the drop in breast cancer after the decreases in usage after publication of the WHI study and an English study. He hypothesized that "it is possible that many subclinical cancer cells may never grow inside a women's breast if she has no estrogen around to fuel that fire."[135]

A different interpretation of the literature came from Tara Parker-Pope, writing in the *Wall Street Journal*. She said that "[m]ost of the scientific data suggest that women who take both estrogen and progestin do have a slightly higher risk of breast cancer than women who don't take hormones." But, she added, "the overall risk to an individual woman is still small," referring to a statement by a task force of the American College of Obstetricians and Gynecologists that she summarized as saying that "a woman's risk of developing breast cancer while using combination hormone therapy was less than one-tenth of one percent a year." Parker-Pope's operational conclusion was that the range of data coming out on health effects did not "necessarily mean women should make the decision to use" hormones—only that they should "go into this decision with an open mind, shaking loose fears about heart attacks and other health problems that have scared so many women away from this treatment."[136]

But the next explosion was not long in coming. It was a confirmation in April 2007 by Ravdin and his colleagues of their hypothesis of the December before. In a "Special Report" in the *New England Journal of Medicine* that provided updated data from 2004, they wrote that "the data are most consistent with a direct effect of hormone-replacement therapy on preclinical disease," although they said that there might be some "contribution" to the effect by changes in mammography.[137] They backed up their thesis with a reference to "anecdotal reports of regression of breast cancer after discontinuation of hormone-replacement therapy."[138] A Wyeth spokesman warned against causal explanations, but Ravdin's coauthor, Donald Berry, called the evidence "a smoking gun."[139]

Cross-Currents on Heart Disease

Simultaneously, more data appeared on heart disease with branches related to age. Jacques Rossouw and coauthors from the WHI had an item of good news for "younger women or women with less than 10 years since menopause" who took hormones: for women between ages 50 and 59, "the risk of total mortality was reduced."[140] However, they suggested that even this statistic must be taken with caution: it did "not necessarily imply an absence of harm over prolonged periods of hormone use."[141] Beyond that, and of great concern, there were "large absolute excess risks" of heart disease for "women more distant from menopause"—risks great enough that, "taken together with their increased risks of stroke, breast cancer, and venous thromboembolism, would in general contraindicate the use of hormones for disease prevention in these groups."[142]

A couple of months later, JoAnn Manson and WHI colleagues reported more encouraging news for women in the 50- to 59-year-old age group, namely that those using estrogen "had a lower prevalence and quantity of coronary-artery calcium than those receiving placebo."[143] This, they suggested, "provid[ed] support for the hypothesis that estrogen therapy may have cardioprotecting effects in younger women."[144] Yet, they raised the possibility that estrogen could "still increase the risk of clinical CHD events," at least in older women, "owing to adverse effects on thrombosis and plaque rupture." And they re-sounded the now-familiar theme that "hormone therapy should not be initiated (or continued) for the express purpose of preventing cardiovascular disease in either younger or older postmenopausal women."[145]

Even given that qualification, there was disagreement among the authors of the calcification study. One of the other authors, Marcia Stefanick, declared that "[t]o extrapolate this subsample of women who are 50 to 59 is a huge mistake," reportedly pointing out that, given that a high number of women in the sample were "obese," it was unclear "how the data apply to thinner women." A press report indicated that both Stefanick and Manson emphasized that there was a significant difference in risk between taking estrogen alone, because of the risk of uterine cancer, and an estrogen-progestin combination.[146] A University of Southern California physician who consulted for Wyeth reportedly suggested that the calcification study indicated that if estrogen were started early, it "could be taken for decades." The WHI's Rossouw called this "[w]ishful thinking."[147]

Tara Parker-Pope of the *Wall Street Journal* weighed in with another critique of the early reports of the WHI, underlining the 2007 findings that indicated a decrease in mortality in women in the 50 to 59 group. She said that "many doctors" thought that "for younger women without a uterus, estrogen should be an option for long-term prevention of heart disease." She quoted Hugh Taylor, a Yale professor who was a principal investigator for the KEEPS study, as saying that "[i]f this is preventing heart disease and saving lives, I think it's really wrong not to consider it."[148]

A War with Many Fronts

Battles for Minds

Thus, after a decade and a half featuring a wave of prescriptions and a cascade of medical studies bridging a steep decline in use of postmenopausal hormones, a battle for women's minds continued. If one takes seriously the idea of an educated consumer making rational choices for herself, one would have to imagine a consumer who makes it a secondary career to study the medical literature on hormone replacement therapy. In colloquial language, now it's in, now it's out; now it's up, now it's down. As varied reports on risk trickle out, how does even a model consumer make a choice?

Battles in Court

We have noted that one stopgap solution, for women convinced that hormone therapy made them sick, was to sue. The results of the early rounds of litigation were mixed. In what may have been the first lawsuit to go to a jury, in a federal court in Arkansas, Wyeth won against a breast cancer victim's claim that the company had sold Prempro without enough research on its risks. Wyeth's Little Rock lawyer said the "jury's decision was consistent with the evidence presented and the body of scientific knowledge around hormone therapy."[149]

In another Arkansas case shortly afterward, the plaintiff won an early technical battle but lost the war before the jury. The trial judge ruled against Wyeth's objection to answers by experts for the plaintiff to questions about whether the company "was negligent in this case?" Both experts said it was their opinion that Wyeth was negligent. The company argued that this allowed an impermissible statement of opinion on an "ultimate issue" in the case, but in allowing the testimony, the judge noted that the lawyer had "first questioned the experts at length regarding the facts and data underlining their opinions."[150] Despite this interim victory for the plaintiff, who also claimed that Prempro caused breast cancer, the jury found for Wyeth. The plaintiff's lawyer promised to fight on.[151]

Less than a week later, a Philadelphia jury awarded $2.4 million to an Ohio woman and $600,000 to her husband in another Prempro breast cancer case.[152] This case had a colorful history: reportedly, the first trial was declared a mistrial because one juror had threatened another juror with a broken table leg while they deliberated.[153] Despite the jury's finding for the plaintiff, the trial judge granted judgment notwithstanding the verdict in favor of Wyeth, which among other arguments contended that the plaintiffs had not shown that the plaintiff wife "would not have developed breast cancer if she had not taken Prempro."[154] These were just the opening rounds. Some 1,800 Prempro cases had been filed in the state court in Philadelphia alone,[155] and there were about 5,000 cases pending nationwide.[156] Through 2007, the verdicts in products liability cases against Wyeth continued to be mixed. A victory for the company came in October when a Minnesota state judge ruled that a breast cancer plaintiff had not proved her causation case by showing general acceptance in the scientific community of the scientific studies she presented or of her experts' methodology.[157] On the other side, a New Jersey trial judge concluded that a plaintiff claiming that Prempro had caused her breast cancer could take advantage of a presumption that she would have heeded an adequate warning if Wyeth had given one.[158] And most strikingly, in October a Nevada jury handed down a $134 million award, including $99 million in punitive damages, to three breast cancer plaintiffs. In the six prior cases brought against Wyeth in the state, the company had won.[159]

Meanwhile, Wyeth struggled to gain approval from the FDA for its nonhormonal drug Pristiq, which it wanted to market not only for menopausal symptoms but also for depression in older women.[160] And the FDA approved two skin patches and a spray that used estradiol for menopausal symptoms. An advantage of such products was that because they avoided initial metabolism in the liver, they could be used in relatively low doses. *The Medical Letter* cautiously commented that "[t]ransdermal administration can be effective and might prove to be safer than oral administration, but prospective comparisons with clinical endpoints are lacking."[161]

Propriety and Practicality

Where there are dollars to be made from medical products that usually require prescription, some sellers will seek to bypass the procedures of the FDA. At the same time the FDA-approved transdermals were coming on the market, the FTC issued complaints against seven sellers of natural progesterone creams. The agency alleged that these firms had made claims for their products that were not supported by scientific evidence. The director of the FTC's Bureau of Consumer Protection accused companies of "violat[ing] their trust by making claims they just couldn't prove." A release by the agency noted that its staff had identified the respondents "through an Internet search of Web sites advertising products that claimed they were natural alternatives to HRT and that they would prevent diseases such as cancer and osteoporosis."[162] This rather routine regulatory episode spotlighted a question that was a focus of Chapter 2: what are the proper—and practical—boundaries of government intervention in lively markets for health care products? The rise of the Internet had presented that question in an especially sharp way.

Conclusion

The history of regulation of postmenopausal estrogens has much to teach us about the use of large populations as experimental vehicles for consumer products, in particular medical products. It presents a remarkable series of rises and falls in the assessment of the risks and benefits of products intended to alleviate discomfort and even suffering. It accentuates the fact that the only way to calculate the long-term effects of certain products is to try them out on mass markets. This history teaches that those effects do not manifest themselves all at once in neat packages. Another lesson is that the measurement of these effects depends on many variables, not all of which will be classified and analyzed at the same time. Thus, even sophisticated scientists dealing with a very large group of people may not think, initially, to focus on subclasses of that group as defined by such characteristics as age, which may appear obvious in retrospect.

Another part of the puzzle is the difficulty of applying a model of informed consumers to chemical formulas. This clearly is so with respect to lay consumers, but in the setting of constant changes in data analysis, it is often even so with respect to physicians. Indeed, even the experts disagree. In fact, a challenging dimension of the subject lies in the chemical complexity of the products themselves. There is a certain irony in the fact that after decades of use, it was still impossible for scientists fully to characterize a best-selling product, Premarin, confected from the urine of mares.

The environment surrounding these products resembled a battlefield with many skirmishes going on at the same time: manufacturers struggling against regulators; scientists disputing against one another; scientists and clinicians at odds; consumers vexed with their doctors, who themselves are vexed with manufacturers, scientists, and regulators in various degrees; and claimants' lawyers on the attack against manufacturers, at least implicitly suggesting that regulators have not done enough—all this in the context of cultural controversies about what it means to be a woman.

In short, the battles over postmenopausal estrogens present a classic recipe for regulation: science drawn into the vortex of politics, a politics itself enmeshed in ways of thinking about the human condition.

CHAPTER 7

Experiments at the Billionth Level: Nanotechnology

Richard Feynman, of whom a leading biography is simply titled "Genius," spanned an uncommonly large realm of modern science with his investigations and speculations. One suggestion that he made in 1959 is the seminal ancestor of a technology—nanotechnology (NT)—that presents a unique set of potential benefits, as well as risks, which at this writing are relatively uncharted. Drawing on his vast knowledge of physics, Feynman said in a talk at the American Physical Society that "[t]here is nothing I can see in the physical laws that says the computer elements cannot be made enormously smaller than they are now." He elaborated on an ambition "to build a billion tiny factories, models of each other, which are manufacturing simultaneously, drilling holes, stamping parts, and so on."[1]

NT received an initial impetus toward commercial development with the accidental discovery of "buckyballs," 60 carbon atoms clustered in a sphere, by scientists working in a Rice University laboratory.[2] This event provided an intellectual framework for a technology that has been defined as "the purposeful creation of structures possessing at least one dimension that is 100 nanometers in size or smaller."[3] There are various ways to specify the scale of this research. A nanometer is a billionth of a meter. The width of a hydrogen atom is about one-tenth of a nanometer. A flea is about a million nanometers, and a red blood cell is about 7,000.[4] Perhaps more understandable to lay persons is a definition of NT as "[t]he study of things 1/1000 the width of a human hair."[5] Nanotechnologists engage in "[t]he design, characterization, production and applications of structures, devices and systems by controlling shape and size at the nanometer scale."[6]

There are several different descriptions of how NT scientists do their atomic level work. One summary described a process in which atoms are "specifically placed and connected, all at very rapid rates, in a fashion similar to processes found in living organisms." In this process, "production would be carried out by large numbers of tiny devices, operating in parallel," to "form products of great complexity at extremely small scale."[7] Another description pictured a tiny world in which scientists were "capable of picking up, sliding or dragging atoms or molecules around on surfaces to build rudimentary nanostructures."[8]

It should be noted that there have been some disputes over the concept of "nanotechnology" itself, quarrels over language that stirred concern over the reputational effects of the term on those who practice and use these processes. An adviser to the Woodrow Wilson Center Project on Emerging Nanotechnologies worried that the lumping of the many uses of the science into one word could blur the distinctions among them with respect to the different kinds of risk they posed. He reportedly suggested that if "a particular use of nanotechnology poses a health concern," it might tar the entire field in the public eye.[9]

Types of Nanoparticles

Nanoparticles come in several flavors. Some are byproducts of various processes, including manufacturing processes. Others are deliberately engineered particles, with those principally relevant to this discussion being two- and three-dimensional particles. Two-dimensional manufactured nanoparticles "include nanowires, bipolymers, inorganic nanotubes, and carbon nanotubes," the latter being "extended graphene sheets that resemble chicken-wire." Carbon nanotubes have been described as having "'one hundred times the tensile strength of steel, thermal conductivity better than all but the purest diamond, and electrical conductivity similar to copper, but with the ability to carry much higher currents.'"[10] Three-dimensional nanoparticles, including buckyballs, have been proposed for use in "surface lubrication, drug delivery, and electronic circuit applications."[11]

Another categorization of nanoparticles divides them into "fixed" particles, which "'are embedded in a matrix and cannot move,'" and free particles. The latter may present safety hazards, for they "can disperse widely in the environment" and sometimes can enter the human body, "bioaccumulat[ing] in tissues and organs."[12] An overlapping classification of nanophenomena includes the suspension of nanoparticles in a gas—for example, as in nanoaerosols; in liquids—for example as colloids or nanohydrosols; or in matrixes, as nanocomposites.[13] Another cross-cutting set of categories are coated and uncoated particles, with coated particles being a potential object of concern because they "remain inert for as long as their coating lasts," giving them a tendency "to persist longer in the environment or in the human body than uncoated nanoparticles." Moreover, coated particles may be difficult for regulators to classify because the coating "could cause them to behave in novel ways, rendering regulations developed for the original nanoparticles of little use."[14]

Commercial Applications

Nanoparticles have a "dramatic increase in surface area" which makes possible new uses of substances at a level where "the laws of physics, biology and chemistry merge."[15] In particular, their relatively large surface property makes them "excellent catalysts."[16] Moreover, one group of authors has said that "nanomaterials are likely to prove potent at far lower concentration levels than envisioned when [current regulatory] thresholds were initially set."[17]

One potential consequence of this technology is that one could "make structures that are 100 times stronger per unit mass." Another is the development of "surgical control to the cellular and molecular level" in medical applications.[18] The "raw materials" of NT would "be simple compounds as inexpensive as petrochemicals and sugar."[19]

Another set of potential applications "could give rise to a 'Hydrogen Economy,'" using nanostructures "to make solar-energy cells cheaper and more efficient." A related advantage would be the production of batteries that are more efficient and much lighter.[20] In general, the technology could provide a basis for much cleaner production techniques "because atom-by-atom control can easily avoid producing unwanted byproducts."[21]

The hoped for improvements in medical technology include enhancement of surgical tools "in the short run" and, in the "more distant future," implanted mechanical devices "to correct auditory, visual, and sensory impairment."[22] One scientist describes a technique of "double imprinting," that is, "making a new molecule from an imprint," a process in which "[w]e mix and match materials poured into a nanovessel created by imprinting, looking to see which combinations have promising properties." He suggests that "[t]his strategy might aid pharmaceutical firms that synthesize medicines related to ones already available."[23] Another report summarizes work of a Harvard physics professor using "a nanopore made of silicon nitride" to develop a much faster way of mapping the human genome.[24]

There has even been a suggestion that "nanotechnology can be used to mobilize the body's own healing abilities to repair or regenerate tissues or organs." A Northwestern neurologist explained that "[b]y injecting molecules that were designed to self-assemble into nanostructures in . . . spinal tissue, we have been able to rescue and regrow rapidly damaged neurons."[25] And scientists at the Lawrence Berkeley National Laboratory, manipulating nanomaterials, constructed a material mimicking mother-of-pearl "that might find use in artificial bone and joints or in tissue regeneration."[26]

There are significant possibilities of innovations in electronics, with possibly the "greatest impact" forecast for display technologies and potentially a near-term "impact on computer memory devices." There also have been hopes for data storage capabilities,[27] with the possibility of "putting the equivalent of the brains of a laptop computer into a smaller volume than a bacterial cell, operating at gigahertz speeds with a power dissipation of about 100 nanowatts."[28]

One catalog of potential applications spoke of "'electronic paper' that could display information on sheets that rolled up like conventional newsprint; chemical sensors; wearable electronic devices; solar cells that could be printed onto rooftop tiles; or scads of simple radio-frequency identification (RFID) sensors for monitoring warehouse or store inventories."[29] A technical article spoke of the possibility of "obtain[ing] the metamaterial-layered structure with hyperbolic dispersion required for supermicroscopy."[30] Another article spoke of the use of "[c]omposites based on conductive or semiconductive nanoparticles" to "augment the use of conjugated organic polymers in flexible electronics, light-emitting displays, and photovoltaics."[31] The writer of a letter to a scientific magazine asked the authors of a published article whether they could apply a technique they had developed to "the creation of solar cells." The authors, MIT scientists, replied that "[s]olar cells are a major focus in our work . . . right now."[32] One commentator pictured a seemingly fantastic application in devices, with "little cameras pointing in every direction" that could "store a century's worth of full-color, high-resolution video and the 360-degree view around" the devices "in one cubic centimeter of molecular density memory!"[33] Another writer summarized the potential benefits of NT as "enormous," with the prospect of "exponential advances in manufacturing, technology, communication, medicine and military applications."[34]

Taking a long view, Mihail C. Roco predicted that around 2010, workers "cultivat[ing] expertise with systems of nanostructures" would create ways "to improve the tissue compatibility of implants . . . or perhaps even to build artificial organs." Roco, senior adviser for NT to the National Science Foundation and described as "a key architect of the National Nanotechnology Institute," saw even more progress after 2015, with the expansion of the field "to include molecular nanosystems": "Computers and robots could be reduced to extraordinarily small sizes. Medical applications might be as ambitious as new types of genetic therapies and antiaging treatments."[35]

What all this promised for the future was staggering, as measured by quantitative estimates of industry growth. The National Science Foundation estimated that by 2015, the technology would have "a $1 trillion impact on the global economy and . . . employ 2 million workers, 1 million of which may be in the United States."[36] Another estimate, by a private firm, was that by 2014, "nanotechnology products [would] account for fifty percent of all electronics and information technology products and sixteen percent of all healthcare products."[37]

Technical Challenges

In the face of these extravagant predictions was the fact that the technical challenges to many applications of NT are enormous. Simply illustrative are two sentences in an essay by a chemistry professor seeking to synthesize a "macromolecule" that would stop cholera "in its tracks." He describes the creation of "a small sugar on each end of rod-shaped bis-peptides that just span the distance between adjacent pockets" in the cholera toxin protein (Ctx). He also notes, however, that his research team had not yet "been able to determine whether each bis-peptide was binding two pockets of one Ctx or binding with pockets on two different Ctx molecules and thus creating a cross-linked network of Ctx molecules."[38]

Another challenge was evident in a report at a symposium dedicated to the late Richard Smalley, the Nobel Prize-winning leader of the Rice University group that discovered buckyballs. The new report summarized the discovery of "a way to clone just a single electronic type of nanotube," which would separate that tube from others that had different physical/chemical properties. That discovery, fulfilling something that was "[h]igh on Smalley's wish list," was said to have the potential of "mak[ing] possible a new generation of sensors and tiny nanoelectronic devices." Yet, that kind of use needed much more research, designed "to produce industrial quantities"; indeed, one chemist said that "the Rice team still has a way to go to prove that the process does indeed produce just a single type of tube."[39] More generally, breakthroughs in such areas as drugs, drug delivery systems, devices, and tissue engineering procedures were likely to be slow, in part because of "many toxicological uncertainties associated with inserting nano-size materials into the human body."[40]

The federal government, already supporting research in the area, began to establish a formal legal frame for NT as the new century opened. President Clinton's budget message for 2001 baptized a federal program called the "National Nanotechnology Initiative."[41] In 2003, Congress passed the 21st Century Nanotechnology Research and Development Act.[42] Setting up a National Nanotechnology Coordination Office,[43] the law sought to "establish goals and priorities" for a National Nanotechnology Program, to "establish program component areas, with specific priorities and technical goals," and to "propose a coordinated interagency budget . . . to ensure the maintenance of a balanced nanotechnology research portfolio and an appropriate level of research effort."[44]

Safety Concerns and Uncertainties

The optimism that these forecasts and government initiatives reflected, however, could not obscure the hazards to safety and health—often only dimly perceived—that might accompany the new technology. The key word, which gives little comfort to the developers of NT—and especially to persons vulnerable to physical risk—is "might." By 2006, a time when hundreds of commercial applications of NT were in use,[45] perhaps the most striking thing about information concerning risk to human beings was how sketchy it was. The language of various reports and commentaries on the subject is revealing, laden as it is with "could's," "may's," "it is likely's," "uncertainty's," and "it appears's."

The new technology had drilled itself into the very teeth of some consumers. Nanoscale silica was "being used in a range of products, including dental fillings." Nanoscale titanium dioxide was "finding uses in cosmetics, sun-block creams, and self-cleaning windows." Other NT products included "stain and wrinkle-free fabrics incorporating 'nanowhiskers'" and tennis balls.[46] The rate of marketplace innovation was evident in the raw numbers. From March to November 2006, there had been a "70 percent increase . . . in the number of products" that manufacturers reported were made with NT—a total of 356 consumer products, of which 197 were made in the United States. Silver was used in 47 of those products, which included disinfectant sprays, a toothpaste, and a "germ free wireless laser mouse."[47] The figure had gone up to 475 products by May 2007.[48]

One risky byproduct was nanomaterials entering the environment during "disposal, recycling, or reclamation." A possible effect that would not occur to most people was the grinding up of old computer screens for use in road building materials. A journal article pointed out that although the exposure of human beings to such nanomaterials from that source was "most obvious" in "workers doing the grinding," particles also could "harm road-construction workers, and perhaps travelers and neighbors, particularly as road surface . . . weathers with time and traffic."[49] Another writer expressed the concern that "nanoparticles may pose a fire or explosion hazard." Laymen presumably would never think that "single-wall nanotubes can be ignited by a camera flash at several centimeters."[50]

Despite these warnings, a persistent drumbeat in the literature echoes and re-echoes ignorance about possible harmful effects. Unsurprisingly, concerns were expressed along the lines of the "Andromeda Strain"—the prospect that "self-replicating nanodevices might escape the laboratory and, in essence, devour everything"—that is, "convert[ing] whatever they contact into more copies of themselves." To be sure, this problem, which NT specialists called the "gray goo" problem, seemed far-fetched and easily preventable.[51]

The less fanciful problems, however, were many, and a pervasive one lay in lack of knowledge. An essay by David Warheit in a DuPont publication in 2004 notes that "[f]ew data exist regarding the health and environmental effects of engineered nanoparticles,"[52] mentions the "paucity" of data on the subject, and refers specifically to the fact that "the inhalation toxicology data base on nanomaterials is rather sparse."[53]

The infant science of NT risks had turned up problems in a few experimental creatures: rats, fish, and water fleas, although some seemingly troubling data was subject to benign interpretation. The data on rats was illustrative. One summary of research indicated that "ultrafine or nanoparticles" " . . . produce more potent adverse effects" on the lungs of rats—specifically, "in the form of inflammation and subsequent tumors"—than "larger-sized particles of identical chemical composition at equivalent mass concentrations" instilled in the trachea.[54] It is clear that there is more than one way to interpret this state of affairs. The author of this summary noted that a small database indicated that "the lungs of larger mammals are less reactive to the dust burden insult when compared with results from experimental toxicity studies in rats," which indeed were "studied, in large part, because of their enhanced lung sensitivity to particulates." He also pointed out that toxicity studies on rats often exposed them "to materials . . . at very high . . . concentration."[55] The author viewed the lack of information as a reason to go slow in drawing "far-ranging conclusions" about the hazards of the technology.[56]

Another focus of research was aquatic life. According to results published by Eva Oberdörster, young largemouth bass gave "significant evidence of oxidative stress" after 48 hours' exposure to buckyballs.[57] She also found that "buckyballs at a concentration of 800 parts per billion," administered over 48 hours, "would kill 50 percent of a test population" of water fleas.[58]

With respect to people, rather than fish and water fleas, there was evidence that the category of ultrafine particles caused various lung problems and was associated, in some studies, with "elevated lung cancer." One could not take too much from these results, because "other studies have not found elevated lung cancer, and the precise contribution of the ultrafine particle fraction in workplace aerosols to . . . observed health effects" was "still open to question and a matter of active research."[59] Yet, the authors of a government study hypothesized, in bold type, that "**[e]ngineered nanoparticles are likely to have health effects similar to well-characterized ultrafine particles with similar physical and chemical characteristics.**"[60]

The same document, published by the National Institute for Occupational Safety and Health (NIOSH) in October 2005, cited early articles by Gunter Oberdörster, in 1992 and 1994, which suggested that for nanomaterials, "mass and bulk chemistry may be less important than particle size, surface area, and surface chemistry (or activity)."[61] The NIOSH document underlined the idea that "[i]n many cases, health end points appear to be more closely related with particle surface area rather than particle number," although it also said that "the number of particles depositing in the respiratory tract or other organ systems may play an important role."[62]

One hypothesis about particle size was that the smaller the particle, the greater the chance of injury to the lung; a possible explanation was that "deep in the lung," smaller particles "may bind to proteins causing unexpected consequences."[63] There was evidence that nanoparticles could penetrate skin cells and could find their way into the digestive tract.[64] A worrisome report on a consumer product was that "titanium dioxide and zinc oxide nano particles used in sunscreens can cause free radicals in skin cells and possibly damage DNA,"[65] although there were unpublished studies indicating that those materials in sunscreens "do not penetrate beyond the epidermis."[66] There were also reports from Gunter Oberdörster that associated the formation of lung tumors in rats with "chronic inhalation of fibrous and nonfibrous particles," administered at high concentrations; these substances included "[e]ven rather benign nonfibrous particles" like titanium dioxide.[67] And Oberdörster had suggested the possibility that "discrete nanoparticles may enter the bloodstream and translocate to other organs" and could go from the nose to the brain "by translocation along the olfactory nerve."[68]

An illustration of the kinds of distinctions about risk that one could make among substances was the observation that "different surface coatings on particles can influence" their toxicity in the lung.[69] This is just an example of how many considerations conscientious researchers had to take into account in determining the hazards of NT. The larger point was how little firm knowledge there was about the new technology. The NIOSH report boldfaced the statement that "**[u]ntil more information is available on the mechanisms underlying nanoparticle toxicity, it is uncertain as to what measurement technique should be used to**

monitor exposures in the workplace."[70] At this point, one commentator wrote in an engineering publication, the "only acceptable respiratory protective equipment" was two types of devices that he described as "cumbersome to use" and as requiring "compliance with rigorous OSHA [Occupational Safety and Health Administration] standards."[71] Perhaps most telling was his observation that studies of biological effects of nanomaterials in animals revealed that "it is possible that similar effects could occur in humans" and that this would "become clearer as researchers begin to study workers who have been exposed to nanomaterials."[72] This was as clear an indication as one could have that workers using those substances were front-line experimental subjects.

The very character of nanoparticles had edges in the direction of both benefit and risk. Because they could "readily penetrate cell membranes," they could "deliver targeted drug therapies." But their size might enable them to "cross physiologic barriers (including the lung-blood, blood-brain, and placental barriers)" and "enter body compartments." "Surface modifications" of the particles might allow them "to bind to cell surface receptors and potentially to interact with internal cell structures." This seemed to promise medical benefits, yet "[s]ubtle variations in nanoparticle surfaces . . . can have dramatic impacts on where and how nanoparticles gain entry into organs and cells, as well as where and how they are transported after entry."[73] This was so whether the variations were "due to intentional coating prior to entry into the body or due to unintentional surface binding" or the degradation of coating once the particles got into the body.

Most of the uncertainties about these biologic actions had not been resolved. By early 2006, an article in a publication dedicated to NT pointed out that there had been "no studies on any nanomaterial's reproductive toxicity, immunotoxicity, or chronic health effects—such as cancer—or developmental toxicity."[74] As to many effects, the puzzle was just that—a puzzle. On the one hand, "[u]ncoated fullerenes [had] been found to cause oxidative stress in in vitro testing systems." On the other hand, "some authors [had] questioned whether observed toxicity is caused by contaminants (specifically organic solvents) rather than the fullerenes themselves."[75]

Regulatory Lag

NT presented itself as a classic of regulatory lag, and for several reasons. With nanomaterials pouring onto the market, it began to appear that these particles were "likely to prove more potent at far lower concentration levels than envisioned when . . . thresholds were initially set." Moreover, by contrast with other kinds of materials for which it was possible to extrapolate toxicity, "too little" was known about nanomaterials "to enable such extrapolation." Beyond that, because "many nanomaterials are being developed in a decentralized fashion," in "small, dispersed facilities," it would be very difficult to direct "any compliance efforts to where they are needed." Thus nanomaterials, for example those used in sunscreens, might "fall through the cracks" of different regulatory agencies—in that case, the FDA and the EPA.[76] The EPA, indeed, was a fine example of the gap between theory and practice. Although it theoretically could request additional data in "Pre-Manufacture Notification" documents, with 85 percent of cases being "submitted without any health data," it "rarely" would do so. It "typically" would employ toxicological estimates that have "little applicability to nanomaterials," because of the "novel and enhanced properties" of those substances.[77]

In a few months bridging 2005 and 2006, concern about the new materials was becoming more fully emergent. During that period, several major documents from governmental and private sources analyzed safety problems, among others, that were wrapped up in the new technology.

In September 2005, NIOSH presented a "Strategic Plan for NIOSH Nanotechnology Research." An agency summary listed several "strategic goals." These included "understand[ing] and prevent[ing] work-related injuries and illnesses possibly caused by nanoparticles/nanomaterials." The document exhibited the mass-experiment nature of the technology. It spoke of the "need to determine the toxicity of nanomaterials," to "identify possible health effects from the early uses of these materials," and to "monitor the ongoing health of individuals working with nanomaterials." A hopeful goal was to "apply[] nanotechnology products" to "prevent work-related injuries and illnesses." The plan also sought to "[p]romote healthy workplaces" and spoke of the "need to develop and evaluate engineering controls, personal protective equipment, and guidance on safe handling of nanomaterials."[78]

Symbolic of the lack of knowledge on the subject was the subtitle of the "Plan": "Filling the Knowledge Gaps." The NIOSH summary of the plan effectively identified these "gaps" when it spoke of the need to "assess possible exposure when nanomaterials are breathed in or settle on the skin" and "determine what happens to nanomaterials once they enter the body." It spoke of the need to "[i]nvestigate and determine the physical and chemical properties (ex: size, shape, solubility) that influence the toxicity of nanoparticles." It mentioned the identification of "knowledge gaps where epidemiological studies could advance understanding of nanomaterials and evaluate the likelihood of conducting new studies."[79]

Somewhat chillingly, the document's list of "critical issues" included determination of "the likelihood that current exposure-response data (human or animal) could be used in identifying and assessing hazards." The summary also listed development and field testing of "practical methods to accurately measure airborne nanomaterials in the workplace" and the evaluation of "the effectiveness of engineering controls in protecting workers from nanoaerosols," as well as the development of "new controls where needed" and the evaluation and improvement of "current personal protective equipment."[80]

One reading this document has the sense of a walk back in time, to the early days of the Industrial Revolution, to the early development of pharmaceuticals, to the widespread use of asbestos in various applications. One can picture, in a less knowledgeable age, public officials and private parties playing catch-up on safety ten to 25 years behind the risk curve. Here, however, we are dealing with a scientific and political community much more aware of toxicity risks and able to set out research agendas for identifying risk. And yet in this new century, before meaningful regulation is in place, risk experiments are being carried out on workers and consumers.

NIOSH: Uncertainties Underlined

Remarkably representative of this state of affairs was NIOSH's October 2005 document, co-issued by the Centers for Disease Control and Prevention, entitled "Approaches to Safe Nanotechnology." NIOSH said that "[t]his document and resulting guidelines will be systematically updated . . . as new information becomes available."[81] Viewed through a positively rosy lens, this is a laudable and frank acknowledgment that accumulation of data on NT is a work in progress. Through a darker lens, it is evident that investigations of the effects of NT on people are simply another scientific project.

Both in summary and explication, the NIOSH "Approaches" document reveals a vast amount of landscape that requires research and description. In a brief summary introducing the document, the agency says that the "information gap is critical because of the unknown risk that nanomaterials pose to workers."[82] In the body of the report, it observes that "**[i]n the case of nanomaterials, the uncertainties are great because the characteristics of nanomaterials may be different from those of the larger particles with the same chemical composition**."[83] It also acknowledges that "**there are many uncertainties as to whether the unique properties of engineered nanomaterials (which underpin their commercial potential) also pose occupational health risks**."[84]

In fact, the document specifies that "**[v]ery little is known about the safety risks that engineered nanomaterials might pose**."[85] With reference to fire and explosion hazards, the language of "could" and "may" is symbolic: "**nanoscale combustible material could present a higher risk than a similar quantity of coarser material, given its unique properties**."[86] The drafters note also that "[s]ome nanomaterials may initiate catalytic reactions that would not otherwise be anticipated from their chemical composition."[87]

The "Approaches" document identifies a large zone of uncertainty about possible workplace hazards. It observes that "[v]ery few studies" have "measured exposure to nanoparticles that are purposely produced and not incidental to an industrial process." It suggests that a probable source of risk will arise from "processes generating nanomaterials in the gas phase, or using or producing nanomaterials as powders or slurries/suspensions/solutions." It also identifies as a source of potential risk "maintenance on production systems (including cleaning and disposal of materials from dust collection systems)." It labels as "minimal risk" devices "comprised of nanostructures," although it says that "some of the processes used in their production may lead to exposure to nanoparticles."[88]

The NISOH document further speaks of various difficulties in measuring aerosol concentrations and "monitor[ing] exposures with respect to aerosol surface area."[89] Indeed, it says that **there is not one sampling method that can be used to characterize exposure to nanosized aerosols.** To overcome these difficulties, it suggests a number of approaches employing the use of complex instruments and techniques, including the use of electron microscopes.[90]

Hopefully, the document refers to the probable effectiveness of "a wide variety of engineering control techniques similar to those used in reducing exposures to general aerosols." These include engineering controls, such as "isolat[ing] the generation source from the worker" and "local exhaust ventilation systems."[91] The report further suggests "the incorporation of good work practices in a risk management program." On another risk avoidance front, it notes that there is a wide range of effectiveness for protective clothing, with "penetration efficiencies" ranging from 0 percent to 31 percent for eight different fabrics.[92]

Finally, the report says that the last trench of defense is respirators, while noting that "there are no specific exposure limits for airborne exposures to engineered nanoparticles." The combination of physical constraints and the complexity of administration of a respirator program is evident in the report's reference to OSHA's general standards for respiratory protection, which include "an evaluation of the worker's ability to perform the work while wearing a respirator," the need for training of workers, maintenance and storage of equipment, and "respirator fit testing."[93] Just one symbol of the primitive condition of the art is the statement that "NIOSH is conducting research to validate the efficiency of HEPA filter media [a type of filter originally developed by the Atomic Energy Commission in World War II for the removal of radioactive dust] used in environmental control systems and in respirators in removing nanoparticles."[94]

Statutory Gaps

Another major document appeared around the beginning of 2006. This was "Managing the Effects of Nanotechnology," written by J. Clarence Davies and published by the Woodrow Wilson International Center for Scholars.[95] This report summarized existing legislation on the subject, including the shortcomings of three major laws with respect to regulation of NT. Referring to the "fragmentary knowledge we have of the adverse effects of NT," the author described that knowledge as "clearly rudimentary."[96]

One of the statutes Davies analyzed was the Toxic Substances Control Act (TSCA). Its weaknesses for NT control included its standard of judicial review, which required support for regulations "by substantial evidence in the rulemaking record." A glaring weakness was what Davies described as the law's implicit assumption that "no knowledge about a chemical" meant "that there is no risk." Davies noted that the effect of the statute was that the EPA, which administered the law, could delay or prohibit the making of a chemical "only if it can show that the chemical 'may present an unreasonable risk,'" which as he pointed out, was "precisely the thing that it cannot show." Finally, Davies illustrated other burdens on the agency with the requirement that it show "that a proposed regulation be the 'least burdensome regulation.'"[97]

Another commentator quoted a NIOSH official's statement about the difficulty of showing an "unreasonable risk" under the statute: "'[n]obody is saying here that it's a minor threat or a major threat—we just don't know.'"[98] That writer also pointed out that the submission of a premanufacture notice under TSCA did not require submission of "new data" or the conducting of "new studies," even though the company would have to disclose hazard data already in hand.[99]

There also were limitations, both technical and administrative, to enforcement under the Occupational Safety and Health Act. As Davies pointed out, "[d]etection of NT products requires expensive and sophisticated equipment," a bad sign for an agency "traditionally... starved for resources." Moreover, with respect to toxicity, "it is often unclear which parameters are the relevant ones."[100] In the same year as the Davies report, 2006, Peter Tomasco pointed out that there were no OSHA rules or "permissible exposure limits" specific to nanomaterials. With respect to the crucial legal question of whether a nanomaterial would be judged to be a "recognized hazard" within the "general duty" clause of the OSHA legislation, Tomasco noted that NIOSH had "thus far offered only noncommittal, conservative statements," instancing NIOSH's statement on its Web site that "[o]ccupational health risks associated with manufacturing and using nanomaterials are not yet clearly understood."[101]

The FDA appeared to be a fringe regulator. Its own Web site noted that the agency "regulates products, not technology": that it "regulates very few materials but many types of products." This, the agency's site document pointed out, would "affect the stage at which the FDA becomes engaged in the regulation of nanotechnology and when, in the process, regulation takes effect." Moreover, the agency said that it regulated "only to the 'claims' made by the product sponsor," and that therefore if a manufacturer made "no nanotechnology claims regarding the manufacture or performance of [a] product, FDA may be unaware at the time that the product is in the review and approval process that nanotechnology is being employed." The agency specifically noted that it had "only limited authority over some potentially high-risk products, e.g., cosmetics."[102] As Davies specified it, cosmetic makers did not have to register with the agency, "are not required to file data on product ingredients, and are not required to report cosmetic-related injuries to FDA." He contrasted the more favorable possibilities for FDA regulation of "NT-based drugs, biologics and medical devices," and probably food additives and packaging.[103]

★ ★ ★

Benefits and Risks, in Tandem

The year 2006 appeared as a great flask in which all the ingredients of the problem were being shaken together. Those ingredients included a surge in beneficial applications of NT, the identification of more risks, and a lot of parallel activity and cogitation by public and private actors concerned with the problem for both public and private reasons.

Illustrative of benefits at the miniature level of NT was a report in *Science* summarizing research that "demonstrated short segments of a superconducting wire that meets or exceeds performance requirements for many large-scale applications of high-temperature superconducting materials." This technique took advantage of "a periodic array of extended columnar defects in complex films of material," those defects being "composed of self-aligned nanodots of nonsuperconducting material extending through the entire thickness of the film."[104] As a reporter interpreted it, the researchers used NT to minimize the strain at the meeting point of lattices of two sets of materials—the combination of yttrium, barium, copper, and oxygen, acronymed YBCO—and the ceramic barium zirconate, known as BZO. They did this by "layering successive BZO nanodots right on top of one another," fashioning "BZO columns that ran vertically through YBCO and efficiently pinned magnetic vortices." The result was "dramatically" to "increase[]" the ability of the YBCO wires to withstand high magnetic fields."[105] This modern necromancy, so far beyond the understanding of laypersons, carried great practical potential to "propel high-temperature superconducting wire into the myriad applications technologists have dreamed of ever since 'high-T_c' materials were discovered two decades ago." A Wisconsin superconductivity expert, David Larbalestier, said that it "put a mark in the sand that is well ahead of where we are now."[106]

Simultaneous with this leap forward came a hazard report indicating that, as one report summarized it, "[u]ltrafine and nanoscale particles can go directly into the brain from multiple parts of the nose." David Dorman of the CIIT Centers for Health Research said it was not clear how this happened, although he reportedly noted that "[c]ertain nerves seem to play a role" in the process. Gunter Oberdörster, then at the University of Rochester, said that the type of metal affected the probability of transfer—for example, manganese could "readily" reach the brain but gold was "less likely" to do so. Dorman and Oberdörster both were reported to say that it was "unknown whether this translocation harms health," but Dorman pointed that a practical point of interest was that "workers exposed to high doses of manganese can get a Parkinson-like disease." Another participant at a meeting of the Society of Toxicology where those researchers spoke was David Warheit, a DuPont researcher quoted earlier, who said his laboratory would work to "refin[e] cellular tests to improve their ability to be used for nanoparticle research."[107]

The deficiencies in basic knowledge about NT materials were evident in pronouncements from various quarters. Remarkably, in November 2005, scientists for the Woodrow Wilson Center's nanotechnologies project said that a database the center was developing on the subject indicated that important safety issues were "not being studied." Indeed, the senior scientist on the project, Andrew Maynard, reportedly said there was "no research focused specifically on safety questions." In particular, he identified as a "major research gap" the lack of research on the effect of nanoparticles on the gastrointestinal tract.[108]

Workplace Exposures

Poignantly illustrative of the fact that experimentation, but not research, was being conducted on human beings was an acknowledgment by a NIOSH official that although the agency was working hard on the issue of the effectiveness of respirators against nanoparticles, he would not even speculate when it would issue a "guidance for those operating nanoparticle work environments." Charles Geraci, the chief of the agency's document development branch, reportedly said that although there was evidence that filters in existing respirators "appear[] to efficiently bar penetration of nano-size particles," the "broader question of demonstrating that various respirators provide real protection to users remains unanswered." A senior scientist at NIOSH was summarized as saying that there was "a great deal of practical information the agency requires in order to fully understand workplace exposure to nanoparticles."[109]

Applications Escalate

In March 2006, the Woodrow Wilson Center launched its database. Its scientist Andrew Maynard noted that the number of nanotech consumer products that researchers had found—212 of them—more than double what was expected, was "probably still less than the actual number . . . sold around the world." The trade publisher BNA reported that "[m]ost" of a dozen companies whose products were in the database did not reply to an inquiry about their toxicity tests, their rationales for selecting those tests, and whether they conducted life cycle analyses of their products. The publication noted that two companies that did not reply were Sharper Image, which sold pillows containing NT materials, and L'Oreal, which used nanoscale ingredients in cosmetics.[110] At the same time, NIOSH announced it was creating a model medical surveillance program. The agency's director, John Howard, reportedly stated as the purpose of the program the identification of "what organs should be monitored and what particles should be examined."[111]

As concerns rose about the lack of understanding of potential hazards, the catalog of benefits from NT, realized and potential, continued to grow. A 2007 report from an advisory committee of the European Parliament listed no fewer than seven categories of applications: coatings, flame retardants, chemicals known as flexibilisers that make things more flexible, products that substitute for solvents, catalysts, chemicals to enhance the effectiveness of drugs, and "remediation tools."[112] MIT researchers used nanoparticles of silica in the creation of a chemical that "aggressively repels water," which might be used in sailcloth to collect humidity for drinking water in desert regions. They were working on applications to repel chemical and biological agents from military clothing.[113]

Consortiums and Congress

Symbolizing the rise of the new technology was the formation of more industry and governmental groups focused on the effects of NT. An umbrella group, created in late 2006, was the International Conference on Nanotechnology Occupational and Environmental Health and Safety. This consortium included industrial giants like DuPont and Dow Chemical, as well as governmental units in the United States and the United Kingdom. The stated goals of the consortium—"deliverables" in its jargon—reflected the need to catch up with accelerating developments in the field. One of these goals was "to generate and characterize aerosol nanoparticles," which a spokesperson for DuPont said was "going well" because a "system developed by the consortium produces very good long-term stability for aerosol nanoparticle synthesis." Another goal was "to determine filtration efficiencies for engineered nanoparticles," a topic on which several tests had been done that were forecast to be published. The consortium also sought to "invent a portable air sampler for nanoparticles."[114] This had not yet been done, though some workers might have thought it long overdue.

On the heels of the starting of the consortium came the formation by the Synthetic Organic Chemical Manufacturers Association of a "new coalition for start-ups" in the nanoscale field that would "provide the perspective of small and medium-sized firms" to various regulatory agencies. Among the goals of this group, besides advocacy, was the establishment of "consistency and accuracy in developing standards, definitions and nomenclature."[115] Again the theme of catching up with effects resounded throughout the national nano-enterprise. Meanwhile, the push for development proceeded internationally: the European Commission announced plans to devote $4.04 billion to a "public-private partnership to promote investment in nanoscale electronics research in the European Union."[116]

A principal index to the level of interest in a developing area of concern about health and safety is the way Congress gets in on the act. By April 2006, a California congressman and a senior staff member of the House Subcommittee on Environment, Technology, and Standards were saying that it was too early to decide whether there should be new legislation on NT but that, as Congressman Mike Honda said, "[e]verything is open to discussion." Another measuring rod for the level of interest is the creation of centers to study a subject. Honda and Marty Spitzer, the staff member, appeared at a conference at the Center on Nanotechnology and Society of the Illinois Institute of Technology. Spitzer referred to a new major report in the offing—one being prepared by the National Academies—concerning the requirements for "responsible development" of NTs and "how well the . . . National Nanotechnology Initiative" founded under President Clinton was "encouraging responsible development."[117]

An interesting phenomenon in the story of NT safety was the coalescence, at least a partial one, of a community of interest among various interest groups that, like porcupines, would usually make love only very carefully, if at all. In May

2006, a DuPont official and an analyst for the organization Environmental Defense presented a draft outline of a strategy for control of NT hazards. This strategy involved description of the physics and chemistry of engineered NT materials, life cycle analyses, identification of potential for changing the characteristics of the materials, assessment of various risk management techniques, and decision making about "whether to proceed with production and how to manage risk." A final phase was to be the use of periodic reviews of NT material, with an eye to further decision making as new data became available.[118]

There obviously was increased sensitivity to not only the primary risks of NT, but also the secondary business risks associated with episodes of injury and illness. In late 2005, Mathew Nordan, the vice president for research of Lux Research, Inc., had noted that "[i]t only takes one bad apple to spoil the bunch." Interestingly, he and an Environmental Defense scientist fully agreed in testimony to the House Science Committee that the government should spend much more on investigating the threats posed by NT to health and the environment.[119] That ad hoc partnership followed on an op-ed essay coauthored by the chief executive officer of DuPont and the president of Environmental Defense advocating more funding for research and a "Joint Statement of Principles" to the same effect from a panel of the American Chemical Council and Environmental Defense.[120]

Proposed Constraints

What was to be done? First, it would be helpful to establish a philosophical framework for analysis of the problem. One overarching idea is the so-called "precautionary principle." J. Clarence Davies, observing that there are "many versions" of that idea, has given as a simplified definition, "you will not undertake any action unless you know that it will not have any unacceptable consequences."[121] With that version seeming impossibly impractical, and indeed potentially quite counterproductive, a somewhat more refined version is "if there is potential for harm to human health or the environment, precautionary measures should be implemented."[122]

Davies outlined a framework that, defining the coverage of the law to include "all **products** containing NT material," would put the burden on manufacturers to show "that the proposed product is safe."[123] The regulating agency "would have to establish testing and reporting requirements which, putting "as small a burden as possible" on manufacturers, would "provide enough continuing information to alert the government if a problem arises." A "sustainability plan" would require— among other things—"life cycle analysis" of proposed products and "testing results." It would place the "burden of proof for showing that [a] product does not pose unacceptable risks" on the manufacturer, with there being several possible tests for acceptability of risk. That burden-shifting criterion would govern a review process that would determine whether to approve the "sustainability plan," "approve it with changes, or disapprove it."[124] A "follow-up stage" would "include provisions for dealing with new uses of a product and for requiring further testing if new evidence comes to light."[125] Davies identified as a particular problem the burden such a scheme would put on manufacturers, "especially small start-up companies." However, he cited a commentary indicating that most such firms would "'seek to partner with large companies in industries that can utilize nanotechnology to improve their commercial products.'"[126]

We have noted that some groups that ordinarily take antagonistic positions on matters of safety policy came together. A recognition had developed that varied "stakeholders" had an interest in safety that required research before "bad apple[s]" emerged from the barrel.[127] This concordance of interests appeared to support a self-regulation approach. The EPA had "proposed a voluntary program for NT" in 2005, but Davies observed that "[a] major disadvantage of voluntary programs is that they may leave out the people who most need to be included." In a remark notably tart in a rather sober document, he explained that "small firms making risky products and large firms with small consciences are not likely to volunteer to do health testing or to give EPA information that might indicate a significant risk."[128]

Risks More Focused

Even as the glow of NT brightened with new applications and optimistic predictions, more gloomy news about specific hazards came along, with gloomy prophecies about broad clusters of hazards as well. A hovering presence was uncertainty about risk.

A researcher told an EPA workshop in late 2005, as a reporter summarized it, that "a variety of engineered nanoparticles" could "pass through human skin and cause inflammatory responses" in cells that were "a primary route of occupational exposure" for nanotubes. Other experts stressed the need to measure "all aspects of nanoparticles," noting, for example, that nanoparticles containing iron could do more damage to immune systems than nanoparticles without iron or less iron.[129]

A year later, the leader of the nanotoxicology program for NIOSH reported on adverse effects of nanotubes on the lungs of mice. The official, Vince Castranova, spoke of the "'very unusual' finding" that "nanoropes" eventuating from the exposure of the mice to nanotubes "induced interstitial fibrosis" in the animals. The oddity of this result was that the fibrosis occurred without "an inflammatory response," something that was "not common" with other substances that were irritants to the lung, like asbestos.[130] A summary of this and other research characterized the effects of nanotubes on mice as "obstruct[ing] their airways, suffocating the animals."[131] Other studies indicated effects on heart muscle and aortic tissue—although, to be sure, the mice used in this research were "genetically predisposed to arterial sclerosis and were fed a high fat diet."[132]

Swiss researchers suggested a potentially broader set of hazards, saying that nanotubes had "the potential to build up in the environment and throughout the food chain." They specifically urged companies to screen employees working with carbon nanotubes for "health effects such as lung inflammation, allergic reactions, and cardiovascular problems."[133]

Reports on the variety of risks, identified and potential, trailed along behind an increasing variety of commercial applications. Friends of the Earth suggested that consumers refuse to purchase sunscreens with nanoparticle ingredients. The organization said that "the mostly cosmetic benefits of nanoparticle sunscreens do not outweigh the potential health risks involved in their use."[134] Concern about very small ingredients of commonly used products extended even to the mundane aspects of modern office life, specifically to "ultrafine articles of toner-like material" in laser printers.[135]

An Infant Science

In late 2006, a British study captured the general uncertainties about risks from nanoparticles, laying out with many particulars the need to dredge out much more information. This report by the Department for Environment, Food and Rural Affairs (Defra)[136] listed no fewer than 19 "Research Objectives" (ROs), most of them with several subparts,[137] for an attack on the problem. Purely illustrative are RO6, titled "optimisation and development of technologies that enable the measurement of occupational and environmental exposure to nanoparticles via air"; RO7, "Understanding of fate and behaviour of nanoparticles in air"; and RO11, "Research to establish a clear understanding of the adsorption of nanoparticles via the lung, skin and gut and their distribution in the body (i.e., Toxicokinetics), identifying potential target organs/tissues for toxicity assessment of nanoparticles in the human body."

The relative infancy of the risk science was evident in the report's statement that there was "little information on the influence of . . . nanoparticle characteristics on basic aspects of toxicology and ecotoxicology, mechanisms of actions and influence on dose-response relationships and toxicokinetic profiles." The authors added that "[w]ork is also needed to enable characterisation and measurement of nanoparticles in different environmental and biological media, including air, water and soil and a potential wide range of organisms and their tissues and organs."[138]

Studding the report were references to the need for "clear understanding" of the effects of nanoparticles on people[139] and the "very little information" that had been collected on environmental effects, including "the influence of particle size, shape and number on basic aspects of ecotoxicology, mechanisms of action, influences on toxicokinetic profiles (adsorption/uptake, distribution, metabolism and excretion)."[140] The authors said that "[t]he extent to which fate, behaviour and ecotoxicology of nanoparticles is governed by specific properties, common to some or all nanoparticles, is largely unknown."[141] Indeed, the report identified several areas "where useful information could be provided from *in vitro* studies," including such basic questions as "what happens to nanoparticles inside cells?" and "what happens to cells after [they] have taken up nanoparticles?"[142] The lack of data on such matters was evident in the statement that "[u]nderstanding the mechanism(s) of particle penetration into cells would be important where NPs [nanoparticles] are shown to induce cellular reactivity and/or are believed to translocate through cells."[143]

Exemplifying the kind of effects that would never occur to most laymen with even basic scientific training was "activation of complement by NPs." The authors explained that "[t]he complement system is a proteolytic cascade that complements and amplifies the antibody response to invading pathogens." One analogy to which the report made reference was that of asbestos exposure, noting that "[c]omplement activation occurs after exposure to fibres such as chyrsotile asbestos . . . , leading to recruitment of macrophages to lung alveoli, potentially contributing to asbestosis lesions."[144] Another gremlin in waiting lay in "[r]ecent data from several research groups" that "demonstrates that nanoparticles can bind the protein lactate dehydrogenase leading to underestimation of inflammation."[145]

Giving further point to the lack of relevant information was a British report on a search of the literature on nanomaterials that spoke to the quite basic point of the lack of technology for the very process of measuring NT effects. The report identified the problem of "the use of instruments that are not compatible with the established personal sampling procedures that are used to assess compliance with exposure limits, or for epidemiological studies." It pointed out that "[v]ery few studies have evaluated these instruments for the measurement of engineered nanoparticles in the workplace" and said that "[m]ost of these instruments are too large to be used for personal monitoring and/or their inlet efficiency does not meet the required criteria."[146] The writers also noted that there had been "very few assessments of exposure level to engineered nanoparticles in the workplace"[147] and "very few peer reviewed papers on the effectiveness of engineering or personal control measures to reduce exposure from engineered nanoparticle aerosols."[148] Moreover, they said that there were "few" publications "on the characterization of nanoparticles in their bulk form, in fluids (biological or water/solvent) or for toxicological evaluation."[149]

Bad Magic

In 2006, a German organization began an investigation into why an aerosol "sealing spray" called "Magic Nano" had "caused so many respiratory problems that it was withdrawn from the market." Emblematic of the tininess of the mini-products was the fact that the aerosol would release a "fog with droplets measuring less than 10 micrometers, or 10,000 nanometers, including droplets measuring less than 100 nanometers." By contrast, the droplets from a pump version of the spray measured 100,000 micrometers. The aerosol droplets could get into the lungs, but the pump droplets could not, and as many as half a dozen Magic Nano users had gone to the hospital with pulmonary edema. As many as 110 others had "reported problems" from the aerosol, which was used to make household fixtures like bathtubs and toilets water-resistant and dirt-repellent.[150]

One hypothesis offered by the German Federal Risk Assessment (BfR) spokesman Jurgen Kundke, was that the respiratory problems were "simply a physical-chemical reaction to the tiny drops being inhaled," with particles bouncing off the surface hit by the aerosol in a way that could "increase the extent to which they get inhaled." Another explanation was that some of the solvent in the product "might cling to the nanoparticles . . . and cause the reported problems when in the lungs." Kundke said that this emphasized "the need for manufacturers to test not only chemical ingredients in products but also formulations of those chemicals under conditions that mimic how consumers use those products."[151] The very mundaneness of the use, and the contrast of nano-products with other products, was symbolic of the new tradeoffs created by NT. The fact that the BfR was reported to be "working with toxicologists and several firms" that made the chemical used in the aerosol to understand its effects indicated the difficulty of causation judgments, either prospective or retrospective.

The Magic Nano episode gave special point to the concern of a private company official, quoted earlier, about "one bad apple." Mathew Nordan, the user of that metaphor, contended that national governments should spend up to $200 million a year on toxicology research because of the possible fallout from a single incident.[152] It was notable, indeed, that some of the most vigorous calls for inquiry into risk came from the private sector. In 2006, a global consulting firm, ICF International, said that federal research funds should be "increased substantially" in the area; according to a news summary, the organization said the government should "move much more aggressively to determine the environmental, worker safety, and human health effects of nanotechnology."[153]

As detailed previously, among the more specific concerns about the effects of nanoparticles on the body was their ability to go through the nose into the brain.[154] One metal on which scientists focused was manganese.[155] Physicians representing environmental and health advocacy organizations stressed the need for studies of nanoscale gold and silver, the latter already being used in bandages, toothpaste, and clothing.[156]

A Lag Continues

Simply illustrative of the number of rocks that researchers wanted to turn over in search of potential dangers was the fact that in 2007, an international committee on nanotechnologies identified 111 projects involving NT risks that it would like to pursue. Vladimir Murashov, a member of Technical Committee 229 on Nanotechnologies of the International Organization for Standardization (ISO), named as a high priority the "identification of standard methods to quickly screen engineered nanomaterials to determine whether they may pose a risk to human health or the environment."[157]

Only representative of the criticisms of the laggard state of hazard information was a 2007 report of the National Resources Defense Council. The organization, saying that "nanomaterials in consumer products remain essentially unregulated in the United States," charged the government as guilty of a "gross failure to use its authority to protect citizens from the potentially dangerous effect of nanoscale chemistry." Its report, "Nanotechnology's Invisible Threat, Small Science, Big Consequences," spoke of consumers being "left ignorant and vulnerable to exposure to an untested and possibly unsafe new generation of chemicals."[158]

Consumer Reports checked in with a cautionary article in mid-2007. It noted that a survey by the International Council on Nanotechnology had discovered that only one in three of 64 NT manufacturers and laboratories "monitored exposure to the substances." A telling quotation came from a Wisconsin researcher who had "interviewed scientists in many labs." This specialist, Maria Powell, said that "[s]ome of the PhDs [doing NT work] think concerns about nanomaterials are being cooked up by a bunch of crazy environmentalists."[159] The same month, the Swiss Federal Office for the Environment and Federal Office of Public Health was reported to say that "[i]nformation on nanoparticles" was "insufficient to conduct risk assessments or craft regulations."[160]

It was only in late 2006 that the EPA had said it was hoping within ten months to begin "a voluntary stewardship program" that would "collect and generate information about intentionally engineered nanomaterials from the companies and research institutes that make them."[161] In early 2007 the FDA, which had been maintaining a Web site on the topic,[162] released a report recommending development of "guidance on drugs, biologics, medical devices, and other products with nanotechnology components." The purpose, the agency said, would be to "clarify what information to give the FDA about these products" and to "suggest when the use of nanoscale materials may change the regulatory status of particular products."[163]

As the development of new consumer applications rolled on, along with inevitable workplace exposures, there appeared to be plenty to data collection in progress, although the calls for data seemed to bulk as large as the information gathered and published. In the fall of 2006, Republican Sherwood Boehlert, then chairing the House Science Committee, declared that "[w]e're not happy," saying that "[t]he government needs to establish and implement a clear, prioritized research agenda and fund it adequately."[164]

One piece of data that came in from Britain in 2007 was particularly disturbing because it challenged a conventional comfort zone. This was the first bulletin on nanoparticles of the U.K.'s Health & Safety Executive. One finding of U.K. studies was that semiconductor nanocrystals, sometimes labeled "quantum dots," "could penetrate skin at an occupationally relevant dose within an average work day." The authors of the bulletin report declared "these findings ... surprising since they contradict the conventional opinion that the skin presents an impervious barrier to materials and that abrasion or mechanical stressors are required for nanomaterial penetration."[165] The U.K. bulletin followed a discordant note in an ISO report on aerosols, which said that "[w]ith only limited toxicity data and negligible exposure data, it is currently unclear how exposure to nanoaerosols should be most appropriately monitored and regulated." The ISO report said there was "insufficient information to determine which physical exposure metrics—size-selective number, surface area and mass concentration—are most relevant, or which are the most appropriate exposure characterization techniques to use."[166] This language seemed especially notable, given that it came several months after the German inquiry into a nanoaerosol that had been implicated in a number of illnesses, including some hospitalizations.[167] It was another cameo of a market tryout before the accumulation of data that scientists, and presumably consumers, would prefer to have in hand.

Symbolic of the belief in the benefits of the technology were federal budget allocations for research and development in the area—a proposed $1.5 billion for fiscal 2008, a figure that would bring total expenditures to $8.3 billion since 2001. However, equally symbolic of the galloping, rather uncontrolled nature of the technology was a proposal by the National Science Foundation (NSF) for what was described as a "new, multidisciplinary Center for Research on the Environmental and Health Safety of Nanotechnology," which would "conduct fundamental research on the interactions between nanoparticles and nanomaterials and the living world on all scales." An NSF statement said that "commercial exploitation" of the technology could "only succeed if credible information exists" on its "environmental and health safety aspects."[168]

Catchup Efforts Continue

The phenomenon of catchup ball was evident in the publication of two major U.S. government documents that bridged the last half of 2007 and early 2008. First came a report by the Nanotechnology Task Force of the FDA.[169] It mixed what were now becoming the standard acknowledgments about the puzzle presented by the new technology with the need for new information and with a cautious indication that it was not time to step up the general level of regulation.

Notable as indexes to the rise of the technology was the report's observation that there had been 22,000 "scientific publications" on the topic and 1,900 patent applications for nano-products.[170] Symbolic of the uncertainty about the subject was the report's notation that "[i]dentifying precisely what qualifies as a nanoscale material is difficult and currently a subject of substantial discussion in the scientific, regulatory, and standards communities."[171]

The breadth of ignorance about the subject was evident in the "mays" in the report. For example, concerning the question of whether there was an "upper size limit" for the biological effects of small particles, the report said that "there may be" such a limit for absorption in the skin, "though that limit may vary based on other factors as well." It also said that "characteristics such as a particle's shape and the location of changes in its surface may affect the interactions of nanoscale materials with chemicals in the body."[172]

An interesting broad framing of the topic was evident in the authors' decision to "address[] scientific issues as distinct regulatory policy issues in recognition of the important role of the science in developing regulatory policies in this area, rapid growth in the field of nanotechnology, and the evolving state of scientific knowledge related to this field."[173] Just the articulation of that distinction empha- sizes the need ultimately to integrate science with regulation.

The catchup-ball aspect of the problem appeared starkly in the report's sum- mary of "[s]everal scientific reviews" as "conclud[ing] that the state of knowl- edge for biological interactions of nanoscale materials is generally in need of improvement to enhance risk assessments and better support risk management decisions."[174] Paralleling that was the report's reference to the need to "[p]romote efforts, and participat[e] in collaborative efforts, to further understanding of bi- ological interactions of nanoscale materials, including, as appropriate the devel- opment of data to assess likelihood of long term health effects from exposure to specific nanoscale materials."[175]

The authors identified a particular set of problems in the FDA's own bailiwick. Although the agency requires premarket approval for a range of drugs and de- vices, it does not have that power over many other products used on or in the body. Illustrative are cosmetics; the report lists more than a dozen products that fall within the statutory definition, ranging from skin-care creams and permanent waves to baby wipes and mouthwashes.[176]

This book often advises a cautionary strategy for the assessment of product and process risks. The FDA Task Force presents another version of a cautionary approach. Carefully, it notes that "[a]s with many new technologies, the use of nanotechnology does not mean that a product's safety or effectiveness is neces- sarily increased, decreased, or affected in any way."[177] But, although consumers "may not always understand whether the use of nanotechnology has a significant effect on the products they purchase," the Task Force authors say that "[b]ecause the current science does not support a finding" of "greater safety concerns" associ- ated with products using nanoscale materials, they do "not believe there is a basis for saying that, as a general matter, a product containing nanoscale materials must be labeled as such"—instead leaving the decision to "case-by-case" analysis.[178]

There are two other things worth noting about the FDA Task Force report. One is that it was not until August 2006 that the Task Force was created[179] —a fact of particular interest since as early as 1990 there had been about 1,000 scientific publications on the topic and 200 patent applications worldwide.[180]

Regulatory concerns about innovation, it appears, may require a critical mass of developments—an accumulation of scientific papers, a sometimes glacial recognition in many quarters that there may be a problem, and concerns that spread across multiple institutions of government. This leads to the second point, which concerns the bureaucratization of governmental assessment of technolog- ical risk. The Task Force report notes that the FDA "is a member agency of the National Nanotechnology Initiative, a federal research and development program established to coordinate multi-agency efforts in nanoscale science, engineer- ing, and technology."[181] The goals of that effort, as summarized by the report, are primarily the advancement and promotion of the technology, with only the fourth of four goals being listed as the support of "responsible development of nanotechnology."[182]

In January 2008, the Congressional Research Service (CRS) entered the literature, with a summary of "Regulatory Challenges" posed by NT.[183] This report to Congress noted a major underlying tradeoff—that "[s]cientific concern is based in part on some of the very properties" of NT materials hoped to provide great social benefits.[184] It made the sweeping generalization that "[i]t is too soon to know whether such questions are serious cause for concern," but noted that "there is scientific evidence that some nanoparticles may be hazardous." It pointed to an instrumental concern that might give pause to critics of a precautionary stance—the specter of "'a nightmare of public backlash'"[185] that might arise from "consumer rejection of the entire range of consumer products incorporating nanotechnology."[186]

The CRS report rehearsed the problem of lack of data: "Even among researchers whose interest focuses on toxicity, there is no agreement about which data might be useful, and therefore few data are collected."[187] It noted the bedrock problem of definition of terms: "A major obstacle to data collection is the absence of consensus on how the materials should be named, how scientific tests should be conducted, or even what constitutes a sample of a particular material."[188] Difficulties in communication and comprehension in the scientific community itself lay in the fact that "[a]ccessing data is one problem, but understanding the meaning of data is another." The author instanced "an EPA workshop on characterizing nanoparticles" at which "toxicologists and physicists struggled to express their concerns to one another, and admittedly frankly their ignorance of others' areas."[189] Further complicating the problem was the fact that private companies developing the technology would not reveal information about their research, with the result that "scientists generally do not have access to data that are needed to detect patterns in the relationship between toxicity and other characteristics of various nanomaterials."[190]

A direct message to Congress of the report appeared in a discussion of possible gaps in the federal laws that various agencies might use to regulate NT. Even if those statutes "probably provide adequate authority for federal regulators over nanotechnology, such laws were not written with nanomaterials in mind." Thus, "agencies would have to develop new policies, produce guidance, and possibly issue regulations to translate" the language of existing laws "with respect to nanomaterials."[191] Beyond that, Congress might have to pass new laws to require the production of information about the technology or to require "manufacturers . . . to determine physical and chemical properties, to conduct toxicity tests, or to report information that already is reasonably available and potentially relevant" to risk analysis in the areas of human and environmental health and safety.[192]

A salient aspect of the CRS report lay in its synthetic quality. Mostly, it drew together a catalog of concerns that had been building up for a decade and more. What was notable was this: after more than two decades of development of the technology, the gaps in knowledge appeared to rival the dramatically accumulating body of knowledge—and, indeed, there were significant disagreements about even the definition of terms.

I note that many of the specters of danger that critics perceive in new technologies pass into oblivion after mass testing on the market and in the workplace. But I offer the case of asbestos as an example of the need for well-funded, close governmental scrutiny of potential hazards. I draw here on the most basic data in a history I recently surveyed as an expert witness.[193] The hazards of asbestos were remarked as early as the first century AD by Pliny the Elder, and a substantial number of research studies as early as the 1920s pinpointed patterns of illness associated with asbestos exposure. It was not until the 1960s that a few personal injury lawyers put their time into suing for asbestos-caused injury. But by the time I began serving as a witness in litigation involving asbestos in 2007, the number of tort claims filed by people alleging asbestos-caused illness approached three-quarters of a million; these included claims by people who attributed terrible diseases like mesothelioma to such indirect exposures as washing the work clothes of family members who had direct workplace exposure to the fibers. Quite as remarkable were predictions that before the surges of asbestos litigation ceased, there would be that many fresh lawsuits, if not more.

I have come to see asbestos as a modern parable of mass market experimentation. It teaches the complex lesson that we must not overreact to prophecies of doom, but that we must be cautious when reputable experts make such prophecies. The need for caution arises from the fact that when the outcome is a bad one, it may involve the deaths or injuries of thousands, even hundreds of thousands—with economic effects on many workers and stockholders in risk-producing industries.

I should note that just after I wrote this paragraph, an advance online study appeared in the journal *Nature Nanotechnology* pointing out that the "nanometre-scale diameter and needle-like shape" of carbon nanotubes (CNTs) "have drawn comparisons with asbestos."[194] Injecting nanotube material into the abdominal cavity of mice, the authors found that "asbestos-like pathogenic behaviour associated with CNTs conforms to a structure-activity relationship based on length, to which asbestos and other pathogenic fibers conform." In other words, long-fibred carbon nanotubes tended to produce disease in mice that looks like some kinds of asbestos-caused disease. The authors were careful to point out that "[a]lthough the study suggests a potential link between inhalation exposure to long CNTs" and mesothelioma—which is almost always associated with asbestos exposure— "it remains unknown whether there will be sufficient exposure to such particles in the workplace or the environment to reach a threshold dose" that would cause disease in people. They noted that their "study did not address whether the mice exposed to long CNTs that developed" inflammations and the lesions called granulomas "would go on to develop mesotheliomas." However, they said in the technical body of their article that this and other questions—including the disease-causing properties of short CNTs—"must be addressed with some urgency before the commercial use of long CNTs becomes widespread."[195] They were somewhat more pointed in the abstract of their article, in which they called their findings of "considerable importance" because of the large investments being made in carbon nanotubes "under the assumption that they are no more hazardous than graphite." Their findings, they said, "suggest the need for further research and great caution before introducing such products into the market if long-term harm is to be avoided."[196] Andrew Maynard, the Woodrow Wilson Center scientist we quoted earlier in the chapter, stressed that this did not establish that multi-walled carbon nanotubes—already in use in consumer products—caused diseases like those associated with asbestos. However, he also said that "it provides a wake-up call; the burden of proof is to show how they can be used safely."[197]

An Instructive Contrast: Recombinant DNA

An interesting set of historical comparisons and contrasts appears in the history of regulation of recombinant DNA technology. That story is one of scientists themselves taking hold of a problem at the very beginning, and it is an inspiring one. In 1972, an article by David Jackson, Robert Symons, and Paul Berg described a recombinant technique they had used.[198] The next year, two American scientists wrote a letter to *Science,* representing several colleagues, that communicated their "deep concern" that "hybrid molecules may prove hazardous to laboratory workers and to the public."[199] And in 1974, Berg and others wrote *Science* of "serious concern that some of these artificial recombinant DNA molecules could prove biologically hazardous" and proposed an "international meeting of involved scientists from all over the world."[200] That meeting, which took on mythic significance, took place in early 1975 in Asilomar, California. It produced a report that emphasized the need for "containment" of the products of recombinant technology—containment that would be matched "as closely as possible" to "the estimated risk."[201]

It was from this seed that there grew federal guidelines, first issued in draft in 1975 and then in more finished form in 1976. These guidelines included a classification system for containment levels, from the "minimal" P1 level to the most stringent P4 level. The P4 level had a tang of science fiction, featuring fully isolated areas that could be entered only through airlocks by workers who had to shower on leaving.[202]

There are notable distinctions between the early history of recombinant DNA technology and the history of NT as it developed. A fundamental difference, as I have suggested, is that in the case of recombinant DNA, a small group of pioneering scientists grasped the nettle early. And they did so before commercial applications of their scientific product began to find their way to the marketplace. Paralleling this science/industry dichotomy was the fact that, by taking early action that soon evolved into federal guidelines, the scientists fostered a meaningful, disciplined regulation of a new technology.

A sharp contrast appears in the case of NT, in which dozens of commercial flowers bloomed over a period of years before serious conversation took place at the national level about regulation. As noted previously in this chapter, researchers had sought to identify some potential threads of risk from NT as early as the early 1990s. President Clinton proposed his "National Nanotechnology Initiative" as he left office in 2001. Congress passed the 21st Century Nanotechnology Research and Development Act in 2003, with a few abstract references to "ethical, legal, environmental, and other societal concerns related to nanotechnology."[203] But as we have also recorded, the first major documents concerning the risks of NT began to be published only toward the end of 2005, and members of Congress were only talking tentatively about safety regulation targeted to NT by 2006.

Thus, NT was in full swing as a mass experiment for several years. The DNA scientists had put a lock on the barn door early. But the "stakeholders" for NT, both public and private, were playing catchup from the beginning. Here was a cautionary tale at one of the tiniest levels to which human ingenuity had reached.

Conclusion

We began this book with just a few examples of issues involving human experimentation at both micro and macro levels. Like a drumbeat, these issues continue to arise. Here are just a few more that have cropped up in the last year or so:

♦ In May 2007, a team of researchers from several institutions concluded, as one report summarized a special supplement to the journal *Cancer,* that "[p]ublic exposure to chemicals that cause breast tumors in laboratory animal studies is widespread, but regulatory responses have been lacking."[1]
♦ That same month, the FDA ordered makers of all antidepressant medications to use "an expanded black-box warning . . . about an increased risk of suicidal symptoms in young adults 18 to 24 years of age." Yet, two commentators referred to data "suggesting that depression play[s] a key role in suicidiality and that antidepressants do not themselves generate new suicidal symptoms."[2]
♦ In October of that year, an FDA advisory panel voted to ban over-the-counter medicines marketed for colds in children under 6 years of age, with a district vice president of the American Academy of Pediatrics saying that "[t]he current labeling of these products is . . . inaccurate, inadequate and dangerous."[3]
♦ In late January 2008, a report from a subcommittee of the FDA Science Board was summarized as saying that the agency "badly needs funds to bolster its scientific capacity and to update its information technology infrastructure."[4]
♦ On the same day, an official of the Government Accountability Office testified about the agency's conclusion that "federal oversight of food safety is a high-risk area that needs a government wide reexamination."[5]

The Elements of Mass Market Experimentation

An insistent set of themes in the assessment of experimentation of all kinds, only represented by this short list of illustrations, has to do with the way we balance individual prerogatives against the welfare of large masses of people. If we operated purely on risk-utility grounds without ethical or legal restraints, we could justify selecting particular individuals for experiments on the premise that any harm to them would represent a sacrifice that redounded to the benefit of society generally. Many may benefit if a few get hurt along the way to innovation. Yet, our social morality does not permit that choice.

Several factors stand out in the broad tapestry of risk in mass market experimentation. One is the theme of consumerism, rooted in the assumption that people have sufficient information to make choices among risks and benefits. Another, constant theme is that of uncertainty. Members of the public are uncertain about topics on which experts disagree. Experts themselves are sometimes uncertain or simply lacking in knowledge about the existence of risk or the dimensions of risk.

The role of information is crucial. Who has it, who needs it, and what are the incentives, as well as the opportunities, to acquire it or to hide it? In this regard, media are significant—both as reporters and as vehicles for triggering desire for products.

The model of a free market, with producers supplying adequate information and consumers intelligent enough to absorb it and act on it rationally, sometimes gives way to a need for regulation. Regulators enter the field when there is a political consensus for government intervention—sometimes because there is insufficient information in the field, sometimes because people paternalistically think that certain risks are too gruesome to be acceptable, and sometimes because it seems unfair to subject a few people to the risks of a product that benefits many more people. An important question about regulation concerns the point in the process of product development where government should intervene. The appropriate point for intervention may vary according to whether the subject area is one where patterns of hazard develop quickly or one where they develop over a long period of time. Some types of hazards may outrun the ability of regulation to respond to them. Politics, generated by pressure groups, may tilt the balance one way or the other.

Some landmarks in food and drug law exhibit strong social tilts toward regulation: the Pure Food and Drug Act of 1906, a creature of the administration of Theodore Roosevelt that prohibited misbranding and adulteration of products; the 1938 Food, Drug, and Cosmetic Act, a creature of the Franklin Roosevelt administration that required a showing of safety for drugs; and the Drug Amendments of 1962, adding the criterion of effectiveness to the ongoing concern with safety. At the same time, a vigorous market in over-the-counter drugs gives personal choice its innings.

In the social centrifuge of mass experimentation, several different groups act and react on each other in the struggle to define the proper boundary between encouragement to innovation and minimizing of risk. Sometimes that process makes for odd sets of antagonists and curious pairings of bedfellows. The groups whirling about in the political and legal worlds include scientists, practicing physicians, product sellers, consumers, media, and regulators. Interestingly, sometimes scientists and medical clinicians—on the surface blood siblings—contend against each other. These groups represent many streams of thought and often they are at odds on practical issues of choice and regulation that come into focus. Yet, sometimes groups that are often natural antagonists, like sellers and consumers, make common cause in the search for information about risk.

Experimentation on the effects of substances and processes on human beings takes various forms. Sometimes, experimentation may be identified as just that, and done in a centralized, controlled way. In its most formal settings, it may employ the so-called "gold standard." There, the people being experimented on—often called "human subjects" in language that this writer finds faintly degrading—are "randomized." Some receive or encounter the substance or process on which an experiment focuses, and the others receive a placebo.

As experimentation extends outward into the community, the process becomes less controlled and more diffuse. A broader randomization occurs because some people in the general market purchase or encounter a substance and some do not. Data relevant to the experiment can be collected only at some expense, sometimes great expense. Often, it only can be gathered retrospectively, although scientists would prefer prospective studies, which for purposes of inquiry on causation begin at the beginning.

An important issue concerns personal choice, a central component in the theory of consumer sovereignty. The principles of the original Nuremburg Code speak of an "understanding and enlightened decision."[6] The wide range among consumers of capacity to ingest and order information presents difficulties with regard to both understanding and enlightenment.

The neediness—sometimes the desperation—of people who may be targets of experimentation affects another factor, the meaningfulness of choice. Indeed, the way in which a product is presented to people may affect their view of their desire for the product: it may turn desire into perceived need. An illustrative situation of true desperation is that of the patient diagnosed with a terminal disease. In one case involving an alleged cancer cure, the FDA—and ultimately the Supreme Court—dealt with this problem in what might be described as a paternalistic way, essentially preventing personal choice. The Court effectively ratified the agency's decision to prohibit the interstate shipment of the product, confected from apricot pits.[7]

A striking contrast in result appears in the history of the speedups of the investigational new drug process achieved by pressure from a small community including a vital cluster of relatively sophisticated people, desperate for relief from a life-threatening disease widely viewed as a terminal one. In this situation, involving HIV/AIDS sufferers, expressed choices for risk-taking overcame conventional "good science" in the process of scrutinizing investigational new drugs. At one border of what were called "treatment INDs," that is, limited permissions to try out "promising" drugs for "desperately ill" patients when there is no "comparable satisfactory alternative"[8]—were so-called "compassionate INDs." Those protocols assured people they could get experimental drugs, rather than placebo, for diseases that afflicted only a few.

The position of government on personal choice works at least in three directions. One type of general regulatory rule constrains choice where there is no rational scientific basis for consumer decisions to choose a product. Another set of general regulatory rules protects human subjects from imposition by experts who hold the main cards of expertise and information. But a notable set of exceptions allows for choices to confront risk by members of a desperate, presumably self-informed subgroup.

Benefits and Costs

Another facet of the story has to do with the benefits from opportunities to experiment. Clearly, one set of beneficiaries is the experimenters, who enhance their resumes and their ability to command grant money. Another is the companies whose products are the objects of experiments, who can learn whether products are marketable or may discover that a product either does not work or creates unacceptable amounts of harm. Overall, society benefits from information derived from experiments—by innovation and also by information about risk, which ultimately saves lives and minimizes suffering.

Society's oversight of experiments of all kinds involves an allocation of costs. These include the costs of the experiments themselves—the expense of doing the tests, which is part of what is often a much greater cost of product development. They include costs to the individuals who suffer injury in experiments—which may stop a product in its tracks or, conversely, lead to a judgment that a risk is, on balance, acceptable. And injuries to individuals entail social costs, including lost work time, families riven by injuries to their members, and sometimes uninsured medical expenses. There are several answers to the question of who pays for experimentation.

On the other side of the picture is the question of which members of the public benefit. Some formal experimentation has the potential to cure clinical subjects themselves, but some research experiments do not even promise the possibility of such benefit: in such cases, a properly advised subject will know that he or she is strictly a vehicle for the acquisition of knowledge that may only benefit others. Going into what proved a fatal experiment, Jesse Gelsinger said that at least it might help the children. Mass markets, by comparison, involve a diffusion of risks and benefits. Consumers typically expect, and often require, benefits. But in the process of mass market experimentation, the discovery of risks through the use of consumers' bodies will benefit others who would otherwise be subjected to those risks.

Most nations have put entirely behind them the kinds of horrors associated with Nazi experimentation. The United States, in particular, has evolved a system that on paper, and often in practice, protects the rights of people who are the subjects of formal clinical experimentation. A principal vehicle for this protection is the Institutional Review Board, which must review each proposal for clinical research in at least federally funded trials.

The composition of these boards, which include lay community representatives as well as scientists and doctors with varying specialties, symbolizes the attempt to involve the public at large in scrutiny of experimentation. My personal experience on IRBs at two universities persuades me that on the whole, board members perform their responsibilities conscientiously. Their diversity tends to offset the lack of precise understanding that many of them, especially the lay members, have of the science involved in particular experiments. The process of institutional review is not foolproof, as witness the deaths of Jesse Gelsinger and Ellen Roche. Yet, any process for reviewing risks will occasionally come to grief on various combinations of ambition, politics, local culture, and slips in oversight.

A theme that continues to sound across the research enterprise, and indeed across the whole field of product and process innovation, is that of the amount of the costs. It often takes a lot of money to find out what "good science" would want to know about the fallout from a novel product or technique. That fact drives researchers to cut costs when they can. It sometimes generates incentives to cut corners in trying things out—corners that include the selection of vulnerable populations for research. Review boards must keep in mind the relative vulnerability of research subjects, especially those—probably the great majority—who do not have medical or scientific training and do not possess a sophisticated understanding of the biochemistry involved in the specific research that uses them. The lure of cheaper research is at the heart of disputes about using prisoners as research subjects. Beyond that, it is not terribly fanciful to suggest that free citizens with serious medical problems who undergo clinical experiments are the cousins of prisoners who may trade the use of their bodies for a few weeks of better food in a cleaner and less stressed environment. The freeness of choice is always a relative concept.

The issues are very different from those involving recruits to clinical trials when some individuals offer themselves as the sacrificial objects, on the basis that they are willing to take the risk of injury in return for a chance that an experiment will benefit them personally. In the case of the treatment INDs that the FDA authorized for HIV/AIDS patients, the preference of scientists clearly was to require all subjects of drug investigations to jump through the hoops of randomized trials, which meant that half of those who were willing to take the chance on a drug would not receive it. Here, the interests of society in "good science" faced off against individual choice—and the individuals won. Consumers voted, in a manner of speaking, to take control.

A separate layer of the case of the AIDS drugs from a lawyer's point of view involved the tension between principle and pragmatism. The principle, taken generally to represent the best balancing of social interests, yielded a rule that enforced the randomized trial. The pragmatic solution, weighing the persuasive force of a small but powerfully articulate political group, and taking into account its expressed desire to avoid the conventional process, was to make an exception.

One could foresee that the exception would give rise to similar requests for individualized treatment from other groups of sufferers. Many nonlawyers tend to concretize the idea of "the law." But lawyers and many practical laymen understand that "the law" is not a set of rigid rules and that on matters that count, there frequently are disputes between advocates of rules—defined in the conventional sense—and those who argue for flexibility according to the elements of particular situations.

Beyond the area of clinical research on drugs and medical devices, it is at least interesting as a thought experiment to consider the use of diverse committees, akin to IRBs, in the effort to identify potential risks in other products and processes destined for the general market. That process often proceeds willy-nilly, centered in the firms that develop products. A striking current example of regulatory lassitude is the field of nanotechnology. Even where a general regulatory process bears on safety, typically it is not nearly as stringent as that involved in clinical experimentation and usually it does not precede broad-scale marketing or other uses.

Desire, and Science

Several of the products analyzed in this book share themes of sex and the desire to be loved—ingredients in especially intense searches for personal perfection. Breast implants are a vehicle for heightening physical attractiveness, in the service of the goal of forming temporary or long-term attachments with a component of what people are willing to call love. Drugs for erectile dysfunction make it possible for men to consummate the sex act when they cannot—or maximize the ability to do so, despite the insistence that this is not their purpose. The goals of users span a range of physical desire and mental longings that include a wish for emotional attachment. Estrogen therapy relieves a variety of symptoms, from the mildly uncomfortable to the agonizing, but for many women it also facilitates their sex lives.

All of these products, in one way or another, help people to achieve goals that, as articulated today, would have caused earlier generations to see us as sadly, even pathetically, consumed with our bodies. They would have reacted to the phrase "feeling good about yourself" as extraplanetary. They understood desires well enough. What might, perhaps, have caused them to doubt the strength of our inner cores is how we submit to the translation of desires into needs. But they understood that process, too. *L'Elisir d'Amore*—the Elixir of Love—is a nineteenth century opera.

With respect to products of this kind, government's most powerful role appears not as a regulator of desire, but as a backup purveyor of information. Yet, sometimes it even appears as a paternalistic, or maternalistic, constrainer of risk-taking.

Regulators respond to patterns of injury. In the early experimental stages for a product, statistics in micro form may determine whether development of a drug or device goes forward. If on the basis of relatively thin data, a product does enter the mass market, with many thousands or even millions of people exposed to its risks, rather than only hundreds of experimental "subjects," it may be difficult at first to discern a problem requiring governmental attention. An "adverse event" in California, a "side effect" in Kentucky; it may take a while for enough red pins to dot the map for observers to find a more macro pattern. Science, medicine, media, politics, and law interact here, when people begin to discern patterns of risk in useful products with all the potential for both social benefit and social mischief that implies.

An important element of the problem is scientific disagreement, and this comes in more than one flavor. It is typical of controversial public policy issues that the data are in conflict, or that scientists disagree, on how to interpret the data. The number and range of statistics may be enormous. Only illustrative is the case of breast implants, where there was so much data that scientists began to do meta-analyses—studies of published studies. Moreover, scientists who deal with issues of public importance are only human in the sense that they may disagree about what is best for patient communities even when there is a basic agreement on the data.

The element of uncertainty pervades many difficult cases, often because the best that economically feasible experiments can do is to indicate a range of possible consequences from a product or process. Tied in with this is the long-term nature of some hazards, which may surface only over periods of years, in public experimentation on large numbers of people. Information about risk, where such products as chemicals and medical devices are concerned, is frequently a matter of accretion. And there is so much data—in some cases, studies in the thousands on the safety of particular products. The ED drugs are illustrative—7,000 articles in an eight-year period. We should remember that the more controversial a product, and the more lucrative its potential market, the better news there is for scientists. The combination of controversy and profit means that there is more research to be done. An important practical constraint on regulators, it should be added, is their limited resources for assessing data and for enforcement.

It may be noted that a fascinating aspect of science lies in stories of discoveries that emerged by accident or only as byproducts of where investigators originally were headed. Alexander Fleming's discovery of penicillin—from the inhibiting effects of mold on bacteria on a culture plate that he happened to observe—is a classic. In the area treated here, the case of oral contraceptives is a good example. Searle, the maker of Enovid, the first "Pill," originally received approval to market the drug as therapy for menstrual disorders in 1957. It was not until three years later that it got approval for large-scale clinical testing of Enovid as a contraceptive. As noted in Chapter 4, Viagra originally had piqued scientific curiosity as a treatment for angina, and it was only the "unique 'adverse event' " of erections that launched a thousand commercials.

It should also be observed that the world of mass experimentation is a world filled with scientific oddities. One might ordinarily think that prescription drugs emerge from a complicated brewing of molecules by people in white coats. Contrast, then, Premarin. Here is a biologically very complex product, but one that is derived from the urine of pregnant mares.

A complicating factor is that of synergistic effects, hazards that arise from combinations of products that may not exist with one product. But there may also be a benign cousin: the positive byproduct of a product designed for another purpose. An example lies in the extra endurance Viagra provides for children with pulmonary hypertension. Layered on top of these phenomena is the problem of information lag; we noted in Chapter 4, in particular, the lag time between the collection of data and the publication of journal articles.

This aspect of the problem is linked, in turn, with the time and expense of doing long-term studies. An important professional aspect of those resource realities is the difficulty they pose for scientists who may tie up a substantial part of their careers in the investigation of questions for which the renewal of funding is an annual ritual. We should also note that costs increase as the need for precise knowledge about effects on particular groups—for example, groups defined by age or aspects of their health history—manifests itself. Threading through the research process is the provision of research grants by manufacturers, which now has given rise to requirements by some medical and scientific journals that investigators must reveal their reliance on such grants in published articles.

These problems replicate themselves outside of the laboratory in the doctor's office. Even the most scholarly physicians may disagree about the meaning of data. Practicing doctors who do not use a magnifying glass on the risk sections of package inserts will disagree on how to compare risks and benefits, and about how much to tell their patients concerning their reservations about a product.

These issues typically move into the public eye because of publication of research results, sometimes with fanfare, in medical journals. The sexier the story—and often, it is literally about sex in some way—the more quickly it will be picked up on Internet media, on TV news, or in the printed press. Once a story is in general circulation, it may pose problems in both directions. As noted in the chapter on breast implants, there has been criticism of "junk journalism"—the tendency of reporters to swallow publicity from manufacturers whole. Another element of the problem, though, is the potential of news of adverse events to create unwarranted panic in patients already using a product.

In all of this, an important reality is that information about product risks, either hopeful or doleful, affects corporate bottom lines. We noted in the chapter on estrogens that within a couple of months of publication of the WHI study, the sales of Prempro declined by a quarter.

Science, Media, and Law

The media-izing of controversy leads inevitably to "spin," the fashioning of stories by advocacy groups—varied mixtures of manufacturers, scientists, groups of persons with particular diseases, different types of feminists, and injured individuals who want to tell their stories for reasons of vindication or vengeance. The spin aims at influencing politics, forcing issues on members of Congress and regulators in sensitive areas where they might prefer to take cover. Individual injury victims also invoke the help of the judicial branch through the vehicle of private lawsuits.

The pressures on the FDA, in particular, become enormous as risk profiles for products become controversial. These pressures extend to scientists doing research on specific products. Illustrative of the political antennae that scientists develop is the attempt of scientists, in the wake of the WHI study, to try to calm down members of the public about the risks of estrogens. That episode is evocative of the difficulty that scientists have in translating technical knowledge for the media and the public more generally.

The history of the HERS study as well as the HRI study has lessons to teach. One is how stunning an effect on the public can occur from the publication of reports about large studies that have been a long time in the research. Another is that even when a topic is science, if not "rocket science," scientists squabble among themselves, exchanging volleys about the meaning of data, and sometimes temporizing about how to interpret data. Scientists want to inform people; but they do not want to scare people unnecessarily.

With this kind of disagreement in the background, the consumer herself plays an important part in these dramas. In some cases, where data collection is strung out over time, large numbers of consumers are actively employed as guinea pigs. And when data comes forth on the results of mass experimentation, ordinary people may simply not be able to understand that data. In that situation, interpreters come to the fore, often with commercial axes to grind. The consumer faces a veritable cross fire of purported information, emerging from well-publicized cross-country conversations among scientists, with attendant questions about who to believe.

The battle for minds and hearts begins in the headlines. The stories themselves may feature wars between people of seemingly impeccable qualifications. A little classic on this topic appears in the opening pages of the majority opinion in *Daubert v. Merrell Dow Pharmaceuticals, Inc.,*[9] in which the Supreme Court established a set of criteria for judging scientific testimony. On the issue of whether the antinausea drug Bendectin causes birth defects, Justice Blackmun's opinion first summarizes testimony by Merrell Dow's expert, whom he calls "well-credentialed." In turn, he encapsules testimony by eight experts for the plaintiff, "each of whom also possessed impressive credentials."[10]

In such cases, courts have invented some techniques for avoiding decisions on the merits. If they are reviewing courts, they may simply say that the lower court acted rationally. Or they may send the case back for more development of the evidence. By contrast, in day-to-day practice, the prescribing physician—and the patient—must make a more definitive decision. Another facet of the individualized consumer stories that together make up the gross product of drug and device sales is what one may presume is the tendency of people to choose doctors who will support their desire for controversial medications.

One aspect of the problem, as hinted earlier, is how the incentives of research scientists and industry may be closely aligned with respect to the conduct of experimentation at various levels. Where potential product dangers are concerned, there are some institutionalized checks on risk, but an important question in any area of controversy is how many investigators there are who are truly at liberty to disseminate findings that may prove uncomfortable for companies. It seems necessary, not just desirable, that there exist a substantial research budget on risk that is provided by government agencies and private foundations detached from incentives for commercial exploitation.

Another relevant part of the business of experimentation—and it is a business—is the medical research establishment—and it is an establishment. Investigators live on their grants, and their grants depend on a review process that involves colleagues from across the country. There is a community of interest among these people. As reviewers, they may be quite critical of the proposals of others, but they also have an interest in maintaining lines of inquiry. As a practical matter, scientists as well as sellers have a financial interest in products in various stages of experimentation.

One problem for consumers is assessing tradeoffs, for example, of increased risk of cancer from estrogens against the benefit of reduction of fractures. True, if someone has an intellectual handle on the approximate numbers of risks and benefits for a product, her decision on whether to use it does not differ markedly from many decisions on tradeoffs that people make for themselves each week. The more foundational issue, though, concerns the lack of ability to assess complex statistics. Just one illustration of the subtlety of medical issues on which consumers must decide was the hypothesis that estrogens could be "promoters," if not primary causes, of breast cancer.

A cross-cutting feature of mass experimentation is a new frankness in society. Not much more than a generation ago, people would have whispered about sexually transmitted diseases, or erectile dysfunction, or breast implants. Now, they shout about their problems and solutions from the rooftops, or at least discuss them over cocktails. This generates a parallel frankness in media. Postmenopausal estrogens became part of the diet of newspaper readers, and a small cottage industry developed of simply written books on the topic. The frankness is particularly evident in advertising. What we have called "erection wars" is illustrative; one cannot view a news program for half an hour without seeing at least one ad for an ED drug.

During the last 15 years, the lines have blurred between traditional concepts of prescription drugs, which assume the physician as a sturdy gatekeeper, and drugs available over the counter. The episode of the IND speedups for AIDS drugs exhibits a situation in which even experimental drugs become available to sufferers who claim they are as knowledgeable as the experts. In the realm of ED products,

Eli Lilly began to offer trial packets of Cialis on its Web site. This was simply symbolic of several revolutions the Internet has wrought on medical care, opening up not only tools for self-diagnosis but tools for what as a practical matter amounts to self-medication.

An established feature of what for scientists is a routine part of their craft is the tentative nature of the endeavor. Science is always a work in progress. Sometimes, scientists may occupy themselves with labeling—is Pluto a planet?—but the quest is largely one for new information. Even lay people who as children watched small rodents develop in classroom settings may not be fully sensitized to this point. Like just about everyone, they desire certainty. In this connection, it should be noted that there is always a drive by scientists to categorize the objects of their inquiry more precisely, and in particular, to specify risks further. As that process continues, the consumers' task of assessing data becomes more complex. The twists and turns in the story of postmenopausal estrogens reflect how the accumulation of information over time changes minds among both scientists and lay persons.

The consumer coin has two starkly different faces. On one side is the smiling consumer who is told she is sovereign—that she can decide for herself. On the other is the frowning consumer who either does not have the basic information on risk before her or lacks the ability to understand it.

Tort law stands in the background of any pattern of injury associated with a product. Information sharing among claimants' attorneys about the science of products and the incidence of injuries can now occur at the touch of a few buttons on the computer. However, one problem prospective plaintiffs in such actions share with both scientists and regulators is the difficulty of linking "causes" with effects.

Uncertainty, Culture, and Rationality

Nanotechnology, recently bursting on the scene with commercial viability, becomes an ironic metaphor for the problem of mass experimentation, at Lilliputian dimensions. Nanotech is on the cusp. In its tiny universe, it has been a prime example of nonregulated experimentation. The puzzle exists in three important settings—the workplace, the market for consumer products, and the environment more broadly. The potential for risks of which people ordinarily would not dream is evident in concerns expressed about disease-causing particles being thrown into the air by the weathering of road surfaces. Workers with nano-products, in particular, have become front-line experimental subjects. This is evident from the many uncertainties identified in the document titled "Approaches to Safe Nanotechnology" issued by NIOSH and the Centers for Disease Control and Prevention[11] and from the statement on NIOSH's own Web site about the workplace risks not being "yet clearly understood."[12] Even in 2008, Lloyd's was warning that "Due to the potential impact to the insurance industry if something should go wrong, nanotechnology features very highly in Lloyd's top emerging risks."[13]

In the NT area, one discerns familiar patterns of uncertainty, for example, questions about the transferability of the results of animal studies to people. Overarching such technical issues, however, is the lack of an overall regulatory structure. Years after nano-things had begun literally to touch human beings, there came a clustering of reports that demonstrate a continuing uncertainty about various risks. That uncertainty arises from the lack of, and lags in, information. The decentralization of both inquiry and oversight stands in contrast to the searching quest for self-regulation by scientists at the dawn of the era of recombinant DNA technology.

Culture stands always in the near background, with all that it implies for needs and desires. Definitions of "womanhood" underlie the cases of breast implants and estrogens, as definitions of "manhood" are crucial to the marketing of ED drugs.

Culture informs politics, involving both legislators and regulators. Topics like those we have surveyed become subjects of lobbying by people with intense financial interests and sometimes desperate personal wishes. The border between tastes and safety is often filled with political gunfire.

Politics looks to science and discovers both more and less than it wants. At once, it discerns a mountain of statistics but also the classic two-handed scientist who often can offer only uncertainty: "On the one hand . . . on the other hand." For scientists, good news is when you can establish probabilities, which are themselves not certainties. For prospective consumers inclined to be risk-averse, data on scientific probabilities often sound like playing at dice.

It must be remembered, as we refer to both clinical experimentation and mass experimentation, that true investigation is a process in which the researcher does not know the outcome. On topics where responsible science requires an incremental massing of data, the frequently long time it takes to do that is frustrating to politicians and members of the public. The fact that some experimentation is on a mass scale requires a recognition that in that setting, as well as the laboratory, we do not know the results in advance.

While mass experimentation proceeds, myths develop—in the press, in the doctor-patient relationship, in the minds of patients. This product seems a panacea; that one gushes with a Fountain of Youth. At the same time, some negative findings are underpublicized.

Politicians must deal with what is sometimes a competition between public health concerns and private wishes expressed through the market. Untrammeled by regulation, sellers may create hazards in the environment at large as well as in consumer goods. They may also inflict welfare costs on society if their products injure individuals who cannot absorb their losses. There are numerous stories of seller resistance to news of developing patterns of injury, resistance which on occasion extends even to stonewalling up to the point that agencies bar products or sharply limit their sale. Sellers argue that regulators should connect lots of dots in order to show patterns of injury that require action. Management also feels constant pressure to push toward the marketing of products that have a margin of uncertainty about risk. "Go slow" is not the watchword of successful entrepreneurship.

Suffusing the landscape are the many devices sellers use to promote their products—always artful, by turns blunt and subtle. One judge has spoken of a background of "advertising, marketing devices and trademarks" by which the consumer is "lulled."[14]

In this environment, the tension between emotions and rationality is high. People are willing to be persuaded that things can be made better for them in what they consider vital parts of their lives. If there is evidence that risks and benefits are roughly in balance, they may seek the benefits and accept, insofar as they can, the risks. Government, often reluctantly, serves as a surrogate decision maker when risks seem unacceptable, even though the numbers look fairly equal. This may happen because there is not much information in the consumer sphere; it may happen because the nature of the risk seems particularly horrendous; it also may occur because of a trained intuition that the injury trends for a particular product or process are likely to get worse. In some of the cases discussed here, that intuition may stem from a belief that altering biological fundamentals is likely, over the long term, to produce significant levels of injury and illness; that belief may itself emerge from religious or philosophical conviction concerning human nature.

Attitudes toward Risk

When should Congress empower further regulation of product and process hazards, and when should regulators move to constrain experimentation, either clinically or on mass markets? The so-called precautionary principle is now a stock phrase, and as noted, it has been defined in different ways. Anthony Giddens has proposed a variation that says that "firms producing goods should think through the whole product cycle before those goods are released onto the market or relevant technical processes utilised."[15]

The principal foundation of these ideas, however phrased, is one of aversion to risk, an idea that often goes to war with innovation. In areas like those analyzed in this book, innovation cannot occur without some risk taking. There is a strong argument that when there are danger signs but research does not yet reveal well-founded data on risk, the risk should be the consumer's. It could be contended that this approach should be applied, for example, to a case like that of estrogens at least up to the time the WHI survey began to be published. The argument would be that without alarm bells being rung for widespread illness, unmistakably related to a product, the case for regulation should require a comprehensive brief rather than some discrete, suggestive research articles.

A contrasting way to apply a risk-averse approach is to ask how experimentation would affect people who are least equipped to assess the possibility of injury or to avoid it.[16] An example at the most basic level of experimentation is the troubling report that there is a new movement to use prisoners as subjects of early investigations. [17]

★ ★ ★

Policy Suggestions

One suggestion that might bear fruit is to create offices within existing agencies specifically tasked with doing critical reviews of risk trends and uncertainties concerning particular products and processes. Beyond that, the tale of nanotechnology might suggest the creation of a superagency on safety to replace existing agencies, although politics and various practical considerations weigh against that idea.

An alternative would be the creation of an elite office charged with critical review across agency lines. This office would be charged generally with early diagnoses of product and process hazards, and would have direct access to the Executive Office of the President for the purpose of suggesting early interventions in areas of developing risk. That kind of access would signal political confirmation of the importance of scrutiny of such hazards. In turn, it would provide a more direct line to media for publicity and at the same time would require at least some focused consideration by the executive branch. It would be relatively difficult to toss off suggestions from the office like hot potatoes. Beyond that, with a broad mandate to identify and publicize dangers to the public safety, the office could focus ongoing attention on the need for remedial action across a spectrum of risks. Just one illustration would be advocacy of a high priority on the development and production of pandemic vaccines.

Among the topics reviewed in this book, a prime example of the potential benefits of this kind of office would be to provide prominent early warning about the uncertain risks of nanotechnology. Indeed, the developing story of nanotechnology illustrates the need for formal interagency linkages. The potential hazards of NT spill into areas over which at least three agencies—FDA, EPA, and OSHA—have some jurisdiction. Yet, one can see various opportunities for fly balls of danger to consumers and workers to drop among these regulators. There might be cases in which the new office could recommend emergency measures to deal with a problem with which existing agencies could not cope, either for reasons of lack of statutory authority or lack of resources.

A parallel point concerns existing resources. As this is written, several influential members of Congress have recognized that various safety agencies—in particular, the FDA—are short of funds and personnel necessary to do their most basic jobs of protecting consumers. It might be useful if both houses of Congress could assign general oversight of federal safety programs to existing committees or, if need be, new committees. In suggesting this, I am aware of the value of having members of different Congressional fiefdoms generate investigations of specific problems. The work of Senator Grassley, the ranking member of the Senate

Finance Committee who has been a persistent critic of the FDA, is illustrative. Yet, there could be significant extra benefit from having a combination of overall Congressional oversight of risks and aggressive scrutiny across traditional departmental lines in a new office in the executive branch.

We spoke at the beginning of this chapter of a drumbeat of issues arising about large- and small-scale experimentation on human beings. The beat goes on, but it is a complicated rhythm.

- Over the past couple of years, an increasing body of information has come to light about conflicts of interest in both biomedical research and the application of that research by practicing physicians. Thus, with respect to conflicts in clinical research—such as investigators accepting "stock or consulting fees" from companies financing the research—an audit report by the inspector general of the Department of Health and Human Services found "[h]undreds of financial conflicts of interest among university researchers" that had "not been investigated by the National Institutes of Health."[18] And one writer noted that 94 percent of doctors "have some type of relationship with industry": 83 percent said that they "receiv[e] food and beverages in the workplace," 35 percent received "reimbursement for costs associated with professional meetings or continuing medical education," and 28 percent "receive[d] payments for consulting, speaking, or enrolling patients in trials."[19]

- One specific product area that yielded surprising findings of various types of hazards was a formerly sacred cow of public health: fluoridation of drinking water. A summary of recent research indicated that Iowa children drinking fluoridated water "were 50 percent more likely to have mild fluorosis"—mottled discoloration of enamel—"in at least two of their permanent front teeth at nine years of age than children living in nonfluoridated areas." And one researcher concluded that "fluoride is a risk factor" for osteosarcoma among boys, although that investigator's dissertation adviser warned readers "to be 'especially cautious' in interpreting" these findings. (At the same time, defenders of the researcher asserted that the adviser had a "conflict of interest because he is editor in chief of a newsletter for dentists funded by Colgate.")[20]

- Despite strong allegations that thimerosal, a preservative used in the diphtheria-pertussis-tetanus vaccine, caused autism, a 2007 study showed there was no support for "a causal association" of the chemical with "deficits in neuro-psychological functioning at the age of 7 to 10 years."[21] A commentator declared that the results of parents refusing immunizations to their children were to "elevate[] a theoretical (and now disproved) risk above the real risk of being hospitalized or killed by influenza."[22]

- Although concerns had been raised about the effects on children of phthalates, chemicals used in pacifiers and bottle nipples, experts speaking at a meeting said that "scientists do not know whether phthalate exposure is harmful to people."[23]

+ A scientist was planning large-scale trials on people to test a hypothesis, developed in rats, that hormone therapy could promote recovery from brain injuries; he had been advised as a student 40 years before not to "waste your time" on trying to heal such injuries.[24]

Thus, we must not ignore the great benefits, established and potential, brought us by human experimentation at all levels. There are many cries of alarm about product and process risks. Some will prove to be genuinely alarming; others will fall into oblivion. One important thing, though, is that we understand the experimental character of these ventures, scientific and entrepreneurial. Another is that we understand that uncertainty is the stuff of science, as it often is of law. *Uncertainty*, a concise book by David Lindley, captures the turmoil that Werner Heisenberg's ideas about the position and momentum of the electron produced in the scientific community.[25] On a less profound scale, uncertainty is at the center of all the controversies we have discussed here. And even on the most global scale, we confront radical uncertainties about the warming of the planet over time.[26]

Lessons

It is a truism that life is risky—Holmes' famous phrase was, "All life is an experiment." We do have to recognize that throughout our lives, we are experimental subjects in many ways—knowingly and often unknowingly—and that we derive useful innovations from various types of mass experiments. But the stories analyzed in this book give us some pointed lessons.

The first set of these lessons is that in a world of uncertainty, you pretty much have to be your own judge of what risks to take. This means you have to decide for yourself how much time and energy you want to spend investigating risks. In fact, it means that you have to assess your own tolerance for risk. That should not faze you. We do that all the time—in deciding whom to date, whom to marry, how fast to drive, and whether to eat something that you know always causes reflux.

So this is not a "be afraid—be very afraid" book. Rather, it is a book about being sensible. A pretty good general approach is to view the unknown with a certain degree of healthy skepticism and to understand what your opportunities are for self-protection. Here is an illustrative, brief checklist:

+ Be careful what you consent to as a patient
  • Certainly, as a subject of clinical research
  • But even about what your doctor suggests in routine medical practice
+ Watch what you buy, especially things that literally touch you
  • Drugs and devices
    • Specifically, be wary of breast implants and estrogens
    • You may feel more comfortable about ED drugs, but you have to cut through the hype

- Over-the-counter consumer products
  - Be wary about nano-products—various kinds of cosmetics, household sealants, sunscreens, even foods and food products
- In your workplace, be skeptical about fumes, aerosols, and dust; if you have a union, press its officials on these matters
- If you think you have been hurt by a product, think about seeing a lawyer (and understand that picking a lawyer may be no easy task—just like choosing a product)
- Be public minded—find out who the senators and representatives are who specialize in consumer protection matters and push them for more oversight of product and process risks.

Many people say that we have become too risk-averse as a society. Some will theorize that market forces themselves, backed up by the civil action for personal injuries, generally provide a sufficient guarantee of a working market for risk. But sometimes it is not enough to say that when you are hurt, you can sue. Many wounds cannot be bound up effectively—or even at all—by lawsuits. A principal theme of this book is that often the consumer lacks the information, or the training, to assess risk. In that regard, the approach I have urged here is in part an effort to enhance consumer sovereignty—to let the consumer truly make up his or her mind not only about established risk but about the level of uncertainty to which living itself exposes us all, every day. The case of the HIV/AIDS drugs is emblematic of the way that ordinary citizens can find their way through thickets of doubt to decisions they can best live with. However, my analysis also recognizes that in some situations it is appropriate for government, representing all of us, to slow down the pace of innovation that carries a potential for high risk, especially to vulnerable groups and individuals.

Postscript

As I finish this book in mid-October 2008, I must note the outsize parallel with its subject matter in the international turmoil resulting from a very long-running experiment: the operation of our financial markets. The histories analyzed in this book—of drugs, medical devices, and a quickly expanding new technology at the atomic level—raise questions related to the complexity of the human animal. The human body is a multitude of interconnected systems, many of which are still mysterious to experts. At another level of complexity, however, are the linked phenomena that make up the financial world across the globe. Within those systems, the activities of experimenters in pursuit of their own gain can generate consequences with grave effects on direct consumers and bystanders alike.

How much more lacking in relevant information are we, and how much more vulnerable to these events, by contrast with the more discrete episodes of experimentation I have examined here. As with the topics reviewed in this book, we find that the expertise of experts runs out at major points of impact and decision. Again similarly to those topics, we find interest groups in fierce conflict as governments—collections of mere human beings—struggle to contain the toxic byproducts of experiments, conducted in this case with dollars, pounds, marks, and yen. The dysfunctions of systems involving intangible financial instruments, and resulting panics, pose challenges that make our efforts to control man-made biological risks appear relatively rational. And they entail erosions of trust that may dwarf those associated with the dangers of tangible consumer products. If there are broader lessons to be learned from the histories we have summarized here, they stress caution in response to innovations whose nature we barely understand. For as we proceed case by case in the effort to improve the human condition, we become aware, sometimes painfully, of the boundaries of our knowledge.

Marshall S. Shapo
Evanston, October 2008

Notes

Introduction

1. Clifford J. Rosen, The Rosiglitazone Story—Lessons from an FDA Advisory Committee Meeting, 357 N. Eng. J. Med. 844, 844 (Aug. 30, 2007).

2. Gardiner Harris, Diabetes Drug Backed, but with Warnings, N.Y. Times, July 31, 2007, at A11.

3. Stephanie Saul, Another Study Finds Diabetes Drug Is Risky for Elderly, N.Y. Times, Dec. 12, 2007, at C2.

4. See, e.g., Adverse Drug Events Reported to FDA up Sharply, JAMA Archives Article Reports, 35 Prod. Safety & Liab. Rep. (BNA) 892 (Sept. 24, 2007).

5. Gardiner Harris, Report Assails F.D.A. Oversight of Clinical Trials, N.Y. Times, Sept. 29, 2007, at A1.

6. Jennifer Couzin, Lapses in Biosafety Spark Concern, 317 Science 1487 (Sept. 14, 2007).

7. Ellen Byerrum, Increase in Bio-Safety Laboratories Raises Concern over Worker, Public Safety, 37 O.S.H. Rep. 880 (Oct. 11, 2007).

8. See, e.g., Alex Berenson, Analysts See Merck Victory in Vioxx Deal, N.Y. Times, Nov. 10, 2007, at A1.

9. See Margaret Gilhooley, Addressing Potential Drug Risks: The Limits of Testing, Notable Risk Signals, Preemption and the Drug Reform Legislation, 59 S.C. L. Rev. 347, 357–359 (2008).

10. Alex Berenson, House Panel Scrutinizes Trial of Drug, N.Y. Times, Dec. 12, 2007, at C1 & C2.

11. Ron Winslow & Sarah Rubenstein, Delays in Drug's Test Fuel Wider Data Debate, Wall St. J., March 24, 2008, at A1 & A11.

12. Michelle Morgan Bolton, A Heavy Toll from Disease Fuels Suspicion and Anger, N.Y. Times, Oct. 6, 2007.

13. Carole Bass, Solving a Massive Worker Health Puzzle, Sci. Am., March 2008, 86, 86 & 93.

14. See Jacques Ellul, The Technological Society 134–135 (1965), citing study by Sigfried Giedion, Mechanization Takes Command.

15. See id. at 327.

16. Anthony Giddens, Risk and Responsibility, 62 Modern L. Rev. 1, 3 (1999).

17. Id.

18. Id. at 4.

19. Id.

20. Id. at 5.

21. See Grimshaw v. Ford Motor Co., 119 Cal. App. 3d 757, 174 Cal. Rptr. 348, 369–370 (1981).

22. 174 Cal. Rptr. at 385.

23. Id. at 384.

24. Id. at 387.

25. Id. at 385.

Chapter 1

1. See, e.g., Gina Kolata, Experts Try to Look at Era in Judging Radiation Tests, N.Y. Times, Jan. 1, 1994, at A1, A7.

2. Doubt Was Cast in 1966 on Radiation Experiment, N.Y. Times, March 3, 1994, at A7.

3. David L. Wheeler, An Ominous Legacy of the Atomic Age, Chronicle of Higher Ed., Jan. 12, 1994, at A6.

4. 44 Years after Radiation Tests, Truth about the "Science Club," N.Y. Times, Dec. 31, 1993, at A8.

5. See Heinrich ex rel. Heinrich v. Sweet, 62 F. Supp.2d 282 (D. Mass. 1999).

6. Schloendorff v. Society of New York Hosp., 211 N.Y. 125, 105 N.E. 92, 93 (1914).

7. Mohr v. Williams, 95 Minn. 261, 104 N.W. 12, 14 (1905).

8. Pratt v. Davis, quoted by *Mohr*, supra, from 37 Chicago Leg. News 213. The quotation appears in 118 Ill. App. 161, 1905 WL 1717 at *3 (Ill. Ct. App. 1905). In the Illinois Supreme Court decision in the case—which Cardozo cites in *Schloendorff*, supra—the court affirmed a judgment in favor of the plaintiff, on whom a physician had performed a hysterectomy without her consent. Pratt v. Davis, 224 Ill. 300, 79 N.E. 562 (1906).

9. See, e.g., Canterbury v. Spence, 464 F.2d 772 (D.C. Cir. 1972).

10. See, e.g., In re Cincinnati Radiation Litig., 874 F. Supp. 796, 819–820 (S.D. Ohio 1995).

11. See George J. Annas & Michael A. Grodin, The Nazi Doctors and the Nuremberg Code 133–137 (Oxford 1992).

12. See id. at 137, quoting General Telford Taylor as saying that the Code was "primarily" the work of Judge Harold Siebring.

13. The Nuremberg Code ¶ 1, reprinted in Annas & Grodin, supra, at 2.

14. Id., ¶ 3.

15. Id., ¶ 9.

16. Id., ¶ 10.

17. Heinrich ex rel. Heinrich v. Sweet, 62 F. Supp.2d 282, 321 (D. Mass. 1999), quoting Nuremberg Code ¶ 1, quoted earlier, text accompanying note 13 supra.

18. Id., referring to Rochin v. People, 342 U.S. 165, 172 (1952).

19. World Med. Assn., Declaration of Helsinki I (1964), reprinted in Annas & Grodin, supra, 331, 332.

20. Id., sec. II (2), Annas & Grodin at 332.

21. Id., sec. III, Annas & Grodin at 333.

22. Declaration of Helsinki II (1975), secs. I & II, reprinted in Annas & Grodin 334–335.

23. Id., sec. III, Annas & Grodin at 336.

24. Declaration of Helsinki IV (1989), Basic Principles I(2), reprinted in Annas & Grodin 340.

25. World Med. Assn., Declaration of Helsinki, Declaration V, reprinted in 277 J.A.M.A. 925 (March 19, 1997).

26. Kenneth J. Rothman & Karin B. Michels, The Continuing Unethical Use of Placebo Controls, 331 N. Eng. J. Med. 394 (Aug. 11, 1994).

27. Id.

28. Id.

29. Benjamin Freedman, Charles Weijer, & Katherine Cranley Glass, Placebo Orthodoxy in Clinical Research I: Empirical and Methodological Myths, 24 J. Law, Med. & Ethics 243, 244 (1996).

30. Id. at 245.

31. Id.

32. See id. at 247–248.

33. Benjamin Freedman, Charles Weijer, & Kathleen Cranley Glass, Placebo Orthodoxy in Clinical Research II: Methodological Myths, 24 J. Law, Med. & Ethics, 252, 252–253 (1996).

34. Id. at 254.

35. Id. at 255.

36. Id. at 258.

37. Peter Lurie & Sidney Wolfe, Unethical Trials of Interventions to Reduce Perinatal Transmission of the Human Immunodeficiency Virus in Developing Countries, 337 N. Eng. J. Med. 853 (1997).

38. Marcia Angell, The Ethics of Clinical Research in the Third World, 337 N. Eng. J. Med. 847 (1997).

39. George J. Annas & Michael A. Grodin, Human rights and maternal-fetal HIV transmission prevention trials in Africa, 88 Am. J. Pub. Health 560 (April 1, 1998).

40. Samiran Nundy & Chandra M. Gulhati, A New Colonialism? Conducting Clinical Trials, in India, 352 N. Eng. J. Med. 1633, 1633–1634 (2005).

41. Id. at 1634–1636.

42. Barry R. Bloom, The Highest Attainable Standard: Ethical Issues in AIDS Vaccines, 279 Science 186 (Jan. 9, 1998).

43. Ronald Bayer, The Debate over Maternal-Fetal Transmission Prevention Trials in Africa, Asia, and the Caribbean: Racist Exploitation or Exploitation of Racism? 88 Am. J. Pub. Health 567 (April 1, 1998).

44. Praphan Phanupak, Ethical Issues in Studies in Thailand of the Vertical Transmission of HIV, 338 N. Eng. J. Med. 834 (1998).

45. Merlin L. Robb et al., Letter, 338 N. Eng. J. Med. 843 (1998). For another argument in favor of placebo-controlled studies, where a particular alternative therapy is not the standard of care, see Salim S. Abdool Karim, Placebo Controls in HIV Perinatal Transmission Trials: A South African's Viewpoint, 88 Am. J. Pub. Health 564 (April 1, 1998).

46. David Brown, AZT's Success in Pregnancy May Help Expand AIDS Treatment for Poor, Wash. Post, Feb. 19, 1998, at A10.

47. Harold Varmus & David Satcher, Ethical Complexities of Conducting Research in Developing Countries, 337 N. Eng. J. Med. 1003 (1997).

48. John Harris, 31 J. Med. Ethics 242, 242 (April 2005).

49. Id. at 243, 245.

50. Id. at 243.

51. Id. at 247.

52. Robert Levine, The Need to Revise the Declaration of Helsinki, 341 N. Eng. J. Med. 531 (1999).

53. Tom Reynolds, Declaration of Helsinki revised, 22 J. Natl. Cancer Inst. 1801 (Nov. 15, 2000).

54. World Med. Assn., revised Declaration of Helsinki paragraph 29 (52nd WMA General Assembly, Edinburgh, Scotland, Oct. 2000).

55. See Susan Okie, Health Officials Debate Ethics of Placebo Use; Medical Researchers Say Guidelines Would Impair Some Studies, Wash. Post, Nov. 24, 2000, 2000 WL 29917819.

56. World Med. Assn., supra note 54, revised Declaration, Note of clarification on paragraph 29, http://www.wma.net/e/policy/b3.htm (printed Oct. 3, 2006).

57. Declaration of Helsinki, paragraph 30 (Edinburgh version, 2000).

58. Note of clarification on paragraph 30 of the WMA Declaration of Helsinki, added in 2004, http://www.wma.net/e/policy/b3.htm. (printed March 7, 2007).

59. See Philip J. Hilts, F.D.A. Rule Questioned By Scientists, N.Y. Times, Oct. 29, 1994, at 7; AP, F.D.A. Offers Stricter Rules on Drug Tests, unidentified newspaper, Oct. 28, 1994, at 9.

60. See 21 C.F.R. § 312.32(c)(1).

61. See id. § 312.32(a).

62. See id.

63. See 21 C.F.R. § 314.80((c)(1)(i)(2006).

64. See id. § 314.80(a) (2006).

65. See Sheryl Gay Stolberg, The Biotech Death of Jesse Gelsinger, N.Y. Times Magazine, Nov. 28, 1999

66. See id.

67. Trial & Error, Paul Gelsinger believes doctor did not fully disclose danger before his son Jesse participated in gene therapy experiment that killed him, Dateline NBC, Sept. 20, 2002.

68. Neil Munro, Nudging NIH, 35 Natl. Journal No. 44 (Nov. 1, 2003).

69. Stolberg, supra.

70. See id.

71. See id.

72. See id.

73. Kristen Philipkoski, Another Chance for Gene Therapy?, Wired News, http://www.wired.com/news/technology/0,1282,31613,00.html, printed July 16, 2003.

74. Stolberg, supra note 65.

75. Sheryl Gay Stolberg, Youth's Death Shaking Up Field Of Gene Experiments on Humans, N. Y. Times, Jan. 27, 2000, at 1, 20.

76. Id.

77. See Dateline NBC, supra note 67.

78. Stolberg, N.Y. Times, Jan. 27, 2000, supra note 75.

79. Institute for Human Gene Therapy Responds to FDA, Feb. 14, 2000, http://www.upenn.edu/almanac/between/FDAresponse.html, printed July 16, 2003.

80. Barbara Sibbald, Death but One Unintended Consequence of Gene-Therapy Trial, 164(11) Canad. Med. Assn. J. 1612 (May 29, 2001).

81. I have changed the spelling of "adnovirus," as it was transcribed from the hearing, with a notation that the transcriber was using a phonetic rendition.

82. FDCHeMedia, Inc., U.S. Senator Bill Frist (R-TN) Holds Hearing on Gene Therapy; Public Health Subcommittee of Senate, Health, Education, Labor and Pensions (Feb. 2, 2000) [hereafter, Gene Therapy Hearing].

83. Id.

84. Dateline NBC, supra note 67.

85. Horace Freeland Judson, The Glimmering Promise of Gene Therapy, 40(8) Technology Review Vol. 109 No. 5 (Nov. 1, 2006).

86. Vicki Brower, Targeted Genetics buys Genovo, Joins with Biogen in Gene Therapy, Biotechnology Newswatch, Aug. 21, 2000, at 4.

87. Rick Weiss, FDA Seeks to Penalize Gene Scientist, Wash. Post, Dec. 12, 2000, at A14, printed from the Internet March 29, 2007.

88. Rick Weiss & Deborah Nelson, Penn Settles Gene Therapy Suit; University Pays Undisclosed Sum to Family of Teen Who Died, Wash. Post., Nov. 4, 2000, at A4.

89. Information Issued by U.S. Attorney's Office for the Eastern District of Pennsylvania: U.S. Settles Case of Gene Therapy Study that Ended with Teen's Death, U.S. Fed. News, Feb. 9, 2005.

90. Id.

91. Feds Use False Claims Act to Punish, Bar Research Violations After Subject Died, Atlantic Information Services, Feb. 21, 2005.

92. Id.

93. Kathryn Senior, Is Gene Therapy Ready for HIV/Ebola Virus-Derived Viral Vectors? 357 (9258) Lancet 776 (March 10, 2001).

94. See Gene Therapy Hearing, supra note 82, printout at 23–24.

95. See id., printout at 26–28, FDA Official J.P. Siegal and NIH Official Amy Patterson in Colloquy with Senator Jeffords.

96. Id., printout at 32, Patterson colloquy with Frist.

97. Judson, supra note 85.

98. Id.

99. FDA, Ctr. For Biologics Evaluation and Research, Guidance for Industry: Gene Therapy Clinical Trials—Observing Subjects for Delayed Adverse Events (November 2006) (printed from the Internet).

100. Stolberg, N.Y. Times Magazine, supra note 65.

101. See Eliot Marshall, Report on Clinical Trial Volunteer's Death, Science Now, July 16, 2001, http://sciencenow.sciencmag.org/feature/data/7161.shtml.

102. See Eliot Marshall, Hopkins Death 'a Mystery,' Science Now, June 19, 2001, http://sciencenow.sciencemag.org/cgi/content/full/2001/619/2.

103. See id.

104. See Eliot Marshall, report of July 16, 2001, supra note 101.

105. See Eliot Marshall, report of June 19, 2001, supra note 102; Johns Hopkins Medical Institutions, Office of Communications and Public Affairs, Volunteer Dies After Participation in Research Study, June 13, 2001, http://www.hopkinsmedicine.org/press/2001/june/010613.htm.

106. See Eliot Marshall, supra, report of June 19, 2001.

107. ABCNEWS.com, Johns Hopkins Takes Blame, July 16, 2001, http://abcnews.go.com/sections/living/DailyNews/hopkins010716.html.

108. Id.

109. See Susan Levine, FDA Faults Clinical Research at Hopkins, Wash. Post, Sept. 8, 2001, at B2; Linda Bren, Human Research Reinstated at Hopkins, With Conditions, FDA Consumer, Sept.-Oct. 2001.

110. See Julie Bell, JHU researcher found to have violated rules; FDA proposes restrictions; study resulted in death, Balt. Sun, April 18, 2003.

111. See Levine, supra.

112. See Levine, supra, and Linda Bren, supra.

113. Edward D. Miller, Our Legacy to Ellen Roche, Hopkins Medical News, Fall 2001, http://www.hopkinsmedicine.org/hmn/F01/postop.html .

114. See Levine, supra.

115. See Healthcare Gamble, Insight, April/May 2003, http://www.insight-mag.com/insight/03/04-05/feat-2-pt-1-Healthcare.asp.

116. See id.

117. Letter from Joanne M. Rhoads, Director, Division of Scientific Investigations, FDA, to Alkis Toglas, stamped March 31, 2003.

118. Id.

119. Julie Bell, supra, note 110.

120. Steve Mitchell, UPI, TGN1412 Clouds Future of Superantibodies, http://www.terradaily.com/reports/TGN1412_Clouds_Future_Of_Superantibodies.html, April 17, 2006.

121. Elisabeth Rosenthal, Inquiries in Britain Uncover Loopholes in Drug Trials, N.Y. Times, Aug. 3, 2006, at A3.

122. Charles O. Choi, Not So Super, Sci. Am. July 2006, at 25.

123. Eliot Marshall, Bioethics Panel Urges Broader Oversight, 292 Science 1466 (2001).

124. See id.

125. E.K. Silbergeld, S. Lerman, & L. Hushka, Human Health Research Ethics, 305 Science 949 (2004).

126. Id., referring to 40 CFR pt. 26 (2001).

127. Id.

128. Rick Weiss, New HHS Panel Makeup Draws Ire of Patient Advocates, Wash. Post, Jan. 5, 2003, at A9.

129. Id.

130. Jennifer Couzin, New Rule Triggers Debate Over Best Way to Test New Drugs, 299 Science 1651 (2003).

131. Id.

132. Id., quoting Beatrice Golomb, Univ. of California, San Diego.

133. Id. quoting Steve Robinson.

134. Andrew Pollack, In Drug Research, the Guinea Pigs of Choice Are Now, Well, Human, N.Y. Times, Aug. 4, 2004, at A1, C3.

135. Id. at C3.

136. Id.

137. Ian Urbina, Panel Suggests Using Inmates in Drug Trials, N.Y. Times, Aug. 13, 2006, A1 & A18.

Chapter 2

1. Http://www.fda.gov/cder/regulatory/applications/ind_page_1.htm.

2. Http://www.fda.gov.cder/about/smallbiz.faq.htm.

3. Center for Drug Evaluation & Research and Center for Biologics Evaluation & Research, Guidance for Industry: Content and Format of Investigational New Drug Applications (INDs) for Phase 1 Studies of Drugs, Including Well-Characterized, Therapeutic, Biotechnology-Derived Products 6 (Nov. 1995).

4. Center for Drug Evaluation and Research, Frequently Asked Questions on Drug Development and Investigational New Drug Applications, http://www.fda.gov/cder/about/smallbiz/faq.htm (printed Feb. 22, 2007).

5. Id.

6. 21 USC 360dd (2006) (printed Oct. 12, 2006).

7. See 21 C.F.R. § 312.36 (printed Oct. 12, 2006).

8. FDA, Guidance for Institutional Review Boards, 1998 Update, http://www.fda.gov/oc/ohrt/irbs/drugsbiologics.html (printed Oct. 12, 2006).

9. Talk by Mary Kremzner & Brenda Kiliany on drug regulatory process, http://www.fda.gov/cder/handbook/develop.htm, at 6–7(printed c. July 2002).

10. See id. at 7–8.

11. FDA Release, Approval of AZT, March 20, 1987.

12. Id.

13. 412 U.S. 609 (1973).

14. Id. at 621.

15. Id. at 629.

16. See id. at 617–619. In a concurrence, Justice Powell said there could be "no doubt . . . that Congress intended to impose standards that would bar reliance upon anecdotal evidence or mere professions of belief by doctors as determinative of a drug's efficacy." Id. at 639 n.2.

17. 442 U.S. 544 (1979).

18. Id. at 557–558.

19. 21 CFR § 312.34(a), 52 Fed. Reg. 19466 at 19476 (May 22, 1987).

20. Id.

21. 52 Fed. Reg. at 19476.

22. Id. § 312.34(b)(3).

23. 52 Fed. Reg. at 19468.

24. Id.

25. Id. at 19469.

26. Benjamin Freedman, Equipoise and the Ethics of Clinical Research, 317 N. Eng. J. Med. 141, 143 (July 16, 1987).

27. Id., quoting A. Schafer, The randomized clinical trial: for whose benefit?, 7(2) IRB: Review of Human Subject Research 4–6 (1985).

28. Id.

29. Id. at 144.

30. Larry Thomson, Experimental Treatments? Unapproved but not Always Unavailable, FDA Consumer, Jan.-Feb. 2000.

31. 53 Fed. Reg. 41516 (Oct. 21, 1988), containing and explaining 21 CFR §§ 312.80–.88.

32. 21 CFR § 312.80.

33. See 53 Fed. Reg. at 41517–41518.

34. Id. at 41519–41520.

35. Id. at 41520, quoting Confronting AIDS: Update 1988 (Inst. of Med. 1988).

36. 21 CFR § 312.84(a).

37. 53 Fed. Reg. at 41520.

38. 21 CFR § 312.83.

39. 53 Fed. Reg. at 41518.

40. Pub. L. 100–607 § 201 (Nov. 4, 1988), adding to the law what is now 42 U.S.C. § 300cc-12.

41. Beth E. Myers, The Food and Drug Administration's Experimental Drug Approval System: Is It Good for Your Health? 28 Houston L. Rev. 309, 329, referencing S. Kazman, Red Tape for the Dying: The Food and Drug Administration and AIDS, at para. 28 (Heritage Foundation Report No. 644, Apr. 8, 1988).

42. See id. at 329–330, referencing sources.

43. Id. at 332, referencing, inter alia, Booth, An Underground Drug for AIDS, 241 Sci. 1279, 1279–1280 (1988).

44. Michael P. Peskoe, Application of AIDS-Related Drug Approval Processes to Other Drug Therapies—A Different View, 45 F.D.C.L.J. 357, 357–358 (1990).

45. Id. at 359.

46. Id.

47. Id. at 361.

48. James J. Eigo, Expedited Drug Approval Procedures: Perspective from an AIDS Activist, 45 F.D.C.L.J. 377, 377 (1990). Eigo's explanation of the role that the nature of AIDS deaths played in his becoming an "AIDS activist" appears id. at 379.

49. David W. Barry, A Perspective on Compassionate Parallel Category C Treatment Track IND Procedures, 45 F.D.C.L.J. 347, 352 (1990).

50. J. Daniel Kiser, Legal Issues Raised by Expedited Approval of, and Expanded Access to, Experimental AIDS Treatments, 45 F.D.C.L.J. 363, 366 (1990).

51. See A. Bruce Montgomery, How the Recent Changes in Expedited Drug Approval Procedures Affect the Work of a Clinical Investigator, 45 F.D.C.L.J. 339, 339–340 (1990).

52. Id. at 340–341.

53. See id. at 342–343.

54. Kiser, supra note 50, at 367.

55. Peskoe, supra note 44, at 360.

56. Kiser, supra note 50, at 373.

57. Montgomery, supra note 51, at 339.

58. Ellen C. Cooper, Changes in Normal Drug Approval Process in Response to the AIDS Crisis, 45 F.D.C.L.J. 329, 338 (1990).

59. Barry, supra note 49, at 351.

60. Id.

61. See Cooper, supra note 58, at 337.

62. See id. at 336.

63. Eigo, supra note 48, at 380.

64. Cooper, supra note 58, at 337–338.

65. See 55 Fed. Reg. 20856 (May 21, 1990).

66. FDA, Proposed Rule, New Drug, Antibiotic, and Biological New Drug Regulations: Accelerated Approval, 57 Fed. Reg. 13234 (April 15, 1992).

67. Id. at 13235.

68. Id. at 13234.

69. Id.

70. Id. at 13235.

71. Id. at 13234.

72. Id. at 13237.

73. See supra, text accompanying note 65.

74. Public Health Service, Expanded Availability of Investigational New Drugs Through a Parallel Track Mechanism for People with AIDS and other HIV-Related Disease, 57 Fed. Reg. 13250 (April 15, 1992).

75. Id. at 13257.

76. Id. at 13256.

77. FDA, Final Rule, New Drug, Antibiotic, and Biological Drug Product Regulations; Accelerated Approval, 57 Fed. Reg. 58942, at 58958 (Dec. 11, 1992), adding 21 CFR § 314.510.

78. See id., 58958–58959, adding 21 CFR § 314.520.

79. Id. at 58945.

80. Id. at 58943–58944.

81. Id. at 58948.

82. Pub. L. 105–115 (Nov. 21, 1997) (subsequent citations to sections now in U.S.C.A.).

83. 21 U.S.C.A. § 360bbb(a).

84. Id. § 360bbb(b)(1).

85. Id. § 360bbb(b)(3).

86. Id. § 360bbb(c)(1)–(3), (5).

87. Id. § 360bbb(c)(6), (7).

88. Id. § 356(a)(1).

89. Id. § 356(b)(2)(A).

90. 42 U.S.C.A. § 282(i)(1), (2).

91. http://clinicaltrials.gov/ct/gui/c/w2b/info/whatis?JServeSessionIdzone_ct=xvasgu6 sp1 (consulted when updated May 14, 2002), further updated at Understanding Clinical Trials, http://clinicaltrials.gov/ct2/info/understand, September 20, 2007 (consulted July 7, 2008), containing 20 questions, with the glossary at http://clinicaltrials.gov/ct2/info/glossary.

92. For a briefer list of questions patients might ask, see Larry Thompson, Experimental Treatments? Approved but not Always Unavailable, FDA Consumer, Jan.-Feb. 2000.

93. See FDA, Proposed Rule, Expanded Access to Investigational Drugs for Treatment Use, 71 Fed. Reg. 75147, 75147, 75150 (Dec. 14, 2006).

94. See id. at 75149, 75157.

95. Id. at 75147, 75148, 75150.

96. Id. at 75149.

97. Id. at 75159. The agency noted that "many studies that are described as open-label safety studies have characteristics that appear to be more consistent with treatment INDs or treatment protocols." Id. at 75155.

98. Id. at 75155.

99. Id. at 75150.

100. Id. at 75151.

101. Id.

102. Id. at 75155.

103. Id. at 75150.

104. Id .at 75160.

105. See id. at 75152.

106. 445 F.3d 470 (D.C. Cir. 2006).

107. Ezekiel J. Emmanuel, Drug Addiction, New Republic, July 3, 2006, 9, at 9–10.

108. Id. at 472 (court's characterization).

109. Id. at 476.

110. Id. at 483.

111. Id. at 483–484, quoting Palko v. Connecticut, 302 U.S. 319, 325 (1937).

112. See id. at 476.

113. Id. at 484, characterizing Cruzan v. Director, Missouri Dept. of Health, 497 U.S. 261 (1990).

114. Id.

115. Id. at 486.

116. Id. at 488–489 (Griffith, J., dissenting).

117. Id. at 496.

118. Id. at 497–498.

119. Id. at 493–495.

120. Id. at 499.

121. Id. at 490.

122. See Abigail Alliance for Better Access to Developmental Drugs v. Eschenbach, 469 F.3d 129, 134–135 (D.C. Cir. 2006), denying petition for rehearing.

123. Rehearing en banc was granted and judgment vacated on Nov. 21, 2006.

124. Emanuel, supra note 107, at 10, 12.

125. See id. at 9, 12.

126. Id. at 12.

127. Id.

128. Abigail Alliance for Better Access to Developmental Drugs v. Eschenbach, 495 F.3d 695, 702–05, (D.C. Cir. 2007).

129. See id. at 705–706.

130. See id. at 712–713, discussing United States v. Rutherford, summarized supra, text accompanying notes 17–18.

131. See, e.g., id. at 714–716 (Rogers, J., dissenting).

132. Id. at 717.

133. See e.g., id. at 717, quoting a 1609 English decision.

134. See id. at 718–719.

135. Id. at 720.

136. Id. at 708.

137. Id. at 709–710.

138. Id. at 709.

139. See id. at 712–713.

140. Id. at 713.

141. Id. at 726.

142. Id. at 713–714.

143. Abigail Alliance for Better Access to Developmental Drugs v. Eschenbach, 2008 WL 114305 (U.S.) 76 U.S.L.W. 3367 (Jan. 14, 2008) (denying petition for certiorari).

144. Susan Haack, Scientific Secrecy and "Spin": The Sad, Sleazy Saga of the Trials of Remune, 69 L. & Contemp. Probs. 47, 54–56 (2006).

145. See id. at 56–57 (quoting James O. Kahn et al., Evaluation of HIV-1 Immunogen, an Immunologic Modifier, Administered to Patients Infected with HIV Having 300 to 549×10^6 /L CD4 Cell Counts: A Randomized Controlled Trial, 284 J.A.M.A. 2193, 2200 (2000)).

146. See id. at 57–59.

Chapter 3

1. See David G. Borenstein, Silicone Breast Implants and Rheumatic Diseases, in Practicing Law Inst., Breast Implants Litigation 1993, 487 PLI/Lit 363, 365 (1993).

2. 21 CFR § 878.3530.

3. www.plasticsurgery.org/mediactr/implants.htm.

4. 21 U.S.C. § 360c(a)(1)(B).

5. 21 U.S.C. § 360c(a)(1)(C).

6. Proposed Rule, 47 Fed. Reg. 2810, 2820 (Jan. 19, 1982).

7. See, e.g., 55 Fed. Reg. 20568, 20570.

8. 47 Fed. Reg. at 2820–2821.

9. Id. at 2821.

10. Id.

11. Id. at 2819.

12. Id. at 2819–2820.

13. Statement from the Dow Corning Corporation, September 1995, "Dow Corning's Disclosure to Breast Implant Complications 1960s–1985," http://www.pbs.org/wgbh/pages/frontline/implants/corp/pkginserts.html.

14. 53 Fed. Reg. 23856, 23862–23863, 23873–23874 (June 24, 1988), which became 21 CFR § 878.3530.

15. 55 Fed. Reg. 20568 (May 17, 1990).

16. See id. at 20570–20571.

17. Id. at 20571–20572.

18. 56 Fed. Reg. 14620 (April 10, 1991), which became 21 CFR § 878.3540.

19. Id. at 14622.

20. Id. at 14626.

21. 56 Fed. Reg. 49098 (Sept. 26, 1991).

22. Id. at 49099. In a section on saline-filled implants, the agency used language that was parallel to, and sometimes identical with, its language on silicone gel implants. See id. at 49101.

23. FDA Release P92-1, FDA Calls for a Moratorium on the Use of Silicone Gel Breast Implants (Jan. 6, 1992).

24. FDA Release P92-11, Breast Implants Available Only under Controlled Clinical Studies (April 16, 1992).

25. 57 Fed. Reg. 22966-01 (May 29, 1992).

26. David Kessler, Special Report: The Basis of the FDA's Decision on Breast Implants, 326 N. Eng. J. Med. 1713, 1713–1714 (June 18, 1992).

27. Id. at 1714–1715.

28. Id. at 1715.

29. 57 Fed. Reg. 45811 (Oct. 5, 1992).

30. See, e.g., id. at 45812-01 ("low bleed gel-filled" device); id. at 45812–02 (combination gel-saline device) (both on the same date).

31. 58 Fed. Reg. 3436, 3436–3439 (Jan. 8, 1993).

32. See V. Mueller & Co. v. Corley, 570 S.W.2d 140 (Tex. Ct. App. 1978).

33. Chronology of Silicone Breast Implants, http://www.pbs.org/wgbh/pages/frontline/implants/cron.html; Cathy A. King-Cameron, Carving Another Exception to the Learned Intermediary Doctrine: Application of the Learned Intermediary Doctrine in Silicone Breast Implant Litigation, 68 Tul. L. Rev. 937, 961 n.157 (1994).

34. See In re Silicone Gel Based Implants Prods. Liab. Litig., 793 F. Supp. 1098 (Judicial Panel on Multidist. Litig. 1992).

35. For brief summaries of this history, see Krista R. Stine, Silicone, Science and Settlements: Breast Implants and a Search for Truth, 63 Defense Csl. J. 491, 491 (1996); Richard A. Nagareda, Outrageous Fortune and the Criminalization of Mass Torts, 96 Mich. L. Rev. 1121, 1141–1142 (1998). A news story reporting the bankruptcy filing is Barnaby J. Feder, Lawsuits Force Implant Maker to Bankruptcy, N.Y. Times, May 16, 1995, at A-1.

36. Natl. Multiple Sclerosis Society, Silicone Breast Implants and Multiple Sclerosis-Like Disorder (May 1993), http:www.pbs.org/wgbh/pages/frontline/implants/medical/positionstate.html.

37. Alan J. Bridges et al., A Clinical and Immunologic Evaluation of Women with Silicone Breast Implants and Symptoms of Rheumatic Disease, 118 Annals of Internal Med. 929 (1993).

38. Council on Scientific Affairs, Am. Med. Assn., Report: Silicone Gel Breast Implants, 270 J.A.M.A. 2602 (Dec. 1, 1993).

39. David Kessler et al., A Call for Higher Standards for Breast Implants, 270 J.A.M.A. 2607 (Dec. 1, 1993).

40. Sherine E. Gabriel et al., Risk of Connective-Tissue Diseases and Other Disorders after Breast Implantation, 330 N. Eng. J. Med. 1697, 1700 (1994). The authors qualified their conclusion by noting that it could not be taken as definitive on the general question because of certain limitations, such as the relatively limited size of the population studied. See also Mark A. Schusterman et al., Incidence of Autoimmune Disease in Patients after Breast Reconstruction with Silicone Gel Implants Versus Autogenous Tissue, http://www.pbs.org/wgbh/pages/frontline/implants/medical/abstract6.html (July 1993) (abstract) ("[t]he incidence of autoimmune disease in mastectomy patients receiving silicone gel implants is not different than in patients who had reconstruction with autogenous tissue"; H.J. Englert & P. Brooks, Scleroderma and Augmentation Mammoplasty—A Causal Relationship?, abstract of 1994 Aust. N. Z. J. Med. 24, http:www.pbs.org/wgbh/pages/frontline/implants/medical/abstract5.html ("study failed to demonstrate an association between silicone breast implantation and the subsequent development of scleroderma").

41. Marc C. Hochberg, Editorial, Silicone Breast Implants and Rheumatic Disease, 33 Br. J. Rheumatology 601, 602 (1994).

42. Philip J. Hilts, Some Reassurance on Breast Implants, N.Y. Times, Oct. 26, 1994, at A8.

43. Jorge Sanchez-Guerrero et al., Silicone Breast Implants and the Risk of Connective-Tissue Disease and Symptoms, 332 N. Eng. J. Med. 1666, 1669 (1995).

44. See Sara Marley, Study Sees No Linkage of Implants, Illnesses, Bus. Ins., July 10, 1995, at 10.

45. See Banaby J. Feder, Lawsuits Force Implant Maker to Bankruptcy, N.Y. Times, May 16, 1995, at A1, C6.

46. Gina Kolata, Legal System and Science Come to Differing Conclusions on Silicone, N.Y. Times, May 16, 1995, at C6.

47. See Marcia Angell, Do Breast Implants Cause Systemic Disease?—Science in the Courtroom, 330 N. Eng. J. Med. 1748 (June 16, 1994).

48. See Kolata, supra note 2.

49. J.A. Goldman et al., Breast Implants, Rheumatoid Arthritis and Connective-Tissue Diseases in a Clinical Practice, 48 J. Clin. Epidemiology 571 (April 1995)(abstract).

50. Heather Bryant & Penny Brasher, Breast Implants and Breast Cancer—Reanalysis of a Linkage Study, 332 N. Eng. J. Med. 1535, 1539 (1995).

51. Sanchez-Guerrero et al., supra note 43, at 1666, citing sources.

52. American College of Rheumatology, Statement on Silicone Breast Implants, Oct. 22, 1995, http://www.pbs.org/wgbh/pages/frontline/implants/medical/positionstate.html.

53. C.H. Hennekens et al., Self-Reported Breast Implants and Connective-Tissue Diseases in Female Health Professionals. A Retrospective Cohort Study, 275 J.A.M.A. 616 (1996) (abstract).

54. Online Focus: Breast Implants, May 30, 1996, http:www.pbs.org/newshour/bb/health/may96/breast_implants_5-30.html.

55. John C. Stauber & Sheldon Rampton, Confidence Game: Burton-Marsteller's PR Plan for Silicone Breast Implants, 3 PR Watch Archives No. 1 (First Quarter 1996)(Ctr. For Media & Democracy), http:www.prwatch.org/node/107/trackback (printed Feb. 16, 2005).

56. Laura Flanders, Beware: P.R. Implants in News Coverage, from Extra: The Magazine of FAIR, Jan.-Feb. 1996, http://www.fair.org/index.php?page=1342.

57. Marcia Angell, Shattuck Lecture—Evaluating the Health Risks of Breast Implants: The Interplay of Medical Science, the Law, and Public Opinion, 334 N. Eng. J. Med. 1513, 1516 (June 6, 1996).

58. Id. at 1515.

59. Id. at 1517.

60. Id.

61. See In re Silicone Gel Breast Implant Prods. Liab. Litig., Submission of Rule 706 National Science Panel Report at 2–3 (Nov. 30, 1998).

62. Id. at I-17.

63. Id. at I-20.

64. Id. at I-25.

65. Id. at I-26.

66. Id. at II-13.

67. See id. at II-25.

68. See id. at II-28.

69. Id. at II-28.

70. See id. at III-5–6.

71. Id. at III-5.

72. Id. at III-14.

73. See id. at III-17.

74. See id. at III-C-7.

75. See supra at text accompanying notes 53–54.

76. See id. at III-C-7–8.

77. Id. at III-19.

78. Id. At IV-3.

79. See, e.g., id. at IV-7–15; IV-26–41.

80. Id. at IV-41.

81. Id. at IV-42.

82. Id. at 7.

83. Id. at IV-42.

84. Silicone Breast Implants: The Report of the Independent Review Group 11 (July 1998).

85. Id. at 10.

86. Id. at 14.

87. Id. at 17.

88. See, e.g., id. at 17–18.

89. See id. at 19.

90. Id. at 20.

91. Id. at 26. Six specific conclusions on CTD appear id. at 22–23, summarized by the general statement that "if there is a risk of connective tissue disease, it is too small to be quantified."

92. Id. at 25.

93. Id. at 26.

94. Id. at 23.

95. Id.

96. Id. at 26.

97. Id. at 29.

98. Id. at 28.

99. Id. at 30.

100. Id. at 32.

101. Id. at 32.

102. See Scott A. Tenenbaum et al., Use of antipolymer assay in recipients of breast implants, 349 Lancet 339 (1997).

103. See Richard Horton, Commentary, Conflicts of Interest in Clinical Research: Opprobrium or Obsession? 349 Lancet 1112 (1997).

104. Report of Independent Review Group, supra, at 32.

105. Institute of Medicine, Safety of Silicone Breast Implants (Natl. Acad. Press 2000), originally released June 2, 1999, see 64 Fed. Reg. 45155, 45156.

106. Institute of Medicine study, supra at 16.

107. Id. at 2.

108. See id., e.g., ch. 7 ("Antinuclear Antibodies and Silicone Breast Implants"); ch. 8 ("Epidemiological Studies of Connective Tissue or Rheumatic Diseases and Breast Implants"); ch. 9 ("Silicone Breast Implants and Cancer"); ch. 10 ("Neurological Disease and its Association with Silicone Breast Implants"); ch. 11 ("Effects on Pregnancy, Lactation and Children").

109. See id., Executive Summary, e.g., at 3–5.

110. Id. at 54, 57.

111. Id. at 19–20.

112. See id. at x.

113. Id. at 3.

114. Id. at 116.

115. Id. at 118–119.

116. Id. at 123.

117. Id. at 135.

118. Id. at 139.

119. Id. at 150–151.

120. See id. at 168.

121. Id. at 189.

122. Id. at 197.

123. Id. at 214.

124. See id. at 232.

125. See id. at 215.

126. Id. at 225.

127. Id. at 226–228.

128. Id. at 232; see also id. at 226.

129. See id. at 233, 237.

130. Id. at 247.

131. Id. at 263.

132. See id. at 284.

133. Id. at 273.

134. Id. at 284.

135. Id. at 10.

136. Id. at 11.

137. Id. at 11–12.

138. Id. at 12.

139. 64 Fed. Reg. 45155 (Aug. 19, 1999).

140. Id. at 45156.

141. Id. at 45158.

142. Id.

143. Id. at 45159.

144. National Center for Policy Research (CPR) for Women & Families, Fact Sheet on the Safety of Silicone Breast Implants, http://www.cpr4womenandfamilies.org/facts1.html (undated, apparently c. 1999).

145. Esther Janowsky et al., Meta-Analyses of the Relation between Silicone Breast Implants and the Risk of Connective-Tissue Diseases, 342 N. Eng. J. Med. 781 (2000).

146. Id. at 788–789.

147. Id. at 786, 788.

148. Rodney J. Rohrich & Arshad R. Muzaffar, Silicone-Gel Breast Implants: Health & Regulatory Update 2000, at 30 (American Council of Science & Health).

149. Id. at 20.

150. Id. at 28–29.

151. Id. at 33.

152. Id. at 31.

153. Patricia Lieberman & Diane Zuckerman, Do Breast Implants Cause Disease: A Review of the Studies Included in the Recent Meta-Analysis, National Ctr. for Policy Research (CPR) for Women & Families, http://www.center4research.org/implantsn.html.

154. FDA, Breast Implants, An Information Update 2000.

155. Id. at 17, quoting the IOM Report.

156. Id. at 19.

157. Id. at 23.

158. See id. at 17–28.

159. FDA, Breast Implant Risks, http://www.fda.gov/cdrh/breastimplants/breast_implant_risks_brochure.html (Nov. 2000).

160. Information Update, supra note 154, at 29.

161. Id. at 33.

162. Id.

163. S.L. Brown et al., Silicone Gel Breast Rupture, Extracapsular Silicone, and Health Status in a Population of Women, 28(5) J. Rheumatol. 996, 1001 (May 2001).

164. Id. at 996 (abstract).

165. S. Lori Brown et al., An Association of Silicone-gel Breast Implant Rupture and Fibromyalgia, 4(4) Current Rheumatology Reports 293, 293 (Aug. 2002) (abstract).

166. Id. at 297.

167. Id. at 294.

168. See Natl. Cancer Inst., Release, Silicone Breast Implants Not Linked to Most Cancers (April 24, 2001), http://www.cancer.gov/newscenter/silicone_othercancers.html, summarizing Louise A. Brinton et al., Cancer Risk at Sites Other Than Breast Following Augmentation Mammoplasty, 11(4) Annals of Epidemiol. 248 (April 2001).

169. Louise A. Brinton et al., Mortality among augmentation mammoplasty patients, 12(3) Epidemiol. 321 (May 2001).

170. NCI Release, supra note 168.

171. Diana Zuckerman & Rachael Flynn, Government Studies Link Breast Implants to Cancer, Lung Diseases and Suicide, Natl. Ctr. for Policy Research (CPR) For Women & Families, http://www.center4research.org/implantgovstdy.html.

172. FDA Notice, 66 Fed. Reg. 35645, 35646 (July 6, 2001).

173. Mentor Corp., Saline-Filled Breast Implant Surgery: Making an Informed Decision (c. 2001, copy in possession of author). [hereafter, Mentor Corp., my printout].

174. See supra, text accompanying notes 154–162.

175. Mentor Corp., supra, my printout, at 2.

176. Id. at 16.

177. See id. at 20–21.

178. See http://www.fda.gov/cdrh/breastimplants/labeling/mentor_patient_labeling_5900.html.

179. Mentor Corp., supra, my printout, at 8–12.

180. See id. at 4.

181. See Gina Kolata, A Sexual Subtext to the Debate Over Breast Implants, N.Y. Times, News of the Week in Review, Oct. 19, 2003, at 4.

182. See Gina Kolata, F.D.A. Defers Final Decision About Implants, N.Y. Times, Jan. 9, 2004, at A1 & A14.

183. See supra, text accompanying notes 57–60.

184. Gardiner Harris, High Rate of Failure Estimated for Silicone Breast Implants, N.Y. Times, April 7, 2005, at A20.

185. See id.

186. Gardiner Harris, F.D.A. Panel on Silicone Breast Implants Hears From Women on Each Side of the Debate, N.Y. Times, April 12, 2005, at A15.

187. Gardiner Harris, Citing Safety Concerns, Panel Rejects Bids to Sell Silicone Breast Implants More Widely, N.Y. Times, April 13, 2005, at A16.

188. Gardiner Harris, F.D.A. Panel Backs Silicone Implant from One Maker, N.Y. Times, April 14, 2005, at A1 & A20.

189. Id. at A20.

190. See Stephanie Saul, F.D.A. Will Allow Breast Implants Made of Silicone, N.Y. Times, Nov. 18, 2006, A1 & A12.

191. See id.

192. See id.

193. Some of the ensuing material in this chapter is based on passages in Marshall S. Shapo, The Law of Products Liability (4th ed. 2001 & Supps. through 2008), including ¶¶ 5.04[5], 12.21[3][b], and ¶ 23.04[1][a].

194. Dow Chem. Co. v. Mahlum, 970 P.2d 98, 106 (Nev. 1998).

195. Douglas McCollam, Last Men Standing, 26 Am. Lawyer No. 2 (Feb. 2004); printed from file: //C:\Prgram%20Files\West%20Group\WestGroup\WestMate\dhtml5. htm.

196. 970 P.2d at 106.

197. McCollam, supra.

198. 970 P.2d at 118.

199. See id. at 106.

200. See id. at 106.

201. Id. at 112.

202. See id. at 112–113.

203. See id. at 118–121.

204. See id. at 108–109.

205. Id. at 109.

206. See id.

207. See Vassallo v. Baxter Healthcare Corp., 428 Mass.1, 4–5, 12–14, 696 N.E.2d 909, 913–914, 917–918 (1998).

208. Hopkins v. Dow Corning Corp., 33 F.3d 1116, 1124–1125 (9th Cir. 1994).

209. Toole v. Baxter Healthcare Corp., 235 F.3d 1307, 1312 (10th Cir. 2000).

210. Giddings v. Bristol-Myers Squibb Co., 192 F. Supp.2d 421, 425 (D. Md. 2002).

211. Meister v. Med. Eng'g Corp., 267 F.3d 1123, 1132 (D.C. Cir. 2001).

212. Id. at 1128–1129.

213. Id. at 1130.

214. Jennings v. Baxter Healthcare Corp., 152 Or. App. 421, 429–430, 954 P.2d 829, 834 (1998).

215. Jennings v. Baxter Healthcare Corp., 331 Or. 285, 307–309, 14 P.3d 596, 608 (2000).

216. Sasha Nemecek, Augmenting Discord, Sci. Am., April 1996, at 36–37.

217. See Settlement Facility and Fund Distribution Agreement between Dow Corning Corporation and the Claimants' Advisory Committee, Pursuant to the Amended Joint Plan of Reorganization of Dow Corning Corporation Dated Feb. 4, 1999, Effective Date June 1, 2004, printed July 12, 2007, http://www.tortcomm.org/downloads/PLAN_FINAL. 5-26-04.pdf.

218. Dow Corning Emerges from Bankruptcy, U.S. Today, June 1, 2004, http://www. usatoday.com/money/industries/manufacturing/2004-06-01-dow-corning_x.htm, printed June 22, 2007.

219. Claimant Information Guide, www.dcsettlement.com/CIG_Docs/Eng/CIG/CIG_ ENG_5.pdf, at 5, printed June 22, 2007.

220. Id. at 6.

221. See id. at 2.

Chapter 4

1. FDA, Revised Viagra Label, Sept. 19, 2004, http://www.fda.gov/cder/foi/label/2002/ 20895s11s15s18lbl.pdf, printed July 4, 2007.

2. Warren St. John, In an Oversexed Age, More Guys Take a Pill, N.Y. Times, Dec. 14, 2003, sec. 9, at 1.

3. Id. at 2.

4. See Graham Jackson et al., Past, Present, and Future: A 7-Year Update of Viagra (Sildenafil Citrate), 59 J. Clin. Pract. 680, 680–682 (2005).

5. John Schwartz, Viagra's Hidden Risks, Wash. Post, June 9, 1998 (4,000 subjects, nine deaths); Kathleen Kerr, Viagra Investigated, Newsday, May 23, 1998 (4,500 subjects, eight deaths).

6. Letter of March 27, 1998, from Robert Temple, M.D., Director, FDA Office of Drug Evaluation, to Sandra J. Croak-Brossman, Ph.D, Pfizer Pharmaceuticals, on Application Number 020895.

7. Physicians' Desk Reference, 53d ed., at 2426 (1999)(label as amended April 1998).

8. FDA Talk Paper, FDA Approves Impotence Pill, Viagra, March 27, 1998; http://www.fda.gov/bbs/topics/ANSWERS/ANS00857.html.

9. Six Deaths Trigger Old Concerns about Viagra, Chicago Sun-Times, May 24, 1998, at 44; Lauran Neergaard, Deaths Limited To Viagra Now 16, FDA Says, AP Story in Chattanooga Times, June 10, 1998.

10. See Irwin Goldstein et al., Oral Sildenafil in the Treatment of Erectile Dysfunction, 338 N. Eng. J. Med. 1397, 1400 (May 14, 1998).

11. See id. at 1398.

12. See, e.g., id. at 1398, 1403.

13. See Richard L. Siegal, "Dear Doctor" letter, dated May 1998, http://www.fda.gov/medwatch/safety/1998/viagra.htm.

14. FDA clears Viagra As Cause of 16 Men's Deaths, Chicago Sun-Times, June 10, 1998.

15. Lauran Neergaard, supra note 9.

16. Kathleen Kerr, 10 More Die While Using Viagra, Newsday, June 10, 1998.

17. Julie Rovner & Sarah Ramsey, US Concerns Mount over the Safety, Effectiveness, and Cost of Viagra, 352 Lancet 124 (July 11, 1998).

18. See id., referring to Goldstein et al., supra note 10.

19. See http://www.fda.gov/medwatch/safety/1998/aug98.html (posted Oct. 1, 1998).

20. See FDA Talk Paper, Pfizer Updates Viagra Labeling, http://www.fda.gov.bbs/topics/ANSWERS/ANS00926html/ (Nov. 24, 1998).

21. Professional Packet Insert, http://www.fda.gov/cder/consumerinfo/viagra/default.htm (revised Nov. 1998). For an example of wry wordplay, see United Press Intl, UPI Focus: New Warnings Issued Viagra, Nov. 24, 1998 ("Pfizer says it is revising the drug's label so users will know of the possibility and seek medical treatment should the condition, known as priapism, pop up").

22. Important Prescribing Information, http://www.fda.gov.cder/consumerinfo/viagra/default.htm (Nov. 24, 1998).

23. Geoff Hackett et al., Long-Term Safety and Efficacy after 2 Years of Viagra [R] (Sildenafil Citrate) Treatment in Erectile Dysfunction, 161 (4S) Suppl. J. Urology 214 (April 1999). (Abstract).

24. MedWatch, Summary of Safety-Related Drug Labeling Changes Approved by FDA, June 1999: Viagra, http:www.fda.gov/medwatch/safety/1999/jun99.htm (posted, Aug. 9, 1999).

25. Id.

26. See id.

27. See Melvin D. Cheitlin et al., Use of Sildenafil (Viagra) in Patients with Cardiovascular Disease, 99[1] Circulation 168, 169–170 (1999).

28. Id. at 175.

29. See id. at 174–175.

30. Id. at 175–176.

31. Gordon Williams, Reply, 87 BJU Intl. 907 (2001). For further details on this exchange, see infra, text accompanying notes 52–56.

32. Rohit Ahora et al., Acute Myocardial Infarction after the Use of Sildenafil, 341 N. Eng. J. Med. 700 (Aug. 26, 1999).

33. Id.

34. Fuminobu Ishikura et al., Effects of Sildenafil Citrate (Viagra) Combined with Nitrate on the Heart, 102 Circulation 2516 (Nov. 14, 2000).

35. United States v. Rutherford, 442 U.S. 544 (1979), discussed supra, Chapter 2, text accompanying notes 17–18.

36. http://www.viagra.com/professionals/summary/pro_pack_insert.asp?n=0 (revised Jan. 2000) (printout Aug. 6, 2001, at 10).

37. Id. (printout at 11).

38. Id. (printout at 13).

39. Mike Mitka, Some Men Who Take Viagra Die—Why?, 283 J.A.M.A. 590 (Feb. 2, 2000).

40. Id.

41. Babak Azarbal et al., Poster, Adverse Cardiovascular Events Associated with the Use of Viagra, 35 J. Amer. College of Cardiology, 553A (Feb. 2000).

42. Bill Hoffman, Court Rule Excites Viagra Rival, N.Y. Post, Nov. 9, 2000.

43. Id.

44. Bradley G. Phillips et al., Sympathetic Activation by Sildenafil, 102 Circulation 3068, 3069 (2000).

45. Id. at 3072.

46. Viagra's Effect on Nerve Activity, USA Today (Oct. 2001), printed July 11, 2007, from http://fndarticles.com/p/articles/mi_m1272/is_2677_130ai_79340021.

47. Howard C. Herrman et al., Hemodynamic Effects of Sildenafil in Men with Severe Coronary Artery Disease, 342 N. Eng. J. Med. 1622 (June 1, 2000).

48. Saad Shakir et al., Cardiovascular Events in Users of Sildenafil: Results from First Phase of Prescription Event Monitoring in England, 322 Br. Med. J. Med. 651 (March 17, 2001).

49. Mike Mitka, Studies of Viagra Offer Some Reassurance to Men with Concerns about Cardiac Effects, 285 J.A.M.A. 1950 (April 18, 2001).

50. Andrew Boshier et al., Cardiovascular Events in Users of Sildenafil: Authors' Reply, 323 Br. Med. J. 51 (July 7, 2001).

51. Jay Cohen, Comparison of FDA Reports of Patient Deaths Associated with Sildenafil and with Injectable Alprostadil, 35 Annals of Pharmacotherapy 285, 287 (2001).

52. Gordon Williams, Editor's Comment on Press Release: Further Research Supports Viagra Safety Profile, 86 BJU Intl. i–ii (Oct. 2000).

53. I. Osterloh & R. Hargreaves, Correspondence: Editor's comment on: 'Press Release: Further research supports Viagra safety profile,' 87 BJU Intl. 905 (2001).

54. Id., referencing Azarbal et al., supra note 39, but perhaps meaning M.A. Mittleman et al., Incidence of Myocardial Infarction and Death in 53 Clinical Trials of Viagra® (Sildenafil Citrate), 35 J. Am. Coll. Cardiol. 302A (2000).

55. Gordon Williams, Correspondence: Reply, 87 BJU Intl. 907, 908 (2001).

56. Id.

57. See Eric G. Boyce & Elena M. Umland, Sildenafil Citrate: A Therapeutic Update, 23 Clinical Therapeutics 2, 11 (2001).

58. See id. at 12, citing R. DeBusk et al., Management of Sexual Dysfunction in Patients with Cardiovascular Disease: Recommendations of the Princeton Consensus Panel, 86 Am. J. Cardiology 175 (2000).

59. See, e.g., Editorial Retraction, 311 Science 335 (Jan. 20, 2006).

60. D. Schultheiss et al., Central Effects of Sildenafil (Viagra) on Auditory Selective Attention and Verbal Recognition Memory in Humans: A Study with Event-Related Brain Potentials, 19 World J. Urol. 46, 49 (2001).

61. William E. Sponsel et al., Correspondence: Sildenafil and Ocular Perfusion, 342 N. Eng. J. Med. 1680 (2000).

62. Juan E. Grunwald et al., Effect of Sildenafil Citrate (Viagra) on the Ocular Circulation, 131 Am. J. Ophthalmology 755 (June 2001).

63. Juan E. Grunwald et al., Acute Effects of Sildenafil Citrate (Viagra) on Intraocular Pressure in Open-Angle Glaucoma, 132 Am. J. Ophthalmology 872 (Dec. 2001).

64. Laura Bell, Viagra's effects on eyes examined; In rare cases, popular impotence drug has been found to alter vision, Dallas Morning News, Nov. 6, 2000, at 1F.

65. See University of Maryland Ophthalmologist Says Viagra May Trigger Permanent Vision Loss in Some Men, AScribe Newswire, March 1, 2001.

66. See supra, Chapter 3, e.g., at text accompanying notes 69 (National Science Panel report on clinical immunology) and 90 (UK report on autoimmune responses).

67. See Peter Mucha, Permanent Vision Loss in 5 Men Raises Question on Viagra Use, Philadelphia Inquirer, April 7, 2001.

68. See, e.g., Horacio Kaufman, Multiple System Atrophy, 11 Current Opinion in Neurology 351 (1998).

69. I.F. Hussain et al., Treatment of Erectile Dysfunction with Sildenafil Citrate (Viagra) in Parkinsonism due to Parkinson's Disease or Multiple System Atrophy with Observations on Orthostatic Hypotension, 71 Neurol. Neurosurg. Psychiatry 371, 373 (2001).

70. David Tuller, Experts Fear a Risky Recipe: Viagra, Drugs and H.I.V., N.Y. Times, Oct. 16, 2001, sec. F, at 5 (quoting Dr. Ken Mayer).

71. See id.

72. Viagra Web site, http://www.viagra.com/professionals/about/faq.asp?n=0 (printed Aug. 6, 2001).

73. Erectile Dysfunction: Exercise Study Confirms Safety of Viagra in Stable Angina Patients, Health & Medicine Week, Dec. 10, 2001, at 21.

74. Culley C. Carson et al., The Efficacy of Sildenafil Citrate (Viagra®) in Clinical Populations: An Update, 60 Urology (Supp. 2B) 12, 25 (Aug. 30, 2002).

75. See id. at 23.

76. See Jay M. Young et al., Efficacy and Safety of Sildenafil Citrate (Viagra®) in Black and Hispanic American Men, 60 Urology (Supplement 2B) 39, 46 (2002).

77. See id. at 44–45.

78. See Diana Wysowski, Comparison of Reported and Expected deaths in Sildenafil (Viagra) Users, 89 Am. J. Cardiol. 1331, 1334 (2002).

79. See id. at 1332, 1334.

80. R.A. Moore et al., Sildenafil (Viagra) for Male Erectile Dysfunction: A Meta-analysis of Clinical Trial Reports, 2002 BMC Urology 2: 6, printout at 4.

81. See id. at 5.

82. Id. at 5–6.

83. Id. at 8.

84. Harin Padma-Nathan et al., A 4-Year Update on the Safety of Sildenafil Citrate (Viagra®), 60 Urology Supp. 2B (2002), at 67, 69.

85. Id. at 78.

86. Id. at 70.

87. Id. at 74.

88. See id. at 75.

89. Id. at 67.

90. Id. at 78.

91. Id. at 84.

92. Id. at 85.

93. Id. at 88.

94. Id. at 67 (credit footnote).

95. Peter H.C. Lim et al., The Clinical Safety of Viagra, 962 Ann. N.Y. Acad. Sci. 378, 380 (2002).

96. Id. at 386.

97. Id. at 382.

98. Id. at 380.

99. Id. at 386.

100. Krishnamurthy Sairam et al., Oral Sildenafil (Viagra™) in Male Erectile Dysfunction: Use, Efficacy and Safety Profile in an Unselected Cohort Presenting to a British District General Hospital, 2 BMC Urology 4, printout page 6 (2002).

101. See id. at printout pages 5, 6.

102. Id. at printout page 5.

103. David G. Birch et al., A Double-Blind Placebo-Controlled Evaluation of the Acute Effects of Sildenafil Citrate (VIAGRA) on Visual Function in Subjects with Early-Stage Age-Related Macular Degeneration, 133 Am. J. Ophthalmology 665, 670 (2002)(supported by Pfizer).

104. Id. at 671.

105. Yoram Vardi, Effects of Sildenafil Citrate [Viagra] on Blood Pressure in Normotensive and Hypertensive Men, 59 Urology 747, 748 (2002).

106. Hypertension: Viagra Significantly Effective, Well-Tolerated for Men Taking Multiple Blood Pressure Treatments, Heart Disease Weekly, June 16, 2002, at 22 (summarizing study reported by Dr. Thomas G. Pickering of Mount Sinai School of Medicine, New York).

107. See Patricia A. Pellikka et al., Cardiovascular Effects of Sildenafil During Exercise in Men with Known or Probable Coronary Artery Disease, 287 J.A.M.A. 719, 723, 724 (Feb. 13, 2002); Erectile Dysfunction: Mayo Clinic Study Shows No Adverse Heart Effect for Viagra, Heart Disease Weekly, March 17-March 24, 2002, at 17 (quoting Dr. Pellikka).

108. See Rakesh C. Kukreja et al., Sildenalfil (Viagra) Induces Powerful Cardioprotective Effect via Opening of Mitochondrial K_{atp} Channels in Rabbits, 283 Am. J. Physiol. Heart Circ. Physiol. 1263, 1267 (Sept. 2002); Myocardial Infarction: VCU Discovery Shows That Viagra Protects the Heart, Heart Disease Weekly, Oct. 6, 2002, at 18.

109. Stroke: Viagra Shown Effective in Reducing Effects, Heart Disease Weekly, April 21, 2002, at 23 (reporting on presentation by Michael Chopp, Ph.D., of Neuroscience Institute at Henry Ford Hospital).

110. See Ken Purvis et al., The Effects of Sildenafil Citrate on Human Sperm Function in Healthy Volunteers, 53 Br. J. Clin. Pharmacol. 53S, 59S (2002).

111. http://www.fda.gov/medwatch/SAFETY/2002/sep02.htm: VIAGRA (sildenafil citrate) tablets.

112. Viagra: S.F. Asks FDA for Gonorrhea Warning on Label, American Health Line, March 18, 2002.

113. See Erectile Dysfunction: New study of Viagra's Onset Finds Most Men Respond within 20 Minutes, Pain & Central Nervous System Week, Jan. 6, 2003, at 17. See also Erectile Dysfunction: Viagra Can Take Effect in As Few As 14 Minutes in Many Men, Study Shows, Clinical Trials Week, Sept. 29, 2003, at 5.

114. See Study Dispels Viagra Eyesight Fears, Health Newswire Consumer, Jan. 6, 2003 (reporting on study by Dr. Tim McCulley, published in Ophthalmologica).

115. Andrea Salonia et al., Sildenafil in Erectile Dysfunction: A Critical Review, 19 Current Med. Research. & Opin. 241, 241 (2003).

116. Id. at 257.

117. Id. at 246.

118. Id. at 249.

119. Id. at 247.

120. Id. at 250.

121. See id. at 251–252.

122. See id. at 253–254.

123. See id. at 254.

124. See id. at 252.

125. See id. at 253.

126. See id. at 255–256.

127. Diane Tran & Laurence Guy Howes, Cariovascular Safety of Sildenafil, 26 Drug Safety 453, 459 (2003).

128. A. Benchekroun et al., A Baseline-Controlled, Open-Label, Flexible Dose-Escalation Study to Assess the Safety and Efficacy of Sildenafil Citrate (Viagra®) in Patients with Erectile Dysfunction, 15 Intl. J. Impotence Research S19, S21 (2003).

129. Id. at S22.

130. Id. at S23.

131. Kim M. Fox et al., Sildenafil Citrate Does Not Reduce Exercise Tolerance in Men with Erectile Dysfunction and Chronic Stable Angina, 24 Eur. Heart J. 2206, 2209 (Dec. 2003).

132. Id. at 2211.

133. B-P Jiann et al., What to Learn about Sildenafil in the Treatment of Erectile Dysfunction from 3-Year Clinical Experience, 15 Intl. J. Impotence Research 412, 416 (2003).

134. See id. at 414.

135. See id. at 416.

136. Sundeep Bhatia et al., Immediate and Long-Term Hemodynamic and Clinical Effects of Sildenafil in Patients with Pulmonary Arterial Hypertension Receiving Vasodilator Therapy, 78 Mayo Clin. Proc. 1207, printout at 9–10 (2003).

137. Id. at printout 5–6.

138. Anousheh Arnavaz et al., Effect of Sildenafil (Viagra®) on Cerebral Blood Flow Velocity: A Pilot Study, 122 Psychiatry Research: Neuroimaging 207, 208–209 (2003).

139. See, e.g., Milton Liebman, The Field Widens, 38(10) Medical Marketing & Media, at 50 (Oct. 1, 2003).

140. See NN Kim, Phosphodiesterase Type 5 Inhibitors: A Biochemical and Clinical Correlation Survey, 15 Intl. J. Impotence Research Supp. 5, S13 at S17–S18.

141. Id. at S16.

142. Id. at S17.

143. See Liebman, supra note 139.

144. See id.

145. Charles Bankhead, Post-Marketing Studies of ED Therapies under Review, 32 Urology Times No. 9, June 15, 2004.

146. See D. Abbott et al., Preclinical Safety Profile of Sildenafil, 16 Intl. J. Impotence Research 498, 498–499 (2004).

147. Id. at 503.

148. See A. Boshier et al., Evaluation of the Safety of Sildenafil for Male Erectile Dysfunction: Experience Gained in General Practice Use in England in 1999, 2004 BJU Intl. 796, 796.

149. Id. at 798.

150. See id. at 799.

151. See id. at 800.

152. R.C. Rosen et al., Quality of Life, Mood, and Sexual Function: A Path Analytic Model of Treatment Effects in Men with Erectile Dysfunction and Depressive Symptoms, 16 Intl. J. Impotence Research 334, 337 (2004).

153. Id. at 339.

154. Herbert Jagle et al., Visual Short-Term Effects of Viagra: Double-Blind Study in Healthy Young Subjects, 137 Am. J. Ophthalmol. 842, 848 (2004).

155. Id. at 849.

156. See id. at 847–848.

157. See id. at 849 ("[a] possible site of origin is the cyclic nucleotide gated (CNG) channels, which are found not only in the membrane or cone outer segments but also at the synaptic terminal").

158. Id. at 842–843.

159. Sildenafil doesn't work for postmenopausal women, 17 Journ. Am. Acad. of Physicians Assistants No. 3 (March 1, 2004) (synopsis) ("no differences in the proportion of women reaching orgasm, orgasm latency, or subjective sexual arousal").

160. Stephen J. Leslie et al., No Adverse Hemodynamic Interaction Between Sildenafil and Red Wine, 76 Clin. Pharmacol. Ther. 365, 369 (2004).

161. R. Crosby & R.J. DiClemente, Use of recreational Viagra among men having sex with men, 80 Sex Transm. Infect. 466, 467 (2004).

162. See id. at 466, summarizing P.L. Chu et al., Viagra Use in a Community-Recruited Sample of Men Who Have Sex with Men, 33 J. AIDS 191 (2003).

163. Id. at 467.

164. Id.

165. Frank Romanelli & Kelly M. Smith, Recreational Use of Sildenafil by HIV-Positive and -Negative Homosexual/Bisexual Males, 38 Annals of Pharmacotherapy 1024, 1025 (2004).

166. Id. at 1026, citing L. Sherr et al., Viagra Use and Sexual Behavior among Gay Men in London, 14 AIDS 2051 (2000).

167. Id., citing G.N. Colfax et al., Drug Use and Sexual Risk Behavior among Gay and Bisexual Men Who Attend Circuit Parties: A Venue-Based Comparison, 28 J. Acquir. Imm. Defic. Syndr. 373 (2001).

168. See id., citing A.A. Kim et al., Increased Risk of HIV and Sexually Transmitted Disease among Gay and Bisexual Men Who Use Viagra, San Francisco, 2000–2001, 16 AIDS 1425 (2002).

169. See id. at 1027.

170. See id.

171. David Kirby, Party favors: Pill Popping as Insurance, N.Y. Times, June 21, 2004, at F-1.

172. See Romanelli & Smith, supra note 165, at 1027.

173. See id. at 1028–1029.

174. Aging with H.I.V.: Four Profiles, N. Y. Times, Aug. 17, 2004, at F-6.

175. Charles Bankhead, Post-Marketing Studies of ED Therapies under Review; AUA Guideline Warns of Conflicts of Interest Influencing PDE-5 Comparison Trials, 32 Urology Times No. 9, June 15, 2004.

176. Josh Weinstein, Why Advocacy Beats DTC: The Battle for Market Share Should Be Waged in Doctors' Offices, 24 Pharmaceutical Exec. No. 10, at 136 (Oct. 1, 2004).

177. Letter from Christine Hemler Smith, Division of Drug Marketing, Advertising, and Communications, Food and Drug Admin., to Robert B. Clark, Vice President, US Regulatory, Pfizer Inc., Nov. 10, 2004 (photocopy in possession of author).

178. See id.

179. See Michael Johnsen, FDA Taking Aim at DTC Claims, 26 Drug Store News No. 17, at 24 (Dec. 13, 2004).

180. See Kenneth Snow, Erectile Dysfunction: A Review and Update, 39 Formulary No. 5, at 261 (May 1, 2004).

181. Graham Jackson et al., Past, Present, and Future: A 7-Year Update of Viagra[®] (Sildenafil Citrate), 59 Int. J. Clin. Pract. 680, 682 (2005).

182. See id. at 683.

183. See, e.g., id. at 687, concluding that "[s]ildenafil has had a unique history and development and remains the leading treatment for ED."

184. K. Shinlapawittayatorn et al., Effect of Sildenafil Citrate on the Cardiovascular System, 38(9) Braz. J. Med. Biol. Res. 1303, 1307 (2005).

185. Id. at 1309.

186. See Robert F. DeBusk & Robert A. Kloner, Rationale for Not Combining Nitrates and PDE5 Inhibitors; Phosphodiesterase Type 5, 54 J. Fam. Prac. No. 12 (Dec. 2005).

187. See Andrew K. Hotchkiss, Aggressive Behavior Increases after Termination of Chronic Sildenafil Treatment in Mice, 83 Physiology & Behavior 683, 685 (2005).

188. Id. at 687.

189. See T. Klotz et al., Why Do Patients with Erectile Dysfunction Abandon Effective Therapy with Sildenafil (Viagra[®])? 17 Intl. J. Impotence Research 2, 3–4 (2005).

190. See DeBusk & Kloner, supra note 186, referring to E.D. Michelakis et al., Long-Term Treatment with Oral Sildenafil Is Safe and Improves Functional Capacity and Hemodynamics in Patients with Pulmonary Arterial Hypertension, 108 Circulation 2066 (2003).

191. See Ben Harder, Potent Medicine: Can Viagra and Other Lifestyle Drugs Save Lives?, 168 Science News No. 8 (Aug. 20, 2005).

192. See, e.g., William B. White, Clinically Relevant Drug-Drug Interactions of the PDE5 Inhibitors, 54 J. Fam. Prac. No. 12, at ss23(9) (Dec. 2005).

193. See 168 Science News Issue 8, supra note 191 (Aug. 20, 2005).

194. See Cardiology: Viagra Blunts the Effects of Stress on the Human Heart, Heart Disease Weekly, Nov. 20, 2005, at 86.

195. Ercan Kocakoc, Effects of Sildenafil on Major Arterial Blood Flow Using Duplex Sonography, 33 Journal of Clinical Ultrasound 173, 174–175 (2005).

196. Raj Akash et al., Association of Combined Nonarteritic Anterior Ischemic Optic Neuropathy (NAION) and Obstruction of Cilioretinal Artery with Overdose of Viagra®, 21 J. Ocular Pharmacol. & Therapeutics 315, 316–317 (2005).

197. See Howard D. Pomeranz & Abdhish R. Bhavsar, Nonartertic Ischemic Optic Neuropathy Developing Soon after Use of Sildenafil (Viagra): A Report of Seven New Cases, 25 J. Neuro-Ophthalmol. 9, 12 (2005).

198. Id. at 13.

199. Robert A. Egan & Frederick W. Fraunfelder, letter, Viagra & Anterior Ischemic Optic Neuropathy, 123 Arch. Ophthalmology 709 (2005).

200. See Murat Koksal et al., The Effects of Sildenafil on Ocular Blood Flow, 83 Acta Ophthalmol. Scand. 355, 356 (2005).

201. Id. at 358.

202. Id.

203. 47 Med. Letter 49 (June 20, 2005).

204. Texas Man Suffers Vision Loss, Sues Pfizer, Alleging Drug Caused Harm, 33 BNA Prod. Liab. & Safety Rptr. 651 (July 4, 2005)(reporting on Thompson v. Pfizer Inc., No. H-05-1985 (S.D. Tex.).

205. Viagra Causes Blindness, Lawsuits Allege, Trial, Dec. 2005, at 14 (reporting on Sansone v. Pfizer, No. L-3369-04 (Camden Cty. Super. Ct.).

206. http://injury-law.freeadvice.com/drug-toxic_chemicals/viagra-lawyer.htm, printed July 30, 2007.

207. See Marc Kaufman, FDA Told of Viagra, Blindness Link Months Ago, Wash. Post., July 1, 2005, business section.

208. Viagra Causes Blindness, Lawsuits Allege, Trial, Dec. 2005, at 14.

209. Viagra (Sildenafil Citrate) Tablets [January 21, 2000, Pfizer], http:www.fda.gov/medwatch/safety/2000/jan00.htm, printed August 3, 2001.

210. See Nicole Ostrow & Kristen Hallam, Bloomberg News, Viagra Label to Include Warning on Vision Loss, Phila. Inquirer, June 28, 2005.

211. FDA Statement, FDA Updates Labeling for Viagra, Cialis and Levitra for Rare Post-Marketing Reports of Eye Problems, July 8, 2005, http://www.fda.gov/bbs/topics/NEWS/2005/NEW01201.html, printed February 14, 2006.

212. FDA Alert [7/2005], http://www.fda.gov/cder/consumerinfo/viagra/default.htm, printed July 4, 2007.

213. Pfizer Inc.; Pharma Company Asserts No Increased Risk of Blindness with Viagra, Women's Health Law Weekly, July 31, 2005, at 78.

214. Group Seeks Strong Vision Loss Warnings on Labels for Erectile Dysfunction Drugs, 33 Prod. Safety & (BNA) Liab. Rep. 1071 (Oct. 31, 2005).

215. Jane Salodof MacNeil, ED Drugs Overprescribed by Primary Care Docs, 35 Fam. Prac. News, Issue 16 (Aug. 15, 2005) (quotation from article text).

216. Id.

217. See Kenneth J. Snow, Erectile Dysfunction: A Review and Update, 39 Formulary No. 5, S-175, at 261 (May 2004), referring to C. Carson et al., 15 Int. J. Impotence Research, Suppl. 5: 5–175, Abstract 31.

218. Tracy Wheeler & Cheryl Powell, Drug Ads and Reps Seem to Be Everywhere, Spending Billions to Influence You and Your Doctor, Akron Beacon J., March 13, 2005. The erection business was a merger and acquisitions item. GlaxoSmithKline, which had

held marketing rights for Levitra, outside the United States, sold those rights back to Bayer AG, a German firm, but at about the same time Shering-Plough acquired the U.S. rights from Bayer. Shawn McCarthy, First They Tried to Play It Safe, Toronto Globe & Mail, March 5, 2005, 2005 WLNR 11923125.

219. Brand Health Check: Viagra—Flagging Sales Signal Hard Time for Viagra, Media Asia, Aug. 26, 2005, 2005 WLNR 13456317.

220. See id.

221. See Alex Berenson, Sales of Drugs for Impotence Are Declining, N.Y. Times, Dec. 4, 2005, A-1 at A-34.

222. See id.

223. See Media Asia, supra note 219.

224. See Berenson, supra note 221.

225. See David Kiley, The Little Blue Pill—and Pals—Have the Blues, Business Week, Feb. 28, 2005, 2005 WNLR 3035632.

226. See Berenson, supra, at A-34.

227. Younger Men Lead Surge in Viagra Use, Study Reveals, Lab Bus. Wk., Aug. 29, 2004.

228. See Berenson, supra.

229. See id.

230. See Shawn McCarthy, supra note 218.

231. Brand Health check: Viagra, Media Asia, Aug. 26, 2005, supra note 219.

Chapter 5

1. Marshall S. Shapo, A Nation of Guinea Pigs 262 (Free Press 1979).

2. See, e.g., Clare Dyer, Pill Claimant Accuses Defendants' Witness of "Cavalier" Attitude, 324 Br. Med. J. 111 (May 11, 2002) (on upcoming decision on statistical risk factors related to third-generation oral contraceptives for venous thromboembolism).

3. See Sherrill Sellman, Hormone Heresy 6 (Get Well Intl., Inc. 1998).

4. Synthetic Generic Conjugated Estrogens: Timeline, http:/www.fda.gov/cder/news/timeline.htm (May 5, 1997).

5. See Wyeth Annual Report 2001 at 8.

6. See FDA Backgrounder on Conjugated Estrogens, http://www.fda.gov/cder/news/cebackground.htm (May 5, 1997).

7. Hormone Foundation, Evolution of Estrogen (Timeline), http://www.hormone.org/public/menopause/estrogen_timeline/index. cfm, last consulted Aug. 14, 2007.

8. Jeremiah Stamler et al., Prevention of Coronary Atherosclerosis by Estrogen Androgen Administration in the Cholesterol-Fed Chick, 1 Cir. Res. 94 (1953).

9. See FDA's Approval of the First Oral Contraceptive, Enovid, http://www.fda/gov/oc/history/makinghistory/enovid/html.

10. M. Evans & Co. 1996.

11. See id. at 40–43.

12. Id. at 165.

13. Id. at 19.

14. Id. at 69.

15. See id. at 25.

16. See, e.g., id. at 19 ("completely preventable" if treatment begun "*before* the onset of menopause"); 206 ("[m]enopause is unnecessary. . . . Younger women need never experience it").

17. See, e.g., id. at 18.

18. Id. at 132.

19. Id. at 105.

20. See id. at 134; see also id. at 15 ("an invitation to all women to start this adventure").

21. Id. at 67. See also id. at 158 "([e]strogen therapy, far from causing cancer, tends to prevent it").

22. Id. at 207.

23. See id. at 204 ("I still come across those persons who would tear the telescope from Galileo's eyes or wrest the dissecting knife from the hands of Vesalius").

24. Evolution of Estrogen, supra note 8.

25. See John C. Burch et al., Effects of Long-Term Administration of Estrogen on the Occurrence of Mammy Cancer in Women, 174 Am. Surg. 414, 414 (1971).

26. Federico G. Arthes et al., The Pill, Estrogens, and the Breast, 28 Cancer 1391 (1971).

27. Burch, supra, at 418.

28. See id. at 416–418.

29. Benjamin F. Byrd et al., Significance of Postoperative Estrogen Therapy on the Occurrence and Clinical Course of Cancer, 177 Ann. Surg. 626, 630 (1973).

30. Arthes, supra note 26, at 1394.

31. Id.

32. Dr. George B. Sanders in Discussion of Byrd et al., supra, 177 Ann. Surg. at 630–631.

33. Dr. Laman A. Gray in Discussion of Byrd et al., supra, 177 Ann. Surg. at 631.

34. Samuel D. Loube & David Kushner, Do Estrogens Cause Breast Cancer? A Critique, 41 Med. Ann. D.C. 158, 160 (1972).

35. Robert Fechner, Carcinoma of the Breast During Estrogen Replacement Therapy, 29 Cancer 566, 572 (1972).

36. Id., citing sources.

37. Id.

38. Id.

39. Victor E. Gould et al., Morphologic Features of Mammary Carcinomas in Women taking Hormonal Contraceptives, 57 Am. J. Clin. Path. 139, 140–143 (1972).

40. Basil A. Stoll, Hypothesis: Breast Cancer Regression under Oestrogen Therapy, 3 Br. Med. J. 446, 448 (Aug. 25, 1973) (italics in original).

41. Id. at 449.

42. Id. at 450.

43. P. Garcia-Webb & M.H. Briggs, Breast Cancer Regression under Oestrogen Therapy, 4 Br. Med. J. 419 (Nov. 17, 1973).

44. Id. at 420.

45. Id.

46. Fechner, supra note 35, at 566.

47. FDA, Certain Estrogen-Containing Drugs for Oral or Parenteral Use, 37 Fed. Reg. 14826 (July 25, 1972).

48. See id. at 14827.

49. See id., a general statement that follows a specific reference to what became recognized as the association between maternal ingestion of the hormone diethylstilbestrol and vaginal cancer in daughters born of women who took that product during pregnancy.

50. See W.H.W. Inman & M.P. Vessey, Investigation of Deaths from Pulmonary, Coronary and Cerebral Thrombosis and Embolism in Women of Child-Bearing Age, 2 Br. Med. J. 193, 198 (1968).

51. A Warning on the Pill, Wash. Post, Sept. 10, 1970, at C-9; AMA to Publish a Pamphlet on the Pill, Am. Med. News, Aug. 10, 1970, at 1.

52. See J.I. Mann & W.H.W. Inman, Oral Contraceptives and Death from Myocardial Infarction, 2 Br. Med. J. 245, 248 (May 3, 1975).

53. Samuel Shapiro, Oral Contraceptives and Myocardial Infarction, 293 N. Eng. J. Med. 195, 196 (1975).

54. Donald C. Smith et al., Association of Exogenous Estrogen and Endometrial Cancer, 293 N. Eng. J. Med. 1164, 1166 (1975).

55. Harry K. Ziel & William D. Finkle, Increased Risk of Endometrial Carcinoma Among Users of Conjugated Estrogens, 293 N. Eng. J. Med. 1167, 1169 (1975).

56. Noel. S. Weiss, Risks and Benefits of Estrogen Use, 293 N. Eng. J. Med. 1200, 1201 (1975).

57. Kenneth J. Ryan, Cancer Risk and Estrogen Use in the Menopause, 293 N. Eng. J. Med. 1199, 1200 (1975).

58. See Morton Mintz, FDA Panel Urges Warnings on Estrogen Instructions, Wash. Post., Dec. 20, 1975, at A2.

59. 306 Lancet 1135 (Dec. 6, 1975).

60. Harry K. Ziel & William D. Finkle, Association of Estrone with the Development of Endometrial Carcinoma, 124 Am. J. Ob. Gyn. 735, 736 (1976).

61. Id. at 739.

62. See the Joint Hearing, Oral Contraceptives and Estrogens for Postmenopausal Use, 1976, before the Subcommittee on Health of the Senate Labor and Public Welfare Committee and the Subcommittee on Administrative Practice and Procedure of the Senate Judiciary Committee, Jan. 21, 1976, at 86–87.

63. Estrogen Prescribing a Dilemma for Physicians, Am. Med. News, March 9, 1976, at 13.

64. Capsule item, Am. Med. News, March 22, 1976, at 3. The "irresponsible" charge also appears in FDA Drug Bulletin, Feb.-March 1976, at 19.

65. Robert Hoover et al., Menopausal Estrogens and Breast Cancer, 295 N. Eng. J. Med. 401, 405 (1976).

66. See id. at 402, 404.

67. Id. at 404.

68. FDA, Physician Labeling and Patient Labeling for Estrogens for General Use, 41 Fed. Reg. 43117, 43118 (Sept. 29, 1976).

69. Id. at 43122. A revision of this document, which contained virtually the same substantive language quoted earlier, appears in FDA, Physician Labeling and Patient Labeling for Estrogens for General Use: Amendment, 41 Fed. Reg. 47573, 47577 (Oct. 29, 1976).

70. FDA Release 76–28, Sept. 27, 1976.

71. Advertisement, Am. Med. News, Oct. 25, 1976, Impact section at 8–9.

72. Capsule item, Am. Med. News, Nov. 8, 1976, at 2.

73. 21 C.F.R.§ 310.515(b)(4), issued at 42 Fed. Reg. 37641, 37642 (July 22, 1977).

74. 42 Fed. Reg. at 37639.

75. Id. at 37637.

76. See FDA, Patient Labeling for Estrogens for General Use, revised guideline text, 42 Fed. Reg. 37645, at 37645–37646 (July 22, 1977).

77. FDA, Estrogens for Postpartum Breast Engorgement, 43 Fed. Reg. 49564, 49565–49566 (Oct. 24, 1978).

78. UPI, Estrogen's Use for Menopause 'Up to Patient,' Chicago Sun-Times, Sept. 15, 1979.

79. HEW News, Feb. 1, 1979, reprinted under headline Study Says Estrogen-Cancer Link May Be Reversible, F.D. Cosm. L. Rep. ¶ 42,445 (Feb. 12, 1979).

80. Ronald K. Ross et al., A Case-Control Study of Menopausal Estrogen Therapy and Breast Cancer, 243 J.A.M.A. 1635, 1637 (1980).

81. Noel S. Weiss et al., Decreased Risk of Fractures of the Hip and Lower Forearm with Postmenopausal Use of Estrogen, 303 N. Eng. J. Med. 1195, 1196 (1980).

82. Id. at 1197–1198.

83. See Alexis de Tocqueville, Democracy in America 248 (J.P. Mayer & Max Lerner eds., Harper & Row 1966).

84. Pharm. Mfgrs. Assn. v. FDA, 484 F. Supp. 1179, 1188 (D. Del. 1980).

85. Id. at 1191 (quoting the Commissioner).

86. Id.

87. Id. at 1192.

88. Pharm. Mfgrs. Assn. v. FDA, 634 F.3d 106, 108 (3d Cir. 1980). For a contemporaneous technical holding that opposes an estrogens manufacturer, see United States v. Articles of Drug . . . Hormonin, 498 F. Supp. 424 (D. N.J. 1980), which upholds the government's seizure of hormone drugs on the basis that they were "new drugs" that had not gone through the FDA's New Drug Application process. Although the court said that it appeared that the firm's drugs were "no more or less safe and effective than other estrogenic drugs," it said that the products fell within the definition of "new drugs" under the statute because they had not been shown by "substantial evidence" to be "generally recognized" as "safe and effective" for their intended uses. See id. at 435.

89. See 634 F.2d at 108 and the specific reference at 484 F. Supp. 1182.

90. 634 F.2d at 108.

91. Lawyers' Medical Report: Estrogens, 24 Personal Injury Newsletter 225 (Feb. 16, 1981).

92. Bernardo v. Ayerst Labs., 99 A.D.2d 430, 470 N.Y.S.2d 395 (1984).

93. Erkki Hirvonen et al., Effects of Different Progestogens on Lipoproteins During Postmenopausal Replacement Therapy, 304 N. Eng. J. Med. 560, 561 (1981).

94. See id. at 562.

95. M.I. Whitehead et al., Effects of Estrogens and Progestins on the Biochemistry and Morphology of the Postmenopausal Endometrium, 305 N. Eng. J. Med. 1599, 1603–1604 (1981).

96. Paul C. MacDonald, Editorial, Estrogen Plus Progestin in Postmenopausal Women, 305 N. Eng. J. Med. 1644, 1644–1645 (1981).

97. Estrogen Therapy Guidelines Approved, Am. Med. News, Dec. 18, 1981, at 12.

98. Joel Alcoff, Estrogen Replacement Therapy, 25(6) Am. Fam. Physician 183 (June 1982).

99. Gina Kolata, see New Puzzles Over Estrogen and Heart Disease, 220 Science 1137 (1983).

100. Alcoff, supra note 98.

101. Kolata, supra, at 1137.

102. See id. at 1138.

103. See id.

104. See Trudy L. Bush et al., Estrogen Use and All-Cause Mortality, 249 J.A.M.A. 903, 904 (1982).

105. Id. at 906.

106. Id. at 905.

107. Victor Cohn, Estrogen Linked to Lower Death Rates in Women, Wash. Post. undated, c. Feb. 1983.

108. D.W. Kaufman et al., Noncontraceptive Estrogen Use and the Risk of Breast Cancer, 252 J.A.M.A. 63, 67 (1984). Reaching the same conclusion was R.I. Horwitz & K. R. Stewart, Effect of Clinical Features on the Association of Estrogens and Breast Cancer, 76 Am. J. Med. 192 (1984).

109. Barbara S. Hulka, "When Is the Evidence for 'No Association' Sufficient, 252 J.A.M.A. 81 (July 1984).

110. No Estrogen Link Found with Breast Cancer Risk, Am. Med. News, July 13, 1984, at 24; Hulka, supra, at 82.

111. See Gordon M. Wardlaw, Putting Osteoporosis in Perspective, 93 J. Am. Dietetic Assn. 1000 (Sept. 1993).

112. Id.

113. Christine Russell, NIH Panel Urges Older Women to 'Consider' Estrogen Therapy, Wash. Post., April 5, 1984, at A2.

114. FDA Talk Paper, summarized in Estrogen Therapy Recommended for Osteoporosis in Postmenopausal Women, F.D. Cosm. L. Rep ¶ 43,316 (May 29, 1984).

115. FDA Notice, 51 Fed. Reg. 12568 (April 11, 1986).

116. FDA, Proposed Rule, 52 Fed, Reg. 37802 (Oct. 9, 1987).

117. FDA, Final Rule, 55 Fed. Reg. 18722 (May 4, 1990).

118. Hormone replacement therapy, 8 Back Letter 3 (July 1993), citing 52 Annals of Rheumatic Disease (1993).

119. Wardlaw, supra note 111, citing B.L. Riggs & L.J. Melton, The Prevention and Treatment of Osteoporosis, 327 N. Eng. J. Med. 620 (1993).

120. Id.

121. Richard L. Prince et al., Prevention of Postmenopausal Osteoporosis: A Comparative Study of Exercise, Calcium Supplementation, and Hormone-Replacement Therapy, 325 N. Eng. J. Med. 1189, 1189 (1991) (abstract).

122. Id. at 1195.

123. Brian M. Walsh et al., Effects of Postmenopausal Estrogen Replacement on the Concentration and Metabolism of Plasma Lipoproteins, 325 N. Eng. J. Med. 1196, 1199 (1991).

124. Id. at 1203.

125. Meir J. Stampfer et al., Estrogen Therapy and Cardiovascular Disease: Ten-Year Follow-up from the Nurses' Health Study, 325 N. Eng. J. Med. 756 (1991).

126. Id.

127. Quotation of Annlia Paginini-Hill in Christopher Tedeschi, Estrogen Replacement May Keep Teeth Healthy, http://www.usc.edu/hsc/info/pr/1vol2/204/estrogen.html, summarizing article in 155 Arch. Intern. Med. (Nov. 1995).

128. Janet B. Henrich, The Postmenopausal Estrogen Breast Cancer Controversy, 268 J.A.M.A. 1900, 1900 (1992).

129. Id. at 1901–1902.

130. Id. at 1902. One negative byproduct of hormone replacement was that it caused an increase in the density of the breast parenchyma, that is, the fundamental breast tissue. This effect, which often would go away when a woman stopped taking hormones, made it more difficult for mammographic examinations to pick up "small malignant masses." See Jack E. Meyer et al., Letter to the Editor, 270 J.A.M.A. 2685 (1993).

131. Scott Fields & William L. Toffler, Estrogen Replacement Therapy for Reducing Cardiovascular Disease, 158 Western J. Med. 515 (May 1993).

132. Peter Collins et al., Cardiovascular Protection by Estrogen—A Calcium Antagonist Effect, 341 Lancet 1264 (May 15, 1993). See also E. Barrett-Connor, Estrogen and Estrogen-Progestogen Replacement: Therapy and Cardiovascular Diseases, 95 Am. J. Med. 5A-40S, 42S (Nov. 30, 1993) ("[t]he reduced risk of heart disease in postmenopausal women who take unopposed oral estrogen is a consistent and biologically plausible finding").

133. Margareta Falkenorn et al., Hormone Replacement and the Risk of Stroke: Follow-Up of a Population-Based Cohort in Sweden (abstract), 153 Arch. Internal Med. 1201 (May 24, 1993).

134. E. Barrett-Connor, Estrogen and Estrogen-Progestogen Replacement—Therapy and Cardiovascular Disease, supra note 132, at 42S.

135. Id.

136. Id., citing D. Grady et al., Hormone Therapy to Prevent a Disease and Prolong Life in Postmenopausal Women, 117 Ann. Intern. Med. 1016 (1992).

137. Diane J. Schneider, Elizabeth Barrett-Connor and Deborah J. Morton, Thyroid Hormone Use and Bone Mineral Density in Elderly Women: Effects of Estrogen, 271 J.A.M.A. 1245 (April 27,1994).

138. Id.

139. Id.

140. Id.

141. Id.

142. Rita Rubin, Estrogen Anxiety: Enter Menopause and Pop Hormone Pills: Not So Fast, Say Researchers, *U.S. News & World Report*, April 4, 1994, at 60.

143. Carol L. Otis & Linda Lynch, How to Keep Your Bones Healthy, 22 Physician & Sportsmedicine 71 (Jan. 1994).

144. Kathi Gannon, Osteoporosis: No. 1 Concern in Menopause (Upjohn Co. telephone survey concerning menopausal issues), 138 Drug Topics 42 (May 9, 1994).

145. Amanda Spake, The Raging Hormone Debate (Estrogen Replacement Therapy), 8 Health 46 (Jan.-Feb. 1994).

146. Id.

147. John R. Lee with Virginia Hopkins, What Your Doctor May *Not* Tell You About Menopause: The Breakthrough Book on Natural Progesterone (Warner Books 1996).

148. See Natural Progesterone, Highlights from an Interview with Dr. John Lee, http://www.yourlifesource.com/progesterone.htm (Loren & Kathy Schiele, 2003, printed May 24, 2006).

149. See, e.g., http://www.hormoneprofile.com/leeoffhrt.htm (printed Oct. 16, 2007).

150. Marvin W. Davis, Drugs for the Prostate and Menopause (continuing education courses, including test question and form for receiving credit), 137 Drug Topics 1242 (Dec. 13, 1993).

151. Katie Rodgers, Hormone Replacement Therapy: Unanswered Questions, Still. (benefits and risks of estrogen therapy should be discussed with physician), 138 Drug Topics 32 (May 9, 1994).

152. What Every Woman Should Know about Menopause and Osteoporosis, PR Newswire p0317PHFNS2 (March 17, 1994) (document written by Dr. Lila E. Nachtigall; listed contact person at Bristol-Myers Squibb).

153. The Writing Group for the PEPI Trial, Effects of Estrogen or Estrogen/Progestin Regimens on Heart Disease Risk Factors in Postmenopausal Women, 273 J.A.M.A. 199 (Jan. 18, 1995)(summary).

154. Francine Grodstein et al., Postmenopausal Estrogen and Progestin Use and the Risk of Cardiovascular Disease, 335 N. Eng. J. Med. 453 (Aug. 15, 1996).

155. Francine Grodstein et al., Postmenopausal Hormone Therapy and Mortality, 336 N. Eng. J. Med. 1769, 1773 (June 19, 1997).

156. Graham A. Colditz et al., The Use of Estrogens and Progestins and the Risk of Breast Cancer in Postmenopausal Women, 332 N. Eng. J. Med. 1589 (June 15, 1995).

157. Francine Grodstein et al., supra note 155, 336 N. Eng. J. Med. at 1775.

158. FDA, Center for Drug Evaluation & Research, Synthetic Conjugated Estrogens: May 5, 1997: Questions and Answers, http://www.fda.gov/cder/news/ceqa.htm [hereafter, Questions and Answers].

159. Janet Woodcock, M.D., Memorandum, Approvability of a Synthetic Generic Version of Premarin, May 5, 1997, http://www.fda.gov/cder/news/celetterjw.htm.

160. Id. section III.

161. Id. (emphasis added in the original).

162. Id. section IV.

163. Id.

164. Id.

165. Id.

166. Id.

167. Id.

168. Id. section V.

169. Questions and Answers, supra note 158, items 2 & 13.

170. FDA Statement on Generic Premarin, HHS News P97–12 (May 5, 1997), http://www.fda.gov/cder/cepressrelease.htm.

171. Richard Eastell, Treatment of Postmenopausal Osteoporosis, 338 N. Eng. J. Med. 736, 736 (1998).

172. See id. at 740. For a developing concern about side effects, see infra, chapter 6, text accompanying note 141.

173. 40 Medical Letter 29–30 (March 13, 1998).

174. See Drug Information: Raloxifene, http://www.nlm.nih.gov/medlineplus/print/druginfo/medmaster/a698007.html.

175. See Eastell, supra, at 743.

176. FDA Talk Paper, FDA Approves Teriparatide to Treat Osteoporosis, http:/www.fda.gov.bbs/topics/ANSWERS/2002/ANS01176.html.

177. Stephen Hulley et al., Randomized Trial of Estrogen Plus Progestin for Secondary Prevention of Coronary Heart Disease in Postmenopausal Women, 280 J.A.M.A. 605, 610 (Aug. 19, 1998).

178. See id. at 609–610.

179. Id. at 610.

180. Id. at 612.

181. See David M. Herrington et al., Effects of Estrogen Replacement on the Progression of Coronary-Artery Atherosclerosis, 343 N. Eng. J. Med. 522, 526 (Aug. 24, 2000) ("a mean of 3.2 years of estrogen replacement did not slow the progression of coronary atherosclerotic lesions in women").

182. Id. at 527.

183. Id. at 528.

184. Elizabeth G. Nabel, Editorial, Coronary Heart Disease in Women—An Ounce of Prevention, 383 N. Eng. J. Med. 572 (Aug. 24, 2000).

185. Id. at 573.

186. Carmen Rodriguez et al., Effect of Body Mass on the Association Between Estrogen Replacement Therapy and Morality Among Elderly US Women, 153 Am. J. Epidemiol. 145, 148, 151 (2001).

187. Estrogen Replacement Lowers Death Rate, Doctor's Guide dated Jan. 8, 2001, http://www.docguide.com/news/content.nsf/NewsPrint/48CE40246EB07D61852569CE0 0648.

188. William D. Dupont et al., Estrogen Replacement Therapy in Women with a History of Proliferative Breast Disease, 85 Cancer 1277 (March 15, 1999)(abstract).

189. Catherine Schairer et al., Menopausal Estrogen and Estrogen-Progestin Replacement Therapy and Breast Cancer Risk, 283 J.A.M.A. 485, 490 (Jan. 26, 2000).

190. Walter Willett et al., Editorial, Postmenopausal Estrogens—Opposed, Unopposed, or None of the Above, 283 J.A.M.A. 534, 534–535 (2000).

191. http://my.athernet.net/~nrsprntg.CoverText.html.

192. Mark Clemons and Paul Goss, Estrogens and the Risk of Breast Cancer, 344 N. Eng. J. Med. 276, 280 (Jan. 25, 2001).

193. Id. at 283.

194. Id. at 282.

195. Id. at 277.

196. Wendy J. Chen & Graham A. Colditz, Estrogen Replacement Therapy and the Risk of Breast Cancer, http://www.uptodatecom/html/tes/may_02/topics/13320P2.htm (current to Sept. 26, 2001), citing L. Bergkvist et al., Prognosis after Breast Cancer Diagnosis in Women Exposed to Estrogen and Estrogen-Progestogen Replacement Therapy, 130 Am. J. Epidemiol. 221 (1989).

197. Elizabeth Barrett-Connor & Donna Kritz-Silverstein, Estrogen Replacement Therapy and Cognitive Function in Older Women, 269 J.A.M.A. 2637, 2641 (May 26, 1993).

198. Annlia Paganini-Hill & Victor W. Henderson, Estrogen Deficiency and Risk of Alzheimer's Disease in Women, 140 Am. J. Epidemiol. 256 (1994)(abstract).

199. NIH News Release, 16-Year Study is Further Evidence that Estrogen Replacement May Be Protective against Alzheimer's (June 18, 1997), citing study in 48 Neurology No. 6 by Claudia Kawas et al.

200. Ruth A. Mulnard et al., Estrogen Replacement Therapy for Treatment of Mild to Moderate Alzheimer Disease, 283 J.A.M.A. 1007, 1013 (Feb. 23, 2000).

201. NIH News, Estrogen Replacement Therapy Not Effective for Treatment of Alzheimer's Disease in Some Women, Feb. 23, 2000, http://www.alzheimers.org/nianews/nisnews27.html. (quoting Dr. Neil Buckholtz).

202. Carmen Rodriguez et al., Estrogen Replacement Therapy and Ovarian Cancer Mortality in a Large Prospective Study of US Women, 2285 J.A.M.A. 1460, 1463 (March 21, 2001).

203. Id. at 1464.

204. Rita Rubin, Hormone Therapy: Doubts Grow, USA Today, June 12, 2001.

205. Id., apparently referring to editorial by Robertson, Women and Cardiovascular Disease, 103 Circulation 2318 (2001). I could not locate this statistic in the editorial but Robertson is quoted on it in various places, including Rubin, supra, and in Poll Finds Majority of Women Unaware Heart Disease Is Their #1 Killer, http://www.lifeway.com/Fit4/Search/ArticleViewer.asp?art_id=701.

206. Lori Mosca et al., Hormone Replacement Therapy and Cardiovascular Disease: A Statement for Healthcare Professionals from the American Heart Association, 104 Circulation 499 (2001).

207. Id.

208. Id., citing E. Hemminki & K. McPherson, Impact of Postmenopausal Hormone Therapy on Cardiovascular Events and Cancer: Pooled Data from Clinical Trials, 315 Br. Med. J. 149 (1997).

209. Susan Okie, Study: Hormones Don't Protect Women from Heart Disease, Wash. Post, July 24, 2001, at A1.

210. Id.

Chapter 6

1. Wyeth, Annual Report 2001, cover.

2. Id. at 8.

3. Id. at 10–11.

4. Id. at 66.

5. See Denise Grady, Scientists Question Hormone Therapies for Menopause Ills, N.Y. Times, April 18, 2002, at 1, 20.

6. Id. at 20. For a review of the position paper, see Rodolfo Paoletti & Nanette K. Wenger, Review of the International Position Paper on Women's Health and Menopause: A Comprehensive Approach, 107 Circulation 1336 (2003)(referring also to the WHI research, results of which are discussed supra at pages 160–180, and to an NCI study released in 2002 that reported a "significantly increased risk of ovarian cancer" for HRT users, especially women who used the drugs for ten years or more, see James V. Lacey Jr. et al., Menopausal Hormone Replacement Therapy and Risk of Ovarian Cancer, 288 J.A.M.A. 334 (July 17, 2002) (abstract).

7. Robert Lindsay et al., Effect of Lower Doses of Conjugated Equine Estrogens With and Without Medroxyprogesterone Acetate on Bone in Early Postmenopausal Women, 287 J.A.M.A. 2668 (May 22/29 2002) (abstract).

8. Deborah Grady et al., Cardiovascular Disease Outcomes During 6.8 Years of Hormone Therapy: Heart and Estrogen/Progestin Replacement Study Follow-up (HERS II), 288 J.A.M.A. 49 (July 3, 2002).

9. See id. at 53.

10. Id. at 55, 57.

11. Stephen Hulley et al., Noncardiovascular Disease Outcome During 6.8 Years of Hormone Therapy, 288 J.A.M.A. 58 (July 3, 2002) (abstract).

12. Denise Grady, A Hormone Therapy Finds No Benefit, N.Y. Times, July 3, 2002, at A14.

13. Writing Group for the Women's Health Initiative Investigators, Risks and Benefits of Estrogen Plus Progestin in Health Postmenopausal Women, 288 J.A.M.A. 321 (July 17, 2002).

14. Id. at 321.

15. See id. at 322, 331–332.

16. Id. at 325.

17. Id. at 327.

18. Id. at 330.

19. Id. at 331.

20. See id. at 327, 330.

21. See id. at 327, 330.

22. See id. at 327, 331.

23. See id. at 322, 327.

24. See id. at 331.

25. Id.

26. Gina Kolata & Melody Petersen, Hormone Replacement Study a Shock to the Medical System, N.Y. Times, July 10, 2002, at A1 &A16.

27. Thomas M. Burton, Hormone Conundrum, Wall St. J., July 10, 2002, at B1 & B3.

28. Judy Peres, Doubts Cast on Hormone Therapy, Chi. Trib., July 10, 2002, at 1, 16.

29. Kolata and Peterson, supra, at A16.

30. Editorial, Hormone Therapy Woes, N.Y. Times, July 11, 2002, at A26.

31. Id.

32. Scott Hensley, Wyeth CEO: Concerned But Hopeful, Wall St. J., July 10, 2001, at B1 & B3.

33. Gina Kolata, Rush to Fill Void in Menopause-Drug Market, N.Y. Times, Sept. 1, 2002, at A1 & A17.

34. Mary Duenwald, Hormone Therapy: One Size, Clearly, No Longer Fits All, N.Y. Times, July 16, 2002, at D1, D6.

35. Kolata, supra note 33, at A17.

36. Despite Safety Concerns, U.K. Hormone Study to Proceed, 297 Sci. 492 (July 26, 2002).

37. 44 Medical Letter 78 (Sept. 2, 2002).

38. Denise Grady, Risks of Hormone Therapy Exceed Benefits, Panel Says, N.Y. Times, Oct. 17, 2002, at A25.

39. See Gina Kolata, Scientists Debating Future of Hormone Replacement, N.Y. Times, Oct. 23, 2002, at A18.

40. David Brown, Doubts Grow About Post-Menopausal Hormone Use, Wash. Post., Oct. 27, 2002, at A12.

41. Gina Kolata et al., Menopause without Pills: Rethinking Hot Flashes, N.Y. Times, Nov. 10, 2002, A1 & A22.

42. 63 Fed Reg. 55399 (Oct. 15, 1998) (notice of availability of draft guidance).

43. FDA, Draft Guidance, 64 Fed. Reg. 52100 (September 27, 1999).

44. FDA, Draft Guidance, 68 Fed. Reg. 5300 (Feb. 3, 2003).

45. 68 Fed. Reg. 17953 (April 14, 2003).

46. Francine Goldstein et al., Understanding the Divergent Data on Postmenopausal Hormone Therapy, 348 N. Eng. J. Med. 645, 645–646 (Feb. 13, 2003).

47. See id. at 648–649.

48. Id. at 649.

49. FDA Approves Wyeth's New Low Dose Prempro (Women's Health, item datelined March 13, 2003), http://www.thewomenshealthsite.org/article_display.jsp?ArticleID=214.

50. Gina Kolata, Hormone Therapy, Already Found to Have Risks, Is Now Said to Lack Benefits, N.Y. Times, March 18, 2003, at A26.

51. Jennifer Hays et al., Effects of Estrogen Plus Progestin on Health-Related Quality of Life, 348 N. Eng. J. Med. 1839, 1852, 1850 (May 8, 2003).

52. Id. at 1852.

53. Deborah Grady, Postmenopausal Hormones—Therapy for Symptoms Only, 348 N. Eng. J. Med. 1835, 1837 (May 8, 2003).

54. Sally A. Shumaker et al., Estrogen Plus Progestin and the Incidence of Dementia and Mild Cognitive Impairment in Postmenopausal Women, 289 J.A.M.A. 2651 (May 28, 2003) (abstract).

55. Sally A. Shumaker et al., Conjugated Equine Estrogens and Incidence of Probable Dementia and Mild Cognitive Impairment in Postmenopausal Women, 291 J.A.M.A. 2947 (June 23/30, 2003) (abstract).

56. Teresa Schaer, M.D., Letter to the Editor, Weighing the Risks of Hormone Pills, N.Y. Times, June 2, 2203, at A20.

57. Rowan T. Chlebowski et al., Influence of Estrogen plus Progestin on Breast Cancer and Mammography in Healthy Postmenopausal Women, 289 J.A.M.A. 3243 (June 25, 2003) (abstract).

58. See Denise Grady, Study Finds New Risks in Hormone Therapy, N.Y. Times, June 25, 2003, at A1 & A19.

59. See id.

60. JoAnn E. Manson et al., Estrogen Plus Progestin and the Risk of Coronary Heart Disease, 349 N. Eng. J. Med. 523, 529 (Aug. 7, 2003).

61. Howard N. Hodis et al., Hormone Therapy and the Progression of Coronary-Artery Atherosclerosis in Postmenopausal Women, 349 N. Eng. J. Med. 535 (Aug. 7, 2003) (abstract).

62. David Herrington & Timothy Howard, from Presumed Harm to Potential Harm—Hormone Therapy and Heart Disease, 349 N. Eng. Med. 519, 520 (Aug. 7, 2003).

63. John Bailar, Hormone-Replacement Therapy and Cardiovascular Diseases, 349 N. Eng. J. Med. 521, 521–522 (Aug. 7, 2003).

64. Jane A. Cauley et al., Effects of Estrogen Plus Progestin on Risk of Fracture and Bone Mineral Density, 290 J.A.M.A. 1729 (Oct. 1, 2003).

65. Anna Mathews & Scott Hensley, Hormone-Therapy Debate Grows, Wall St. J., Oct. 8, 2003.

66. Id.

67. Tara Parker-Pope, The Case for Hormone Therapy, Wall St. J., Oct. 21, 2003.

68. See supra, text accompanying note 44.

69. See 69 Fed. Reg. 7492 (Feb. 17, 2004) (notice).

70. Menopausal Hormone Therapy, FDA Consumer, Nov.-Dec. 2003, at 36.

71. Menopause and hormone therapy information available, F.D. Cosm. L. Rep. (CCH) No. 2184, Report Letter at 6 (2004).

72. Milo Geyelin, Wyeth's Prempro Problems Galvanize Plaintiffs' Lawyers, Wall St. J., July 16, 2002, at B1.

73. See Tobias Millrood, The Rise and Fall of Hormone Therapy, Trial, Aug. 2003, at 42.

74. Id. at 47, citing In re Prempro Prods. Liab. Litig., MDL 4:03cv01507 (E.D. Ark. Mar. 4, 2003).

75. http://injury-law.freeadvice.com/drug-toxic_chemicals/prempro-lawsuit.htm, printed Aug. 3, 2007.

76. Web site of Monheit Law, http://www.monheit.com/prempro/, printed Feb. 24, 2006.

77. Web site of Ennis & Ennis, P.A., http://hrt.side-effect.com, printed May 30, 2006.

78. NIH News, March 2, 2004, NIH Asks Participants in Women's Health Initiative Estrogen-Alone Study to Stop Study Pills, Begin Follow-up Phase.

79. Women's Health Initiative Steering Committee, Effects of Conjugated Equine Estrogen in Postmenopausal Women with Hysterectomy, 291 J.A.M.A. 1701 (April 14, 2004) (abstract).

80. NIH News, supra note 78.

81. Id.

82. Denise Grady, Estrogen Study Stopped Early Because of Slight Stroke Risk, N.Y. Times, March 3, 2004, at A15.

83. See Leila Abboud & Andrea Petersen, Rethinking Hormone Therapy—Again, Wall St. J., March 3, 2004, at D1 & D3.

84. Warnings to Marketers of Alternative Hormone Therapies, F.D. Cosm. L. Rep. (CCH) No. 2240 (2005) (referencing FDA News).

85. See Leslie Berger, On Hormone Therapy, the Dust is Still Settling, N.Y. Times, June 6, 2004, sec. 15, at 1, 10.

86. Susan Love, New Looks at Old Questions, N.Y. Times, June 6, 2004, sec. 15, at 10.

87. FDA, Draft Guidance, Guidance for Industry: Noncontraceptive Estrogen Drug Products for the Treatment of Vasomotor Symptoms and Vulvar and Vaginal Atrophy Symptoms—Recommended Prescribing Information for Health Care Providers and Patient Labeling, Revision 4 (Nov. 2005—Labeling), http://www.fda.gov/cder/guidance/6932dft.htm (printed May 30, 2006).

88. Id., printout at 3.

89. See id., printout at 11–14.

90. Id., printout at 16.

91. Id., printout at 21.

92. Id., printout at 24.

93. Id., printout at 21.

94. Shelley Salpeter, Invited editorial, Hormone Therapy for Younger Postmenopausal Women: How Can We Make Sense out of the Evidence?, 2005 Climacteric 307, 309.

95. Po M. Lam et al., Where Are We with Postmenopausal Hormone Therapy in 2005? 21(5) Gynecological Endocrinology 248, 248 (abstract portion) (Nov. 2005).

96. Id. at 254.

97. Salpeter, supra note 94, 2005 Climacteric at 309.

98. Id. at 309.

99. Id. at 307.

100. Id. at 308.

101. Id. at 309.

102. The Women's Health Initiative, Judith Hsia et al., Conjugated Equine Estrogens and Coronary Heart Disease, 166 Arch. Internal Med. 357, 360, 362 (2006).

103. Id. at 364.

104. Harvard Health Letter, June 2006, at 4–5.

105. Pamela Ouyang et al., Hormone Replacement Therapy and the Cardiovascular System, 47 J. Am. Coll. Cardiology 1741, 1741 (2006).

106. Id. at 1750.

107. Id. at 1751.

108. Francine Grodstein et al., Hormone Therapy and Coronary Heart Disease: The Role of Time since Menopause and Age at Hormone Initiation, 15 J. Women's Health 35, 42 (2006).

109. Id. at 39.

110. Id.

111. Id. at 43.

112. Michael C. Craig et al., The Women's Health Initiative Memory Study: Findings and Implications for Treatment, 4 Lancet Neurol. 190, 192 (2005).

113. Id. at 193.

114. P.M. Maki, Hormone Therapy and Cognitive Function: Is There a Critical Period for Benefit?, 138 Neuroscience 1027, 1027 (2006).

115. Id. at 1028.

116. Id. at 1029.

117. Id.

118. M. Grigorova & B.B. Sherwin, No Differences in Performance on Test of Working Memory and Executive Functioning Between Healthy Elderly Postmenopausal Women Using or Not Using Hormone Therapy, 2006 Climacteric 181, 189 (2006).

119. Id. at 191–192.

120. James Douketis, Hormone Replacement Therapy and Risk for Venous Thromboembolism: What's New and How Do These Findings Influence Clinical Practice?, 12 Curr. Opin. Hematol. 395, 396 (2005).

121. Id. at 397.

122. Id.

123. See id. at 397–398.

124. Jody E. Steinauer et al., Postmenopausal Hormone Therapy: Does It Cause Incontinence?, 106 Obstet. & Gyn. 940, 942–943 (2005).

125. Id. at 944.

126. See F.O. Aina et al., Hormone Replacement Therapy and Cataract: A Population-Based Case-Control Study, 20 Eye 417 (April 2006) (abstract).

127. Tara Parker-Pope, In Study of Women's Health, Design Flaws Raise Questions, Wall St. J., Feb. 28, 2006, A1 at A13.

128. Id. at A1.

129. See infra, chapter 7, at pp. 209–210. See, more generally, Marshall S. Shapo, A Nation of Guinea Pigs ch. 8 (Free Press 1979).

130. See Gina Kolata, Drug for Bones Is Newly Linked to Jaw Disease, N.Y. Times, June 2, 2006, at A1, A15.

131. *Angeliq* for Treatment of Menopausal Symptoms, 49 Medical Letter 15–16 (Feb. 12, 2007).

132. P.M. Ravdin et al., A Sharp Decrease in Breast Cancer Incidence in the United States in 2003, Abstract 5, 29th Annual San Antonio Breast Cancer Symposium; Gina Kolata, Reversing Trend, Big Drop Is Seen in Breast Cancer, N.Y. Times, Dec. 15, 2006, at A1, A22.

133. Christina A. Clarke et al., Recent Decline in Hormone Therapy Utilization and Breast Cancer Incidence: Clinical and Population-Based Evidence, 24 J. Clin. Oncology e49 (Nov. 20, 2006).

134. Kolata, supra note 132, at A22.

135. Gina Kolata, Hormones and Cancer: Assessing the Risks, N.Y. Times, Dec. 26, 2006, D1 at D2.

136. Tara Parker-Pope, The Hormone Decision: How to Weigh the Risks, Wall St. J., Jan. 11, 2007, D1 at D4.

137. Peter M. Ravdin et al., The Decrease in Breast-Cancer Incidence in the United States, 356 N. Eng. J. Med. 1670, 1673 (April 19, 2007).

138. Id. at 1672.

139. Gina Kolata, Sharp Drop in Rates of Breast Cancer Holds, N.Y. Times, April 19, 2007, at 22.

140. Jacques Rossouw et al., Postmenopausal Hormone Therapy and Risk of Cardio-vascular Disease by Age and Years Since Menopause, 297 J.A.M.A. 1465, 1471 (April 4, 2007).

141. Id. at 1476.

142. See id. at 1473–1475.

143. JoAnn E. Manson et al., Estrogen Therapy and Coronary-Artery Calcification, 356 N. Eng. J. Med. 2591, 2598 (June 21, 2007).

144. Id. at 2599.

145. Id. at 2600.

146. See Jennifer Couzin, Seeking Clarity in Hormones' Effect on the Heart, 316 Science 1826 (June 29, 2007).

147. AP, Study Finds Some Heart Benefits of Estrogen, N.Y. Times, June 21, 2007, at A15.

148. Tara Parker-Pope, Now NIH Misread Hormone Study in 2002, Wall St. J., July 8, 2007, at B1, B2.

149. Wyeth Wins First Case Alleging That Prempro Caused Patient's Breast Cancer, 34 Prod. Safety & Liab. Rep. (BNA) 938, 939 (Sept. 25, 2006)(summarizing Reeves v. Wyeth, E.D. Ark., No. 05-163, verdict on Sept. 15, 2006).

150. In re Prempro Prod. Liab. Litig., Rush v. Wyeth, 474 F. Supp. 1040, 1043–1044 (E.D. Ark. 2007).

151. Woman to Challenge Defense Verdict in Second Federal Prempro Trial, 35 Prod. Safety & Liab. Rep. (BNA) 186 (Feb. 26, 2007).

152. Pennsylvania Jury Awards Couple $3 Million, Finds Prempro Caused Wife's Breast Cancer, 35 Prod. Safety & Liab. Rep. 185 (Feb. 26, 2007) (summarizing Nelson v. Wyeth Pharms., Inc., Pa. C.P. No. 04-01-01670).

153. See Eckert Seamans, Philadelphia Report (Summer 2007) 1–2, www.eckertseamans.com (printed Dec. 5, 2007), reporting on Nelson v. Wyeth.

154. Pennsylvania State Court Throws out Prempro Verdict, $3 Million Damage Award, 35 Prod. Safety & Liab. Rep. 578 (June 18, 2007).

155. See Pennsylvania Jury Awards Couple $3 Million, supra note 152.

156. See Wyeth Wins First Case, supra note 149.

157. See Minnesota Trial Court Dismisses Suit, Finds Causation Proof Inadmissible, 35 Prod. Safety & Liab. Rep. (BNA) 1028 (Nov. 5, 2007) (summarizing Zandi v. Wyeth, Inc. (Minn. Dist. Ct. Hennepin Co., No. 27-cv-06-6744, Oct. 15, 2007).

158. See Heeding Presumption Applies to Claim Alleging Failure to Warn of Prempro's Risks, 50 AAJ Law Reporter 311 (summarizing ruling in Deutsch v. Wyeth, Inc. (N.J. Middlesex Super. Ct., No. MID-L-998-06, June 20, 2007).

159. See Nevada Jury Finds Drugs Caused Cancers; Wyeth Vows to Challenge $134 Award, 35 Prod. Safety & Liab. Rep. (BNA) 982 (Oct. 22, 2007).

160. See Sarah Rubenstein, Wyeth's Pipeline Hits a Snag, Wall St. J., Aug. 13, 2007, at A11.

161. See 49 Med. Letter 71–72 (Aug. 27, 2007).

162. See FTC Release, FTC Charges Seven Online Sellers of Alternative Hormone Replacement Therapy with Failing to Substantiate Products' Health Claims (Oct. 5, 2007).

Chapter 7

1. James Gleick, Genius: The Life and Science of Richard Feynman 355 (First Vintage Books ed. 1993).

2. See, e.g., Nell Greenfieldboyce, 'Buckyball' Nobel Laureate Richard Smalley Dies, http://www.npr.templates/story/story.php?storyId=4983474.

3. John T. Monica Jr. et al., Preparing for Future Health Litigation: The Application of Products Liability Law to Nanotechnology, 3 Nanotechnology L. & Bus. 54, 54 (2006).

4. See, e.g., Emery E. Knowles III, Nanotechnology: Evolving Occupational Safety, Health and Environmental Issues, 51 Professional Safety 20, 20 (2006).

5. John Miller et al., A Realistic Assessment of the Commercialization of Nanotechnology: A Primer for Lawyers and Investors, 1 Nanotechnology L. & Bus. 10, 10 (2004).

6. Knowles, supra, at 20.

7. Frederick A. Fiedler & Glenn H. Reynolds, Legal Problems of Nanotechnology: An Overview, 3 So. Calif. Interdisciplinary L.J. 593, 597, 599 (1994).

8. Peter J. Tomasco, Manufactured Nanomaterials: Avoiding TSCA and OSHA Violations for Potentially Hazardous Substances, 33 B.C. Envtl. Affs. L. Rev. 205, 209 (2006), quoting The Royal Society & The Royal Acad. Of Eng'g, Nanoscience and Nanotechnologies: Opportunities and Uncertainties 6 (2004).

9. Pat Rizzuto, Expert Urges 'Decoupling' of Nanotechnology to Help Public Discern Uses, Potential Risks, 37 Prod. Safety & Liab. Rep. 785 (BNA) (Sept. 6, 2007).

10. Tomasco, supra, at 209–210, in part quoting Cientifica report, Nanotubes 12 (2004), (on file with Tomasco).

11. Id. at 210–211.

12. Id. at 211.

13. See Natl. Inst. for Occupational Safety and Health Centers for Disease Control & Prevention, Approaches to Safe Nanotechnology: An Information Exchange with NIOSH 7–8 (distributed only for "pre-dissemination peer review") (hereafter, "NIOSH Approaches").

14. See Tomasco, supra, at 211.

15. Id.

16. Miller et al., supra note 5, at 15.

17. Karen Florini et al., Nanotechnology: Getting It Right the Right Time, 3 Nanotech. L. & Bus. 39, 45 (2006).

18. E. Eric Drexler & Jason Wejnert, Nanotechnology and Policy, 45 Jurimetrics 1, 8–9 (2004).

19. Id. at 10.

20. Miller et al., supra, at 19.

21. Drexler & Wejnert, supra, at 9.

22. Miller et al., supra, at 21.

23. Klaus Mosbach, The Promise of Molecular Imprinting, 295 Sci. Am. No. 4, at 86, 91 (October 2006).

24. Elizabeth Gudrais, A Personal Genome Machine? Harvard Magazine, March-April 2007, at 11–12.

25. Megan Fellman, Nanotechnology May Be Used to Regenerate Tissue, Organs, Northwestern Observer, May 10, 2007, at 3.

26. Charles Q. Choi, Material Progress: Designers Have Crafted New Structures Ranging from Nanorods to Mimics of Mother-of-Pearl, 295 Sci. Am. No. 6, at 58 (Dec. 2006).

27. See Miller, supra, at 17–18.

28. Drexler & Wejnert, supra, at 9.

29. George Gruner, Carbon Nanonets Spark New Electronics, 296 Sci. Am. No. 5, at 76, 78 (May 2007).

30. Nader Engheta, Circuits with Light at Nanoscales: Topical Nanocircuits Inspired by Metamaterials, 317 Sci. 1698, 1702 (Sept. 21, 2007).

31. Anna C. Blazas et al., Nanoparticle Polymer Composites: Where Two Small Worlds Meet, 314 Sci. 1107, 1108 (Nov. 17, 2006).

32. Charles Barney, letter, Viral Ingenuity, and reply by Angela Belcher, 296 Sci. Am. No. 2, at 11 (Feb. 2007).

33. Drexler & Wejnert, supra note 18, at 12–13 (2004).

34. Knowles, supra note 4, at 25.

35. Mihail C. Roco, Nanotechnology's Future, 295 Sci. Am. No. 2, at 39 (Aug. 2006).

36. NIOSH Approaches, supra note 13, at 4.

37. Monica et al., supra note 3, at 55 (2006).

38. Christian E. Schafmeister, Molecular Lego, 296 Sci. Am. No. 2, at 76, 82 (Feb. 2007).

39. Robert F. Service, Cut-and-Copy Approach Clones Nanotubes, 314 Sci. 46–47 (Oct. 6, 2006).

40. Miller, supra note 5, at 19.

41. See e.g., MIT News Office, Research, Financial Aid Raised in Clinton Budget, Feb. 16, 2000, http://www.mit.edu/newsoffice/2000/budget-0216.html.

42. Pub. L. 108-153, 117 Stat. 1923 (2003).

43. Id. sec. 3.

44. See id. sec. 2(c).

45. See e.g., J. Clarence Davies, Managing the Effects of Nanotechnology at 8 (Woodrow Wilson International Ctr. for Scholars, Project for Emerging Technologies) (undated, c. early 2006) (hereafter, Davies).

46. See NIOSH Approaches, supra note 13, at 6–7.

47. See Pat Phibbs-Rizzuto, Consumer Goods Made with Nanotechnology Up 70 Percent Since March, Analysis Finds, 36 OSH Rep. (BNA) 1102 (Nov. 30, 2006).

48. See Nearly 500 Products on Market Made with Nanotechnology, Inventory Indicates, 35 Prod. Safety & Liab. Rep. 489 (May 21, 2007).

49. Florini et al., supra note 17, at 44.

50. Knowles, supra note 4, at 24.

51. See Fiedler & Reynolds, supra note 7, at 605–607.

52. David B. Warheit, Nanoparticles: Health Impacts? Materials Today, Feb. 2004, 32, at 32 (DuPont Co.).

53. Id. at 35.

54. Id. at 34.

55. Id.

56. See id. at 35.

57. Knowles, supra, at 23, summarizing E. Oberdörster, Manufactured Nanomaterials (Fullerenes, Cfft) Induce Oxidative Stress in the Brain of Juvenile Largemouth Bass, 112 Env'l Health Perspectives 1058 (2004).

58. Id., summarizing E. Oberdörster, Toxicity of nCgrj Fullerenes to Two Aquatic Species: Daphnia and Largemouth Bass, Presentation at 227th ACS National Meeting, Washington, D.C., American Chem. Soc. 2004.

59. NIOSH Approaches, supra note 13, at 10, summarizing studies.

60. Id. at 11.

61. Id. at 15.

62. Id. at 18.

63. Knowles, supra, at 23, summarizing K. Donaldson et al., Editorial, Nanotoxicology, 61 Occup'l & Env'l Med. 727 (2004).

64. Id., summarizing R.J. Aitken et al., Nanoparticles: An Occupational Hygiene Review, U.K. Inst. of Med. Research Report 274 (2004).

65. Id., summarizing R. Dunford et al., Chemical Oxidation and DNA Damages Catalyzed by Inorganic Sunscreen Ingredients, 418 FEBS Letters 87 (1997).

66. NIOSH Approaches, supra note 13, at 9, summarizing source from Royal Society & Royal Acad. Eng'g 2004.

67. See G. Oberdörster, Toxicokinetics and Effects of Fibrous and Nonfibrous Particles, 14 Inhalation Toxicology 29 (2002) (abstract).

68. See NIOSH Approaches at 9, summarizing studies.

69. Warheit, supra note 52, at 35.

70. NIOSH Approaches at 15.

71. Knowles, supra note 4, at 24.

72. Id.

73. Florini et al., supra note 17, at 41–42.

74. Id. at 42.

75. Id. at 43.

76. See id. at 45.

77. See id. at 48.

78. Nanotechnology: Strategic Plan for NIOSH Nanotechnology Research: Filling the Knowledge Gaps, http://www.cdc.gov/niosh/topics/nanotech/strat_plan.html.

79. Id.

80. Id.

81. NIOSH Approaches, supra note 13, at 5.

82. Id. at 3.

83. Id. at 4.

84. Id. at 8.

85. Id. at 12.

86. Id.

87. Id. at 13.

88. Id. at 13–14.

89. See id. at 17.

90. See id. at 20–21.

91. See id. at 21–22.

92. See id. at 22.

93. See id. at 23–24.

94. Id. at 24.

95. Davies, supra note 45. A reference to a "standing room only" briefing on this report at the Woodrow Wilson Center, held in early 2006, appears in Susan R. Morrissey, Managing Nanotechnology: Report Evaluates Ability of U.S. Regulatory Framework to Govern Engineered Nanomaterials, 84 Chem. & Eng'g News No. 5 at 34 (Jan. 30, 2006).

96. Davies, supra, at 9.

97. See id. at 11–12.

98. Tomasco, supra note 8, at 237.

99. See id. at 235.

100. Davies, supra, at 12.

101. Tomasco, supra, at 240.

102. FDA Regulation of Nanotechnology Products, http://www.fda.gov/nanotechnology/regulation.html, c. 2006 (logo at top labeled 1906/2006 FDA Centennial), printed June 13, 2006.

103. See Davies, supra, at 13.

104. S. Kang et al., High-Performance High-T_c Superconducting Wires, 311 Sci. 1911 (March 31, 2006) (abstract).

105. Robert F. Service, Nanocolumns Give YBCO Wires a Big Boost, 311 Sci. 1850, 1851 (March 31, 2006).

106. Id. at 1850.

107. Pat Phibbs, Researchers Find Ultrafine Particles Can Go Directly to Brain Through Nose, 36 Occup. Safety & Health Rep. (BNA) 244 (March 16, 2006).

108. Pat Phibbs, Database on NanoTechnology Research Shows Important Issues Not Being Studied, 34 Prod. Safety & Liab. Rep. (BNA) 1098 (Dec. 1, 2005).

109. Michael Bologna, NIOSH Declines to Predict Release Data for Respirator Guidance for Nanotech Firms, 36 OSH Rep. (BNA) 454–455 (May 18, 2006).

110. See John Gannon & Pat Phibbs, Wilson Center Launches Online Database of Products Made with Nanotechnology, 34 Prod. Safety & Liab. Rep. (BNA) 278 (March 20, 2006).

111. NIOSH to Focus on Nanotechnology Best Practices, Assessment, Surveillance, 36 OSH Rep. (BNA) 174 (March 2, 2006).

112. Pat Rizzuto, Benefits of Green Nanotechnology Cited in Reports from U.S., European Scientists, 37 OSH Rep. (BNA) 632 (July 12, 2007).

113. Mark Fischetti, Call It Beetle Guard, 295 Sci. Am. No. 6, at 33 (Dec. 2006).

114. See Lauren Couillard, Nanoparticle Consortium Reaching Goals, But Portable Air Sampler Proves Difficult, 36 OSH Rep. (BNA) 1149 (Dec. 14, 2006).

115. Coalition Formed for Nanotech Companies, 37 OSH Rep. (BNA) 501 (May 31, 2007).

116. EU Nanoelectronics Partnership to Provide Funds for Research Across Multiple Fields, 35 Prod. Safety & Liab. Rep. (BNA) 623 (July 2, 2007).

117. Pat Phibbs, Lawmakers Await National Academies Nanotechnology Report to Pinpoint Problems, 3 Prod. Safety & Liab. Rep. (BNA) 478 (May 8, 2006).

118. See Pat Phibbs, Strategy to Evaluate Nanomaterial Risks Outlined by DuPont, Environmental Group, 36 Occup. Safety & Health Rep. (BNA) 474–475 (May 25, 2006).

119. See Robert F. Service, Calls Rise for More Research on Toxicology of Nanomaterials, 310 Sci. 1609 (Dec. 9, 2005).

120. See Florini et al., supra note 17, at 50, text accompanying notes 62, 63 (citing sources).

121. Davies, supra note 45, at 23.

122. Knowles, supra note 4, at 25.

123. Davies, supra, at 18.

124. See id. at 19–20.

125. Id. at 20.

126. Id. at 21, citing John C. Miller et al., The Handbook of Nanotechnology 37 (John Wiley & Sons 2005).

127. See, e.g., the reference in NIOSH Approaches 5 ("[t]his document has been developed to provide a resource for stakeholders who wish to understand more about the safety and health applications and implications of nanotechnology in the workplace") and Florini et al., supra, at 50 (the "call for increased research comes from a wide range of stakeholders").

128. Davies, supra, at 22.

129. Pat Phibbs, Some Nanoparticles Pass through Skin, Cause Inflammation, Researcher Finds, 35 OSH Rep. (BNA) 978 (Nov. 2, 2005).

130. Lauren Couillard, Nanoparticle Studies Finds Health Hazards; Link to Human Exposures Not Established, 36 OSH Rep. (BNA) 1169 (Dec. 21, 2006).

131. See Robin Fretwell Wilson, Nanotechnology: The Challenge of Regulating Known Unknowns, 34 J. Law Med. & Ethics, 704, 708 (2006).

132. See Couillard, supra.

133. Carbon Nanotubes Persist, Bioaccumulate, Could Harm Lungs, Scientists Say in Study, 37 OSH Rep. (BNA) 452 (May 17, 2007), summarizing Reviewing the Environmental and Human Health Knowledge Base of Carbon Nanotubes and Supplemental Materials, in the journal Environmental Health Perspectives, published May 19, 2007.

134. Pat Rizzuto, Advocates Urge Consumers to Avoid Sunscreens with Nanoscale Ingredients, 35 OSH Rep. (BNA) 771 (Aug. 20, 2007).

135. See Lauren Couillard, Particles from Common Laser Printers Are Major Source of Office Air Pollution, 37 OSH Rep. (BNA) 692 (Aug. 2, 2007).

136. Dept. for Environment, Food and Rural Affairs, Characterising the Potential Risks Posed by Engineered Nanoparticles (Oct. 2006).

137. See id. at 7–13.

138. Id. at 14.

139. See id. at 32, referring, among other effects, to adsorption in various organs, oxidative stress, inflammatory effects, genotoxicity, and "pathogenicity and translocation potential and pathways for nanoparticles in the airways and lung and their potential impacts on the cardiovascular system and brain."

140. Id. at 42.

141. Id.

142. See id. at 36. (In the text, the bracketed word "that" is "they.")

143. Id. at 68.

144. Id. at 83.

145. Id. at 86.

146. Health & Safety Laboratory, Buxton, UK, Health & Safety Executive NanoAlert Service, Issue 1, at 5–6 (Dec. 2006).

147. Id. at 11.

148. Id. at 14.

149. Id. at 16.

150. David Graber & Pat Phibbs, German Institute Working to Understand Why 'Magic Nano' Cleaner Caused Ailments, 34 Prod. Safety & Liab. Rep. (BNA) 390–391 (April 17, 2006).

151. Id.

152. Robert F. Service, Calls Rise for More Research on Toxicology of Nanomaterials, 310 Sci. 1609 (December 9, 2005).

153. See Swift Action Urged to Assess Nanotechnology Risk, 36 OSH Rep. (BNA) 1121 (Dec. 7, 2006) (referring to report, Characterizing the Environmental, Health, and Safety Implications of Nanotechnology: Where Should the Federal Government Go from Here?).

154. See text accompanying note 68.

155. See Pat Phibbs, Researchers Find Ultrafine Particles Can Go Directly to Brain through Nose, 36 OSH Rep. (BNA) 244 (March 16, 2006).

156. See Pat Phibbs-Rizzuto, Physicians Back Request to NTP to Study Chemicals, Nanoscale Metals, 37 O.S.H. Rep. (BNA) 306 (April 5, 2007).

157. Pat Phibbs-Rizzuto, International Standards Organization Selects More Than 100 Nanomaterials Projects, 35 O.S.H. Rep. (BNA) 42 (Jan. 15, 2007).

158. Group Finds 'Gross Failure' on Citizen, Worker Protection, 35 Prod. Safety & Liab. Rep. (BNA) 489 (May 21, 2007).

159. Nanotechnology: Untold Promise, Unknown Risk, Consumer Rep., July 2007, 40, at 44.

160. Data Insufficient to Regulate Nonparticles, But Management Possible, Swiss Report Says, 37 O.S.H. Rep. (BNA) 632 (July 12, 2007).

161. Pat Rizzuto, EPA Plans to Launch Stewardship Program for Nanomaterials by Middle of Next Year, 36 O.S.H. Rep. (BNA) 951 (Oct. 26, 2006).

162. FDA Regulation of Nanotechnology Products, http://www.fda.gov/nanotechnology/regulation.html (last consulted, Jan. 11, 2008).

163. See FDA nanotechnology task force issues report, F.D. Cosm. L. Rep. (CCH), Report No. 2326, at 4 (Aug. 6, 2007).

164. See Pat Rizzuto, Legislators Scold Agencies for Inadequate Action on Risks Nanotechnology May Pose, 36 O.S.H. Rep. (BNA) 862 (Sept. 28, 2006).

165. U.K. Bulletin Summarizes Science on Toxicity, Measurement, Control of Nanoparticles, 37 O.S.H. Rep. (BNA) 477 (May 24, 2007).

166. Lauren Couillard, Nanoparticle Inhalation Exposure Assessment Published by ISO, Available for Purchase, 37 O.S.H. Rep. (BNA) 63 (Jan. 25, 2007).

167. See supra, text accompanying notes 150–151.

168. Bush Seeks $1.5 Billion for Initiative on Nanotechnology; $8.3 Billion Spent So Far, 35 Prod. Safety & Liab. Rep. 143–144 (Feb. 12, 2007).

169. Nanotechnology: A Report of the U.S. Food and Drug Administration of the Nanotechnology Task Force (July 25, 2007).

170. See id. at 8.

171. Id.

172. Id. at 10–11.

173. Id. at ii.

174. Id. at 13.

175. Id. at 15–16.

176. See id. at 27.

177. Id. at 34.

178. See id. at 34–35.

179. See id. at 5.

180. See id. at 8.

181. Id. at 4–5.

182. See id. at 5.

183. Linda-Jo Schierow, CRS Report for Congress, Engineered Nanoscale Materials and Derivative Products: Regulatory Challenges (Jan. 22, 2008).

184. Id. at 4.

185. Id. at 5, quoting Vicki L. Colvin, Testimony before the Committee on Science, U.S. House of Representatives, Hearing on "The Societal Implications of Nanotechnology," 109th Cong., 1st Sess., April 9, 2003.

186. Id. at 5.

187. Id. at 7.

188. Id. at 8.

189. Id. at 10.

190. Id. at 9–10.

191. See id. at 12–13.

192. See id. at 21.

193. I provided testimony on the law in the bankruptcy estimation litigation in In Re W.R. Grace & Company, on behalf of future claimants for asbestos-caused illness.

194. Craig A. Poland et al., Carbon nanotubes introduced into the abdominal cavity of mice show asbestos-like pathogenicity in a pilot study, Nature Nanotechnology, advance online publication, 20 May 2008, dol:10.1038/nnano.2008.111, printout at 1.

195. Id. printout at 5.

196. Id., abstract, printout at 1.

197. Pat Rizzuto, Multi-Walled Carbon Nanotubes Exhibit Asbestos-Like Behavior in Mouse Study, 38 Occup. Safety & Health Rep. (BNA) 418 (May 29, 2008).

198. David A. Jackson, Robert H. Symons & Paul Berg, Biochemical Method for Inserting New Genetic Information into DNA of Simian Virus 40, 69 Proceedings of Nat. Acad. Sciences of U.S. 2904 (1972).

199. Maxine Singer & Dieter Soll, Guidelines for DNA Hybrid Molecules, 181 Sci. 1114 (1973).

200. Paul Berg at al., Potential Biohazards of Recombinant DNA Molecules, 185 Sci. 303 (1974).

201. For a more detailed record of this history, see Marshall S. Shapo, A Nation of Guinea Pigs 218–226 (Free Press 1979).

202. See Department of HEW, NIH, Recombinant DNA Research, Guidelines, 41 Fed. Reg. 27,902 (July 7, 1976). For more details on the history and content of the Guidelines, see Shapo, supra, at 226–240.

203. See Pub. L. 108-153, § 2(b)(10), 15 U.S.C.A. § 7501(b)(10) (repeating these adjectives in various sequences in subsections (A), (B), and (C)).

Conclusion

1. 35 Prod. Safety & Liab. Rep. (BNA) 488 (May 21, 2007).

2. Richard A. Friedman & Andrew C. Leon, Expanding the Black Box—Depression, Antidepressants, and the Risk of Suicide, 356 N. Eng. J. Med. 2343, 2343–2344 (June 7, 2007).

3. Gardiner Harris, F.D.A. Panel Urges Ban on Medicine for Child Colds, N.Y. Times, Oct. 20, 2007, at A1, A11.

4. Bronwyn Davis, House Panel Told FDA Critically Needs Funds to Boost Scientific Capacity, IT Infrastructure, 36 Prod. Safety & Liab. Rep. (BNA) 114 (Feb. 4, 2008).

5. GAO-08-435 T, Statement of Lisa Shames, Federal Oversight of Food Safety, Testimony before the Subcommittee on Oversight and Investigations, Committee on Energy and Commerce, House of Representatives, Jan. 29, 2008.

6. See supra, chapter 1, text accompanying note 13.

7. United States v. Rutherford, 442 U.S. 544 (1979).

8. 52 Fed. Reg. 19466 (May 22, 1987).

9. 509 U.S. 579 (1993).

10. Id. at 582–583.

11. See supra, Chapter 7, text accompanying notes 60–70.

12. See supra, Chapter 7, text accompanying note 101.

13. See Pat Rizzuto, Emerging Technology's Potential Risks Often Unknown, Leading Insurer Reports, 38 OSH. Rep. (BNA) 29 (Jan. 10, 2008).

14. Lechuga, Inc. v. Montgomery, 467 P.2d 256, 262 (Ariz. Ct. App. 1970) (Jacobson, J., concurring), citing Nalbandian v. Byron Jackson Pumps, Inc., 399 P.2d 681, 686–687 (1965) (Lockwood, J., concurring).

15. Anthony Giddens, Risk and Responsibility, 62 Modern L. Rev. 1, 9 (1999).

16. This idea borrows from John Rawls, A Theory of Justice (Harvard 1971).

17. See supra, pages 31–32.

18. Jeffrey Brainard, NIH Turns Blind Eye to Academics' Financial Conflicts, Audit Says, 54 Chron. Higher Ed., No. 21, Feb. 1, 2008, at A8.

19. Eric G. Campbell, Doctors and Drug Companies—Scrutinizing Influential Relationships, 357 N. Eng. J. Med. 1796 (Nov. 1, 2007).

20. See Dan Fagin, Second Thoughts about Fluoride, Sci. Am., Jan. 2008, 74, at 79, 80.

21. William W. Thompson et al., Early Thimerosal Exposure and Neuropsychological Outcomes at 7 to 10 Years, 357 N. Eng. J. Med. 1281, 1281 (abstract) (Sept. 27, 2007).

22. Paul A. Offit, Thimerosal and Vaccines—A Cautionary Tale, 357 N. Eng. J. Med. 1278, 1279 (Sept. 27, 2007).

23. Pat Rizzuto, Research Finds Link Between Exposure to Phthalates, Children's Health Unclear, 35 Prod. Safety & Liab. Rep. (BNA) 997 (Oct. 22, 2007).

24. Thomas M. Burton, Medical Mystery: One Doctor's Lonely Quest to Heal Brain Damage, Wall St. J., Sept. 26, 2007, A1 & A17.

25. See generally David Lindley, Uncertainty (first Anchor Books ed. 2008).

26. See Richard Kerr, Mother Nature Cools the Greenhouse, but Hotter Times Still Lie Ahead, 320 Science 595 (May 2, 2008) (reporting on computer model that "even predicts a slight cooling of the globe" over the next several years, related to ocean currents, a prediction the author points out is not the first forecast "to herald a slowdown or even a temporary cessation of global warming," although "by 2030, forecast global temperatures bounce back up to the warming predicted with greenhouse gases alone").

Index

About the Author

MARSHALL S. SHAPO is the Frederic P. Vose Professor of Law at Northwestern University School of Law. His scholarship over 40 years has focused on how society deals with injuries through the legal system and on the interrelationship of science and law. He is the author of 25 books, including his magisterial 3,500-page treatise on products liability, *The Law of Products Liability* (4th edition, 2006). His titles on law and society include *Compensation for Victims of Terrorism* (2005), *Tort Law and Culture* (2003), and *A Nation of Guinea Pigs* (1979). He was a Visiting Fellow at Oxford and Cambridge Universities and has lectured extensively in Europe and Asia. The American Bar Association bestowed the Robert B. McKay Law Professor Award on Professor Shapo in 2005. He has served as a consultant in liability and injury cases involving asbestos compensation, medical devices, rocket motors, anti-terror products, swimming pools, and Pan Am 103.